Law and Morality
in
Ancient China

SUNY Series in Chinese Philosophy and Culture
David L. Hall and Roger T. Ames, editors

Law and Morality
in
Ancient China

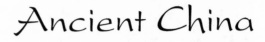

The Silk Manuscripts
of
Huang-Lao

R. P. PEERENBOOM

State University of New York Press

Published by
State University of New York Press, Albany

© 1993 State University of New York

For information, address State University of New York Press,
State University Plaza, Albany, N.Y., 12246

Production by Marilyn P. Semerad
Marketing by Theresa A. Swierzowski

Library of Congress Cataloging-in-Publication Data

Peerenboom, R. P. (Randall P.). 1958–
    Law and morality in ancient China: the silk manuscripts of Huang-
Lao / R. P. Peerenboom.
        p. cm.—(SUNY series in Chinese philosophy and culture)
    Includes bibliographical references and index.
    ISBN 0-7914-1237-7.   —ISBN 0-7914-1238-5 (pbk.)
    1. Huang Lao po shu.   2. Philosophy, Chinese—To 221 B.C.   3. Law
(Philosophy)—Early works to 1800.   4. Taoism—China—Early works to
1800.   I. Huang Lao po shu.   1993. II. Title.   III. Series.
B126.P38   1993
181′.11—dc20
                                                                    91-47541
                                                                        CIP

10   9   8   7   6   5   4   3   2   1

For Calla

Contents

✳

Preface

The 1973 archeological discovery of important documents of classical thought known as the *Huang-Lao Boshu* (Silk Manuscripts of Huang-Lao) coupled with advancements in contemporary jurisprudence make possible a reassessment of the (legal) philosophies of pre-Qin and early Han China. This study attempts to elucidate the importance of the Huang-Lao school within the intellectual tradition of China through a comparison of the *Boshu*'s philosophical position, particularly its understanding of the relation between law and morality, with the respective views of major thinkers of the period—Confucius, Han Fei, Lao Zi, Zhuang Zi, and to a lesser extent, Shen Dao, Shen Buhai and the authors of the *Guan Zi* and *He Guan Zi*. So doing reveals Huang-Lao to be a unique and sophisticated social and political philosophy that, until its expulsion from court by Emperor Wu and subsequent adoption by Daoist religion, served as the ideological foundation for the post-Qin reforms of the early Han.

Chapter I consists of two sections. In the first, I review the current state of Huang-Lao studies, summarizing the efforts of leading sinologists to clarify textual issues such as the title, date, and authorship of the lost work. In the second, I present a methodological overview in which I develop the distinctions in contemporary philosophy of law that will provide the conceptual apparatus, the hermeneutic framework as it were, for sorting out the relation of Huang-Lao to other schools of classical Chinese thought. Chapters II and III explicate Huang-Lao thought as exemplified in the *Boshu*. The former treats the general character of Huang-Lao, with special attention to metaphysics, philosophy of language, and epistemology; the latter treats Huang-Lao social and political philosophy, with special attention to jurisprudence.

Chapters IV to VII examine the intellectual, historical, and political context. In Chapter IV, I examine the relation of Huang-Lao to the Confucianism of Confucius; in V, to the Legalism of Han Fei; in VI, to the Daoism of Lao Zi and Zhuang Zi. Chapter VII sketches a wider portrait of the evolution of Huang-Lao thought. After exploring the intellectual importance of the Jixia Academy (Zou Yan, Shen Dao, the authors of the *Guan Zi*) and Shen Buhai for Huang-Lao, I consider the political influence of Huang-Lao in the early Han. Finally, I offer potential explanations for the demise of Huang-Lao during the reign of Emperor Wu and reflect on its transformation and adoption by Han dynasty religious Daoists.

In Chapter VIII, the epilogue, I ask what contributions, if any, Huang-Lao can make to contemporary philosophy or jurisprudence. In the Appendix, I take up the relation between the *He Guan Zi* and Huang-Lao. Since the Mawangdui discovery of the *Boshu*, many texts have been declared Huang-Lao works. Of these, the *He Guan Zi*, long considered to be an eclectic, post-Han apocryphal work, is the best candidate. However, because of its eclectic, multi-author character, determining which parts belong to Huang-Lao and which to other schools requires careful analysis. Further, there is no clear evidence as to whether the *Boshu* preceded the *He Guan Zi* or vice versa. Thus, rather than attempting to integrate the *He Guan Zi* into the historical narrative of the main text, I have chosen to append a separate discussion.

Citations

Citations of the Mawangdui silk manuscripts of Huang-Lao will be of the following form: page number of 1980 Wen Wu (volume 1) edition:line number of original text. Citations of Confucius follow the numbering in D. C. Lau's *Confucius: The Analects* (New York: Penguin Books, 1979). Citations of Lao Zi are to chapter number of the *Dao De Jing*. I have found Chen Guying's edition (translated by Young and Ames) useful in that it presents in one handy volume the original Chinese, a translation, and commentary. Citations of Xun Zi, Zhuang Zi, and Han Fei Zi follow *Concordance to Philosophers* (Nan Yu Press, n.d.), volumes 1, 2, and 5, respectively. For Xun Zi and Zhuang Zi, they are of the following form: page number/chapter number/line number; for Han Fei, page number/line number. Citations to the *Chun Qiu Fan Lu* are of the following form: chapter number/*juan*/line of the *Sibu beiyao*, Zhonghua press edition. Citations to the *Huai Nan Zi* are of the form chapter/page/line of Yang Jiage (Taibei: Shijie Press, 1985) edition. Citations to Shen Dao are according to the fragments as numbered in Thompson's *The Shen Tzu Fragments*. Citations of the *Guan Zi* are to the *Sibu beiyao* edition. Citations to the *Shi Ji* are to the Dingwen edition and of the form *juan*:page number of Dingwen text. Citations to the *Han Shu* follow Dubs. Citations to *He Guan Zi* are to the *Sibu beiyao* edition, chapter number/page number/line number. I abbreviate the *Shi Ji* as *SJ* and the *Han Shu* as *HS*.

In addition, I cite (if available) an English translation, using the following abbreviations for the translators:

C: Chan
D: Duyvendak
Ds: Dubs
F: Bodde's translation of Feng's *History of Chinese Philosophy*.
G: Graham
L: Liao
R: Rickett
T: Thompson
W: Watson

I am responsible for all translations. Where necessary, I have retranslated passages or modified existing translations to reflect advances in sinology and to ensure consistency in the rendering of key terms. A corollary of the coherence approach to hermeneutics advanced in this book is that translation is itself interpretation. How one translates a term depends on one's reading of the ideas and philosophy of the text. Ultimately, the adequacy of one's translation can only be assessed in light of the overall coherence of the textual interpretations to which it gives rise. As our philosophical interpretations change, so must our translations.

Brackets, [ ] indicate elaboration interjected by me to render the translation intelligible. Brances, { }, indicate lacunae in the text, for which the enclosed word(s) are interpolated for reasons explained in an accompanying note. Leaders, . . . , indicate common ellipsis. Bold face leaders, **. . .** , indicate lacunae in the original text. I give the number of missing characters in an accompanying note.

Romanizations are in Pinyin, with the exception of citations of works using Wade-Giles and proper names of authors who use other systems.

Acknowledgments

✳

Many persons and institutions have contributed to this project. I would like to thank the East-West Center and the Pacific Cultural Foundation, Republic of China, for funding the preliminary research in Asia and the subsequent writing.

I have been aided in the translation of the Mawangdui Huang-Lao manuscripts by Yang Youwei, Roger T. Ames, Angus Graham, and Russell McLeod, all of whom provided detailed, line by line commentary. In addition, I benefitted from the clarifying responses of Qiu Xigui and Zhu Dexi to several of my questions.

Roger Ames, Carine Defoort, Angus Graham, Kenneth Kipnis, Victor Hao Li, Steve Odin, Graham Parkes, and James Sellmann all made valuable suggestions for improving the content, organization and style of this work. For this I am most thankful. I would also like to thank Tim Engstrom for opening up the world of pragmatism and contemporary Continental thought, and Henry Skaja for pointing out and elucidating the relevance of Peirce for my interpretation of classical Daoism. In addition, I have made use of the philosophical, jurisprudential, and sinological efforts of others too numerous to mention here. Their appearance in the bibliography and notes marks my gratitude.

Without the support of all the preceding, the quality of this work would have been considerably lessened. I owe a special debt of gratitude, however, to Professors Yang Youwei and Roger T. Ames. Both have transmitted much more than the ancient grammar and arcane ideas of a distant civilization. In embodying the living tradition of classical Chinese thought, each in his own way exemplifies a world-view compelling in the quality of life it makes possible. My life has been enriched through knowing them.

Parts of this book were published in various journals. Passages from chapters II and III are from "Natural Law in the *Huang-Lao Boshu*," *Philosophy East and West* 40, no. 3 (1990). Much of Chapter IV is drawn from "Confucian Justice: Achieving a Humane Society," *International Philosophical Quarterly* 30, no. 1 (1990). Passages from "Beyond Naturalism:

A Reconstruction of Daoist Environmental Ethics" (*Environmental Ethics* 13, 1 [1991]), appear in Chapter VI. Passages from Chapter VII are drawn from "Han Dynasty Cosmology: The Emergence of Naturalism," *Asian Culture Quarterly* 16 (1988), and "Naturalism and Immortality in the Han: The Antecedents of Religious Daoism," *Chinese Culture* 29, no. 3. A slightly edited version of the appendix appears in *Early China* 16 (1991).

I. Introduction

*

December 1973, Hunan province, near Changsha, ancient state of Chu. Working on a site known as Mawangdui Han Tomb Three, archaeologists make a discovery that promises to dramatically alter and enrich our understanding of the life and philosophy of ancient China. They excavate from the tomb of a prince—the son of Li Cang, prime minister of Changsha—over 300 pieces of lacquerware, some 100 wooden figurines, bamboo containers of food, silk paintings, and most important for students of intellectual history, silk scrolls dating back to the early Han. In addition to charts, maps, and diagrams, the scrolls contain more than 120,000 characters, including the two oldest known versions of the *Lao Zi* (called *Lao Zi* A and B) plus many previously lost essays on a wide variety of topics: yin yang, five phases, medicine, Daoist yoga, astronomy and astrology. Perhaps of greatest concern for philosophers, however, are the four silk manuscripts of the Huang-Lao school that precede the *Lao Zi* B.[1]

1. The Silk Manuscripts of Huang-Lao

Prior to the Mawangdui discovery, sinologists were more confused than clear about the school of thought known as Huang-Lao. In the absence of extant texts, knowledge of the school, gleaned from a handful of citations in historical records and other classical works, was fragmented and contradictory.[2] One knew that the *Huang* (黃) refers to Huang Di, the mythical Yellow Emperor; the *Lao* (老) to Lao Zi, the alleged founder of Daoism. One knew that Huang-Lao doctrines dominated both the worlds of politics and thought in the early Han: Sima Qian notes in the *Shi Ji* that in addition to Han Emperors Wen and Jing and the Empress Dowager Dou, many prominent political figures—including Cao Can, Chen Ping, and Tian Shu—favor Huang-Lao and take it as the basis of their policies.[3] Intellectually, several important philosophers such as Shen Buhai, Shen Dao, and Han Fei are, according to Sima, former students of Huang-Lao thought.[4]

Prior to this find, one also knew that the Huang-Lao school lost favor

1

abruptly around 140 B.C. when Han Wu Di, siding with the Confucians and Dong Zhongshu, prohibited other ideologies and banned Huang-Lao thought from court.[5] And one knew that by the late Han, Huang-Lao was associated with Daoist religion, immortality, sexual yoga, and traditional medicine. Apart from these tantalizing tidbits, little was known.

With the discovery of the Mawangdui Silk Manuscripts of Huang-Lao, the world of sinology has gained one of the key pieces to the classical puzzle. After two millennia, it is now possible to resolve many of the mysteries of Huang-Lao and answer such queries as why what were thought to be esoteric immortality teachings would be so popular among leading Han political figures and philosophers. Contrary to the picture painted by the scattered references to Huang-Lao and the Yellow Emperor in the late Han, Huang-Lao thought is first and foremost a sophisticated political philosophy that, on a most general level, represents a synthesis of classical Daoism and Legalism.

Yet although the Mawangdui discovery has enhanced understanding of ancient Chinese philosophy, several factors have conspired to diminish the returns reaped from this extraordinary find. First, although many scholars have repeatedly called for close study of the silk manuscripts of Huang-Lao (hereafter *Huang-Lao Boshu* 黃老帛書 or simply *Boshu*), little has been published, particularly in Western languages. Only a handful of articles, generally of an introductory character, have appeared in English.[6] Although numerous articles have appeared in Japanese and Chinese, there are but two book-length treatments of this important topic.[7] Further, there is as yet no complete translation of the text in English, Japanese, or even modern Chinese.[8]

The obstacles to translation and analysis, moreover, are formidable. Though the silk scrolls have held up remarkably well considering the circumstances, parts of the text have been lost to water damage and others rendered unintelligible by the obliteration of all or parts of a key word or words. When faced with such predicaments in other classical texts, one is often able to turn to an extensive commentarial tradition to fill in the lacunae. In the case of the *Boshu*, however, there are no extant commentaries. Only rarely is it possible to reconstruct a damaged passage on the basis of a similar passage in the classical corpus.

The lack of commentaries contributes, moreover, to a larger problem for Huang-Lao studies. So little is known about Huang-Lao thought that it is difficult to determine how to approach the text. In working with classical writings, one can usually rely on the work of previous scholars to provide a hermeneutical framework to guide one's interpretive efforts. Yet with the *Boshu*, one is for all intents and purposes on one's own. There are no other extant texts from the school. The few references to Huang-Lao in the classical literature are of little assistance in that they link Huang-Lao to a wide variety of political and philosophical figures: one is left wondering how a single system of thought could possibly serve both the harsh Legalism of Han Fei and the lenient laws and relaxed governing style of Cao Can. Even where there is an abundance of information, it hinders more than helps: in the late Warring States and Han periods, the Yellow Emperor is broadly claimed as patron saint. The *Han Shu* alone lists works with *Huang Di* in the title under the categories of Daoism, yin yang, five phases, militarism, calendars, astrology, astronomy, medicine, sexual yoga, immortals, and more.[9] With such a wide range of Yellow Emperor images, one is hardpressed to state definitively which "Huang Di" is signaled by *Huang-Lao*.[10]

As for the text itself, although unquestionably a great boon, it too is a source of difficulties: for starters, we do not know the title, author(s), or date. Whereas the four individual sections are titled, the text as a whole is not. Indeed, not only is the title uncertain, one cannot even be sure that the four sections form a single work. Similarly, with respect to authorship, not only is the author unknown, but single authorship is itself a matter of debate. And although archeological evidence constrains the latest possible date of copying to 168 B.C., the date of composition of the original remains much contested.[11]

Further, the synthetic nature of the text compounds the translation-interpretation problem: one finds in the *Boshu* many strands of thought. Recognizing the vocabulary of a particular school or philosopher, scholars have rushed to interpret Huang-Lao in terms of that school or philosopher. Unfortunately, however, one finds in the *Boshu* the technical jargon of Daoism, Legalism, Confucianism—even Mohism. There are words and expressions redolent of Lao Zi, Han Fei, Shen Dao, Shen Buhai, Guan Zi, Mo Zi, Xun Zi, Yin Wen Zi, and the authors of various chapters of the *Huai Nan Zi, Lu Shi Chun Qiu,* and the "Outer Chapters" of the *Zhuang Zi.*

As a result, the enormous potential of the discovery of the *Huang-Lao Boshu* to assist in clarification of the relationship between the various pre-Han and Han philosophical schools is being compromised by the willingness on the part of contemporary scholars to appeal to it without first clearly delineating its conceptual content. In the absence of a clear statement as to the unique philosophical import of the *Boshu* in particular and Huang-Lao thought in general, all late Warring States and early Han literature that has any Daoist-Legalist content is being relegated to the Huang-Lao school. To illustrate, many recent articles have centered on the legal philosophy of the new text, arguing that the author represents a "close parallel" to Han Fei Zi,[12] that he differs from Han Fei Zi but is similar to Shen Dao and Shen Buhai,[13] that his legal philosophy is based on Lao Zi's dao,[14] that it is basically the same as the Jixia Daoism of parts of the *Guan Zi*, and so on.[15] Others have applied the label *Huang-Lao* to the *Huai Nan Zi*,[16] *Lu Shi Chun Qiu*,[17] *He Guan Zi*,[18] *Yin Wen Zi*[19] and "Tian Dao" chapters of the *Zhuang Zi*.[20]

Given the current state of disarray in Huang-Lao studies, what is needed is a careful discussion of the differences between the various pre- and early Han philosophical systems as well as a comparison of their similarities. Paying close attention to how the *Boshu* differs from other works allows one to appreciate the novelty of Huang-Lao thought. It then becomes possible to stipulate what one means by *Huang-Lao* and to provide criteria for distinguishing Huang-Lao from other schools, thus clarifying rather than obfuscating the relations among ancient Chinese philosophers and schools. Further, by reexamining one's ideas about classical Chinese philosophies in light of the recent discovery, one not only comes to a better understanding of the *Boshu* but of the other schools as well.

In the following chapters, I argue that Huang-Lao promotes a foundational naturalism[21]: the way of humans (*ren dao* 人道) is predicated on and implicate in the normatively prior way of the natural order (*tian dao* 天道). Correlated to this foundational naturalism is the natural law theory of the *Boshu*: the laws that govern society are construed as objective laws of a predetermined natural order discoverable by humans.

Foundational naturalism coupled with a natural law theory differentiates Huang-Lao thought from that of other ancient schools, including classical Daoism. Ironically, however, the standard practice has been to read Lao Zi and Zhuang Zi as if they were Huang-Lao Daoists, attributing to them the metaphysical view of a single, predetermined natural order to be followed by humans. The view I explicate as that of the *Boshu* will therefore seem familiar to those acquainted with the standard reading, or misreading as I argue, of Lao Zi and Zhuang Zi. One of the main objectives of this work is then to challenge the traditional account of classical Daoism and demonstrate that the differences between classical Daoism and Huang-Lao thought go well beyond the latter's adoption of a rule of law rejected by the former.

The import of the thesis that Huang-Lao advocates a foundational naturalism is that it not only saves the phenomena, as it were, by accounting for the significant differences and similarities between Huang-Lao and other figures and schools, but does so—to borrow the terminology of scientific theory valuation—in an elegant and fertile fashion in that it offers a concise explanation as to *why* Huang-Lao would adopt and reject those features that it does. It provides, in short, a clearly delineated conceptual statement as to what is unique about the philosophy of Huang-Lao.

Yet the thesis is philosophically important not only for its hermeneutical value in understanding the *Boshu* and explicating the relationship between Huang-Lao and other schools of thought. It is equally important because it sheds light on previously inexplicable developments in Chinese thought. For instance, Derk Bodde and Clarence Morris were at a loss to account for the "naturalization" of law in China. They had discovered that, "because the spheres of man and nature were thought of as forming a single continuum," violations of law in the Chinese world represent not just transgressions of the human social order but disruptions of "the total cosmic order." Yet they further note that such a concept of law could not have arisen from early Confucians because "law to them was itself a violation of the social order. Nor could it have started with the Legalists, since these men used law quite consciously to destroy and remake the old social order."[22] The classical Daoists, for their part, rejected codified law as a means of effecting social order. Who, then, was responsible for the "naturalization" of law? Writing before the Mawangdui discovery, Bodde and Morris had no way of knowing that the primary force was the school of Huang-Lao whose natural law theory grounded the laws governing the human order in the cosmic natural order.

Finally, the claim that Huang-Lao advances a natural law theory predicated on foundational naturalism is philosophically significant in that it challenges many commonly held views about "Chinese" philosophy. Joseph Needham has argued that, whereas natural law does exist in ancient China in the form of Confucian rites or *li* (禮) (a misreading of Confucius, I argue), natural law is not grounded in the laws of nature. He asserts this in part because he does not think that "Chinese" organismic cosmology allows for a conception of natural laws in the natural science sense.[23]

Roger T. Ames and David Hall have claimed that order in (classical) Chinese thought is best characterized as aesthetic rather than logical in part on the grounds that classical Chinese philosophy, Confucianism in particular, lacks the notion of transcendence that has dominated Western thought and undergirds logical order.[24] In a similar vein, Chad Hansen has argued that the Chinese have no concept of truth. More specifically, Chinese philosophy lacks the notion of semantic truth that has been so dominant in the Western philosophical tradition.[25]

I argue that there is a notion of transcendence in Huang-Lao thought. That is, in the Huang-Lao system the natural order has normative priority over the human world. It is not a matter of humans fashioning the Way, but of following the Way. Although this is not the ontological transcendence that one finds in certain readings of Plato or Christianity, it neverthe-less contrasts sharply with the interactive, mutually determining *tian ren he yi* (天人合一—interrelation of human and *tian*: nature/heaven) model that dominates much of Chinese thought—even, incidentally, that of cosmolo-gists such as Dong Zhongshu with whom Huang-Lao shares, I contend, a common ancestry. Further, this conception of transcendence obviates Needham's objections against natural laws in the natural science sense and a fortiori against juristic natural law grounded in the laws of the natural order. It also underwrites Huang-Lao's realist or semantic theory of lan-guage, attesting to a semantic conception of truth that Hansen claims does not exist in Chinese thought.

That Huang-Lao thought fails to conform to the positions of the pre-ceding renowned scholars need not undermine the validity of their views as generalizations about (classical) Chinese philosophy. Rather, Huang-Lao is the exception to the rule. It constitutes a major countercurrent in the flow of Chinese intellectual history. Therein lies its value. As a challenge to many textbook generalizations about the nature of Chinese thought, it forces one to rethink and qualify previously held views and, in the process, to develop a greater appreciation of the richness and diversity of thought in ancient China.

1.1 Text

The *Huang-Lao Boshu* consists of four sections, each with title and number of characters appended: *Jing Fa* (經法 -Canonical Laws)[26] 5000 characters; *Shiliu Jing* (十六經 —Sixteen Classics) 4564 (or 4354) charac-ters; *Cheng* (稱—Weighing by the Scales) 1600 characters; *Dao Yuan* (道原—Origins of the Way) 464 characters. The exact numbers cannot be verified because water damage has destroyed parts of the text.

A coterie of mainland Chinese scholars including Zhang Zhengliang, Zhu Dexi, Qiu Xigui, Tang Lan, and Gu Tiefu began the onerous task—as crucial as it is demanding—of transcribing the silk manuscripts into mod-ern characters. A transcription into simplified characters appeared in *Wen Wu* (1974).[27] In 1975, Tang Lan produced his seminal work on the *Huang-Lao Boshu* in which he discusses the title, dating, authorship, and content of the text. In addition, he produced a simplified character version of the text with photocopies of the original silk manuscripts. To this he appended a section by section table of passages in the classical corpus similar or iden-tical to passages in the *Boshu*.

In 1980, Wen Wu Publishers came out with a three volume hardback edition of the silk manuscripts in modern complex characters. Volume 3 contained the Huang-Lao texts as well as the two versions of the *Lao Zi*.

Extensively annotated, this edition also contained high-quality photo-reproductions of the original manuscripts. The state of the art in textual criticism, it is the version I have relied on for my translations.

1.2 Title

Tang Lan believes the silk manuscripts are the *Huang Di Si Jing* (黃帝四經—Yellow Emperor's Four Classics). His arguments are complex and at times difficult to follow. He notes, first, that of possible works listed in the *Hanshu* bibliography, the "Yi Wen Zhi," only the *Huang Di Si Jing* is in four sections. Listed under the category of Daoism are, in addition to the *Huang Di Si Jing* in four *pian* or sections, the *Huang Di Ming* (黃帝銘) in six sections, *Huang Di Jun Chen* (黃帝君臣) in ten sections, and *Za Huang Di* (雜黃帝) in fifty-eight sections. The latter three are rejected by Tang primarily on the basis of the number of sections, as is one other possibility, *Li Mu* (力牧) in twenty-two sections.[29]

Second, Tang suggests that an honorific title in which the accolade *jing* (經—classic) is conferred on works attributed to the Yellow Emperor would be appropriate given the circumstances. First, two of the sections—*Jing Fa* and *Shiliu Jing*—contain the word *jing*. The other two sections, although not referred to as *jing*, are, Tang claims, written in the style of classics. Second, the scrolls were copied in the early Han, most likely in the time of Wen Di, during the period when Huang-Lao is emerging as the dominant court ideology. Tang reiterates that Han Emperors Wen and Jing and Empress Dowager Dou are all said to have studied or been fond of the teachings of Huang-Lao. Further, the arrangement of the texts suggests that the work is indeed of the Huang-Lao school in that the four Yellow Emperor sections precede the *Lao Zi*. As a subargument, Tang notes that

> the 'Dao Jing' section of the *Sui Shu*, 'Records of Jing Ji,' states: 'In the Han, there were in circulation texts by the masters of thirty-seven schools. . . . The four parts of the Yellow Emperor and the two parts of the *Lao Zi* were the most profound.' The *Yellow Emperor* in four parts mentioned here obviously refers to the *Yellow Emperor's Four Classics*. . . . It can be seen that the doctrine of Huang Di and Lao Zi is the four parts of the *Yellow Emperor's Four Classics* and the two parts of *Lao Zi*. Scholars of the Southern Dynasty most likely were still able to encounter the Huang-Lao text in this combined form. From this record, it can be further established that the four parts concerning the Yellow Emperor and the doctrine of *xing ming* (形名—forms and names) which precede the *Lao Zi* B must indeed be the *Yellow Emperor's Four Classics*.[30]

The fact that the Yellow Emperor is a major character in one of the sections, the *Shiliu Jing*, further supports Tang's claim that the four sections represent the doctrines attributed to the Yellow Emperor. Drawing the various strands of the argument together, Tang contends that it is reasonable that a text espousing Huang-Lao ideas favored by the ruling elite would be accorded the title *jing*, especially in that by the early Han the *Lao Zi* was already considered a "classic" (*jing*). Thus the four silk manuscripts preceding *Lao Zi* B are, Tang concludes, the *Yellow Emperor's Four Classics*.

Gao Heng and Dong Zhian offer a second hypothesis.[31] They suggest that the *Shiliu Jing* section is the *Huang Di Jun Chen* (The Yellow Emperor on the Ruler and Ministers) in ten sections. In the initial stages after the discovery, the *Shiliu Jing* (Sixteen Classics) was read as *Shi Da Jing* (*Ten Great Classics*)—the characters *liu* (六—six) and *da* (大—great) being very similar in appearance. This may have been a factor in Gao and Dong's reasoning. At any rate, as they point out, there are in fact fourteen rather than sixteen sections. Moreover, nine sections contain discussions between the Yellow Emperor and his ministers or descriptions of their activities. It is possible that a scribe divided what were originally ten sections into fourteen sections. And, given the content of the chapters, particularly the interplay between ruler and ministers, it is possible that the *Shiliu Jing* section could be the lost *Huang Di Jun Chen*.

Both the Tang and the Gao and Dong claims are, however, problematic. As for the latter, there are fourteen sections rather than ten. Further, the *Shiliu Jing* section already has a title. If it is to be taken as a separate work, there would be no need for a second title. Finally, if the *Shiliu Jing* is the *Huang Di Jun Chen*, then what are the other sections?

Tang's claim, although much more probable, simply cannot be verified. As many have pointed out, it is possible that the early bibliographies are not complete.[32] Given Huang-Lao's status as the ideology favored by leading philosophers and politicians alike, there were surely many works written about or under the aegis of Huang-Lao. Indeed, the Yellow Emperor is cited so often in the Han that it would be surprising if some Huang-Lao texts were not overlooked. The *Boshu* could be one of those which escaped the attention of the early bibliographers. To be sure it is unlikely that a work of such sophistication and philosophical import would go unnoticed by scholars who, toiling in the service of politicians, have available the vast resources of the state. Of all academicians, they would seem the most likely to be aware of a major treatise in political philosophy.

Nevertheless, that the *Boshu* might have been missed by the bibliographers remains a possibility, albeit a remote one. As little hinges on a final determination of the title, I will avoid begging the question by referring to the Mawangdui silk manuscripts preceding the *Lao Zi* B as the *Huang-Lao Boshu* or simply *Boshu*.

1.3 Authorship

There are two fundamental issues with respect to authorship. First, are the four sections penned by a single person or more than one person, or perhaps written by several but edited by one? Second, who is this person(s)?

Tang Lan believes one hand is responsible. He claims that, although the writing styles of the four parts differ, the parts are all interrelated and, judging by the content, form a single whole. Tu Wei-ming also comments that the four sections "exhibit a remarkably unified pattern of thought."[33] Long Hui, based on a philological study, seconds Tang's assertion. In particular, he argues that the occurrence in different sections of several unusual phrases indicates that they are composed by a single person.[34]

Others take exception to Tang and Long's assessment. Qiu Xigui and Uchiyama Toshihiko contend that, although the works exhibit a unity of thought, that does not necessarily entail that they are by one person.[35] Wu Guang and Wei Qipeng deny not only that they are the work of a single hand but that they are composed at one time. Wu notes that the *Cheng* section is composed of brief passages edited together and suggests that the various sections evidence different trends of thought.[36]

The issue of authorship, like that of title, does not appear resolvable given the evidence now available. Even the criteria are problematic. That certain unusual phrases are repeated, although suggestive, is not sufficient to prove the essays are the work of a single author. People of the same school often employ similar phrases, especially if they are meant in a technical sense relative to that school. Lacking other texts from the Huang-Lao school, it is difficult to rule out this possibility. Students likewise often adopt the jargon of their teachers for a variety or reasons. They may do so because that is how they have come to frame the issue or, alternatively, to cover up the fact that they have not thoroughly understood the ideas. Or they may simply be compelled to employ terminology agreeable to the teacher. In the highly deferential master-disciple relation that existed in ancient China, that a disciple would parrot the words of his master is unexceptional. A third explanation of the repeated occurrence of unusual language is that one person may have edited all four essays, thereby bringing a measure of consistency in terminology and thought to the work. Whereas a more detailed philological analysis might reveal patterns of speech so idiosyncratic that they could not be but from one person, the repetition of a few unusual phrases is insufficient to demonstrate single authorship.

The second main criterion for judging the works to be of one person is consistency of thought. But consistency is largely in the eye of the beholder. On a very general level, the text can be said to be consistent—but then so can many works by different people of roughly the same orientation.

What degree of consistency is required to demonstrate single authorship? There are several inconsistencies between and within the four sections. For instance, in the "Lun Yue" section of the *Jing Fa*, the author states that the way of heaven is for achievements to be pursued and realized in three seasons and for punishments and killings to be carried out in one season (57:66a). In the "Guan" section of *Shiliu Jing*, however, the author states that, although spring and summer are the time for rewards, *both* fall and winter are the seasons for punishments (62:85b).

Similarly, in the "Guo Tong" section of *Shiliu Jing*, the author has the Yellow Emperor arguing for a Shen Nung-like egalitarianism. All are to be treated equally and to share the same standard of living—with the exception of the ruler.[37] Yet this contradicts the many statements throughout the four sections that class distinctions—economic, social, and political—are natural and necessary.[38] In fact, Guo Tong raises precisely this counter-argument, though to no avail as the Yellow Emperor repeats his order that all are to be made equal.[39]

Further, as even those who claim the four essays to be the product of a single hand acknowledge, the styles differ markedly. *Jing Fa* is a straightforward, somewhat mechanical exposition of a political philosophy. There is very little cosmology. *Dao Yuan*, on the other hand, is primarily cosmology. In contrast to the rather tight, discursive argumentation of *Jing Fa*, *Cheng* is a collection of short, largely unconnected reflections. *Shiliu Jing*, for its part, is a wordy piece dealing with the mythology and hagiography of the Yellow Emperor.

It is of course possible for one person to discuss a range of topics and to write in notably different styles, particularly when the topics differ. The style one employs when relating popular legends about the Yellow Emperor need not, and in the hands of a good writer, probably would not, coincide with that used to compose a treatise in political philosophy. Yet again one must ask at what point do differences in style become, if not themselves differences of content, at least proof of different thinkers or authors?

There is no clear cut answer. Different people will assess the issue differently. For my part, I believe, as many have claimed, that the four essays do evidence a high degree of unity of thought. There are certainly no more numerous or egregious inconsistencies than in many other philosophical works. After all, few, if any, achieve perfect marks for consistency when subject to the kind of critical scrutiny that the *Boshu* has undergone. Indeed, that the level of consistency is as high as it is speaks well of the author(s) when one considers the difficulty of the writing process in the days before word processors: writing on silk and bamboo permits little opportunity for editing and revision. Nevertheless, one cannot say for sure whether the four essays are the work of one person or not. For that reason, it would be more accurate to refer to the author(s) of the *Boshu*. Stylistically, however, that approach is unappealing. Consequently, I will simply refer to the author, though one should bear in mind the possibility of multiple authors.[40]

The second issue has to do with the identity of the author. Tang, noting the long history of Legalism in Zheng, suggests he is a Legalist recluse from that state. Long Hui, however, has compiled considerable philological evidence to support the claim that the author is from Chu. He notes that the *Boshu* contains many sayings, proverbs, and expressions of Chu. The author also evidences a familiarity with Chu geography, mentioning such places as Bowang Mountain. Third, the pattern of quotations suggests a Chu author: there are many quotations from other Chu works, especially the *Guo Yu*; and many Chu authors cite the *Boshu*, including the authors of the *Wen Zi*, *Huai Nan Zi*, and *He Guan Zi*. Fourth, the *Boshu* displays rhyme patterns similar to *Huai Nan Zi*, some of which are peculiar to the Chu dialect.[41]

Wu Guang concurs with Long's assessment, noting that the *Boshu* exemplifies considerable Daoist influence, and that Daoists such as Lao Zi, Huan Yuan, He Guan Zi, and the authors of the *Huai Nan Zi* are all associated with the state of Chu. That the writings of a Huang-Lao Daoist from Chu would turn up in a tomb near Changsha is not surprising as Changsha is a major capital and center of learning in the Han.[42]

Zhong Zhaopeng suggests a third possibility, that the author is a Huang-Lao scholar from Qi. The *Shi Ji* (87.2436) provides the following lineage: "Le Chen Gong studied the Yellow Emperor and Lao Zi, his original teacher was called He Shang Zhang Ren (Old Man of the River), whose origins are unknown. He Shang Zhang Ren taught An Qisheng who taught Mao Xi Gong who taught Le Xia Gong who taught Le Chen Gong who taught Gai Gong. Gai Gong taught at Gao Mi and Jiao Xi in the state of Qi and served as instructor to prime minister Cao Can." Zhong then documents that in the historical records, Gai Gong, Le Cheng Gong and An Qisheng are all linked to the state of Qi.[43]

Zhong and Long/Wu's positions, strictly speaking, are not incompatible. The author could be a person from Chu who studied and wrote in Qi, most probably at the Jixia Academy, a known center of intellectuals and Huang-Lao scholars. Or he could be a person who spent time in Qi and then moved to or back to Chu. Although I discuss the relation of Huang-Lao thought to the Jixia Academy in greater detail later, it seems safe to say that the author was either from Chu or had spent considerable time there and that he was familiar with, perhaps even partially responsible for, the Huang-Lao thought of the Jixia Academy.[44] At any rate, Tang's suggestion that the author was a Legalist recluse from Zheng is unlikely given the philological evidence compiled by Long.

1.4 Dating

The date of composition of the original text of which the Mawangdui *Boshu* is a later copy is hotly debated. Assessments congregrate around the following four periods:[45] mid-Warring States (394–310 B.C.),[46] late Warring States (309–221 B.C.),[47] late Warring States to Qin-Han (309–140 B.C.),[48] early Han (206–135 B.C.).[49]

Mid-Warring States

In arguing for a mid-Warring States dating, Tang Lan points to the *Shi Ji* (63.2146), which states that "Shen Buhai's studies were based on Huang-Lao and took *xing ming* (forms and names; performance and stipulated duties) as central." Shen Buhai was born in 405 B.C. according to Tang[50] and came to power in 354 according to Herrlee Creel.[51] As it took some years for Huang-Lao to become known, the Huang-Lao school, Tang reasons, must have originated about 400 B.C. The *Shi Ji* (74.2347) adds: "Shen Dao was a person from Zhao, Tian Pian and Jie Zi from Qi, Huan Yuan from Chu. All studied the arts of Huang-Lao Daoism. . . . Shen Dao wrote a work on twelve topics." Though Shen Dao's work is no longer extant, enough fragments are available to gain some impression of his thought.[52] Several scholars have pointed out similarities between his ideas and those of Huang-Lao.[53] Tang notes, moreover, that several fragments attributed to Shen Dao are similar or identical to passages in the *Boshu*. He then suggests that Shen Dao cited the *Boshu*. Because Shen Dao is associated with the Jixia Academy during the reign of the Qi rulers Wei and Xuan, the *Boshu* must be earlier and therefore must be a work of the early fourth century B.C.[54]

Tang also offers a second line of argument. The *Shi Ji*, as noted previously, traces Huang-Lao thought from He Shang Zhang Ren to An Qisheng to Mao Xi Gong to Le Xia Gong to Le Chen Gong to Gai Gong who taught Cao Can, the prime minister of Qi appointed by Liu Bang, the first Han emperor. Tang argues that there are five generations of master-disciple relations from He Shang Zhang Ren to Gai Gong, which he calculates adds up to about 100 years. Tang claims Gai Gong instructed Cao Can in the early third century B.C. and adding 100 years to that pushes the origins of Huang-Lao back to the early fourth century B.C.[55] Long Hui, for philological reasons, concurs with Tang's mid Warring States dating. He contends that phonetic considerations, particularly rhyming of -*io* with -*ie(g)*, supports a fourth century B.C. date of composition.[56]

Many scholars have challenged this early dating. The argument that early philosophers such as Shen Dao and Shen Buhai studied Huang-Lao is problematic. First, it is possible that Sima Qian is anachronistically reading Huang-Lao ideas into the thought of these thinkers. He does, after all, have a vested interest. Several have pointed out that both he and his father, Sima Tan, the author of "On the Essentials of the Six Schools," praise Huang-Lao doctrines and refrain from any criticism.[57] By contrast, though quick to point out the strengths of the other schools, the Simas do not hesitate to balance their remarks with specific criticisms. Further, they are writing under the patronage of rulers known to have been partial to Huang-Lao doctrines. They might feel compelled to portray Huang-Lao thought in the best possible light to please those in power. One way to do so would be to push the origins of Huang-Lao thought as far back as possible in that within the Chinese world ideas are revered more for their lasting power than their novelty. That subsequent major thinkers draw on Huang-Lao as the source of their ideas enhances the status of the Huang-Lao school.

Second, there is no way to verify that it is the *Boshu* that these early thinkers are studying. The *Boshu* need not be the seminal work of the Huang-Lao school. Indeed, one suspects on the basis of its sophistication alone, quite apart from the many other reasons for dating it later, that the *Boshu* represents a culmination of Huang-Lao thought rather than an exploratory early work. As for the similarities of the *Boshu* to the fragments of Shen Dao—or for that matter to other works such as the *Guan Zi, Guo Yu* and *He Guan Zi*—there is no prima facie reason that the passages in the *Boshu* could not be citations of the others. One must first ascertain which work precedes which to know who is citing whom.

With respect to Tang's second argument, Zhong Zhaopeng and Wu Guang have compiled extensive historical documentation demonstrating that all of the figures from He Shang Zhang Ren to Gai Gong are late Warring States to early Han persons.[58] This leaves Long's argument based on phonetic considerations as the main justification for a mid-Warring States dating. Nobody has directly challenged Long on this point, most likely because few have the expertise to evaluate his claim. Conversely, however, it is difficult to place much confidence in a dating based solely on a few abstruse philological points, particularly when there are strong arguments to contrary.

Late Warring States to Qin-Han

The arguments for the claim that the *Boshu* belongs to the late Warring States are much the same as those for the claim that it belongs to the late Warring States to Qin-Han. Hence I will consider them together, examining first the common arguments. There are basically two types of arguments: one based on the content of the *Boshu*, where it is suggested that the ideas fit the intellectual, historical and political conditions of the late Warring States to early Han; the other based on features or terms of the text.

As for the latter, Wu Guang notes that early and mid-Warring States texts do not add titles to chapters. This practice starts with Xun Zi and Han Fei, who generally append two-word titles, as is most often the case in the *Boshu*. Second, Wu points out that the *Boshu* draws heavily on the *Lao Zi*, which is not compiled until the mid-Warring States. Actually, many sinologists date the appearance of the *Lao Zi* even later, around 250 B.C.,[59] making Wu's argument all the stronger—though of course the ideas could have been disseminated in oral form for much longer. Wu also calls attention to the phrase *qian shou* (黔首—"black-heads," that is "commoners" who are dark-skinned from working in the fields). Wu contends that this term originates in the Warring States. Uchiyama seconds this notion. In addition, Uchiyama comments that the phrases *san gong* (三公—three dukes) and *wu di* (五帝—five emperors) are also Warring States terms.[61]

While the place of Huang-Lao thought in general and of the *Boshu* in particular within the intellectual, legal, and political history of ancient China is a major theme of the following chapters, a brief statement at this point may help clarify the dating issue. Intellectually, the *Boshu* exemplifies the late Warring States and early Han trend toward syncretism. Whereas in the mid-Warring States the leading schools of thought— Confucianism, Mohism, Daoism—joust with each other, by the end of the Warring States there is a marked tendency toward unification, cross pollination, and synthesis. Wu refers to this tendency to appropriate ideas from one's intellectual rivals as "the flowing together of the 100 schools" (*bai jia he liu*— 百家合流). Indeed, Sima Tan describes Huang-Lao as a synthesis of the best ideas of all schools (*Shi Ji* 130.3289): "[Huang-Lao] practice accords with the great order of the Yin Yang school, selects what is good from the doctrines of Confucians and Mohists, and combines them with the essential points of the School of Names and the Legalists."[62]

That the *Boshu* incorporates yin yang theory further suggests, as Uchiyama contends, a late rather than mid Warring States dating.[63] A. C. Graham has argued that yin and yang, historically part of the six *qi* (氣),[64] are used primarily as classificatory terms up to 300 B.C., when philosophers begin to construe them as the primal pair of cosmological forces underlying the natural processes.[65] In the *Boshu*, yin and yang are used in both a classificatory and a causal sense.[66] The author does not, however, develop the implications for human control over the natural processes through manipulation of *qi* that plays such a central role in Dong Zhongshu's interactive microcosm-macrocosm philosophy and the immortality practices of the *fang shi* (方士 —often referred to as "magicians").[67] This suggests that the author of the *Boshu* might have been writing at about the time yin and yang are undergoing the transformation from primarily classificatory terms to causal cosmological forces, which by Graham's reckoning, is the late Warring States.[68]

The political ideas of the *Boshu* also appear to reflect the political conditions of the late Warring States to Han. One of the central tenets of the *Boshu* is that it is the ruler's responsibility to bring peace to the people by unifying the empire—even if that requires the use of force. The unification of the empire is the political counterpart of the intellectual movement toward unity in thought. Much as the intellectual jousting must be put aside in favor of a common solution to problems, so must the territorial predation of warlords be brought to an end to curtail the losses of war and allow for rebuilding the economy. That a Warring States author would see the need to end the feuding and rejuvenate the economy is not surprising. And indeed the *Boshu* not only puts forth economic policies aimed at restoring prosperity, but limits the ruler's deployment of the military to just causes.[69]

Many mainland scholars, employing the tools of Marxist historiography, contend the emergence of Huang-Lao can be traced to the transition from "slave" to feudal society.[70] Greatly oversimplified, the view is that, as society changed in the Warring States, a land-owning class began to arise with the nascent feudal order. The newly arisen land-owning class requires its own ideology to replace the Confucian ideology that served the nobility of the old system. As a meritocracy, the Huang-Lao system allows for the upward mobility of the new ruling class. On the other hand, Huang-Lao upholds class distinctions. In fact, its foundational naturalism provides an unshakable basis for class distinctions by grounding them in the natural order: in nature, valleys complement mountains, yin complements yang; in society, the lowly complement those of superior character. In a similar way, the Huang-Lao legal system, designed to diminish the power ceded the nobility under the Confucian system in which "the *li* (rites) do not reach down to the common people, penal law does not reach up to the great officials,"[71] serves the interests of the new elite. Though Huang-Lao ideologists justify their laws by claiming them to be "natural," implicate in the natural order or the Way (dao) as it were, they are only natural given the class perspective—attitudes, beliefs, and values—of the emerging power group.[72]

As for the military philosophy of Huang-Lao, Gao Heng and Dong Zhian argue that the right to engage in just wars represents the right of the newly arisen land-owning class to defeat in the name of justice the noble class of the former slave order and unify the empire. They and many others suggest that it is no coincidence Huang-Lao emerged out of the Jixia Academy in Qi.[73] The ruling house of Qi belonged to the infamous Tian family that usurped power from the established ruling house of Jiang, which traced its legitimacy back to the founding of the Zhou dynasty. As Benjamin Schwartz points out, the murder of the legitimate ruler by Tian Wen Zi in 481 B.C. constituted one of the stock examples of illegitimate use of force to seize political power.[74] Some suggest that the rulers of Qi then became patrons of the arts and humanities in an attempt to regain public support. Others suspect that the real motives for sponsoring intellectual debate and new ideas was to generate an ideology that will justify their usurpation. The views are not incompatible. Liu Weihua and Miao Runtian argue that Qi rulers, realizing that military might would not be sufficient to maintain the empire, sponsored the Jixia Academy in hopes of stimulating debate between schools. This debate would generate a new ideology that synthesized the best of each school and that could serve as a basis for a new empire that the people would support. Huang-Lao, with its call for an active if people-oriented government and its support of righteous wars and unification of the empire, is the result.

It is worth noting as supporting evidence for this view that the first authenticated reference to the Yellow Emperor is a bronze inscription attributed to King Xuan of Qi in which the king claims the Yellow Emperor as the ancestor of the Tian clan.[75] The Yellow Emperor is often portrayed in the literature as the ultimate ancestor of the Chinese people and a gallant warrior who was the first to unify the empire.[76] That a leader looking to justify rule by conquest would claim the Yellow Emperor as ancestor would be reasonable. It would be equally reasonable for scholars working under the patronage of such rulers to present their new political philosophy under the aegis of the Yellow Emperor.

In any event, those who favor a late Warring States as opposed to a late Warring States to Qin-Han dating believe there are good reasons to rule out a Qin to Han dating. The main one is that the *Boshu* never mentions the harsh Qin regime by name. There is no doubt that the author of the *Boshu* is opposed to the austere Legalist policies of Qin. As I argue later, his foundational naturalism is an attempt to provide a theoretical basis for limiting the all-powerful Legalist sovereign.[77] Further, his call for lenient laws and a government that relies on moral suasion and benevolence to complement military strength is readily understandable as an attempt to redress the imbalances of the strict Qin dictatorship. Were the author writing after the collapse of the Qin, he would have no reason to avoid reference to Qin. On the other hand, were he writing during the Qin, he would have the best of all reasons to avoid direct criticism: if caught, he would face certain execution. Yet for that very reason it is unlikely that someone would write a work so critical of Qin's Legalist policies during the height of Qin's powers. Thus, the most likely date of composition is the late Warring States.

Early Han

Arguments for a Han dating are primarily contextual. Many of the conditions that lead to a Warring States dating continue to exist in the Han. Post-Qin society was still plagued by social instability and the threat of war. The need for a single ruler to unify the empire and put an end to the destruction remained, making a Han dating possible.

In fact, the Han seems a more likely candidate in some ways. It is, after all, during the early Han that the Huang-Lao school reaches its zenith of popularity and political power—a likely time for a sophisticated political work such as the *Boshu* to appear. Further, that so many Han political figures adopt Huang-Lao policies is itself proof that the philosophy of the *Boshu* fits the times.

No doubt the lenient laws and people-oriented policies promoted in the *Boshu* are warmly welcomed after the despotic brutality of the Qin. As Nishikawa Yasuji observes, the *Boshu*'s policy of respecting local customs is typical of Han politicians said to favor Huang-Lao. Rather than simply enforcing the whims of the ruler, one first consults with the local officials to determine the specific needs and conditions of the people. And in contrast to the dictatorial Qin government that sought to regulate the lives of the people in great detail, Han Huang-Lao leaders were known for their noninterventionist, hands-off style of government (*qing jing wu wei* 清靜無为).[78] From a economic perspective, the *Boshu*'s emphasis on lower taxes and moderation in the ruler's use of the people's labor as well as its call for frugality on the part of the ruler make sound fiscal sense for a state seeking to recover from the ravages wrought by Qin.

Thus both politically and economically, the government-for-the-people policies of the *Boshu* fit the post-Qin era. Indeed, Jiang Guanghui argues that the willingness of the author and Huang-Lao proponents to circumscribe the power of the ruler and to redirect the resources of the state to the people reflects the insecurity of Han rulers who, in the wake of the power struggle following the collapse of Qin, feared rebellion.[79] The demise of Qin created a power vacuum. In the ensuing struggle, Liu Bang, the eventual victor and first Han emperor, was forced to make concessions to local power brokers to gain their support. In the early years of his rule, he lacked the strength to impose his will. He was forced to acquiesce to the demands of the local leaders and masses. Hence he turned to Huang-Lao policies in an effort to consolidate his power base by gaining the support of the people through lenient laws and favorable economic measures of the type advocated by the author of the *Boshu*. This works so well, the story goes, that by the time of Han Wu Di, the state was once again prosperous and the people's faith in the government restored. As a result, Han Wu Di was able to pursue a more active role for the government and try to regain some of the authority for the central government that the early Han leaders had been forced to relinquish to local authorities. To do this required, however, a new ideology. Dong Zhongshu with his New Text Confucianism was waiting in the wings to answer the call.

The abrupt demise of Huang-Lao is the subject of a later chapter. For now, the issue at hand is the dating of the *Boshu*. Although the Huang-Lao policies of the *Boshu* fit early Han conditions, they also fit the conditions of the late Warring States. Those seeking to unify the state in the turbulent Warring States period confronted the same need to gain the support of the people and local power brokers. Further, an author of the late Warring States would surely have been aware of the theoretical and practical limitations of Qin's Legalist policies. Qin was a dominant state long before it unified the empire in 221 B.C. It would not be difficult to project the future of the empire under Legalist rule by observing life within the Qin state. Therefore the author of the *Boshu* could have written a work critical of Qin policies that constrained the power of the Legalist sovereign and reconfirmed the commitment of the government to serve the people before Qin unification. Given the other arguments cited previously—particularly, the absence of any mention of Qin—the *Boshu* would appear to be a late Warring States rather than a Qin or Han product.

In the matters of dating and authorship, however, there is room for disagreement. Hence I avoid as much as possible basing my interpretation of the *Boshu* on a narrowly defined period. How one dates the text of course will affect one's interpretation. Nevertheless, inasmuch as the conditions between the late Warring State and early Han are in many ways similar, my interpretation of the *Boshu* is compatible with either a late Warring States or a Qin to early Han dating.

2. Methodology

The nature of Huang-Lao thought as a deliberate synthesis of the best ideas of other schools makes it difficult to clearly articulate its uniqueness within the tradition. One must examine not only the ways in which Huang-Lao is similar to other schools from which it borrowed ideas, but how it differs from them. I argue that the uniqueness of Huang-Lao lies in its promotion of a foundational naturalism. The foundational character of Huang-Lao is manifest in various ways: in the *Boshu*'s epistemology, metaphysics, philosophy of language, jurisprudence, and so on. Although I discuss each of these areas, a few words may be in order as to why I have given such a central place to law and morality and the relation between them as illustrative of the differences between the philosophy of Huang-Lao and other classical schools.

To begin with, the importance of law within the Huang-Lao school is widely acknowledged. Indeed, as noted earlier, many commentators have made law the centerpiece of their analysis, arguing for a similarity between the author of the *Boshu* and Han Fei, Shen Dao, Shen Buhai, and so on. Organizing the analysis around each philosopher's views about law and morality offers easy access to the differences between them, in part because law and morality are central concerns of Chinese philosophers. It is a commonplace that Chinese philosophy is predominantly social and political philosophy: rather than being preoccupied with metaphysical quandaries, Chinese thinkers tend to center their aim on the Socratic question of how we as individuals and as a society (ought to) live. This is not to claim that Chinese philosophers are completely unconcerned with metaphysics. Most thinkers engage in some metaphysical speculation, and some more than others. The author of the *Boshu* is one of those more inclinced toward metaphysical musing. Indeed, his social and political views are grounded in his metaphysics. Yet when all is said and done his primary philosophical concerns remain social and political—one of the most important being the role, nature and normative basis of law as a means for effecting sociopolitical order.

Law, for better or worse, is a cornerstone of social and political philosophy, and not only for those schools such as Huang-Lao that favor a rule of law. Even those schools that consider law and morality to be nothing more than the will to power of the ruling class and hence deny the normative legitimacy of law take a philosophical stand in their rejection of law and morality. One learns much about the differences between the thought of Huang-Lao and Lao Zi, for instance, from the latter's dismissal of laws and his reasons for doing so.

2.1   Philosophy of Law: A Hermeneutical Framework

To understand the claim that Huang-Lao sponsors a natural law theory, we must first determine, as far as possible, what constitutes natural law. This is not as straightforward as one might suppose. The natural law tradition is extremely heterogeneous, arguably embracing such unlikely bedfellows as Plato, Hamurabi, Mohammed, Aquinas, Kant, and some have suggested, Confucius, Han Fei, and Shang Yang.[80] To clarify what I intend by natural law, it may be helpful not only to examine key features of natural law theory as construed by contemporary jurisprudes, but to contrast it with other philosophies of law such as legal positivism and Dworkin's interpretive account of the law as integrity.

A fundamental tenet of natural law theory is that there is a necessary relation between law and morality.[81] Advocates of natural law on the whole take exception to the legal positivists' notion that "what pleases the prince has the force of law."[82] They do not believe that one is obligated to obey the law simply because it is the will of a sovereign or sovereign body that has the power to enforce it. Nor do they allow that such an obligation is generated solely on the grounds that certain specified institutional procedures were followed in legislating the law.[83] There need to be, they contend, some ethical or rational reasons underlying our laws and our obligation to obey the law—hence their rallying cry: "an unjust law is no law at all."[84]

More specifically, these reasons that justify the law, create an obligation to obey the law, or simply account for the nature and origin of the law, are, at least on what I shall call a strict reading of natural law theory, foundational reasons. To clarify the foundational nature of natural law arguments, it might be instructive to first contrast it with an alternative methodology, that of coherence, as exemplified in the works of John Rawls and Joel Feinberg.[85]

For Rawls and Feinberg, the objective of the ethical reasoning process is to achieve an equilibrium between one's judgments and one's personally and communally held moral beliefs or intuitions. Coherence theories aim to make one's system or web of beliefs coherent by bringing one's ethical judgments into line with one's intuitions. They are nonfoundational in that no belief is privileged as most basic or fundamental. There are no first principles that serve as the foundation on which to build up an edifice of moral argument, no axiomatic moral truths from which one spins out a moral system through deduction or formal logical argument.

To justify one's position, one simply appeals to other beliefs in the web. There are no claims that one's beliefs correspond to objective reality, that one's theory "cuts at the joints of nature," that one's ethical principles correspond to objectively true principles existing in Nature or Platonic Heaven or some other nonhuman realm. Were someone to challenge one's beliefs, one could bring forth arguments and reasons that one believes to be persuasive in hopes of convincing the other person. But there are no guarantees of resolution. The conversation could continue until agreement is reached or break off with the parties agreeing to disagree. As Feinberg observes, foundational philosophers are likely to object to this approach: "They will find no semblance of a complete moral system, no reduction of moral derivatives to moral primitives, no grounding of ultimate principles in self-evident truths, or in 'the nature of man,' the commandments of God, or the dialectic of history. . . . [One may] appeal . . . to all kinds of reasons normally produced in practical discourse, from efficiency and utility to fairness, coherence, and human rights. But I make no effort to derive some of these reasons from others, or to rank them in terms of their degree of basicness."[87] Whereas coherence theorists look to all kinds of reasons to make their case—from pragmatic considerations of efficiency and utility to intuitions to contextual considerations such as existing customs and political structures—natural law theorists seek to base their arguments and their ethical system on firmer foundations.

Natural law is often grounded in some ultimate source of value that is beyond further questioning; it is derived from some transcendent order or first principles that determine the human order and are discovered by humans, not created by them to suit their purposes or to bring coherence to their system of beliefs.[88] Natural law, unlike conventional or positive law, is often held to be universal and immutable; it does not change from context to context as the particular beliefs, customs, and social institutions change.[80] Natural law is often the language of privileged vocabularies, of final vocabularies; it is the language of the Absolute Good, of Inalienable Rights, Divine Commandments, and Categorical Imperatives.[90]

To illustrate the foundational dimension of natural law, we can isolate four main varieties, though in practice they often overlap. The first is divine law. One is obligated to obey the law because it is the command of God. Islamic law is a good example, as is Judaism in which God reveals the law to Moses. It is foundational in that the laws are the direct commands of a transcendent deity who represents an ultimate source of value. Having discovered it to be the word of God, it is unnecessary and indeed fruitless to continue asking for further justification. Needham speaks for many when he observes that the Chinese lack an "autochthonous idea of a supreme being" who could serve as a transcendent divine lawmaker.[91]

The laws of nature are a second prominent basis for natural law. As Needham has pointed out, natural law and the laws of nature go back to a common root in many Western traditions.[92] This attempt to ground law in the universal and immutable laws of the natural order, he argues, never occurred in China. I dispute this claim, arguing that Huang-Lao thought as represented in the *Boshu* does indeed ground its theory of natural law in the objective laws of the natural order.

Third, natural law is commonly defended on moral grounds: the law reflects fundamental ethical principles that we are obligated to obey. It is foundational to the extent that these principles are not justified on pragmatic grounds, as reasonable in light of one's particular context, goals, web of beliefs, but rather are seen as self-evident or to reflect some ultimate value that cannot be compromised or questioned. Some argue, for instance, that abortion should be illegal because it violates a fundamental moral principle—the taking of (innocent) life—which is never permissible.

Indeed it is often asserted that the linkage of law with ethics distinguishes natural law from legal positivism.[93] But this assertion stands in need of clarification. It is true that for many, Hart among them, a defining trait of legal positivism is captured in the minimum separation thesis: "the simple contention that it is in no sense a necessary truth that laws reproduce or satisfy certain demands of morality."[94] But to insist that the law reflect some consideration of ethical matters need not make one a natural law proponent in the strict sense. The choice is not simply either legal positivism or natural law.

Ronald Dworkin's interpretive theory of the law as integrity provides a middle ground.[95] It requires judges interpret the law in the way that makes the law the best it can be. For Dworkin, this means that the judge must make the law coherent in principle, so far as possible. In so doing, due consideration must be given to the ethical issues of justice, fairness, due process, and political integrity—the demand that the law be made consistent with past rulings and decisions.

Although ethical concerns play a prominent role in Dworkin's theory, their role is not a foundational one. Justice, fairness, due process, and political integrity are to be brought into an equilibrium. No one of them is privileged as the most basic. It is the duty of the judge to balance them in light of the particular circumstances. It may be that concern for fairness outweighs the need for due process, or that justice must be traded off to secure political integrity. In the end, what justifies a particular law or legal decision is not some unverifiable correspondence to foundational moral principles, but that in the eyes of the judge the decision reflects the best balance of the various concerns, all things considered.[96]

Our fourth and final kind of natural law attempts to provide rational grounds for law and legal obligations by deriving them from "pure reason" or from first principles that are self-evident, or at least self-evident given some account of human nature, social organization, or morality. A recent version of this type of natural law theory is that of John Finnis, who maintains that theories of natural law are "theories about the rational foundations for moral judgment."[97] As he sees it, "principles of natural law explain the obligatory force . . . of positive laws, even when those laws cannot be deduced from those principles."[98] Rather than relying on strict rational deduction of laws from moral principles, Finnis bases his natural law on "principles of practical reasonableness that call for co-operative life in the wide 'political' community, and for the authority that alone makes life practicable."[99] A system of laws is morally justified on the grounds that it is necessary to make social living possible.

Finnis's theory is supported by two pillars: first, "a set of basic practical principles which indicate the basic forms of human flourishing as goods to be pursued and realized." These "basic goods" are, we are told, self-evident. Second, "a set of basic methodological requirements of practical reasonableness . . . which distinguish sound from unsound practical thinking and which . . . provide the criteria for distinguishing between . . . ways of acting that are morally right or morally wrong."[100] Finnis's system is foundational in the sense that it starts from an axiomatic assumption about rationality, rational rules, and human nature and then builds a case for law and legal obligations on that basis. Although he attempts to diminish the foundational nature of his project by appealing to "practical reasoning," what he means by this is something far different from the pragmatic practical reasoning of most coherence theorists: "By 'practical' . . . I do not mean 'workable' as opposed to unworkable, efficient as opposed to inefficient; I mean 'with a view to decision and action.' Practical thinking is thinking about what (one ought) to do."[101] The underlying belief is still that legal and moral principles are rationally discoverable and that these then generate morally obligatory rules of conduct: "If anything can be said to be required by or contrary to natural law, then everything that is morally . . . i.e. reasonably . . . required to be done is required by natural law."[102] Once one determines—based on Finnis's indemonstrable, self-evident basic goods—what is reasonable, one knows what is one's moral and hence legal duty.

Two additional points may be made about this fourth type of natural law theory. First, such theories are often teleological in that laws are held to be morally justifiable if they promote, or at least accord with, our nature or end as human beings, hence their description as "natural" laws. Finnis, for instance, ties what is reasonable and hence moral/legal to basic goods that are forms of "human flourishing." To illustrate more concretely, some maintain, as does Aquinas, that the purpose of sexual activity is procreation. Therefore laws prohibiting sexual activity between homosexuals or the use of birth control devices in sexual activity gain support on grounds that they violate our natural ends.[103]

Second, theories of this type are called *natural* in that knowledge of the laws is often held to be acquired through special "natural" human faculties—through sensation and reason, as with Locke, for example. Similarly, Aquinas maintains that humans have an innate disposition—*synderesis*—to grasp the precepts of natural law.[104] By using our innate faculties and capacities—usually not shared with animals—we humans are somehow able to discover natural laws.

The epistemological assumption that our minds mirror nature is the central form of foundationalism criticized by Richard Rorty, as well as by Alan Donagan who, following Wilfrid Sellars, deems it the Fallacy of the Naturally Given: "Knowledge is either of the sort of entity naturally suited to be immediately present to consciousness, or of entities whose existence and properties are entailed by entities of the first sort."[105] The assumption is that, because our minds naturally perceive the world to be a certain way, the world is indeed that way. Or, to relate it more directly to natural law, it is the assumption that because we are led by our reason (as with Locke) or innate dispositions (as with Aquinas) to hold certain laws to be true or naturally valid, they are indeed so.

To attempt to justify natural laws by appeal to a special relation between the person and the object known—that is, the natural laws—however, is to elide a causal explanation of how one came to have the belief with a justification for that belief. As Sellars points out, "in characterizing an episode or a state as that of knowing, we are not giving an empirical description of that episode or state; we are placing it in the logical space of reasons, of justifying and being able to justify what one says."[106] To maintain that one has grasped by innate disposition that abortion is illicit explains why one has that belief in the sense of how it is one came to hold it, but it does not justify it.

Although I believe the Rorty-Sellars critique seriously undermines the foundationalism of natural law doctrines, I do not intend to pursue this further in that it is not my purpose here to attack or defend natural law theories per se. Rather I am interested in providing a hermeneutical framework for sorting out the relation between the legal philosophy of the author of the *Boshu* and that of his contemporaries. Consequently, although much remains to be said about natural law theories by way of exposition and elaboration as well as criticism and defense, I believe enough has been said for the present purpose. I will argue that Huang-Lao espouses natural law in a strict, foundational sense; Confucius, a Dworkinian interpretive theory of law; and Legalism, positive law.

Having stated what I wish to accomplish by appeal to contemporary jurisprudence, I should make clear what I am not attempting. First, apart from the potential benefit of providing a systematic account of a natural law theory grounded in the objective laws of the natural order, I do not intend for this work to make significant contributions to Western philosophy of law. I have developed the hermeneutical framework of legal positivism, natural law, and Dworkin's coherence/constructive interpretation theory of law only to the extent necessary to serve my purposes of explicating the differences between Huang-Lao thought and the thought of other major figures in the Chinese tradition. This is not to say that the explication of natural law in terms of foundationalism and the contrasting of this with Dworkin's coherence theory could not make a contribution to Western philosophy of law if further developed. Yet this is not the appropriate forum.

Nor will this work make a direct contribution to comparative philosophy of law. First, I do not believe that the natural law theory presented in the *Huang-Lao Boshu* is philosophically tenable—it is certainly out of step with the current postmodern trend away from natural law theories to a more hermeneutically sensitive theory à la Dworkin. Though it might be of interest to the comparative philosopher to compare Huang-Lao natural law with Western natural law theories, I will not take up that project in great detail here. Any such comparisons will be solely for the purpose of explicating Huang-Lao. Second, although the Confucian and to a lesser extent Daoist and Legalist traditions might be of interest and value to Western philosophers of law, I will not be able to present here the kind of sophisticated comparisons between, say, Confucius and Dworkin, that would be necessary to demonstrate just what it is about the Chinese traditions that might be of value and why. At best my remarks can be only suggestive. Again, though I believe a thorough comparison of Confucius and Dworkin would be of great interest to jurisprudes both Eastern and Western, it must await another forum.[107]

Comparative philosophy has, in my view, three distinguishable though not completely distinct stages. In the first, the most sinological for those of us doing Chinese comparative philosophy, one simply tries to get a line on what the Chinese text is about. Although one can never escape one's own tradition and avoid asking those questions that are of interest to oneself, one must nevertheless attempt as much as possible to understand the text from a culturally sensitive perspective.[108] Having gained a context-sensitive interpretation of the text, one can in the second stage make more explicit comparisons to Western works.[109] Finally, one can utilize the insights gained in the first two stages to contribute to Western philosophy without necessarily attempting to link the ideas appropriated to an interpretation or a set of terminology of a particular Chinese text. One simply makes one's argument about the merits of a coherence approach to law without defending the ideas as Confucian, for example.

Given the newness of the *Boshu* and the relative neglect of law in ancient China, we are now in the first phase. If I am successful at explicating the Huang-Lao theory of natural law and contrasting it to other ancient Chinese legal philosophies, I will have provided the necessary groundwork for the second and third stages.

II. The Natural Way of Huang-Lao

In this chapter, I argue that Huang-Lao philosophy is best understood as a foundational naturalism. The first section is devoted to an explication of this concept, the following ones to a demonstration that the philosophy of the *Boshu* does indeed fit the description. In the second section, I examine the nature of nature; in the third, the place of humans within the cosmic natural order. Finally, in the fourth section, I explore the relationship between humans and nature by investigating how humans go about following the Way.

1. Foundational Naturalism

Naturalism is a much abused term. Used in conjunction with a wide variety of theories, its precise meaning, shrouded in a dense layer of conceptual mist, often eludes us. In contending that Huang-Lao espouses a foundational naturalism, I intend the following. First, as a *naturalism*, humans are conceived of as part of the cosmic natural order understood as an organic or holistic system or ecosystem. In the language of Huang-Lao, dao as the cosmic natural order embraces both the way of humans (*ren dao* 人道) as well as that of nonhuman nature (*tian dao* 天道).[1] Second, Huang-Lao privileges the cosmic natural order: the natural order has normative priority. It is taken to be the highest value or realm of highest value. Third, and correlate to the second, the human-social order must be consistent and compatible with the cosmic natural order rather than nature and the natural order being subservient to the whims and needs of humans.

Huang-Lao advances a *foundational* naturalism in that the cosmic natural order serves as the basis, the foundation, for construction of the human order. This means, in the case of the *Boshu*, not simply that human behavior and social institutions are to be modeled on the way of nature. The natural order constitutes the foundation for the human social order in the more radical sense that the correct social order is held to be implicate in

27

the cosmic order. The task of humans is to discover and implement it. In this way, the *Boshu* naturalizes the human order by grounding it in a predetermined natural order. The foundational character of Huang-Lao naturalism is signaled primarily in three ways: by the transcendence of the cosmic natural order, the realist underpinnings of Huang-Lao philosophy, and the author's correspondence theory of language and epistemology.

1.1   *Huang-Lao Naturalism*

I have suggested that Huang-Lao conceived of the cosmic natural order (*dao*) as an holistic or organic system that consists of both humans (*ren*) and nonhuman nature (*tian*). Alternatively, one might conceive of humans as apart from nature, as dualistically opposed to nature. One might then construe the universe in mechanical terms, as a machine operated by humans. In the *Boshu*, however, *tian-di-ren* 天地人—heaven, earth, and humans—form an integrated system: "The way of one who realizes kingly rulership of the empire consists of a heavenly component, a human component and an earthly component. When these three are employed in line with each other . . . one will possess the empire."[2]

The emphasis on the *tian-di-ren* triad attests to the integrated character of Huang-Lao naturalism, supporting the claim that Huang-Lao does indeed conceive of humans as part of the cosmic natural order. The relationship between the cosmic natural order, the human order, and the order of nonhuman nature is muddied, however, by the ambiguity of the terminology. The problem, which plagues many naturalists, the author of the *Boshu* included, lies in the failure to consistently distinguish between *natural* and *nature* as pertaining to the cosmic natural order as opposed to that part of the cosmic natural order that is nonhuman. In the *Boshu*, *tian* (*tian dao*: natural-heavenly way; *tian zhi dao*: the way of nature-heaven; *tian di zhi dao*: the way of heaven and earth/nature) is sometimes used as a synonym for dao, the cosmic natural order. At other times it is used to indicate one part of the cosmic natural order, nonhuman nature, in contrast to the human-social part (*ren*: human; *ren dao*: humanly way; *ren zhi dao*: way of humans). In fact, *tian* is even more ambiguous than the English *nature* in that it may also refer to a particular part of nonhuman nature, the sky, firmament, or heavens, in contrast to *di*, the earth. In assessing the naturalism of the *Boshu*, one does well to keep in mind this linguistic ambiguity and the possibility that it might signal conceptual equivocation on the part of the author. In this work, unless otherwise specified, *natural order* is to be understood as the cosmic order that embraces both humans and nonhuman nature, and *nature* to refer to the nonhuman component of the cosmic natural order.

That the natural order is normatively privileged, the second defining trait of Huang-Lao naturalism, differentiates it from both theisms and humanisms. Roughly, theisms pit God and the sacred religious order over and against the profane, with nature and humans often making up the latter. Nature and humans have value to the extent that they partake of the sacred; their value is predicated on their relation to the sacred. Human behavior is evaluated according to ethical standards that derive their validity from the holy, being, if not the word of God, sanctioned by religious powers.

Humanisms, or more accurately, anthropocentricisms—historically often a response to theisms—privilege humans and the human-social order. Not only are the concerns of humans given priority but humans are given responsibility for determining what constitutes a proper order. The universe can be shaped to fit human needs. Nature, if valued at all, is so for its utility, its ability to serve one's interests. One's concern for nature need not go beyond self-interested worry as to whether nature will prove amenable or resistant to one's attempts to bend it to human will.[3]

In the *Boshu*, the natural order is the primary realm of value. One indication of this is the attempt to justify behaviors, institutions, or relations by claiming them to be "natural."[4] For instance, the author argues that just as there are differences between things in nature, some are high, some are low, so there are differences between humans: some are noble, some are lowly. The *Boshu* seeks in this way to justify a human pattern of social organization, the "feudal" or bureaucratic class society, as natural.[5]

Ancillary to the normative privileging of the natural order is the belief that the human order must be compatible with the natural order. Any "way of man" that destroys the natural order, that undermines the ecosystem as a whole, making human life impossible, would be unacceptable to the author of the *Boshu*—as it would be, I presume, to most of us.[6] Nature and the natural order as a whole do not exist simply to serve the needs of humans. Indeed, rather than nature being subservient to humans, humans are by and large subservient to nature.

Imitative and Nonimitative Naturalism

The demand that the human order be compatible with the normatively privileged natural order allows for a variety of possible relations between humans, nonhuman nature, and the natural order as a whole. Specifically, one can distinguish between *imitative* and *nonimitative* naturalism. In imitative naturalism, human behavior, social institutions, relations, patterns of organization, and so on are modeled on nonhuman nature. For instance, the *Boshu* contends that nature has its times for promoting life and for curtailing life. In the spring and summer, life is nurtured: flowers blossom, crops grow, animals thrive. In fall and winter, death prevails: flowers wither, crops are harvested, animals perish or hibernate. Human society, analogously, must have its times for promoting and curtailing life. In the spring and summer, when the life forces of yang are in ascendancy, rulers should be generous in distributing society's largesse and lenient in implementing punishments. In the fall and winter, when the yin forces of death reach their apex, rulers should strictly enforce laws and diligently carry out punishments and executions.[7]

In nonimitative naturalism, the human social order need not emulate the ways and processes of nature. To be sure the human order must be sufficiently compatible with the order of nonhuman nature to ensure that the system as a whole is able to function in a way that allows for the continued existence of humans. Yet humans may have their way, nonhuman nature, its own. While nonhuman nature may be a realm of contention where only the strong survive, human society need not be.

Nonimitative naturalists take the natural order to be a result of negotiation between nature and humans. Human interests are important, but so are the interests of nature. One must find a balance between the two. Of course, it is ultimately humans who must assess the interests and value of nature. This does not preclude one, however, from taking into consideration the possibility that nature has its own value and interests: in planning a new construction project, one gives thought to the animals that would be disadvantaged by having their current habitat destroyed and so forth.

Imitative naturalists, on the other hand, have a tendency to conceive of not only the cosmic natural order as normatively superior to the human order but of the nonhuman natural realm as superior as well. This often leads to the denigration of the human, of anything human-made, of society. What does not imitate nature is artificial, bogus, bad; what does is natural, real, good.

Huang-Lao, although it does not overtly denigrate the human realm, favors a naturalism that is heavily imitative. Of course, not every human action or social practice has a natural correlate. And there are some instances in the *Boshu* where humans do not simply acquiesce to nonhuman nature. Thus "imitative"–"nonimitative" are ends of a continuum rather than either-or antithetical propositions. Nevertheless, there is in the *Boshu*, as will be demonstrated more fully later, a strong emphasis on the need to comply with nature, in addition to sufficient examples of behavior and institutions being required to imitate nature, to merit the label *imitative*. Whoever the author of the *Boshu* may be, he is clearly not Xun Zi, who, criticizing his Daoist counterparts, beseeches humans to take control of nature and employ it in their interests (64/17/44):

You glorify nature and meditate on her,
Why not domesticate and regulate her?
You obey nature and sing her praises,
Why not control her course and use it?
You look on the seasons with reverence and await them,
Why not respond to them by seasonal activities?

1.2   Huang-Lao Foundationalism

Understanding Huang-Lao as a naturalism according to our three criteria provides a foothold into the philosophy of *Boshu*, but it is at best an initial step. As noted, there are many possible naturalist philosophies consistent with the criteria. To gain a deeper appreciation of Huang-Lao thought, it is necessary to explore its foundational character. This is brought out in part by the transcendence of the natural order.

Transcendence

By *transcendent* I mean the following: *A* is transcendent with respect to *B* if the meaning or import of *B* cannot be fully analyzed and explained without recourse to *A* but the reverse is not true.[8] Normatively, the natural order is transcendent in two senses. First, it is transcendent in that it is privileged as the fundamental realm of value. That is, the natural realm is transcendent in its normative priority. Its value is independent of human value judgments. Humans do not determine the value of the natural order. Rather it is simply taken to be good, indeed, to be the good. It is the right Way.

Though Huang-Lao is foundational in its privileging of the natural order as transcendent, as normatively prior, this may for many be unobjectionable. We all would probably agree that destroying the ecosystem to the point where life, particularly human life, no longer could be sustained is something to be avoided. Philosophically, however, a thorough-going pragmatist or coherence theorist would argue that, although preservation of a life-sustaining ecosystem is unquestionably of vital interest to us, there is no theoretical reason to privilege it as most fundamental, to take it as a given, as an absolute value. It still must be located in the logical space of our reasons, weighed in light our other beliefs, values, goals, and so forth. Granted, it is a value that is likely to be high on all our lists. It is one of those core values most difficult to dislodge in our web of beliefs and norms. Nevertheless, were one to exercise one's creative powers, one could perhaps imagine a scenario in which destruction of the universe as we know it would be a normatively viable option.

We need not, however, dwell on such science-fiction-like possibilities in that Huang-Lao is transcendent in a second, more telling sense. To clarify this aspect of Huang-Lao's foundationalism, it is helpful to draw a distinction between *correspondence* and *interpretive* naturalisms.

Correspondence versus Interpretive Naturalism

Both correspondence and interpretive naturalism are naturalisms in that they conceive of humans as part of the cosmic natural order, privilege the natural order and insist that the human order be compatible with the natural order. The essential differentia is that the former conceives of the natural order as predetermined whereas the latter does not. That is, correspondence naturalists contend that there is a single, preconfigured, normatively correct Way, dao, cosmic natural order. Just as nature is rule governed, structured by constant, impersonal, universal laws of nature, so is human society rule governed, structured by constant, impersonal laws that arise from and are implicit in the cosmic natural order. Humans must simply discover and abide by these laws.

In contrast, interpretive naturalisms reject the notion that there is a single correct order. Although they may allow that the nonhuman component of the natural order is preconfigured—that nature is impersonal, constant, and rule governed—interpretive naturalists contend that there are, at least in theory, many possible natural orders. The reasoning is that the constraints imposed on humans by nature and the natural order are underdetermining: many social arrangements meet the requirement of compatibility with the survival of the ecosystem as a whole. They believe, in short, that there are many viable human ways within the cosmic Way. It is up to humans to create their own way, a way that most adequately suits their particular needs, interests, and sociopolitical-historical context.[9]

Huang-Lao naturalism is correspondence naturalism. There is a correct Way (*zheng dao* 正道). This differentiates the dao of Huang-Lao from the multiple daos of Zhuang Zi. Chad Hansen has argued that dao for the latter refers not to an absolute metaphysical entity, to some predetermined natural order, but to perspectival discourse. It is more a linguistic than metaphysical concept.[10] Although some might wish to take issue with this interpretation, it does capture the insight that for Zhuang Zi each person has in some sense his own way, his own dao. Thus in the *Zhuang Zi* there are arguably as many rights (*shi* 是) and wrongs (*fei* 非) as there are daos.[11] In the *Boshu*, by contrast, there is just one.[12]

In addition to being singular, the Way of Huang-Lao is rule governed; dao is defined by laws (*fa* 法), standards (*du* 度), patterns (*ze* 則), principles (*li* 理), forms, and names (*xing ming* 形名) that are not the product of humans but generated by the Way itself. *Fa*, *li*, and *xing ming* in the hands of the author of the *Boshu* are not mere Legalist techniques for governing, mere tools for protecting the ruler. They are normative concepts grounded in dao, in the normatively correct natural order. Indeed, they are that order. They are alternative expressions for dao, ways of verbally articulating the natural order.

Neither the Way nor the laws, principles, rules, and so forth that constitute the underlying structure of the Way are open for negotiation. They are simply taken as given, something to be discovered rather than created. In this respect, the normative universe of Huang-Lao is metaphysically predetermined. Unlike Confucius, who urges humans to extend the way,[13] the author of the *Boshu* time and again exhorts one just to hold fast to the Way. Instead of creatively determining a novel way to fit one's particular circumstance, one merely instantiates a preconfigured pattern.

Dao, then, is transcendent in the sense stipulated previously: *A* (the normatively correct Way) is transcendent with respect to *B* (human society) if the meaning or import of *B* cannot be fully analyzed and explained without recourse to *A* but the reverse is not true. In the *Boshu*, the normatively correct Way exists independent of the actual order created by humans and is therefore transcendent.

Huang-Lao Naturalism and the Logical-Aesthetic Distinction

The distinction between correspondence and interpretive naturalisms runs parallel to but is not completely isomorphic with that between a logical and aesthetic order, the latter terminology introduced by Whitehead and developed by Hall and Ames.[14] As a rule of thumb, what I would call a *foundational*, *correspondence theory*, Hall and Ames would call a *logical order*; what I would call a *pragmatic*, *interpretive* or *coherence theory*, Hall and Ames would call an *aesthetic order*.[15]

In privileging the natural order, an interpretive naturalism is foundational. Assuming a priori the normative priority of the natural order constrains the possibilities of the emergent order in a way that is neither necessary nor allowable within the aesthetic framework of Hall and Ames. To be sure, given the high stakes involved and the generality of the requirement that the natural order be given sufficient priority to ensure that (human) life is sustained, many might find this to be a relatively inoffensive form of foundationalism. Yet a foundationalism it remains. Apart from this feature, however, interpretive naturalisms—in calling for a judicious balance between the interests of humans and nature, in placing on the shoulders of humans the responsibility to create and bring about such a harmonious order, and most important, in allowing that multiple normatively acceptable orders are possible—exemplify those traits central to an aesthetic order.

An aesthetic order has the following features:[16]

1. It begins with the uniqueness of the one particular as it collaborates with other particulars in an emergent complex pattern of relatedness and, as such, will permit of no substitutions: plurality is prior to unity and disjunction to conjunction.

2. It takes as its focus the unique perspective of a concrete, specific detail revealing itself as productive of harmony or an order that is expressed by a complex of such details in their relationship to one another.

3. Given that it is concerned with the fullest disclosure of the particularity for the emergent harmony, it necessarily entails movement away from any universal characteristic to the concrete detail.

4. It is an act of "disclosure"—the achieved coordination of concrete details in novel patterns that reflect their uniqueness—and hence is describable in the qualitative language of richness, intensity, and so forth.

5. It is fundamentally anarchic and contingent, and as such, is the ground for optimum creativity, where creativity is to be understood in contradistinction to determination.

6. "Rightness" in this context refers to the degree to which the insistent particularity of the detail in tension with the consequent unity of these specific details is self-evidently expressive of an aesthetical pleasing order.

A logical order, in contrast, has these features:

1. It begins with a preassigned pattern of relatedness, a "blueprint," wherein unity is prior to plurality as determinative of the construction (of order).

2. It registers concrete particularity only to the extent and in those respects necessary to satisfy this preassigned pattern and will permit of substitution by any particular that can satisfy these same conditions.

3. Given that it reduces the particular to only those aspects needed to illustrate the given pattern, it necessarily entails a process of formal abstraction, moving away from the concrete particular towards the universal.

4. It constitutes an act of "closure"—the satisfaction of predetermined specifications—and is hence describable in a quantitative terminology of completeness.

5. Being characterized by necessity, it limits creativity to conformity, renders novelty defect.
6. "Rightness" in this context refers to the degree of conformity to the preassigned pattern.

For Hall and Ames, the best example of an aesthetic order is the philosophy of Confucius, though that of Lao Zi and Zhuang Zi are also so interpreted. In fact, they suggest the character of Chinese thought as a whole is best understood as aesthetic rather than logical.

To illustrate the logical model, Hall and Ames point to the "transcendent formalism" that Stephen Pepper ascribes to Plato, which entails "a preassigned pattern that registers particular phenomena as 'real' or 'good' only to the extent that they satisfy the pre-existent Ideas" or Forms.[17] Yet they need not have gone beyond the bounds of the Chinese tradition to find instances of the logical order. Huang-Lao correspondence naturalism falls, with minor qualifications, rather neatly under this heading.

We have already observed that dao for Huang-Lao is understood as a preconfigured natural order. There is a well-articulated cosmic blueprint replete with laws, patterns, principles, standards, and measures: the universe is, in a word, rule governed. In fact, the Way is even discussed in quantifiable terms. We are told that the natural order grasps the one, fixes the two, illumines the three, ensures the standard duration of the four seasons, implements the seven laws, establishes the eight measures, and so forth (53:48a–50a). In a similar vein, the author repeatedly calls attention to the importance of fixed measures (*du*):

> The area circumscribed by a compass is called a circle; that within a carpenter's ruler is deemed a square; that marked off below the plumbline is dubbed straight; that under the carpenter's water level is said to be flat. Measuring by the standards of foot and inch, things are said to be large and small, long and short. Weighing by the balances and scales, things are said to be light and heavy and to be correct. Measuring the volume in terms of bushels and piculs, things are said to be many and few and of a given quantity. These eight measures are the models to be applied. (51:42b)

Further, the Way, as a preassigned, rule governed pattern, is to be instantiated, not created. It is characterized by necessity:[18] one must hold fast to the Way. As expected of a logical order, "rightness" is not a matter of appropriateness in the particular context but of correspondence to the determinate order, of conformity to the law. Following the Way, therefore, constitutes an act of "closure." Instead of a novel expression of one's particularity, a *dis*closure of one's uniqueness, one merely adheres to a predetermined pattern.

In the logical order, unity is prior to plurality and the whole takes precedence over the parts. In the foundational natural order of Huang-Lao, this is also so. The integration of humans into the natural order exemplified by the heaven-earth-human triad attests to the unity of the system: as the all-encompassing natural order, dao is characterized by a constant, pervasive unity, and hence deemed "the one" (*yi* 一).[19] And the normative privileging of the natural order reflects the priority of the whole to any of the parts: as the source of all things, dao is said to be an independent, unchanging standard (87:169b).

Though Huang-Lao naturalism evidences many of the key features of a logical order, one might nevertheless hesitate to declare it a perfect fit. Whereas dao as the cosmic Way that encompasses both the way of humans and of nature is "universal," and whereas humans are required to comply with a rule governed, preconfigured Way, it is not clear that the author of the *Boshu* would wish to denigrate the particular to the extent that it becomes nothing more than an interchangeable part. In fact, some scholars, Teng Fu among them, have argued that each thing in the Huang-Lao universe has its own unique place within the cosmic harmony.[20] For Teng, *li* (principle) serves this individuating function. Each thing has its inherent regularity, law, order: its own *li*. For the cosmos to be perfectly ordered, each particular must find its preassigned place within the overall cosmic structure. Although this view still assumes a preconfigured universe, it provides the particular with a uniqueness and value vis-à-vis the whole that runs counter to the decidedly inferior status of the substitutable particular of the logical order.

The appropriateness of applying to Huang-Lao the universal-particular relationship of the logical order may also be questioned from a reverse angle. To this point I have made much of the singular and predetermined character of the Huang-Lao Way. But one must take care not to overstate the *Boshu*'s position. The author, having painted with broad stokes the outline of a preconfigured normatively correct Way, may have intended to leave some of the details to be filled in by others. In particular, and *contra* Teng, although each thing comes into existence with a form and a name, and falls under a *li*, it is not clear whether each thing has a *unique* form, name, or principle. Consequently, it is not clear whether each thing has a predetermined place and path in the cosmic structure peculiar to it alone such that realization of cosmic perfection entails each thing's finding its particular place in the preconfigured cosmic pattern. Though the Way, laws, principles, names, and forms serve as predetermined constraints on human possibilities, they may nevertheless allow room on a localized level for more than one possible arrangement within the more universal constraints.[21]

Although the emphasis remains on accommodation, on compliance with the natural order, there may be, within the broad restrictions imposed on humans by the Way, laws, principles, and so forth, some room for human "initiative," albeit in a limited sense. At the very least, it is up to humans to determine whether they will comply with the natural order and, if so, with what attitude. That one has to accommodate the natural order need not be construed as particularly burdensome or confining. Nature provides humans with tremendous bounty. Taking advantage of the resources nature has to offer is most certainly within the interests of humans. To reap the benefit offered by mother nature, however, it is necessary to respect her ways. In planting the right crops in the right place at the right time, we go along with nature. At the same time we serve our own ends. The lesson to be drawn is that one need not regard the need to comply with the natural order as inevitably detrimental to one's life possibilities, to one's opportunities for personal disclosure and to one's hopes for self-realization.

A final point of qualification in regard to the appropriateness of reading Huang-Lao as a logical order concerns the relation of novelty to change. That the Huang-Lao universe is predetermined does not mean it is unchanging and static. This is not Plato's world of unchanging eternal Forms in which the phenomenal world of becoming is relegated to a secondary, less real, less true, status. Quite the contrary. The Huang-Lao universe is one of constant change. The key, however, is *constant* change. Change itself is rule governed and built into the system. It is grounded, as it were, in the natural processes themselves.

Weak versus Strong Transcendence

Having stated in what sense Huang-Lao naturalism is transcendent, a few words of clarification are in order as to the way in which it is not transcendent. As defined, the Judeo-Christian conception of God, Aristotle's Unmoved Mover, and Plato's Forms as well as the Huang-Lao conception of the natural order are all transcendent. But clearly dao is not God, and Huang-Lao is not Plato.

A further distinction needs to be drawn between transcendence in a strong sense (*chao jue* 超絕) and a weak sense (*chao yue* 超越). The former suggests a radical ontological disparity or separation. The *creatio ex nihilo* cosmogonic paradigm of Genesis in which God, ontologically distinct and temporally prior to the world, creates the world out of nothing is perhaps the clearest example. The interpretation of Plato's Forms as external, existing in some ontologically independent realm, would be another instance of the strong sense, whereas the reading of Aristotle's universals as indwelling, internal to phenomena, though still teleologically predetermining, would be an example of the weak sense.[22]

Huang-Lao advances transcendence of the weak sense. In that it does not, therefore, entail a radical ontological separation between the source of the determining order and the human realm that complies with this order, it can still be construed in terms of an organismic or holistic natural cosmology. The order is certainly not derived from a deity outside the system as a whole. Yet neither is it the interactive organismic cosmology of Confucius in which humans participate in defining the social and natural orders—the latter most notable with Dong Zhongshu. That is, we do not have in the *Boshu* a cosmology in which humans are responsible for the creation and achievement of a social order that emerges out of their own aesthetic-normative judgment rather than in accordance with preestablished principles. Nevertheless, this does not preclude one from considering Huang-Lao a variation of the *tian ren he yi* 天人合一 notion, where this is understood to embrace any kind of organicism or natural order that encompasses both humans and nonhuman nature, including a weak transcendent one.[23]

Correspondence Realism

That the *Boshu* advances a form of correspondence realism provides a second indication that Huang-Lao naturalism is indeed foundational (correspondence) naturalism.[24] The author believes that faithful adherence to nature is not only desirable but possible. By overcoming one's subjective biases, one can mirror nature: one can directly perceive "objective" reality.

'Objective' and 'subjective' have served many masters. They have even been retooled to fit this postmodern era in which hope of escaping one's human perspective to directly access reality has been abandoned. No longer is it considered possible, at least among postmodernists, to leap out of one's skin—one's cultural, linguistic, historical tradition—to compare one's theories with something absolute, with nature's own vocabulary. As a result, the terms have taken on new meanings to fit the times. In an effort to set off the old from the new, Rorty has contributed the following analysis:[25]

objective 1: representing things as they really are
subjective 1: a product only of what is in here (the heart, mind, soul)

objective 2: characterizing the view that would be agreed on as a result of argument undeflected by irrelevant consideration

subjective 2: what has been, or would be, or should be, set aside by rational discussants—[what] is seen to be, or should be seen to be, irrelevant to the subject matter of the theory

The second set reflects the new postmodern consciousness. The difference between subjective and objective in this view has to do with how well something fits one's framework and its degree of confirmation within one's conceptual scheme. We attribute the accolade *objective* to that which is, by our lights, so well confirmed that it seems to be indubitable.[26] This interpretation of subjective and objective, although perfectly coherent within the framework of contemporary postmodern hermeneutics, is not the sense of subjective-objective operative in Huang-Lao thought.

In referring to the *Boshu*, I intend *subjective* and *objective* in the traditional epistemological sense captured in the first of Rorty's pairs. Subjective is what one perceives, experiences, knows based on one's limited, biased perspective. Objective is what corresponds to "the world out there," to reality. This sense of objective brings out the realist foundations of Huang-Lao thought and most accurately reflects the *Boshu*'s correspondence epistemology and theory of language.

Huang-Lao's Correspondence Epistemology

Although I examine Huang-Lao epistemology[27] and philosophy of language in detail later, I offer here a preliminary sketch to further clarify the foundational character of Huang-Lao naturalism. The author of the *Boshu* believed that it is possible to directly apprehend and understand (*jian zhi* 見知) objective reality. To do so, one must overcome all subjective biases. One must become empty (*xu* 虛) and tranquil (*jing* 靜). This will enable one to be impartial, without personal biases (*wu si* 無私), and to directly apprehend objective reality understood as the Way, principles (*li*), laws (*fa*), or forms and names (*xing ming*) of things.

One will then be able to distinguish right from wrong, reality from pretense. One will be able to *wu wei* 無為, comply with the natural order, make punishments match the benchmark of heaven, know the origins of fortune and misfortune, ensure that names correspond to reality. One will, in short, be able to govern, to rule over a properly regulated empire. Having discovered the Way, one will be able to carry it out.

In reading the *Boshu* one cannot help but note the total absence of the kind of vertigo that plagues many post-Nietzschean thinkers. In the wake of God's demise, countless philosophers seem to be lost and adrift in a sea of nihilism. Having given up transcendent sources of knowledge, and accepting that the inability to escape the human perspective undermines the foundationalist project, they find themselves staring into a normative abyss. It is as if depriving values of their transcendent foundations has reduced all values to an equal footing, creating a moral free for all.

Though I do not believe the death of God need entail either cognitive or normative egalitarianism—the views that any idea or value is as warranted or as good as any other—I do find it striking that one discerns in the *Boshu* none of the concern for the inherent fallibility of our limited perspectival views that so dominates the *Zhuang Zi*.[28] Whereas Zhuang Zi seems wholeheartedly bent on demonstrating the inevitable restrictions on one's perspective, the author of the *Boshu* appears equally confident that universal objective truth is within one's immediate grasp. To discover it, one need only empty oneself of subjective biases. Though this may not be a feat readily accomplished by anyone but a sage, that it is considered possible at all merits attention in that it betokens the kind of realist world-view and correspondence epistemology that is associated with foundationalism. One is able to be certain as to what is right and wrong in a given situation— what form of social organization or distribution of wealth is correct, for example—because one has direct access to the normative order. One is able to immediately (that is, unmediatedly) penetrate to the truth of the matter as expressed in the forms, names, principles, and laws that are a direct manifestation of dao.

Huang-Lao's Philosophy of Language

In keeping with its realism and correspondence epistemology, the *Boshu* champions a realist theory of language. Names are grounded in dao, in the objective foundations of the natural order. This distinguishes Huang-Lao's theory of *xing ming* from that of Han Fei. For the latter, the doctrine of *xing ming* (names and forms; stipulated duties and performances) is an expedient political technique designed to protect the ruler. Names, titles, and duties are defined by the ruler and those in charge as they see fit given the political circumstances. For the author of the *Boshu*, however, things arise from dao replete with form and name.[29] When names match forms, the empire is well ordered. It is the job of the sage-ruler to ensure that names correspond to reality. He is able to do this because he has language-independent access to the Way. By emptying himself of personal bias, he is able to discover objective reality and know whether or not names correspond.

Huang-Lao's realist theory of naming stands in stark contrast to the conventionalism of many of his classical counterparts. Xun Zi, for instance, advances a thorough-going conventionalism: "Names have no inherent appropriateness. Naming is done through convention. When the convention is established and the custom is formed, they are called appropriate names. If they are contrary to convention they are called inappropriate names. Names have no inherent actuality. The actualities ascribed to them are given by convention. When the convention is established and the custom formed, they are called names of such and such actualities" (83/22/25, C126). Xun Zi's conventionalism is noteworthy in that it incorporates both a weak and a strong version.[30] A weak conventionalism holds that the sounds and symbols we use to name something are social conventions. One could just as easily call a horse by the name *cow* and vice versa. A strong conventionalism holds that the way we divide reality in naming is conventional as well. If we grew up in some far away land, we might not divide the world along the lines of 'rabbit' but instead cut it up into 'rabbit-legs' and 'rabbit-torso.' Xun Zi's conventionalism embraces both versions: both the sounds and the distinctions picked out by the sounds are conventional.

Huang-Lao's theory of naming differs on both scores. In the world of Huang-Lao, each thing comes into existence with a form, and each form has a name. One cannot willy nilly decide to call a horse *cow*. More important, names refer to reality; they reflect real distinctions in the world itself.

Rather than a pragmatic, performative theory of attunement of names,[31] Huang-Lao's theory of names is a decidedly realist doctrine of rectification of names (*zheng ming* 正名). It is not simply a matter of names working as judged by the standard of pragmatic success. Huang-Lao is not primarily concerned with the ability of people to carry on their lives with the linguistic tools that happen to be available to them, to get by within a linguistic system that just so happens to name things in certain conventional ways. The standard is much more demanding. Names must be correct. They must reflect objective reality: they must correspond to the normative Way. As a result, there are rectified or correct names (*zheng ming*) and irregular or perverse ones (*qi ming* 奇名), and never the two shall meet: "Rectified names will never be irregular. Irregular names will not endure" (76:132b). When names and reality are properly aligned, one has correct names and the empire is set aright.

2. The Nature of Nature

Having sketched an overview of Huang-Lao philosophy as a foundational naturalism, I must now begin to fill in the sketch. In this section, I examine the nature of nature for Huang-Lao, documenting that nature is indeed understood to be impersonal, constant, and rule governed.

2.1   Nature as Impersonal

As noted previously, the author of the *Boshu* refers to nature as *tian*, employing a host of expressions built around that root: *tian dao* (the natural way), *tian zhi dao* (the way of nature), *tian di zhi dao* (the way of heaven and earth), *tian di zhi heng dao* (the constant way of heaven and earth). It is often difficult to state definitively the precise meaning of *tian* in a particular classical text. In part, this is due to the ambiguity mentioned previously: *tian* can refer to the natural order as a whole, to nonhuman nature, or to the sky/heavens. But it is due perhaps in even greater measure to the wide range of meaning of *tian* in the classical corpus. For early Confucians, *tian* is an anthropomorphic moral agency with the ability to sanction governments through its mandate (*tian ming* 天命).[32] For Lao Zi, it is an impersonal nature that treats humans like straw dogs, like so many scraps of waste paper leftover from a celebration.[33] For Mo Zi, it is a fully personified, religious like force that when displeased brings down ruin on the world. For Xun Zi, it is once again an impersonal nature operating impervious to the machinations of humans: "Are order and chaos due to *tian*? I say, the sun, moon, stars, planets, and auspicious periods of the calendar were the same in the time of sage-king Yu as in that of wicked king Jie" (62/17/19–20).

In the *Boshu*, *tian* is an impersonal nature: "Heaven and earth are impartial; the four seasons continue unceasingly" (45:10a). To this the author adds: "Heaven has its brightness. It is not concerned with the darkness in which the people live. The people open their doors and windows and each takes his light from it, but heaven takes no active part in this. The earth has its bounty. It is not concerned with the poverty of the people. The people fell trees and cut firewood and each takes his riches from it, but the earth as well takes no active part in this" (82:158a).

Despite these unambiguous statements as to the impersonal nature of nature, several modern commentators have claimed that *tian* is an anthropomorphic heaven similar, some say, to Confucius's *tian*.[34] In support, they point out that the author on numerous occasions speaks of *tian* sending down punishments, calamities, disasters, and the like. Yet not only does this interpretation saddle the author with a blatantly contradictory position, it fails to appreciate the fundamental thrust of the text as a whole.

Disaster occurs not because an anthropomorphic heaven wills it but because there is an objective proper order predetermined by the natural order. Failure to comply with the natural order leads to disorder and eventually to misfortune. But this, for the *Boshu*, is not the result of some mysterious interaction between humans and heaven. On the contrary. It is an entirely understandable and commonplace result. Humans might temporarily be able to gain the upper hand over nature but in the long run they will suffer for their abuses of the environment and the proper natural order. If during a drought for commercial purposes one diverts water from a lake to a river, a short-term financial gain might be won but in the end the damage to the ecosystem may be such that on balance one loses. Similarly, if a strong man uses his control of the military to serve his own interests to the detriment of the people, he may benefit for a while, but, as the author states, the people will eventually rebel. And "even though the people may not be able to succeed for the moment, they are certain to do so by the time of their descendants" (82:159a).

One need not, then, take the author's statements about *tian* sending down disasters as being any more indicative of an anthropomorphic conception of nature than the mundane comments of people today that "mother nature" is responsible for the latest natural disaster. The use of such metaphorical language need not entail an anthropomorphic worldview. It is nothing more than a *façon de parler*. We gain a better understanding of the text by paying less attention to such conventional phrases and more to the notion of compliance and what this tells us about the *Boshu*'s conception of nature and the natural order.[35]

2.2 Nature as Constant

Nature in the *Boshu* is not only impersonal, it is constant: "Heaven and earth have their constant norms. . . . The constant norms of heaven and earth are the four seasons, brightness and darkness, the giving and taking of life, hardness and softness" (43:6a–b). Nature has its perpetual cycles, permanent processes, unchanging patterns, fixed standards: "The operations of the heavens are regular and reliable: the sun and moon do not stop in a fixed position; in continual motion, never remiss, they oversee the empire" (67:100a). In fact, the author explicitly states that there is "a constant way to heaven and earth" (*tian di zhi heng dao* 天地之恒道 — 57:69a), supplementing this with the metaphorical description of heaven as the constant trunk and earth as the branches (66:96a).

2.3 Nature as Rule Governed

Impersonal and constant, nature is in addition rule governed. The issue of whether or not Chinese thinkers of the classical period conceive of nature in terms of laws of nature in the natural science sense has been much debated. On one side is Joseph Needham arguing they did not; on the other side is Derk Bodde arguing they did. The latter's case seems the stronger. Bodde provides impressive textual support for his claim that *ze* is used in a variety of pre-Qin texts as a noun to mean "rule," "law," "pattern," in the requisite sense. He concludes on the basis of this textual evidence that "at least a few early Chinese thinkers viewed the universe in terms strikingly similar to those underlying the Western concept of 'laws of Nature.'"[36]

Needham, on the other hand, bases his counterarguments primarily on theoretical considerations about the nature of the Chinese world-view, in particular the absence of a supreme deity in organismic pre-Qin cosmology. As he sees it, laws of nature in the scientific sense are "external" whereas in a Chinese organicism model, regulation is "internal."[37] I will present my own theoretical arguments against Needham's position in the following chapter where I take up Huang-Lao natural law jurisprudence.[38] In this section, I will simply add to the weight of textual evidence in support of Bodde's position.

The *Boshu* provides many general statements of the rule governed character of nature, including the following:

> The sun reliably rises and sets, north and south have their limits: these are the models for measurement. The moon reliably waxes and wanes, there is a constancy to advancement and withdrawal: these are the models for calculation. The stellar formations have their quantifiable relations and do not deviate from their paths: these are the models for reliability (53:49a)

> That the four seasons have their standard periods is the principle of heaven and earth. That the celestial bodies—the sun, moon, stars, and constellations—have their quantifiable relationships is the guideline of heaven and earth. To realize achievements during three seasons and to punish and execute during one season is the way of heaven and earth. Timely and determinate, the alternations of the four seasons are without discrepancy or error. They always have their model. (57:65b)

For the author, mother nature is reliable, predictable—so reliable and predictable that one can use her as a standard, as a model for calculation. It bears noting in this regard that the Yellow Emperor is often credited in classical myths and philosophical literature with originating calendars.[39] In fact, in the *Boshu* he is said to have "enumerated the days, calendared the months, and calculated the duration of the year to match the movements of the sun and moon" (61:79a). He is able to do this because nature is not a chaotic domain presided over by an anthropomorphic deity who, whenever displeased, summons up the elemental forces of rain and wind. There is a constancy to nature, an underlying pattern to what may appear to the uninformed to be whimsical madness. It is up to the sage to discover this under-lying pattern and to structure society accordingly. Were nature not rule governed, this would not be possible.

Yin and Yang

That the author conceives of nature as rule governed is not only con-firmed by general statements like those just cited but through his use of specific terms that delineate the determinate order of nature. One of the primary means of articulating the inherent structure of the natural order is through yin and yang.

Yin and yang originally referred to brightness and darkness, to the sunny and shady sides of a mountain or tree.[40] Passages in the *Boshu* ex-hibit this early sense:

> Since heaven illumined the three, thereby fixing the two, brightness and darkness alternate. (53:49b)

> Heaven has its constant trunk; earth has its regular norms. The conjoining {of heaven's trunk and earth's regular} norms is the source of brightness and darkness, yin and yang. (66:96a)[41]

Significantly, yin and yang are discussed in conjunction with the regular patternation of the constant natural order. Brightness and darkness alter-nate in a predictable, reliable fashion because the cosmos is regulated.

Over time, yin and yang themselves became paradigmatic symbols of the underlying order of the cosmos. All phenomena, human or non-, are classified as either yin or yang.

> As a rule, discussions must {pursue} the essential meaning through the cate-gories of yin and yang.[42] Heaven is yang, earth yin. Spring is yang, fall yin. Summer is yang, winter yin. Daytime is yang, nighttime yin. The larger state is yang, the smaller yin. . . . The ruler is yang, the minister yin. The superior is yang, the inferior yin. The male is yang, the female yin. The father is yang, the son yin. The elder brother is yang, the younger brother yin. . . . All of the yang categories emulate heaven. Heaven exalts proper order. Overstep-ping proper order is dissemblance. . . . All of the yin categories emulate the earth. The virtue of the earth is its being placid and quiet, properly ordered and tranquil. First establishing the characteristics of softness, that which is adept at giving does not contend. This is the standard of the earth and the characteristics of femininity. (83:164b)

The entire natural order is delineated in terms of the bipolar yin and yang. The way in which the author slides from an articulation of the order of nonhuman nature as yin or yang to an articulation of the human order in the same terms reveals the underlying unity of the natural order. Both the human and nonhuman spheres are under the jurisdiction of the Way and as such are subject to the same kinds of regulations.

The normative priority of the natural order is indicated by the author's description of the nature of yin and yang. That which is yang emulates heaven, which in turn values proper order (*zheng* 正). Hence those of yang value things in their right place. Yang, however, is usually associated with aggressiveness: those who take the lead are said to be yang. But to be the initiator runs counter to the author's cardinal belief that one must comply with the natural order. To resolve this difficulty, the author praises one for being yin, for manifesting "feminine characteristics" (*ci jie* 雌節), while rehabilitating yang in a positive sense as compliance with proper order.

Further, the proper order is predetermined. The yin-yang configuration of the natural order is fixed in that phenomena come into existence with their yin and yang quality in tow. It is inherent in their very being. Heaven is by nature yang, the earth yin, the sun yang, the moon yin. . . . Humans cannot declare by fiat that this will be yin and that yang. They must simply put things in the place they are meant to go.

On the level of praxis, it is incumbent upon humans to shape their social practices in accordance with the natural patterns of yin and yang. "Where one kills when the yang phase is at its apex and gives life when the yin phase is at its apex—this is called acting contrary to the determinant conditions (*ming*) of yin and yang. Where one kills abroad when yang is at its apex and promotes life at home when yin is at its apex, one has already acted contrary to yin and yang and, moreover, is acting contrary to his proper place. At the worst, the state will perish. At the very least, the ruler will personally meet with disaster" (51:40b). The natural forces of yin and yang are a direct manifestation and expression of the normative Way. As such, they impose constraints on the behavior of humans and have the normative force of commands (the conventional translation of *ming* 命). Humans must operate within the natural and determinate conditions of yin and yang. Should humans ignore these conditions and seek to forge their own way rather than conform their behavior to the prescribed standards of the Way, trouble is sure to follow.[43]

Li: Principle

Etymologically, *li* first referred to the patterns inherent in jade. In the *Boshu*, *li* are underlying patterns inherent in nature; they are the principles that structure the natural order. Though "pattern" retains more of the concrete image of the original sense of *li*, I favor "principle" with its Aristotelian associations as a translation for *li* in the *Boshu* because it brings out more forcefully the function of *li* as a means of expressing the intrinsic order of the prescribed Way.

For Aristotle, a principle is that from which a thing can be known, that from which a thing first comes into being, or that by which what moves is moved or what changes is changed. As David Hall points out, "principles both establish and account for the order of the world . . . a first principle functions as a determining source of order."[44] Accordingly, Huang-Lao *li* are regulative; they perform a governing function in that they are expressions of the preconfigured normatively correct order or Way.

Although the notion of first principle is not applicable to Confucianism and Daoism,[45] it fits well with the foundational character of Huang-Lao naturalism. Significantly, though *li* is a central concept in the *Boshu*, it occurs only rarely in classical texts—its absence in the *Analects*, *Dao De Jing*, and *Zhuang Zi*, all of which promote an understanding of dao as emergent rather than predetermined, being particularly noteworthy.[46]

In the *Boshu*, nature has its principles:

> That the four seasons have their standard periods is the principle of heaven and earth. (57:65b)

> Breaking land in the initiating of large-scale construction projects during the summer is called violating principle. Transgressing prohibitions and violating principle, the punishment of heaven will surely reach one. (55:61a)

There is an underlying structure to nature, an inherent pattern to the natural order. Humans must discover this implicate order. They must come to realize that they are part of a holistic system, that the natural order is an integrated, unified whole: "Understanding the oneness [of the natural order] lies in the investigation of heaven and earth. The principle of the oneness extends throughout the four seas" (72:221b). *Li*, as a determining source of the natural order, is all pervading. The entire cosmos has its structuring principles. Humans must investigate nature to determine these principles, and then structure their person and society accordingly: "Only after one lines it up in accordance with the constant way of heaven and earth will one determine wherein lies the cause of disaster and fortune, life and death, survival and demise, prosperity and decline. For this reason, one will not deviate from principle in one's actions but will sort out the empire without neglecting any plans" (57:69a). Having discovered the principles inherent in the natural order, one must abide by them—or suffer the consequences. Again, the natural order is taken to be the normative standard. Humans are merely called upon to put their house in order by following the guidelines: "In holding fast to the Way and following principles, one must start from the foundations: in taking compliance as the keynote, one is certain in prohibiting and punishing those whose crimes deserve it to hit the principles of the natural order (*tian li* 天理) dead on" (51:39b).

Fa: Law

Fa, like *tian*, covers a broad spectrum of meaning. At times, it is best translated as "method," at other times as "model," "standard," "law," or even "penal law." For our purposes, we need not be overly concerned with whether or not *fa* is better rendered as "law" rather than "standard." What matters most is that *fa* serves as a means of articulating a determinate and determining order.

Although generally used in conjunction with the social order, there is one instance where *fa* is applied to the natural order. The passage is difficult, in part because of textual corruption, but also because of the inherent obscurity of the topic and prose. Nevertheless, it is sufficiently intelligible to be worth citing, particularly in light of the importance of *fa* as a possible functional equivalent of "laws of nature":

> The natural order holds fast to the one to illumine the three. . . . Since the natural order fixed the two to establish the eight norms, the four seasons all have their standard duration, action and repose have their respective places, internal and external their respective locations. The natural order establishes the eight norms to implement the seven laws (*fa*): Illumined and thereby rectifying is the way of nature; appropriate is the measure of nature; reliable is the periodicity of nature; reversing after reaching the limit is the life process of nature; necessary are the determinant conditions of nature; . . . is the way in which nature constitutes the determinant conditions for the myriad things.[47] These are called the seven laws. (53:49a–51a)

Although opaque, this passage does shed light on several important issues. First, the author does not consider himself to be offering an interpretation of natural phenomena, but to be reporting objective truths about the very nature of nature. Nature operates in a certain, necessary way; characterizable in terms of these seven laws, it constitutes a determinate order. Further, the "laws" themselves are noteworthy, demonstrating as they do that nature is reliable, constant. One of the trustworthy rules of nature is that once things reach their limit, they will begin to reverse. Finally, it is worth noting that nature is considered to be a source of standards or measures, and that these standards and measures are taken to be appropriate, presumably as a model for the social order.

Ze: Pattern

Ze, as previously noted, played a pivotal role in the Bodde-Needham debate, with Bodde taking great pains to document instances of *ze* as "law," "rule," or "pattern." In the *Boshu*, there is one occurrence of *ze* as the pattern of the natural order: "In not becoming the initiator, nor monopolizing [the power] for himself, nor planning in advance, nor acting for gain or rejecting fortune, the sage accords with the pattern of the natural order (*tian zhi ze*). [The ruler] who loses sight of the natural order as his model will perish" (81:144b). Though brief, this passage offers much. In addition to the use of *ze*, there is once more the insistence on human compliance with the natural order. That one is advised to avoid becoming the initiator speaks to the foundational character of the Huang-Lao system. Humans are not responsible for generating the proper order in light of their own ends and best judgment but required merely to adhere to the prescribed Way. The description of the sage as one who does not plan in advance nor act out of self-interest reminds one of the need within the epistemology of the author to overcome personal biases and respond to objective reality. One must always be prepared to react to the changing conditions. Plans prejudice. They influence one's ability to observe and hence obscure the Way.

Tian Ji

Another phrase used by the author to delimit the natural order is *tian ji* 天極. Rare in classical literature, it refers to the limits or extremities of heaven-nature-the natural order. In the *Boshu*, one is instructed to fulfill the limits of the natural order after engaging in a normatively sanctioned punitive attack on another state. Failure will spell one's downfall: the vanquished state will rise up once more and misfortune will redound upon one's own head (45:9b). Only the sage, we are told (45:11b), is able to fulfill the limits of the natural order and make use of the natural order's benchmark (*tian dang* 天當). Perhaps the sage is uniquely able to accomplish this because he alone is able to become empty and tranquil and thereby to apprehend the lineaments of the natural order's benchmark.

At any rate, the limits of nature are nonnegotiable standards:

Heaven and earth are impartial; the four seasons continue unceasingly. When heaven and earth reside in their proper stations, the appearance of the sage ruler is recorded. When one transgresses the limits and fails to hit the mark, mother nature will send down calamities. When man forcefully prevails over nature, he must be careful to avoid missing the mark. When nature, on the other hand, prevails over man, man ought to accommodate and act in consort with nature. First bending and then stretching, one is sure to fulfill the limits of the natural order without usurping nature's achievement. (45:10a)

In the outer chapters of the *Zhuang Zi*, there is an interesting passage that makes reference to the limits of nature:

The knave sacrifices himself for possessions, the gentleman for reputation. That which brings them to alter what is essential in them and to change their inner nature (*xing* 性) differs, but when it comes to casting aside what is one's end in life and becoming a sacrifice for something that is not, they are as one. Hence I say,
> Never be a knave,
> return and abide by the natural order.
> Never be a gentleman,
> follow the principles (*li*) of the natural order.
> Whether crooked or straight,
> be in tandem with the limits of the natural order (*tian ji*).
> Observe face to face the four directions,
> in accord with time (*shi* 時) ebb and flow . . .
> in accord with dao walk your meandering path (83/29/70, G240)

This passage strikes many sympathetic chords with the *Boshu*. Most noticeable, there is the call to comply with the natural order. Whatever one's individual nature, one is still part of a larger natural order. One must act within the constraints of the natural order, complying with its principles. Further, one must do so in a timely fashion—echoing a prominent theme of the *Boshu*.[48] The very terminology with which this is expressed resonates with that of the *Boshu*: *tian ji, li, shi*. Even the mention of face-to-face observation of the four directions is redolent of the four faces of the Yellow Emperor of the *Shiliu Jing* section (61:78a).

Yet ultimately the position in this particular passage and in the whole of the "Robber Zhi" chapter from which it is drawn differs in important respects from that of Huang-Lao. When all is said and done, the author is no Huang-Lao disciple: he denigrates the Yellow Emperor for introducing warfare and destroying the Golden Age while exalting Shen Nung, the mythic symbol of an egalitarian communal society. A. C. Graham classifies the chapter as part of the Yangist miscellany, concurring with Guan Feng who suggests that "Robber Zhi" does not really belong to Daoism at all.[49]

Supporting Graham and Guan's reading is the conspicuous absence in the *Boshu* of the "Robber Zhi" emphasis on one's inner nature or character (*xing*). Though Teng has attempted to restore respect for the particular in Huang-Lao thought by arguing that *li* serves a comparable function of individuation, his arguments, as noted earlier, are not entirely persuasive. Even allowing that the particular has more importance in the Huang-Lao scheme of things than might at first appear, the emphasis is still clearly on the natural order as a whole and on one's duty to assume one's place within both the natural and the derivative social order.

The author of "Robber Zhi," in keeping with his Yangist inclinations, is more concerned with maintaining one's person intact than with serving one's state. His support for Shen Nung coupled with his disdain for the Yellow Emperor suggest that he prefers the communal anarchism associated with the former to the centralized, bureaucratic state instituted by the latter.[50]

Most telling, the author's invocation to wander along one's own meandering path reflects not only his Yangist, individualist leanings but his sympathy with interpretive rather than correspondence naturalism. Although one must act within the constraints of the natural order, there are many ways to do so. Each must find his or her own. The "Robber Zhi" passage poignantly continues, "in accord with the way walk your meandering path. Do not strive to make your conduct consistent, do not strive to make your dutifulness too perfect, or you will miss your end in life." In the final word, one is not to follow a prescribed path common to all but to find one's own way in light of one's own particular ends and character.

3. The Place of Humans Within the Natural Order

Like the nonhuman component, the human-social component of the natural order is also thought of as constant and rule governed: the way of humans (*ren dao*) lies within the cosmic Way. The social order, articulated primarily in terms of *xing ming* (names and forms), *li* (principles), and *fa* (laws), arises from and is a manifestation of dao, the natural order.

3.1 Dao

To appreciate the place of humans within the natural order, one must come to grips with dao as the mysterious metaphysical source or ground of all things, both human and nonhuman, and as the natural order itself. As a metaphysical entity, dao is, the *Dao Yuan* section tells us, an uncaused, independent, unchanging standard. It is nameless, formless, empty and unfathomable. With harmony as its function, it operates in a *wu wei* (nonimpositional) fashion. It is the undifferentiated ground from which the phenomenal world of the myriad things arises (87:168a–174b):

> At the outset of constant undifferentiatedness,
> there was a far-reaching indeterminacy, a great emptiness.
> In its emptiness and indeterminacy, it constituted the oneness.
> Perpetually one, it abided . . .

> Obtaining it, birds fly.
> Obtaining it, fish swim.
> Obtaining it, animals run.
> Obtaining it, the myriad things are engendered.
> Obtaining it, all undertakings are completed . . .

> Heaven and earth, yin and yang,
> the four seasons, sun and moon,
> the stars, constellations, clouds and *qi*,
> things that crawl, those that move like worms
> and those that have roots—

> all take life from it
> yet the Way does not become diminished;
> all return to it
> yet the Way does not become augmented.

This passage, both in style and content, echoes the *Lao Zi*.[51] All things arise from dao. Each is what it is because of the Way. The myriad things are able to coexist and flourish—to realize their inherent potential as fish, birds, humans—because dao as the natural order is an all-pervading, universal harmony. As the underlying unity of the cosmic natural order, dao is labeled *yi*—the one, oneness. "As for all manner of creature—those that crawl, breathe with beaks, fly with fanlike wings, or wriggle like worms— . . . Their not losing their constancy is due to the oneness of the natural order" (53:48b).[52] As the universal natural order, as the tripartite system of heaven-earth-humans, dao, the one, encompasses both the way of humans and of nature.

Further, as an all-pervading harmony, dao holds out the possibility that humans will be able to flourish in and along with nature. Humans need not be at odds with nature. It is possible to realize the underlying harmony, to obtain the Way such that "all undertakings are successfully completed" (87:169a). But to do so, one must first realize that dao is also "one standard, unchanging" (ibid.). A harmonious coexistence is obtainable only if one follows the one prescribed Way that underlies the surface plurality.

> Now a hundred words have their root; a thousand words have their crux; ten thousand words have their gist. The multitudes of the myriad things all pass through a single opening.[53] Who is able to properly govern them if not a person who is himself correctly ordered? Only if one is truly able to put oneself in order will one be able to manipulate the orderly to put in order what is out of line, to grasp the one to understand the many, to eradicate what brings injury to the masses and to maintain what is appropriate for them. Getting a hold of the essence and preserving the one, identifying with the limits of the natural order, one will be able to understand the course of fortune and misfortune in heaven and on earth. (72:123a)

Dao and *Tian*

A hotly debated topic in contemporary Huang-Lao studies is the precise relationship between dao and *tian*. The discussion centers by and large around two sets of issues. The first begins with the questions: Are dao and *tian* the same? If not, what are the differences, and which is more important? The second set focuses on a crucial distinction in Marxist thought, namely, that between materialism and idealism, and asks which is materialistic and which idealistic: dao, *tian*, neither, or both?

On one side of the first set is Liu Xiaogan who contends that the dao of Huang-Lao is the dao of nature (*tian dao*). Moreover, he suggests that *tian* is for Huang-Lao more important than dao whereas with Lao Zi dao is more important.[54] Teng Fu concurs with Liu that *tian* is of secondary importance in the *Dao De Jing*, arguing that Lao Zi's *tian* is derived from dao: nature exists within or as a part of dao. For the Huang-Lao school, by contrast, dao is a materialistic *qi* that exists within *tian* as the natural order, between heaven and earth as it were.[55]

In rebuttal, many have argued that dao is "most important" for Huang-Lao and Lao Zi alike. Further, it would appear that dao and *tian* (or *tian dao*) cannot be the same because the former is said to give rise to the latter. As we have seen, dao is the source of all things, including *tian*. *Tian* and dao must then refer to different things.

As for the second set of issues, Teng stakes out one extreme: for Huang-Lao, both dao and *tian* are materialistic. Yu Mingguang takes up the other: both dao and *tian* are idealistic.[56] Ge Rongjin, in contrast, contends that, whereas Huang-Lao's dao refers to the objective laws of nature, it is still a mysterious spiritual entity that cannot be known empirically.[57] For similar reasons, Wu Guang concludes that Huang-Lao is best characterized as an objective idealism.[58] Jin Chenfeng, seeking a compromise position, suggests that it is not clear whether dao is materialistic or idealistic. It is materialistic in that it is a kind of *qi* yet idealistic in that it is formless and nameless.[59]

The ambiguity of *tian* is responsible for much of the conceptual confusion. *Tian* (*tian dao, tian zhi dao, tian di zhi dao*) is used as a synonym for dao, the natural order. At other times, however, it refers to nonhuman nature or to the sky-heavens. Hence both sides are at least partially right: Liu is right that Huang-Lao's dao refers to a natural order; yet the other side is also right in that dao may be differentiated from *tian* when the latter refers to nonhuman nature as one component of the natural order or to the sky, one part of nature.

The debate as to which is more important, dao or *tian*, turns out to be a specious one. Dao is still "more important" in that it constitutes the underlying unity of the cosmos and is the ontological source as well as normative standard for all things. But in the *Boshu* dao signifies the natural order that is alternatively referred to as *tian, tian dao*, and so on.

In that the *Boshu* promotes not just correspondence but imitative naturalism, nonhuman nature does often serve as the standard for humans, thereby increasing the philosophical profile of *tian*. *Tian* is undoubtedly referred to more often than dao. Yet this hardly entails that it is more "important." The ultimate standard remains dao: "standing on its own, it has no counterpart (87:170a). . . . One standard, unchanging, it may be appropriately applied to everything from crawling insects to wiggling, wormlike creatures" (87:169a).

The second debate suffers from inadequacy of terminology as well. As Ge points out, dao does refer to the objective laws of an impersonal, constant nature. In this day and age, one assumes that such a view would go hand in hand with a materialistic conception of the universe. Yet Ge correctly observes that, as a metaphysical entity, dao is something mysterious and unfathomable. Formlessness and namelessness are not traits one usually associates with materialism.

But is the culprit not our impoverished conceptual categories? Either something is objectively knowable in a positivist empirical sense or else we have a mysterious, spiritual idealism. This is a false either-or. The Huang-Lao position is not on this score all that different from our current way of thinking. Most people nowadays think of the world in positivist, materialist, naturalist terms. We reject the notion that a supernatural deity created the world. We believe that scientific investigation, even if it has not necessarily produced theories that mirror objective nature, has by and large shown dividends both pragmatically and in respect to our understanding of nature. Yet we still marvel at the mystery of life. We still wonder what existed before the big bang and how it got there. As the unfathomable metaphysical source of all things, dao reflects the mystery of life and our sense of wonder; as the natural order, dao is the way that can be known, that must be known if humans are to realize the harmonious world that the heaven-earth-human structure implicitly holds to be possible.[60]

To allow that science, while useful, may not be able to respond to all of our questions need not make one a simple-minded idealist. The *Zhuang Zi* puts it well:

> There are things of which names and substances can be recorded, of which even the most quintessential and least discernible can be noted. . . . There are regularities that things possess, words exhaust, knowledge attains. . . . Yet the one who observes dao does not pursue them to where they vanish or explore the source from which they arise. This is the point where discussion stops. . . . The ultimate both of the Way and of things neither speech nor silence is able to convey:
>> In what is neither speech nor silence,
>> May discussion find its ultimate (72/26/71, G152)

In terms of understanding Huang-Lao thought, to impose the materialist-idealist hermeneutic framework on the text is not most illumining.[61] The end of the Warring States period witnessed, on the one hand, a steadily declining belief in supernatural spirits and deities and, on the other, a dramatic increase in the understanding of the universe in naturalist terms—the latter stimulated by the yin-yang five phases thinking of Zou Yan and his fellow Jixia Academy philosophers. Relying on the materialist-idealist distinction does not allow one to differentiate among the *Boshu*, *Guan Zi*, *He Guan Zi*, and other texts of the period that conceive of the natural order as impersonal, constant, rule governed, non-supernatural, and yet nevertheless differ in important ways.

3.2 Xing Ming: Forms and Names

As one would expect from a realist theory of language, each thing in the Huang-Lao world has a name. What is remarkable about the *Boshu*'s position, however, is that each thing has a predetermined name: "things" (events, actions and ideas in addition to material objects) come into existence with a preassigned form together with a corresponding name: "Dao is

55

without beginning but is responsive. Before it arrived, there was not it. Having already arrived, it is what it is. When something is forthcoming, its form (*xing*) precedes it. Established in accordance with its form, it is named in accordance with its name (*ming*)" (81:143a). Things emerge from the Way preconfigured: "*tian* rectifies names and initiates them" (66:97a). Disorder occurs, however, because each of us tries to name reality from his or her own perspective: "In all matters, whether great or small, each thing assumes its own perspective. Uncompliance and compliance, life and death: each thing names them in light of its own circumstance. Once names and forms have been fixed, each thing corrects itself accordingly" (44:8a). In interpreting events by one's own lights, one imposes subjective biases on experience. To a farmer, that today is rainy is "good" because his crops need water. To me, it is "bad" because I want to play tennis. For each to have one's own names, however, generates chaos. To have social order, it is essential that names be fixed (*ding* 定).

But names cannot be fixed by convention; we cannot merely agree to a common usage. The sage must investigate the situation and rectify names according to objective reality. The epistemology is one of correspondence. By emptying oneself of subjective bias, one is able to apprehend the correct relation between name and reality: "The way to apprehend and understand (*jian zhi*) is simply to be empty (*xu*) and have nothing. Being empty and having nothing, even the minute new autumn hair once completed must have form and name. As soon as form and name are established, there are distinctions such as that between black and white" (43:3a). Once formed, each thing, down to the most minute hair, has a name. But it can be discovered only if one overcomes personal bias. Managing that, the distinctions implicit in the practice of naming cut at the joints of nature: they reflect real distinctions in the world. Names are in this way grounded in the objective natural order, in dao, *tian*, *li*.

> Thus, as for the observations in the empire of one who holds fast to the Way, . . . one apprehends the correct Way (*zheng dao*) and the principle (*li*) to be followed.[62] One is able to judge the crooked and the straight, the beginning and the end, and hence to follow names (*ming*) and thoroughly penetrate the principle (*li*). (58:75a)

> Thus as for the observations in the empire of one who holds fast to the Way, one is sure to observe with particular attention how affairs begin to arise and to thoroughly examine their forms and names. Once forms and names have been fixed, compliance and contrariness have their designated positions, life and death their distinction, survival and demise, prosperity and decline their

lodging places. Only when one lines them up with the constant way of heaven and earth (*tian di zhi heng dao*) will one determine wherein lies the cause of disaster and fortune, life and death, survival and demise, prosperity and decline. (57:68b)

Because there is an objective standard, namely, the natural order, names can be rectified rather than merely attuned or rendered consistent. There are, as noted previously, correct or rectified names (*zheng ming*) and deviant or perverse names (*qi ming*). If one fails to rectify names, chaos results as people attempt to manipulate the deviant or irregular names for their own benefit: "If one alters the constant norms and exceeds the proper measure, people will use the irregular to control each other. Where regularity (*zheng*) and irregularity (*qi*) have their respective positions, names {and titles} are not lost" (43:7a).[63]

If, on the other hand, one is able to overcome subjectivity and apprehend how names correspond to reality, all goes well: the empire is well governed, people do not contend, all know right from wrong:

When the names and reality correspond to each other, there will be stability; when names and reality do not correspond to each other, there will be contention. (54:65a)[64]

Where forms and names are given voice and what is said corresponds to what actually is, misfortune and disaster are eliminated. It is like shadow following form, echo following sound, scales not concealing heavy and light. (58:75b)

Truth

Chad Hansen has put forth what at first blush seems to be a highly implausible view: Chinese philosophy has no concept of truth. But as is often the case, what initially appears to be a radical claim turns out to be, on closer analysis, decidedly less so. To assess the validity of Hansen's position in light of the philosophy of language of the *Boshu*, one must begin by carefully sorting out precisely what that position is.

Hansen is not claiming that the truth of a doctrine or statement is of no importance to the Chinese. He is offering, rather, "a theoretical interpretive claim about the general character of pre-Han philosophical activity."[65] Following Peirce, Hansen distinguishes between three ways of philosophizing about language: we may relate language to the world—this is *semantics*, the relation of strings of language and states of affairs; we may relate language to itself—this is *syntax*, the relation of strings of language symbols to other strings of language symbols; or we may relate language to its social context—this is *pragmatics*, the relation of language and the users of language. The claim that the Chinese philosophy—read pre-Han Chinese philosophy—has no concept of truth means for Hansen that pre-Han philosophers did not do philosophy in the way we do. As he puts it, "the significance of the claim about truth lies in Chinese philosophical focus on pragmatic rather than semantic issues."[66]

Restated as a theory about the general nature of pre-Han Chinese philosophy, Hansen's claim becomes much less radical and much more plausible. To suggest that Chinese philosophy differs in important ways from Western philosophy is, although surely not trivial, hardly unexpected. Indeed, even this revised claim is less exotic than it at first appears. It relies for its power on the rhetorically effective practice of portraying entire traditions in terms of a general dichotomy. Such a generalization, however, ignores the richness of both traditions.[67] What better proof of this than that Hansen himself employs the conceptual tools of American pragmatism to describe classical Chinese philosophy. There is, then, at least one school within the Western tradition that does philosophy in a way sufficiently similar to its Chinese counterpart to serve as a hermeneutical framework.

Further, that the pragmatists offer an alternative conception of truth to the semantic theory that no doubt has dominated Western philosophy of language suggests that Hansen's claim that the pre-Han Chinese have *no* concept of truth also requires qualification. To argue that the pragmatist conception of truth as "warranted assertability" rather than correspondence to reality is not a true theory of truth is circular: it assumes that truth *is* semantic truth, that there can be only one kind of truth—if a theory is not sufficiently similar to the semantic theory of truth, it is not a theory or truth at all.[68]

In support of the claim that Chinese have no, or rather a pragmatic, conception of truth, Hansen offers two types of argument: the first centers on the nature of classical Chinese language, the second on the nature of classical Chinese philosophy. As for the first, the claim is that there are features of Chinese grammar that explain why Chinese philosophers would hold a pragmatic rather than a semantic theory of truth. Most important is the sentence. Hansen contends that Chinese philosophers did not focus their philosophical attention on the sentence. The "reasonably straightforward" explanation of this is that "Chinese is not written in ordinary (subject-predicate) sentences."[69] This and several other features contribute to the view that words have only a naming function. The argument is that subject-predicate sentences lead to a semantic theory of truth: one seeks to ascertain whether the relation predicated between subject and predicate does in actuality hold. Understanding language as a string of names, on the other hand, pushes one in the direction of a more pragmatic theory: for some not clearly stated reason one is less concerned with whether or not names pick out objective reality than with acceptable uses of the word-name within one's linguistic practice—"When words, rather than sentences, command our attention, we *naturally* stress the social, conventional nature of language. We learn words."[70]

We need not stop to puzzle over the intricacies of the first argument. Even allowing that Hansen has indeed properly interpreted Chinese grammar and that the lack of subject-predicate sentences together with the emphasis on names does actually contribute to a pragmatic theory of truth, this line of argument is at best suggestive. Hansen takes considerable pains to distance himself from the Whorf-Sapir thesis, or more accurately, the received Whorf-Sapir thesis: namely, that language determines thought. This is often interpreted to mean (i) that a or several feature(s) of a language determine(s) thought such that one can act or think only in a certain way or (ii) that one is "locked into" one's language such that one can act or think only in a restricted way.

Given Hansen's oft-repeated rejection of linguistic determinism, his claim that "the salient properties of the Chinese language *explain* the pragmatic focus" cannot mean that classical Chinese philosophers *have* to think of truth pragmatically rather than semantically.[71] Rather, the point seems to be that one's language increases the probability of thinking in certain ways, not that it determines the possibility. Classical Chinese language is such that it leads people to "go on" about language in a pragmatic rather than a semantic way. However, one could use classical Chinese to go on in a semantic way. The nature of the language does not preclude this.

One cannot prove that pre-Han Chinese did not have a semantic theory of language simply from examining classical Chinese language. Hansen acknowledges this, stating that his "is not a straightforward empirical claim capable of direct textual confirmation."[72]

The key to determining whether one has a semantic or pragmatic theory lies in one's epistemology: "The relative importance of 'is true' in each tradition reflected, in part, the importance *and the nature* of its epistemology" (his emphasis).[73] To illustrate, he points out that even though Greek philosophers, like their classical Chinese counterparts, talked more about names than sentences, the quintessential Greek philosopher, Plato, has a semantic theory of truth and philosophy of language—as evidenced by his epistemology.

Hence to make his case, Hansen must show that interpreting Chinese texts as pragmatic rather than semantic makes more sense in light of the

epistemology and overall philosophy of the various thinkers. I do not believe this is so for Huang-Lao, though I do agree that the philosophy of
language of many thinkers within the classical tradition—Confucius, Lao
Zi, Zhuang Zi, and Han Fei Zi among them—is more pragmatic than
semantic. Indeed, I agree that as a generalization, pre-Han philosophies
as a whole tend to be pragmatic, coherence rather than foundational,
correspondence theories: in the language of Hall and Ames, they tend to
express aesthetic rather than logical orders.[74]

That the *Boshu* runs counter to the norm makes it all the more philosophically intriguing. In the following chapters, I will examine Huang-Lao
thought within its historical-intellectual context, showing how it constitutes
a response to the failure of contemporary, more philosophically pragmatic,
schools. Here I simply note that interpreting Huang-Lao philosophy of
language as a semantic, correspondence theory is consistent with and supported by its realist correspondence epistemology.

My claim is that, given the foundational character of Huang-Lao's
philosophical naturalism, to attribute to it a semantic theory of language is
not only entirely consistent but makes the most sense: it is the most coherent interpretation. Were one to disagree, one could not simply point
to the nature of classical Chinese language. One would have to show that
reading Huang-Lao as a pragmatic rather than foundational system makes
more sense. This would, however, be difficult. As we have seen, the author
is adamant that language correspond to reality. Language refers to the real
world, not to itself, not to us, not to our own practices. The standard is not
pragmatic success. One is not concerned with whether or not a name is
allowable (*ke* 可) by one's own particular social standards and conventions. One is concerned with the reality behind the names, with the *truth* of
the matter in the old fashion sense of "fitting the facts."

Significantly, *dang* 當—to hit dead on, to directly correspond—
which according to Hansen, "should be thought of as the concept of truth
appropriate to the language and philosophy of language of pre-Han
China," plays an important role in the text.[75] *Dang* is often used in association with *tian*. One is told to judge events in accordance with the benchmark of nature (*tian dang*) and to take care not to exceed the limits
(*ji*—cf. *tian ji* earlier) and miss the mark (*shi dang* 失當).[76] Of particular
concern is the reliable and just application of punishments and rewards.
They too must "hit the mark."[77]

Although the author time and again insists on names corresponding
to reality,[78] he never explicitly applies *dang* to language—but then neither
does he speak of language in terms of *ke* (admissibility), as is typical of
nonfoundational philosophers such as Zhuang Zi. There is then no direct

textual support that the author thought of *dang* as the functional equivalent of *truth*. Nevertheless, as Hansen points out, the question is not whether there is a single, directly translatable term. *Truth* in English plays many roles within our language games. Some of the roles may be played by, as he puts it, a host of separate characters, compounds, or phrases. The issue is whether the concept of truth occurs, and that depends on one's epistemology and the overall character of one's philosophy.[79] This leads in the case of the *Boshu* to the conclusion that Huang-Lao did espouse a semantic theory of truth and ipso facto to the conjecture that had the author addressed the issue he would have spoken of language in terms of *dang* rather than *ke*.

3.3   Li: Principle

While *li* (principle) occurs relatively infrequently in pre-Han philosophical texts, perhaps because of their general aesthetic or pragmatic character, it is of great importance in Huang-Lao.[80] We have already examined *li* as an ordering principle of nonhuman nature. The scope of *li*, however, is not restricted to nature. The human way has its principles as well: "When one, losing the ruler's way and abandoning the principles of humankind, abides in a state of wildness and confusion and yet is unaware of it, he will certainly get himself assassinated" (52:45a).

As in the *xing ming* passages cited in the previous section, names and principles occur together. The author insists that one investigate names and penetrate to the underlying principles. As alternative ways of articulating the natural order, *xing ming* and *li* are intimately related. Just as everything has a form and name, so does it have a principle: "Where each thing {corresponds to the Way} it is called instantiation of principle.[81] Wherein lies the principle is called {compliance}.[82] Where things do not correspond to the Way it is called deviating from principle. Wherein lies deviation from the principle is called contrariness" (53:51a). The *li*, like forms and names, are manifestations of dao. As such, they are prescribed standards for human behavior. They are to be instantiated, followed, complied with, not created, if one is to realize the Way: "Where one follows names and penetrates the principles underlying them, this is sure to lead to fortune. Not doing so is sure to lead to disaster" (58:74b).

3.4   Fa: Law

Fa (law, standard, method) is primarily a means for delineating the human social order. A key concept in Huang-Lao natural law jurisprudence, *fa* is discussed in considerable detail in the following chapter. It merits attention at this point, however, as an indicator of the rule governed character of the human order.

Like forms, names and principles, laws are implicate in the natural order. They arise from and are a manifestation of the Way. Thus the very first sentence of the text declares: "The Way generates the laws" (43:1a).

Laws reflect the natural order understood in terms of dao, principles, forms, and names. Though distinguishable, the Way, laws, principles, forms, and names constitute a tightly woven whole. One cannot realize the Way by according with names while ignoring laws: "When one is without laws in daily living, one's activities will fail to accord with names. One will for this reason be executed in disgrace" (69:111b).

As guideposts of the Way, laws constitute an objective standard of right and wrong: "There is a distinction between right and wrong: use the law to adjudicate between them. Being empty, tranquil and listening attentively, take the law as the tally" (58:74b). The human social order, delimited by laws, is one half of the tally. The normatively correct order, reality, the Way, is the other half. The two halves must fit: laws must correspond to reality, to the Way. One knows if laws accurately reflect the normative order because one is able to rid oneself of subjectivity, to become vacant and at ease and to become thereby directly aware of what is right and what is wrong.

Consequently laws are foolproof indicators of the right Way, which, if relied on, ensure success: "Having instruments and using them properly, one will not err. Relying on the gauge and checking it, one will not be confused. Governing according to the law, one will not be disordered" (81:144a).

4. Following the Way

I have argued that the *Boshu* advances a foundational naturalism: it calls for compliance with a natural order that is not only preconfigured and rule governed but normatively prior to the social order. In this section, I explore in greater detail this latter dimension of Huang-Lao thought.

4.1 Naturalist Foundations of Social Institutions

To realize the Way is to instantiate or implement the preestablished natural order. It is more a matter of holding fast to the Way than of creating a way. The need to comply with the normatively prior natural order is unambiguously put: "Because achievements exceed the natural order (*tian*), there are punishments and executions; where achievements do not measure up to the natural order, one fades into anonymity; where achievements correspond to the natural order, one's reputation will be fully established" (57:66a).

To illustrate the point, the author provides several examples of social institutions and practices that are to be brought into line with nature and the natural order. Perhaps the clearest is that of punishments and rewards, which we are told must fit the proper season: "Spring and summer are the seasons of reward, fall and winter the seasons of punishment. To nourish life, begin with rewards and follow with punishments" (62:85b).

But punishments and rewards are only one aspect of a more comprehensive theory of government correlated to the natural cadence of the cosmic order. The author, living as he did sometime in the turbulent Warring States to early Han periods, believed that a military presence is essential to survival. At the same time, there is more to good government than a strong army. A humane state encourages cultural achievement as well as military prowess. Therefore there is a military (*wu* 武) and a civil or cultural (*wen* 文) component to proper government. They too must be implemented in accordance with the natural order: "Nature has its times for giving and taking life; the state has government policies for giving and taking of life. When the state nourishes life in accordance with the life giving of nature, it is called *civility*. Where the state acts as executioner in accordance with the killing of nature, it is called *martiality*. When civility and martiality are utilized in tandem, the empire is obedient" (47:19a).

The author is particularly concerned that rulers will misuse the military.[83] Hence he stresses that one must engage only in righteous wars—those wars in accordance with principle and sanctioned by heaven cum natural order. "Where military affairs are not formed in accordance with heaven, the military cannot be mobilized. Where they are not modeled on the earth, the military cannot be wielded. Where military affairs are not modeled on humans, they cannot succeed. . . .[84] Heaven and earth forms them and by accommodating the sage takes advantage of this to complete them. The contribution of the sage lies in his application of timeliness" (71:116b). One must engage in war only against those who deserve to be punished and only when the time is right. Further, having vanquished one's opponents, one must exercise great caution to fulfill rather than exceed the limits of the natural order (*tian ji*). If not, one will, as we have seen, bring disaster down on one's own head.

That the preconfigured Way acts as a restraint on the ruler is surely not accidental. As will be discussed in Chapter V, this is one of the ways in which Huang-Lao political philosophy differs from that of Han Fei. The Legalism of Han Fei gives free rein to the ruler. He is able to make law as he sees fit and to change it when it suits him. A Huang-Lao ruler, however, must abide by the Way: "Where the ruler does not treat heaven as heaven he loses his synoptic intuition. Where he does not give proper weight to earth he loses his roots. Where he does not comply with the measured periods of the four seasons the masses suffer as a result. Where he neither abides in the proper position internally or externally nor responds to the alteration between the times for action and inaction his domestic affairs are in turmoil as are his operations abroad" (53:46b).

4.2 Metaphors of Compliance

The author employs a host of terms, expressions and phrases to indicate the normative priority of the natural order and the need for humans to comply with *tian*: *cheng yi quan heng, can yi tian dang* 爯以權衡, 參以天當 (weigh according to the standardized scales, align with the benchmark of the natural order), *zhong tian li* 中天理 (hit the principles underlying the natural order dead on), *shun si shi* 順四時 (comply with the four seasons), *xun tian chang* 循天常 (follow the constancy of nature), *yin tian* 因天 (accord with the natural order), *yin tian shi* 因天時 (accord with heavenly timeliness, the natural seasons), *yin shi* 因時 (accord with timeliness), *jin tian ji* 盡天極 (fulfill the limits of the natural order).

Other phrases underscore the notion of compliance with the natural order articulated in alternative ways: *shun dao* 順道 (comply with the Way), *zhi dao* 執道 (hold fast to the Way), *shun li* 順理 (comply with principle), *cha ming li* 察名理 (investigate names and principles). Conversely, the author castigates those who turn their back on the natural order (*bei tian zhi dao* 倍天之道), who lose or deviate from the Way (*shi dao* 失道) or principle (*shi li* 失理), who act contrary to or go against principle (*ni li* 逆理) or forms (*ni xing* 逆形).

These phrases contain images of two kinds: those that indicate the need for compliance—*ni, shun, yin, shi, xun*; and those which indicate the nature of that compliance and of the order to be complied with—*cheng, zheng, dang, zhong, can*.

Ni (contrarity)—Shun (compliance)

Ni 逆 and its antonym *shun* 順 are central terms in the *Boshu*: "In holding fast to the Way and following principles, one must start from the foundations: taking compliance (*shun*) as the guideline, one is certain, in prohibiting and punishing those whose crimes deserve it, to hit the principles of the natural order (*tian li*) dead on" (51:39b). Karlgren notes that in the *Shu Jing*, *ni* means "to go against," as in "to go against the flow." To swim upstream or to head into the wind illustrate behavior that is *ni*. In the *Shi Jing*, *ni* is used in the sense of "rebellious." The *Guan Zi* (Fa Fa) states: "where something is prohibited and yet it is not stayed, it is called opposition (*ni*)."

In the *Boshu*, because the correct social order is implicate in the natural order, *ni* incorporates both the *Shu Jing*'s going against the natural flow along with the *Guan Zi*'s running counter to the correct sociopolitical order. To act contrary to one is to act contrary to the other. Thus one often finds the author moving seamlessly from the need to comply with the natural order to the need to comply with the social order:

> Where one, not timely in his action and repose, departs from the appropriateness of the earth in planting trees, one runs counter (*ni*) to the way of heaven and earth. Where the ministers do not have an abiding affection for the ruler, where those below do not have an abiding affection for their superiors, and where the clans do not have an abiding affection for their occupations, they run counter (*ni*) to domestic principle. Where there is this contrariness (*ni*), it is called a dead state: engage military expeditions against it. As for the opposite, namely where there is compliance (*shun*), it is called a living state: with a living state, nourish it. Where compliance and contrarity are in accord with principles (*li*), reality and pretense are intimately related. (53:55a)

Be it the Way itself or particular manifestations of the Way such as principles, the call is for compliance. Humans are not to initiate the Way but to follow it.

The *Er Ya* and *Shuo Wen* lexicons define *ni* as *ying* 應 —to welcome. In the *Shu Jing* as well it is used in this sense of "going to meet" and in the *Yi Li* as "to receive." In the *Lun Yu*, it has the sense of "to anticipate." To go out to meet someone or to anticipate is for the author the *Boshu*, however, to initiate action; it is to take the lead rather than to stay behind and respond to the situation in a timely fashion that conforms to the natural order. It is therefore *ni*:

> As a rule, those who in encountering calamities and adversities take the lead are of constant bad omen; those who follow behind, of constant good omen. (70:113b)

> Not usurping the initiative in carrying out affairs, one thereby waits for contrary (*ni*) traits to run their course. . . . To make use of minimum effort to achieve glorious reputation is the optimum of compliance (*shun*). (79:140a)

Because each thing in the determinate normative order has its proper form and name, it is essential that one comply with names in setting up social institutions: "For the ruler and the minister to exchange positions is called contrariness (*ni*). For the person of superior and inferior character to occupy the same position is called disorder. For action and repose to be untimely is called contrariness. For life and death to be dealt out inappropriately is called tyranny" (51:35b). There is by definition but one ruler. To have minister occupy the place of the sovereign in the cosmic hierarchy is to violate the cosmic order.

Yin (to accommodate)

Yin 因—to go along with, to accommodate—is an important concept not only in the *Boshu* but in Huang-Lao thought in general.[85] In *Lun liujia yao zhi*, Sima Tan declares it to be one of the defining characteristics of Huang-Lao thinkers: "they take compliance (*yin xun* 因循) as their function," adding that "whether they have laws or not, they take going along with timeliness (*yin shi* 因時) as their business; whether they have standards or not, they go along with things (*yin wu* 因物) and join them. Thus it is said, the sage is not craftily skillful—the changes of time, this is what he holds fast to."[86] A similar phrase to this last appears in the *Boshu* which, as we shall see shortly, places great importance on acting in a timely fashion.

Etymologically, *yin* means to go along or comply with. It is glossed as *shun* in a commentary to *Lu Shi Shun Qiu*, (Jun Shou). The *Shuo Wen* defines it as *jiu* 就 —to accommodate, adapt. Applied to the *Boshu*, one goes along with the natural order. One adapts to the way of the world and arranges one's life accordingly, suggesting another connotation of *yin*—to rely on. Humans not only follow but rely on nature.

Yet as pointed out earlier, in the *Boshu* to rely on and accommodate the natural order is not a completely passive or negative process. *Yin* has the additional connotation of "to avail oneself of" or "to make the best of something." One is not merely at the mercy of natural processes beyond one's control. More positively, one is able to rely on the natural order as a means for structuring one's life: in spring it is time to plant, in summer to weed, in fall to harvest, and in winter to rest. Obviously the natural order and processes do limit one's options. But at the same time nature provides human kind with tremendous bounty both in terms of material wealth and resources and in respect to the possibility of a good life should the human-social order realize its place within the natural order. To do so, one must learn to take advantage of what nature has to offer by accommodating rather than struggling against it.

In the *Boshu*, one is told to *yin tian* (the natural order), *tian di* (heaven and earth), *shi* (timeliness), *min* 民 (the masses), and *wu zhi xing*

物之形 (the forms of things). Illustrative of the positive dimension of *yin* is the following: "There is that which {when entrusted to one} is heavy but when entrusted to one hundred is light.[87] Humans have their centrality; the myriad things have their forms. Taking advantage of these (*yin*) leads to success" (66:97a). One could try to force something or someone to serve one's purpose. Or one could be more accommodating, more adaptable. Rather than attempting to impose one's will on others, one could employ others to do what they do well and are themselves inclined to do. The *Boshu* believes that by taking advantage of that for which something or someone is inherently suited, one benefits oneself and others the most.

Shi (timeliness)

Another indicator of the normative priority of the natural order and the need for human compliance is the importance given to timeliness. One of the dangers in life, along with acting contrarily, according to the author, is not acting timely. Used verbally, *shi* means "to adapt oneself to circumstances, to come at the right moment, to fuse with a particular 'state' of affairs, to be in harmony with things at the right time."[88] In the *Boshu*, this entails that one act in step with the natural order: "Nothing should mature in advance of its natural course (*tian*). Nothing should flourish when it is not its time. What matures in advance of its natural course will be destroyed. What flourishes before its time will not bear fruit. The sun provides us with light; the moon with darkness. When it's dark, we rest; when it becomes light, we arise. Never deviate from the natural limits. With full awareness of the natural constraints, abide therein" (82:153b).

If one proceeds in a timely fashion, one will be successful. If not, trouble awaits: "When action and inaction are timely, heaven and earth assist one. But when they are untimely, heaven and earth snatches away its assistance" (69:111a).

Timeliness is, moreover, double edged. When it is time to act, one must. To not act when it is time is as dangerous as to act at the wrong time: "Taking advantage of natural timeliness (*tian shi*), everything is decided in light of it. When one ought to decide but does not, disorder will redound upon him" (71:117b).

Cheng (weighing up)

The previous metaphors attested to the importance of compliance. Others indicate that it is compliance of a particular kind; namely, with a predetermined, objective standard. *Cheng* 稱 is one such term.

According to the *Guang Ya*, *cheng* means *du* 度 —(v): to measure, (n): a measure, standard. The *Shuo Wen* defines it as *quan* 權 —to weigh, estimate, calculate. In the *Boshu*, it means weighing things in accordance with a standardized scale.

> The area circumscribed by a compass is called a circle; that within a carpenter's ruler is deemed a square; that marked off below the plumbline is dubbed straight; that under the carpenter's water level is said to be even. Measuring by the standards of foot and inch, things are said to be large and small, long and short. Weighing by the balances and scales, things are said to be light and heavy and to be correct. Measuring the volume in terms of bushels and piculs, things are said to be many and few and of a given quantity. These eight standards are the models to be applied. (51:43a)

There are fixed standards for judgment. One is not left to rely on one's own judgment as to what would be best, what would be most appropriate, in the particular context. This is not a Confucian aesthetic order where the sage as moral exemplar generates and defines the standards.[89] That would be entirely too subjective to suit the author. Instead of exercising one's discretion (*quan*) as called for by Mencius, one simply measures against the objective, universally applicable standards. To not *cheng*—to not weigh things up according to the standardized scale—like acting uncompliantly and failing to act timely, constitutes one of the dangers of life.

Although the concrete image of the objective standard is the scale, the ultimate standard is by extension the natural order itself.

> If one weighs by means of the scale and aligns by means of nature's benchmark, when there are matters to attend to in the empire one is sure to have the skill for testing them. The matters to be attended to are as many as the planted trees, as numerous as the grains of millet stored in the granary. Yet once the volumes of peck and piculs have been standardized and the lengths of foot and inch laid out, there is nowhere to flee from one's synoptic intuition. Therefore it is said, once the measurements of length and volume have been standardized, one regulates things by putting them in order. . . . The way to respond to transformations is to stay once the scales reach equilibrium. When light and heavy are not weighed up this is called losing the Way. (43:4b)

Zheng (proper order)

Definitions of *zheng* 正 in classical lexicons include the following: correct, right, straight, exact. In the *Shi Ji* it refers to the center of a target.

The *Guang Yun*, a later lexicon, glosses it as *dang*: to hit the mark, hit the target dead on. We have already observed how *dang*, in referring to a correspondence between the human-social and natural orders, is indicative of the author's correspondence epistemology and semantic theory of language. The importance of *zheng* in the text further substantiates this interpretation. The author does not ask that one realize an appropriate order but rather the right order.

Names must be rectified (*zheng*); there are correct (*zheng*) name and deviant names. When names are rectified, when they correspond to reality, there is proper order: "Once forms and names are set up and reputations and titles established, there is no longer any place to escape without trace, nowhere to conceal correct order (*zheng*)" (43:4a).

There are objective standards for determining what constitutes the proper sociopolitical order. Among these are the eight standards referred to a moment ago as well as laws: "As for laws and standards, they are of utmost importance for correct order (*zheng*)" (47:20b).

Zheng 政—correct, exact—is a homophone of and a loan word for *zheng* 政—government.[90] This last passage brings out the intimate relation between the two. It is not so much that *zheng* refers to two different concepts, "correctness" and "proper sociopolitical order." Rather, for the author of the *Boshu*, one implies the other. To be correct is to effect proper sociopolitical order. When names are rectified, laws enforced and affairs weighed in accordance with the standardized scales the empire is sure to be properly ordered. The kingly Way will be realized and all will prosper.

✳

Despite the general character of Huang-Lao philosophy, the many direct statements that one is to comply with nature and the natural order, the numerous examples of institutions modeled on nature, and the cluster of metaphors indicating the need to conform to a predetermined order, some commentators have argued that the author of the *Boshu* differs from Lao Zi in allowing humans to actively determine their own way by overcoming nature.[91] Their reading relies primarily on the following statement: "When man forcefully prevails over nature, he must be careful to avoid missing the mark." Even taking the statement in isolation, it is apparent that humans are under some sort of constraint in dealing with nature and the natural order in that they must take care not to miss the mark (*dang*). When one considers the statement in its context, this is all the more evident: "When one transgresses the limits and fails to hit the mark, mother nature will send down calamities. When man forcefully prevails over nature, he must be careful to avoid missing the mark. When nature, on the other hand, prevails over man, man ought to accommodate and act in consort with nature. First bending and then stretching, one is sure to fulfill the limits of the natural order without usurping nature's achievement" (45:10a).

Considering just the one statement alone, it would seem that the author supports a nonimitative correspondence naturalism. One must comply with the Way as the cosmic natural order that embraces both the way of humans and of nature. But the way of humans need not be modeled after nature. At times the relation between nature and humans may alter, with humans—still complying with the Way—gaining temporarily the upper hand over nature. This is consistent with a preconfigured cosmos that is changing constantly according to a rule-governed pattern. When one thing reaches its limits, it begins to descend and its opposite, conversely, to ascend.

In general, however, the naturalism of the *Boshu* is imitative: the human-social order imitates nonhuman nature. We have observed many instances where social institutions are modeled on what is unambiguously nonhuman nature—punishments and rewards correspond to the seasons and so forth. But as pointed out earlier, imitative and nonimitative naturalism are not to be understood as antithetical either-or propositions. Not all human behavior need by modeled on nonhuman nature. Indeed, it cannot be in that not every aspect of human behavior has a nonhuman nature correlate.

Further, and more important, nonhuman nature is not the ultimate standard. Rather, the natural order is. The confusion again seems to arise from the failure to be clear as to the referent of *tian*. In the *Boshu*, the Way cum natural order, whether referred to as *dao*, *tian*, or *tian zhi dao*, remains the ultimate ground for not only the human order but that of nature as well. In the final word, humans are not free to shape the world according to their fancy. Compliance, rather, constitutes the cornerstone to Huang-Lao philosophy: "Contrariness and compliance are determined on the basis of the same dao but are different in principle. To thoroughly understand compliance and contrariness—this is called the guideline to the Way" (51:41b).

4.3   *Huang-Lao Epistemology*

The basics of Huang-Lao epistemology are by now familiar: it is a correspondence epistemology that entails direct, language-independent access to objective reality. The method can be summarized as a progression from *xu* 虛 to *jing* 靜 to *wu si* 無私 to *shen* 神 (or *shen ming* 神明) to *jian zhi bu huo* 見知不惑; that is, one proceeds from "emptiness" through "tranquility" to "elimination of personal bias" and on to "intuitive clarity," which consists of the "apprehending and understanding without confusion" the objective natural order variously articulated as dao, *li*, *xing ming*, or *fa*.[92] The result is that one is able to *wu wei*, comply with the natural order, make punishments match nature's benchmark, know the origins of fortune and misfortune, ensure that names correspond to reality and so forth. In a word, one will know the Way and how to implement it.

Several passages evidence this process: "The way to apprehend (*jian*) and understand (*zhi*: know in the sense of discover) is simply to be empty (*xu*) and have nothing. . . . In his observations in the empire, the one who grasps the Way is without grasping, without fixed positions, without impositional action, without personal biases (*si*)" (43:3a). One must resist falling into the trap of viewing the world from an intransigent perspective, of clinging to old and biased ways of thought. Only then is one able to observe what is presented as it really is, without the obfuscating influence of personal prejudice.

In emptying oneself of prejudice, one becomes tranquil, at ease. When one is not blinded by one's own interests, one is able to observe with detachment, with a levelheaded equanimity that for the author ensures a spiritual-like intuitive clarity (*shen* or *shen ming*). This intuitive clarity—which Schwartz has insightfully described as a synoptic or gnostic intuition[93]—leads to a direct discovery of reality such that one "apprehends and understands without confusion": "Where there is tranquility, there is equanimity; where there is equanimity, there is peace; where there is peace, there is unadorned purity; where there is unadorned purity, there is focus on the essence; where there is focus on the essence, there is gnostic intuition (*shen*). The zenith of utmost gnostic intuition is to apprehend and understand (*jian zhi*) without confusion" (53:52a).

The result, as we have seen earlier, is that one knows, that is, discovers, the correct Way to proceed as determined by forms, names, principles, and laws. The author weaves together the various strands in the following passage, bits and pieces of which have been cited earlier:

> Where issues arise in the empire, one must look into their names thoroughly. . . .[94] Where one follows names and penetrates the principles underlying them, this is sure to lead to fortune. Not doing so is sure to lead to disaster. There being a distinction between right and wrong, use the law to adjudicate between them. Being empty, tranquil, and listening attentively, take the law as the tally. To thoroughly investigate names and principles and the beginning and the end is called penetrating the principle. Only where one, being fair-minded and without personal bias, is not confused in his apprehension and understanding will one know how to set forth resolutely. Thus as for the observations in the empire of one who holds fast to the Way, . . .[95] one will apprehend the correct Way and the principle to be fol-

lowed. One is able to judge the crooked and the straight, the beginning and the end, and hence to accord with names and thoroughly penetrate the principle. (58:74a)

Indicative of his correspondence epistemology, the author employs ocular metaphors traditionally associated with such theories from Plato to Descartes. One directly apprehends or sees (*jian*) how names correspond to reality: knowledge is as indubitable as one's perception is incorrigible. One is clear (*ming*) about the Way. The Way is bright, illumined, obvious, readily apparent to all who are empty and at ease.

Schwartz's characterization of Huang-Lao epistemology as synoptic or gnostic intuition is particularly apt: that it is a kind of intuition captures the directness of the discovery of Huang-Lao knowledge and the inner certainty that accompanies it; that it is synoptic intuition marks the breadth of scope of the sage's understanding; that it is gnostic intuition affirms the sage's ability to fathom the unfathomable.

Only the sage is able to scrutinize the formless,
to hear the soundless.
Having discovered the repleteness[96] of emptiness,
one is able to realize great emptiness.
One will then penetrate the essence of heaven and earth,
and thoroughly identify with the seamless sameness. . . .
One of clarity will surely be able to
scrutinize the extremities,
discover what others cannot discover,
and follow what others cannot obtain.
This is called scrutinizing the model and knowing the limits. (87:171a)

The sage is distinguished by his ability to go beyond the confines of subjective biases to penetrate the mysteries of the Way itself. He attains an intuitive clarity (*shen ming*) that might be considered to constitute a kind of spiritual enlightenment (as *shen ming* is often translated).

The Way is the source of intuitive clarity (*shen ming*). One who is intuitively clear dwells within the standards yet perceives beyond them. By dwelling within the standards, one is credible without speaking. By perceiving beyond the standards, what one says is unimpeachable. By dwelling within the standards, in one's repose one is immovable. By perceiving beyond the standards, in one's acting one is not transformed. Being immovable in repose and untransformable in acting, one is thus said to be intuitively aware. Intuitive clarity is the epitome of apprehending and understanding. (58:70a)

Intuitive clarity is grounded in the Way. One who attains it is able to go beyond the standards, to fathom the Way. Knowledge within the boundaries is everyday, fallible, perspectival-knowledge—or as Plato would call it, *doxa*: opinion. When one becomes empty, one overcomes the limits of one's own perspective and gains a synoptic, gnostic awareness of reality itself, of the Way that is beyond the boundaries of the everyday limited awareness. One discovers an objective, common ground available to all such that no one need be of two minds.

The claim is that by becoming empty one attains intuitive clarity and thus apprehends and discovers the Way—how names, correspond to reality, the principles underlying the names, and so forth—*without confusion* (*bu huo*). *Huo* indicates confusion of a particular sort. As the composition of the character (*huo*: 或—"some," disjunction + *xin* 心 —heart-mind) suggests, it refers to being of two minds about something. One is not clear which way to go, which path to choose. One is uncertain. In the mind's eye of the author, however, there are no two ways about it. Or rather, there is the right Way and wrong ways. Having ridded oneself of deluding self-bias, one has no doubts as to what the truth of the matter is. One clearly and directly apprehends the Way.

One attains in one's empirical observations (*guan* 觀) what Tu Wei-ming has called a *penetrating insight* into reality.[97] Yet the author of the *Boshu* is not advocating a mystical experience within the confines of one's own room or mind. His sage is not the sage of Lao Zi who "without going beyond his doors knows the world, without looking out the window apprehends the heavenly Way."[98] Rather, his epistemology is intended for the ruler who oversees the empire and must make practical decisions about concrete affairs of state. As Jan Yun-hua has remarked, the sage-ruler begins with empirical observation and ends by applying his insights to the world.[99] It is simply that one's empirical observation will be accurate only if one is able to be clearheaded and free from subjective bias.

The issue then is not—as some commentators have framed it— whether the penetrating insight and gnostic intuitive clarity of the sage leads to empirical or a priori knowledge. In contrasting the epistemology of the author to that of his contemporaries, the key differentia is correspondence as opposed to coherence, foundationalism as opposed to aesthetic pragmatism.[100] It is Huang-Lao's attempt to naturalize the Way—to ground knowledge, language, personal behavior, social practices, and politics in the natural order—that sets it apart from other classical philosophies.

III.   The Social and Political Philosophy of Huang-Lao

*

The demonstration that Huang-Lao philosophy is best characterized as foundational naturalism required a sounding of its metaphysical depths. Yet, as is true of most classical Chinese philosophy, the *Boshu* is concerned primarily with the normative questions of how to live and, more important, how to govern. In this chapter therefore I turn to Huang-Lao's social and political thought.

I focus first on Huang-Lao's philosophy of law, arguing that Huang-Lao promotes a natural law theory in which laws are grounded in the objective natural order. The reasons for this are twofold. First, my thesis challenges a popular view that pre-Han Chinese philosophers did not, indeed could not given certain features of the "Chinese" world-view, hold such a theory.[1] Second, philosophy of law is one area where the differences between Huang-Lao and other pre-Han schools of thought become most apparent. The *Boshu* is a syncretic text. The author freely borrows concepts and terminology from other schools. This has led many commentators to overemphasize the similarities between Huang-Lao and other schools in general and between the author of the *Boshu* and other thinkers in particular. To demonstrate that the philosophies differ despite the shared terminology, one must show that the terminology is being put to a different use. Examining the contrasts in a key area of social and political thought such as jurisprudence permits this.

Having narrowed the focus in the first section, I then widen it in the following to consider the nature of the Huang-Lao state. I demonstrate that the author envisions a centralized feudal bureaucracy that although not a government by the people is very much a government for the people. This accounts for the "Huang" in Huang-Lao because Huang-Di, the Yellow Emperor, is a symbol of a centralized state unified through military conquest by a worthy ruler.

1. Huang-Lao Natural Law Jurisprudence

The conventional wisdom about Chinese philosophies of law has it that, insofar as natural law existed in China, it was Confucian natural law predicated on universal ethical principles or *li* (禮—conventionally translated "rites," and not to be confused with *li* 理—principles).[2] Needham, a leading spokesperson for this view, adds that although in the West "the ideas of natural law (in the juristic sense) and of the laws of nature (in the sense of the natural sciences) go back to a common root," the Chinese natural law tradition did not tap the laws of nature as its source.[3] I will take exception to this characterization of Confucianism in the following chapter, arguing that Confucius's Confucianism, properly understood as an ethical system that relies on the discretionary judgment of exemplary persons (*jun zi* 君子) who create an emergent order from the particular context rather than by appeal to universal ethical principles, cannot be construed as natural law understood in a foundationalist sense. While it shares with traditional natural law theories the requirement that the law be moral, its pragmatic coherence character makes it more similar to Dworkin's interpretive theory of the law as integrity than to natural law theories in a strict sense.[4]

My more immediate goal, however, is to challenge Needham on another score; namely, that the natural law tradition in China did not attempt to ground law in the natural order. I claim that the *Boshu* espouses precisely such a natural law theory. To make my case, I must demonstrate firstly that the Huang-Lao of the *Boshu* is a rule of law rather than a "rule of man," and second that it is natural law grounded in a foundational natural order.

1.1   Rule of Law

That the *Boshu* represents a rule of law is affirmed by the prominent place given to *fa* (law) in the text.[5] The first of the four sections is called *Jing Fa*, the first subsection is titled "Dao Fa" and the opening line is "Dao gives rise to the laws." So impressed have some scholars been by the importance of *fa* that they have considered Huang-Lao in general and this work in particular to be part of the Legalist school (*fa jia* 法家).[6] Still others, led by Qiu Xigui, have for similar reasons suggested that this text does not represent Huang-Lao Daoism but another school best labeled *dao-fa jia* (道法家—Daoist-Legalism).[7]

While maintaining that Huang-Lao is actually something fundamentally different from the Legalism of Shang Yang and Han Fei, I do appreciate the point that law is sufficiently central to the respective systems to consider both Huang-Lao and Legalism rule of law philosophies (though the latter is perhaps best understood as rule *by* law rather than rule *of* law). Indeed, the author of the *Boshu* states "as for laws and standards, they are of utmost importance for correct order. Moreover, where proper socio-political order is realized through laws and standards, it cannot be over-turned" (47:20b).

To say that law is important for social order is an understatement. The author maintains that because people are naturally contentious law is necessary if society is to survive. In the "Xing Zheng" (Battling Among the Clans) chapter of the *Shiliu Jing*, Gao Yang and Li Mu, two subordinates of the Yellow Emperor, are discussing the lack of peace in the empire. The former complains that his state is riddled by strife: various clans are feud-ing, factions plot to overthrow each other, the Way has been abandoned. Li Mu assures him that there is no cause for alarm: "Since heaven and earth became settled, all creatures from those with toes to those like worms have contended. While the instigators of conflict are of bad omen, those who do not contend are also without means to succeed. Those who accord with the natural order will prosper while those who act contrary to it will perish. Do not act contrary to the way of nature and you will not lose what is yours to keep" (69:107b). Contention is inevitable. It is part of the natu-ral order. There has always been competition and there always will be. To survive, one must struggle. The key is to do so in a way consistent with the normative natural order.

Although struggle is part of the natural order, it may very well be that humans are particularly prone to conflict. One reason for this, the author suggests, is that the Way is formless and difficult for most people to grasp.

There is a thing that, beginning to . . . ,[8] is established on earth and exceeds heaven. No one has perceived its form. Its great fullness fills the whole of space between heaven and earth and yet no one knows its name. Because no one is able to see it, there are things that develop contrarily. Because there are things that will grow perversely, there are punishments for contrariness: misfortune reaches each one of them. They cultivate that whereby things die and assail that whereby the live. Assailing their foundation, one distances oneself from one's own kin; assailing one's fellow participants . . .[9] the result is sure to be chaos and one will end up without reputation. (58:71a)

Whatever the reason, human society is characterized by competition and a clash of conflicting interests. To ensure stability, laws are needed.

More specifically, impartial publicly promulgated laws are needed if society is to function. We have already witnessed the importance of impartiality and the overcoming of subjective bias for the author in regards to epistemology. It is equally crucial in respect to the law: "In this age it is never acceptable to abandon the laws and rely on personal biases. Relying on one's personal biases is unacceptable because it will give rise to disasters" (81:149b).

The laws are the standards for maintaining social order. Like the scale or compass, they constitute a common measure applicable to one and all alike.

> Retaliating with {partiality} harms one's authority;[10] giving in to desires harms the law; not following them harms the Way. A ruler who frequently falls prey to the above three is not even able to take care of himself. How could he preserve a state? (81:143a)

> . . . Having instruments and using them properly, one will not err. Relying on the gauge and checking it, one will not be confused. Governing according to the law, one will not be disordered. (81:144a)

Significantly, *contra* Legalist thought, even the ruler must abide by the law: "The one who holds fast to the Way, having generated the standards, does not dare to violate them nor to abrogate them once they have been established. Only after {the ruler} is able to bring his own self into line with the guidelines does he apprehend and understand the world without confusion (43:1a).[11]

The law is not merely a political tool to be used by the ruler to further his own ends. He cannot change the law willy nilly. Nor can he circumvent it by issuing pardons. The author is adamant that punishments and rewards be reliable and certain.

> Regulating through punishments means executing the guilty without pardon. (47:16b)

> To be purely impartial (*gong*), without personal bias, and for punishments and rewards to be reliable is how to effect sociopolitical order. (47:21a)

Gong 公 not only means "impartial" but has as well the connotation of "just" and "fair" as evidenced by the modern binomials *gong zheng* 公正 and *gong ping* 公平, respectively. As one would expect given the Huang-Lao world view described in the previous chapter, to be just and fair is to adjudicate conflicts according to the objective natural order. The law, it is to be remembered, is the tally of the Way. This implies what I shall now demonstrate, that Huang-Lao rule of law is rule of natural law.

1.2 Rule of Natural Law

Natural law means different things to different people. As pointed out in Chapter I, one of the key differentiae of natural and positivist law is that the latter does not require the law to display any necessary relation to morality to be valid. Hart, speaking for the legal positivists, captures the difference in "the simple contention that it is in no sense a necessary truth that laws reproduce or satisfy certain demands of morality."[12] In contrast, the rallying cry for natural law proponents has traditionally been "an unjust law is no law at all."[13]

I have suggested that to rely solely on the differentia of Hart's minimum separation thesis and the distinction between natural and positivist law does not allow one to fully appreciate the complexity of the various pre-Han philosophies of law. In examining the relation between morality and the law, one must further distinguish between foundational and pragmatic-coherence systems.

However, as a point of departure, it will repay us to show that Huang-Lao is natural law in the minimal sense of repudiating the minimum separation thesis. That law and morality are inextricably interrelated is borne out in several ways. The author insists that *de* (德—virtue, magnanimity, reward)[14] is an essential component of the kingly art of rulership:

> Even where one's accomplishments are substantial, if his virtue (*de*) is shallow he will be overthrown. (55:58b)

> As for the three evils: the first is to be found of evil instruments of war; the second is to act contrary to virtue; the third is to give free rein to one's heart's desires. (55:64a)

As observed in the last chapter, to simply rely on military strength to keep one's enemies at bay is insufficient. Hence the author calls for both military strength (*wu*) and cultural refinement (*wen*). Nor will it do to rely solely on harsh punishments to control one's subjects. One must supplement punishments with rewards: "Solemn and awful are mother nature's punishments. Yet not to reward (*de*) spells certain downfall. When punishments and rewards complement each other, compliance and uncompliance will be realized" (69:109a).

By being virtuous and rewarding as well as punishing, the ruler gains the support of the people. As a result, the people develop a sense of shame. They come to view laws as their own customs. Internalizing the laws as social norms worthy of respect, they do not feel the inclination to violate them. In this way the legal and normative orders come to coincide.

"Where the ruler exercises moderation in his use of the strength of the masses, riches abound. Where taxes are levied with due measure, the masses prosper. Where the masses prosper, they have a sense of shame. Where they have a sense of shame, edicts and orders become the customs, penal laws and penalties are not violated. Where edicts and orders become customs and penal laws and penalties are not violated, this is the way to be staunch in defense and victorious in battle" (47:20a).

Of course, the ruler must not only reward as well as punish but must do so fairly and reliably. If rewards and punishments do not hit the mark (*dang*), if they do not fit the crime, one violates the natural order, further disrupting cosmic harmony, and as a consequence is sure to bring down disaster on one's own person.[15] "Where punishments and prohibitions miss the mark, misfortune redounds on one's own head. If one prohibits punitive expeditions against those who deserve censure, who deserve to die, one is certain to ruin one's state" (45:9b). On the other hand, when punishments and rewards are impartially applied and on the mark, they are accepted without comment. The people express neither gratitude nor resentment (47:18a). They simply feel as if they have been given their just deserts.

Foundational Natural Law

The emphasis on virtue and the need to balance military strength with cultural achievement, punishments with rewards, indicates that law and morality are integrally connected for the author of the *Boshu*. Yet the most powerful argument for a necessary linkage of the sort denied by the minimum separation thesis—and hence for Huang-Lao law as natural law in the traditional sense—is that laws are grounded in the objective, normatively correct natural order.[16] "The Way generates the laws. The laws apply a guideline to gain and loss and illumine crooked and straight. Hence, the one who holds fast to the Way, having generated the laws, does not dare to violate them nor to abrogate them once they have been established" (43:1a). As evidenced in this statement and discussed at length in the previous chapter, laws arise from dao; they are part of the fabric of the natural order that constitutes the normative standard. As such, to be a valid law, a law must correspond to the Way.

Laws are therefore determinate normative standards to be discovered by the sage. "There is a distinction between right and wrong: use the law to adjudicate between them. Being empty, tranquil, and listening attentively, take the law as the tally" (58:75a).

Just as the sage is responsible for discovering the law but not for creating it, so is he responsible for impartially applying the law but not for interpreting it. In the legal empire of Huang-Lao, the scales of justice are finely calibrated objective standards. Discretion is eliminated. It is neither the sage's duty nor his role to balance the arguments pro and con in light of the particular circumstances. Unlike his Confucian and Daoist counterparts, the Huang-Lao sage is not called upon to build a consensus out of dissension, to realize a harmony amenable to all concerned parties. He is a judge, not a mediator. His task is to decide who is right and who is wrong, nothing more, nothing less. On one side of the scales of justice goes the deed, on the other the Way.[17] The burden on the sage is to eliminate subjective bias so that he is able to apprehend the deed as it actually is and the Way as it should be.

Needham

I have argued that Huang-Lao law is natural law grounded in the natural order and that the natural order is to be understood as constant and rule governed. Huang-Lao laws are then both a reflection and a manifestation of the rule governed natural order. As a reflection of the natural order, laws for governing society are modeled on the laws that govern nature: "Spring and summer are the seasons of reward; fall and winter are the seasons of punishment. To nourish life, begin with reward and then follow with punishment" (62:85b). As a manifestation of the natural order, they are implicit in the normatively correct Way. They constitute the infrastructure of the Way.

Needham, as pointed out previously, denies that in China "the ideas of natural law (in the juristic sense) and of the laws of nature (in the sense of the natural sciences) go back to a common root." He does so primarily on the grounds that the early Chinese do not conceive of the "laws of nature" in a physical science sense. In due fairness to Needham, he did not have available the *Boshu* at the time he made this claim. Nevertheless, his statements are broad sweeping, speaking to the premodern Chinese intellectual tradition as a whole. Thus they would, it seems, pertain to all works of that period. Further, and more important, in characterizing the Chinese tradition as organismic, Needham does have an important insight, but one that needs to be clarified and qualified. That the *Boshu* paints a different picture need not undermine the validity of Needham's view as a general characterization. It merely suggests that Huang-Lao thought represents a countercurrent within the history of Chinese intellectual thought.

Needham approaches the issue of natural law and laws of nature from the perspective of his larger problematic of scientific development, or rather the relative lack of it, in China. To summarize his argument, he points out that in many Western traditions, such as Islam and Judaism, natural law and the laws of nature often flow from the same source: a divine lawmaker who made laws for all things to obey. It was not permissible for human law to run contrary to divine law, including the God-given laws of nature. He then states: "In so far. . . . as natural law came to be overwhelmingly dominant in China, and positive law reduced to a minimum, one would expect that so different a balance might have had important effects on the development of the formulation of the regularities of Nature in the natural sciences. . . . The stronger the role of natural law, the greater facility there might have been in conceiving of the Laws of Nature as a kind of inescapable natural *li* [rites] in which the whole non-human world concurred."[18] China, however, did not develop scientifically. Why not?

The reason, suggests Needham, is that the Chinese were not concerned with the laws of nature. He attributes this to lack of a divine lawmaker, of an "autochthonous idea of a supreme being" to act as source for such laws. Further, and less understandable, this is also to account for their not making the move from natural law based on universal ethical principles—the Confucian *li* in Needham's reading—to natural law based on universal laws of nature.[19]

Needham is partially correct. The lack of a transcendent deity who lays down the law, thereby establishing a predetermined order with which humans must comply in their social order, is consistent with and encourages an organismic cosmology. Nevertheless, despite the absence of this kind of deity, some Chinese—as Derk Bodde has meticulously demonstrated in conjunction with several pre-Han works and as I have shown for the author of the *Boshu*—do conceive of the laws of the natural order as transcendent and predetermined in the sense that they determine the cosmic order, including the order of nonhuman nature and the human order, without being themselves determined by humans or the human order.[20]

Viewed from the *Boshu*'s perspective requiring compliance with a constant, impersonal natural order underlying the social order, Needham's objection that there are no laws of nature in the sense necessary to support natural law cannot be sustained. He contends that, given the organismic character of Chinese cosmology, although "law could not be said to be *in* non-human Nature. . . the laws of human society should be modelled *on* non-human Nature."[21] Although agreeing that the social order is often based on nonhuman nature, we must, in light of this analysis of the *Boshu*, take issue with the first part of his statement. There are "laws of nature." The natural order is regular and reliable and guided by constant norms.

It seems that Needham feels compelled to deny the status of laws of nature to any Chinese conception of the constant forces and principles of nature and the natural order because of a confusion as to the relationship between these laws and organismic cosmology. He seems to think the existence of the former precludes the latter.

He denies, for instance, the existence of the laws of nature in Chinese thought on the grounds that humans, as part of the cosmos, are not governed from the outside but must obey the "internal necessity" of their own natures "in accordance with their positions in the greater patterns (organisms) of which they are a part."[22] But Needham's metaphorical distinction between laws being in things or in nature, and hence external to things, is misleading here. The issue is not one of internality or externality but of conceptual primacy. To the extent that the natural order is normatively primary, which is to say it requires compliance on the part of humans, one could, perhaps, say it is imposed on humans "from outside." That is, it can be looked on as a transcendent order in the general sense elaborated previously.

However, in clarifying the nature of transcendence operative in Huang-Lao we found it helpful to draw a further distinction between transcendence in a strong sense, (*chao jue*), and a weak sense, (*chao yue*).[22] The former entails a radical ontological disparity or separation. By way of illustration, we considered the *creatio ex nihilo* cosmogonic paradigm of Genesis in which God, ontologically distinct and temporally prior to the world, creates the world out of nothing.

Huang-Lao advances transcendence of the weak sense. In that it does not, therefore, entail a radical ontological separation between the source of the determining order and the human realm that complies with this order, it can still be construed, to use Needham's term, as an organicism—as what I would call an organic or holistic natural order. There is no deity, no autochthonous supreme being, that exists apart from the natural order and imposes order on the cosmos. Dao simply is the natural order.

The distinction between transcendence in a weak sense and a strong sense vitiates Needham's basic objection that for the Chinese natural law cannot be grounded in the laws of nature because their organismic worldview prohibited such a conception.

Having argued against Needham that natural law based on the objective natural order does exist in classical China, perhaps I owe at least a few words in response to his broader query as to the lack of scientific development in China. Indeed, this becomes even more difficult to explain in light of my contention that there were Chinese schools that emphasized a law governed natural order. It should be pointed out, first, that there was a brief flourishing of scientific activity around the early Han, as Needham himself documents. However, one reason why it did not continue may very well be that the schools that looked on nature in this way did not endure. The Huang-Lao school fell from power during the reign of Han Wu Di (140 B.C.). With the reemergence of Confucianism during that period, yin yang five phase thinking of the causal correlative cosmology kind that supported predetermined laws of nature was subsequently reinterpreted in a more nonfoundational, mutually determining (*tian ren gan ying* 天人感應) organismic fashion by Dong Zhongshu.[24] Such correlative thinking was subject to further attack during the later Han by skeptics such as Wang Chong.

Further, *pace* Needham, Confucian law is not, as I will show in the next chapter, natural law in a foundationalist sense. Rather than appealing to a predetermined order in the form of abstract, ahistorical, universal ethical principles, Confucianism stresses a dynamic, interactive, emergent sense of order understood as an achievement of harmony in a particular social-historical context. This precludes the progression from universal ethical principles to universal laws of nature to natural law. In short, Confucianism sponsors an aesthetic (organismic) cosmology that, as Needham has so painstakingly documented, is not as conducive to scientific development as the dominant Western conception of nature.

2. The Huang-Lao State

The centerpiece of social and political philosophy is the state. Much can be learned of a philosopher's views by examining the nature of the social order, the manner in which society's resources are distributed, the way in which the political hierarchy is structured. Perhaps even more revealing, however, is the justification offered for these choices. In the case of the *Boshu*, the author envisions a hierarchical feudal bureaucracy with political positions grounded in the natural order and assigned according to merit.

2.1 Yellow Emperor as Symbol

For two plus millennia, the nature of Huang-Lao thought puzzled scholars. The discovery of the *Boshu* provides a key piece to the puzzle and allows us to reply with some confidence that Huang-Lao is a well-developed political philosophy that bases the social order on the natural Way. Now one wonders why *Huang-Lao*?[25] The *Lao*, obviously, refers to Lao Zi. But in many ways the philosophy of Huang-Lao seems antithetical to that of Lao Zi, most noticeably in respect to laws. Whereas Huang-Lao takes laws to be necessary for social order, Lao Zi counts them a leading factor in the appearance of thieving scoundrels and a major source of disorder.[26]

Despite the differences, the author appears to have turned to Lao Zi for his epistemology and the idea of a natural Way that could serve as the metaphysical basis for Huang-Lao social and political theories. As for the former, Huang-Lao's discovery of the Way by eliminating partiality through the attainment of emptiness (*xu*) and tranquility (*jing*) is paralleled in Lao Zi's meditative epistemology in which one discovers the way to effect harmony through the attainment of emptiness and tranquility.[27] As for the latter idea, inasmuch as Lao Zi does portray *tian* as an impersonal nature,[28] the *Dao De Jing* is a likely source for the natural Way of Huang-Lao where dao is elided with *tian dao*: the way of the natural order. However, as I argue later, dao for Lao Zi is not a predetermined order as it is for Huang-Lao. Rather, Lao Zi's dao is emergent. There is an ineradicable element of spontaneity and contingency to dao that undermines any attempt to reduce it to determinate rules.[29]

In any event, at this point we are only interested in the origination of the name. And the appropriation of *Lao* by Huang-Lao is understandable even if we think the author has misrepresented Lao Zi. After all, many a sect has resulted from a creative misreading of an earlier school of thought.

But what of the *Huang* component? It refers to the Yellow Emperor, that much we know. But why the Yellow Emperor? There are various explanations all of which have some measure of plausibility and when taken together go a good distance toward dispelling the mystery.

First is the "keeping up with the competition" theory. Other schools had mythical heroes: the Confucians and Mohists had Yao and Shun, the Agrarians Shen Nung. Huang-Lao, not wanting to appear culturally deprived, needed its own.

Along the same lines is the view that a new system of thought like Huang-Lao requires an ancient authority figure for legitimation. In a tradition that values cultural continuity over novelty, to trace an innovative concept back to legendary figures of personal and cultural achievement constitutes an argument. As a result, cultural icons like Yao, Shun, or the Yellow Emperor come to serve as patrons of new ideas. Though arguments from authority are highly suspect for most today, that they held considerable sway over many pre-Han Chinese cannot be denied. The writings of Mo Zi provide ample testament. He not only repeatedly invoked ancient authority but explicitly discussed it as one of three types of valid argumentation.[30]

It may be that Mo Zi and others invested such importance in ancient persons in part because of the widely held belief that the Golden Age of China lay in the past. As the *Huai Nan Zi* states, "Vulgar people by and large honor the past above the present; therefore those who cultivate a

Way have to credit it to Shen Nung or the Yellow Emperor before it can be taken seriously" (19/11a/5). Although the Huang-Lao school rejects the notion of a utopian good old days it might have discovered that to gain a sympathetic hearing it was necessary to adopt a mythical sponsor for its views.

A third theory addresses a shortcoming of the first two; namely, why the Yellow Emperor rather than some other figure? The answer, most everybody in the late Warring States and Early Han periods was citing the Yellow Emperor—as borne out by the historical records. The *Han Shu* alone lists works that mention the Yellow Emperor *in the title* under the categories of Daoism, Legalism, yin yang, five phases, military, mythology, astrology, calendars, divination, medicine, pharmacy, sexual yoga, and immortality.[31]

Yet that Huang-Lao adopted the Yellow Emperor because he won a popularity contest is not entirely satisfying. Although his mass appeal surely counted for rather than against him, there are more specific reasons for choosing him as the symbolic representative of Huang-Lao thought. Examination of the images of the Yellow Emperor in the literature and mythology of the period suggests that his appeal to the proponents of Huang-Lao lies primarily in his symbolic value as the first ancestor of the Chinese people, who put an end to battling among the clans through military conquest and the establishment of a centralized bureaucratic state replete with ministers, laws, and other such accouterments of feudal bureaucracy.[32]

Since the discovery of the *Boshu*, considerable scholarly effort has been poured into compilation and analysis of Yellow Emperor images in the classical corpus.[33] Charles Le Blanc and Jan Yun-hua have noted that many of the references to the Yellow Emperor portray him as a political figure. In this regard three major themes merit attention for our study of the *Boshu*: the Yellow Emperor as originator of a centralized bureaucratic state; the Yellow Emperor as sole ruler of an empire unified through military conquest; the Yellow Emperor as ideal ruler.[34]

Originator of a Centralized Bureaucratic State

The image of the Yellow Emperor as the one who brought organized government to the people is found in the Legalist writings of Shang Yang.[35]

> In the age of Shen Nung, the people were fed by the ploughing of the men, clothed by the weaving of the women. He ruled without the use of punishments or administration; he reigned without resorting to weapons and armor.

When Shen Nung died, some took advantage of their strength to conquer the weak and of their numbers to oppress the few. Therefore, the Yellow Emperor instituted the formalities of ruler and minister and superior and inferior, the rites for father and son and elder and younger brother, the union of couples as husband and wife. At home he put to work the executioner's axe, abroad he employed weapons and armor. So it was a change in the times.[36]

Shang Yang believes in the existence of a Golden Age when people lived together in cooperative harmony and laws were not needed. Though Shang Yang and the author of the *Boshu* differ on this point, they both portray the Yellow Emperor as a positive force who rescues the people from chaos. The Yellow Emperor responds to the breakdown in the moral and sociopolitical order with the establishment of formal government. Whereas Shen Nung did not need to rely on administrative supervision or punishments to maintain social order, the Yellow Emperor did. He initiated the use of penal laws.[37] As we have observed, laws, though condemned by Lao Zi, play a central role in the political scheme of the *Boshu*. Similarly, the prominent place ceded to military strength and the need for social and class distinctions are also features instituted by the Yellow Emperor that find their counterpart in the *Boshu*.[38]

Like the Legalist Shang Yang, the Yang Zhu disciple who penned the "Robber Zhi" chapter of the *Zhuang Zi* sees the Yellow Emperor as the initiator of a process culminating in a centralized bureaucratic state:

> In the age of Shen Nung
> They slept sound,
> They woke fresh.
> The people knew their mothers
> But did not know their fathers,
> And lived together with the deer . . .

However, the Yellow Emperor was unable to maintain virtue at its utmost, he battled with Chi You in the field of Zhuo Lu and made the blood stream for a hundred miles. Yao and Shun arose, and instituted the ministers; Tang exiled his lord, King Wu killed Zhou. From this time on men took advantage of strength to bully the weak, of numbers to oppress the few. Since Tang and Wu they have all been the trouble-making sort. (81/29/29, G237)

Far from being a hero to the individualist Robber Zhi, the Yellow Emperor is the villain who began the downfall from the giddy heights of the utopian past by instigating war. The *Shiliu Jing* also describes the battle at Zhuo Lu. There, however, the Yellow Emperor is celebrated as a savior of the Chinese people, who were being repressed by the cruel and tyrannical Chi You.[39]

The different assessments of the Yellow Emperor reveal much about the political philosophy of the authors. Whereas the Yellow Emperor was a symbol of centralized government, Shen Nung was, as Graham has demonstrated, the representative of an egalitarian, communal anarchism.[40] Between them, they exemplify two radically different responses to the chaos of the Warring States and early Han periods and to the harsh Legalist regime of Qin.[41] The first response is a call for the dismantling of the centralized bureaucratic feudal state. How this was to be accomplished and what was to replace it varies, however, from thinker to thinker.

For Shen Nung, the goal was to establish an agrarian community in which all till the fields side by side. Class distinctions would be eliminated. Nobody was to receive special privileges. There would be no need for punishments because people would be too busy working the land to commit crimes or lust after the possessions of others. There would be no need for rewards because people would realize it was in their self-interest to work. Having been allotted a parcel of land, they would be content to farm it.

For others, the ideal is a return to the simple communal life of antiquity depicted in the "primitivist" chapters of the *Zhuang Zi* and in the *Dao De Jing* (80):[42]

> Reduce the size and population of the state.
> Ensure that even though the tools of war are available they are not used . . .
> Bring it about that the people return to the use of knotted rope,
>> find relish in their food
>> and beauty in their clothes;
>> find contentment in their daily life
>> and joy in their customs.
> Though neighboring states are within sight of one another
> and the sounds of dogs barking and cocks crowing are heard across the way,
> the people of one state will reach old age and pass away
> without having had any dealings with those of another.

For still others, perhaps judging the state to be too firmly entrenched to be eradicated, the solution was to simply withdraw from the political arena, to retreat from society to the solitude and solace of the countryside.

Stories of Daoist recluses and hermits who lived out their days riding the wind and sipping the morning dew lace the classical literature. It fact, many argue that Zhuang Zi himself is to be counted among this group.[43] This explains, they add, the relative lack of attention paid to the *Zhuang Zi* during the turbulent days of the late Warring States and Han periods. When searching for political advice as to how to set aright the empire, one is unlikely to turn to someone who prefers the pleasure of dragging his tail in the mud to holding the highest office.[44]

Rather than withdrawing from or abolishing the state, the other major alternative is to reform it. As we shall see, this is the choice of the author of the *Boshu*.

Unifier Through Military Conquest

The Yellow Emperor is portrayed not only as the first to institute centralized government. He is also depicted both in the *Boshu* and in other pre-Han texts as being the first to unify an empire that had hitherto consisted of rival, constantly feuding, clans.[45] To ensure peace and stability, the Yellow Emperor was called upon to bring the contending factions to heel through military force.

References to the Yellow Emperor as victorious warrior go back to the *Zuo Zhuan* where in the twenty-fifth year of Duke Xi (635 B.C.) his battle at Ban Quan is mentioned. Though we are not told that his foe was Chi You, that the Yellow Emperor was summoned to subdue the rebellious Chi is well attested in the literature, including the *Boshu* that presents this grisly account:[46]

> When the war was raging full on, the commissioner of Mount Tai said, "Alright, now is the time." Thereupon the Yellow Emperor lifted his halberd, snatched up his weaponry and personally confronted Chi You. Capturing him in due course, the Yellow Emperor peeled off his {skin} to make a target and ordered the people to shoot at it.[47] Those who most often hit it were rewarded. He then cut off Chi You's hair, hung it above the heavenly gate and called it the Banner of Chi You. Stuffing his stomach in order to make a ball, he ordered the people to kick it. Those who most often kicked it were rewarded. He fermented his bones and flesh and threw it into the bitter broth and had the people drink it.[48] In this way, the emperor above established the prohibitions. (67:104a)

The Yellow Emperor's main contribution as a warrior was not the conquest of Chi You itself, however, but the unification of the empire. According to the *Boshu*, forceful unification was necessary because the various clans from the very beginning were unable to live together peacefully: "Heaven and earth having been formed, the black-headed masses were engendered. Once the various clans arose and became established, rival families began to conflict. If not suppressed, the situation would be unstable.[49] In general, the best way to suppress them lies in utilizing both punishments and rewards" (69:108a).

The author maintains that contention is if not inevitable at least the historical norm. All creatures, humans included, have through the ages fought with each other. Those who are not prepared to defend themselves do not survive. The secret to success, as noted earlier, is to take up arms only when the moment and the cause are right. That the Yellow Emperor was victorious in his battles with Chi You and in his quest to bring peace to the masses through military unification is therefore a testimony not only to his military prowess but to his capacity as a wise ruler who unerringly walks the Way.[50]

Ideal Ruler

Though not all hold the Yellow Emperor in high esteem, he is for many not just any ruler but an ideal ruler.[51] His excellences are manifold. As an innovator he is said to have created gardens and designed the *ming tang* 明堂 —the ceremonial hall and spiritual center of the people during the Han.[52] In fact, he is even credited with originating music, rites, and *ren yi* (仁義 —benevolence and righteousness), all distinctly Confucian concerns.[53]

Further, though the Yellow Emperor was the sole ruler of the empire, he is, as Jan has pointed out, often portrayed as an open-minded person willing to listen to and learn from his ministers.[54] "In the old days the Yellow Emperor was able to understand the way of heaven once he retained Chi You, able to examine the resources of earth once he retained Da Chang. He was able to know the east when he retained She Long, the south when he retained Zhu Yong, the west when he retained Da Feng, the north when he retained Hou Tou. . . . After the Yellow Emperor retained these six ministers the world was well governed" (*Guan Zi* 2:82).

Perhaps most important, however, the Yellow Emperor constituted the ideal ruler in that he had the support of the people. This is the aspect in which Huang-Lao thought most clearly reflects the positive influence of Confucianism. The Yellow Emperor was able to unify the people because he, like the best of Confucian rulers, had won their hearts: "In ancient times the Yellow Emperor ruled the world by making the hearts of the people one."[55] Similarly, he was able to institute penal laws because the people had confidence in his leadership and judgment: "When the Yellow

Emperor ruled, people went to him without any pulling, came to him without any pushing, accomplished works without employment and stopped wrongdoings without prohibitions. Therefore the Yellow Emperor ruled by establishing laws (*fa*) that he did not change, allowing people to find security and pleasure in them."[56]

The Yellow Emperor was no despotic tyrant who reigns through terror. Though laws, punishments and military strength are necessary given the tendency of the people to conflict, they must be counterbalanced.[57] The ruler reduces the need for laws by inspiring the people's virtuous behavior and personal development. He accomplishes this not only by personally setting an example but by officially encouraging cultural achievement through sponsoring the arts. To offset punishments the ruler liberally disburses rewards. Because he does so impartially and fairly, the people have no complaints. To diminish the dangers and costs of war the ruler restricts himself to only those battles that are for a just cause and cannot be avoided.

A ruler of such great wisdom and exemplary character is like a god to the people. And indeed the Yellow Emperor was portrayed as a divine being in many texts.[58] He achieved this lofty status because he was, as the *Boshu* puts it, the counterpart of heaven (61:78b). Le Blanc notes that the Yellow Emperor was referred to as the god of Saturn.[59] Comparative mythology reveals that the god-planet of Saturn is often conceived of as the initiator and preserver of order. In Chinese, 'Saturn' is *zhen xing* 辰星—the regulating, governing star. As the god of the regulating star, the Yellow Emperor represented the source of primordial order, responsible for not only social but cosmic order. One wonders whether it could be coincidence that in *Huang*-Lao thought social order is predicated on cosmic order.

Le Blanc, observing that the Yellow Emperor appears as a symbol of the center in Yin Yang Five Phase correlative cosmology as well as of the beginning of society and the universe, concludes that "the ultimate symbolism of Huang Ti would thus appear to be the assertion that the world of man and society abides by the same rules as the world of nature and is structured by the same principles."[60] Through a study of myth, Le Blanc arrived at the same conclusion arrived at here through philosophical analysis of the metaphysics, epistemology, jurisprudence, and political thought of the *Boshu*. The social order is an instantiation of the natural order. The Yellow Emperor is the ultimate sage-ruler, the one to realize the Way and the shape society accordingly.

In sum, as a symbol of a wise ruler who unifies the empire and establishes a centralized government, the Yellow Emperor is an obvious choice for Huang-Lao thinkers such as the author of the *Boshu*. Associated with cosmic and natural order, the main function of the Yellow Emperor is to provide the political superstructure to be grounded in the natural way derived from the *Lao Zi*. In adopting the Yellow Emperor as its patron saint, the Huang-Lao school was able in a single stroke to deliver a statement of its political views and in so doing to distinguish itself from the anarchistic, anti-rule-of-law social and political philosophy of Lao Zi and Zhuang Zi.[61]

2.2   *Centralized Feudal Bureaucracy*

The ideal state promoted in the *Boshu* exhibits, as one would expect, many of the salient features of the government of the Yellow Emperor. It is a centralized bureaucratic state presided over by a single paternalistic ruler who unifies the empire militarily and wins the support of the people through his enlightened policies and upright character. It is a feudal class society with clearly delineated social rankings. And perhaps most important it is a government for the people, less harsh than the brutal Legalist regime of Qin, and concerned first and foremost with the interests of the people rather than the ruler.

The Centralized Bureaucracy

The ruler of the *Boshu* oversees a complex, highly sophisticated feudal bureaucracy. Earning kudos for the design and implementation of the system is the Yellow Emperor who immodestly proclaimed: "Since I and I alone stand as a counterpart to heaven, I have enthroned the kings, appointed the three highest ministers, founded the kingdoms and put a ruler in place along with his three ministers of state. I have enumerated the days, calendared the months, and calculated the duration of the year to match the movements of the sun and moon" (61:78b). Confirming our earlier observation, the relationship between the political order and the natural order in the *Boshu* is an intimate one.[62] The Yellow Emperor laid down both political and natural regulations for social order. Given the foundational naturalism of the author, the political hierarchy of the *Boshu*'s feudal bureaucracy is as much a part of the natural order as is the pattern of day following night.

In unifying the empire, the Yellow Emperor was the first to implement the organizational structure and institutional mechanisms of a centralized state. As we have seen, in the general literature he was often given the honor or, depending on one's philosophical allegiance, the dishonor of being the first to establish laws and punishments to go along with a bureaucratic hierarchy. Each person has an assigned place and must faithfully perform the duties attached to that position or face certain punishment as stipulated in advance. In assigning a central place to laws, punishments, and clearly delineated roles, the author of the *Boshu* indicated his approval of the Yellow Emperor's policies.

While the author's concern for impartially applied punishments and morally just laws has been well documented, his endorsement of class distinctions merits further attention. That he believes such distinctions are legitimate is undeniable. People inevitably perform different functions in the bureaucracy. Along with the different roles come different titles and compensation: "There is a distinction between noble and lowly, this is the difference between persons of superior and inferior character. Styles of dress do not overlap, this is the ranking of noble and lowly" (47:18a).

One is to be afforded perquisites and privileges consonant with one's duties and position. If each person is treated appropriately, the system as a whole operates smoothly and all are content. Nobody is jealous because each feels fairly treated. "Where the ruler classifies them according to their lots the myriad people will not be contentious. Where the ruler compensates them consonant with their titles the myriad things will settle themselves" (87:173a).

That social distinctions would be of such concern to the author is not surprising given his correspondence philosophy of language, which holds that each thing comes into existence with form and name assigned.[63] The political corollary is that one is to be assigned to one's appropriate place in the bureaucratic hierarchy. One is allotted a certain place in the sociopolitical structure and must fulfill the duties that fall to one in that position. As we have noted, for a ruler and a minister to exchange positions or even deviate from their respective posts is anathema to the author and sure to spell disaster. It is, the author tells us, the very definition of "contrariety" (*ni*),[64] and to be contrary is to run counter to the Way; it is to violate the natural order. Of course, not only the ruler and minister must abide in their proper posts. Each slot in the governmental hierarchy must be properly filled: "For persons of superior and inferior character to occupy the same position is called disorder. . . . When disordered, one fails in one's duties of office. . . . When one fails in one's duties of office, one will have one's domain encroached upon. . . . [Conversely,] for the person of superior character and the unworthy to assume proper positions is called proper order. . . . When there is proper order, there is proper government. . . . Where there is proper government the support of the people is attained" (51:35b).

Though hierarchical, the author's centralized bureaucracy is a meritocracy. The talented and superior in character get promoted regardless of class origin, the most important criterion being that one is able to stay within the limits of one's abilities and perform the task for which one is chosen: "The constant way in managing officials is to appoint those who are able to refrain from going beyond their own strengths" (43:7a).

Because the system depends on appointing people held to be worthy, the author insists that reputation be based on past achievement and not simply on pretense. "Where reputation and achievement do not warrant each other such that reputation marches ahead while substance lags behind, this is called losing the Way" (52:45b). If one does not earn one's reputation and is appointed to a high position under false pretenses, one injures both one's own person and the state. One puts one's own person in danger in that one is constantly at risk of being exposed as incompetent and subsequently punished for failing to live up to one's stipulated duties. One injures the state in accepting a position one is not qualified for because others feel slighted. In such slights are sown the seeds of rebellion. People feel they have been cheated, passed over, treated unfairly. As a result, they begin to resent those in power. Those above and those below become estranged. The rift grows until finally the disenfranchised attempt to overthrow their oppressors. Thus the author concludes, "For reputations to be glorious while the substance is scant is to imperil the state and cause the territory to be lost" (55:61a).

Reputations and titles are of course a kind of naming. As such, they must correspond to reality. When social status is not in keeping with real achievements and political positions are assigned on grounds other than merit, the very enterprise of naming is threatened: "Where reputation exceeds the facts, it is called the undermining of names" (51:40b). Although the doctrine of *xing ming* extends well beyond political titles and performances to include every thing in the universe, the importance of names matching reality in the political arena deserves to be underscored. It is after all largely through political channels that the power of society courses and its wealth and resources flow. To control political allotments is in effect to possess the empire. Not only can one set the agenda by placing one's own supporters in key posts but one can win the people over by enriching them through tax breaks and the like.

Yet the most remarkable aspect of the relationship between the author's correspondence theory of *xing ming* and his political hierarchy is perhaps the way the former serves to legitimate the latter.[65] Just as names arise from the Way and are a direct manifestation of the normative natural order, so are class distinctions. They are as constant and inevitable as the laws of nature:[66] "Heaven and earth have their constant norms; the masses have their constant occupations; the noble and lowly have their constant positions; in the managing of ministers, there is a constant way; in the employing of the masses, there is a constant measure" (43:6a).

The author attempts to legitimate his feudal class society by grounding it in the normatively privileged natural order. He justifies the social distinction between upper and lower classes, the noble and base—and ipso facto the distribution of social resources that goes along with the distinction—by declaring it to be natural. Like the laws, principles, names, and so forth discussed earlier, the feudal hierarchy is a direct manifestation and instantiation of the Way. For the author, the hierarchical bureaucratic order is not only the way it is, it is the Way it should be. That there are rulers above ministers above officials above scholars above the masses is the inherent structure of the sociopolitical order implicate in the natural order or dao. The sage-ruler is merely to realize it by assigning the right persons to the right positions.[67]

This is not to belittle the role of the sage-ruler. To appoint those who are worthy is no mean feat. The ruler must be impartial and evenhanded. He must investigate the reality behind the names in order to determine who is worthy of the reputation and appoint accordingly. He must put the interests of the state before his own. Any ruler who manages all this has mastered much of the kingly way and is sure to be a success. "Since the one who realizes the kingly way pays little attention to wealth while exalting those who are knowledgeable, success and prosperity are obtained. Since he pays little attention to his own person while exalting those of the Way, his person is exalted and his orders carried out" (50:33b).

Significantly, the author favors the feudal practice of enfeoffment: "The sage, in his military expeditions, annexes other states . . . and divides up their lands to enfeoff those of superior character" (45:12a). This is one of the characteristics of the rule of Han Emperor Liu Bang to which some have pointed as evidence of Huang-Lao influence on his policies and on Han politics more generally.[68]

One Empire: One Ruler

In the political world of the *Boshu* there must be but one ruler.

> When there are two rulers clarity is lost, men and women contend for power and the state is faced with an unruly military—this is called a doomed state. (49:24b)

> When there are two rulers and man and woman share authority it is called "being utterly lost" and there will be military operations within the state. If

this happens in a powerful state, it will be crippled; if in a mid-size state, it will perish; if in a small state, it will be annihilated. (49:26b)

Where the various officials are at cross purposes and high-ranking officials assume the prerogatives of the ruler this is called "being obstructed." If this happens in a powerful state, it will be pared away; if in a mid-size state, it will be crippled; if in a small state, it will perish. (49:24b)

Further, the ruler is to preside over a unified empire. The author on several occasions has the Yellow Emperor emphatically declare: "I, one man alone, having unified the empire, possess all under heaven" (66:95b; 72:119b). And as we have seen, the author recounts with favor the Yellow Emperor's military exploits made necessary by the incessant warring between factions and culminating in unification. The Yellow Emperor is able to succeed because he complies with the normative Way: "Embracing dao and holding fast to the standards, the empire can be unified" (87:173b).

Although there is to be but one ruler, he is not to be an authoritarian despot able to have his way with his subordinates and to run rough-shod over the interests of the people. Like the Yellow Emperor, the ruler of the *Boshu* has a good working relation with his ministers and the support of his subjects. One reason for this may be that he is ever eager to seek assistance from his ministers. This is evidenced on several occasions in the *Shiliu Jing* where the ruler, none other than the Yellow Emperor himself, petitions his ministers Li Mu, Yan Ran, and Guo Tong for guidance on a range of topics from military affairs to legal matters to personal cultivation. The author even makes it a point to explicitly warn the ruler of the dangers of trying to go it alone: "Not taking advantage of the help of the assistants nor heeding the considerations of the sagacious and worthy ones, but instead to depend on the firmness of the inner and outer city walls and to rely on boldness and strength for defense—this is called being personally aggressive. Being personally aggressive, one will be endangered. Defending the state in this way, one will not be secure. Waging war in this way, one will not be victorious" (82:160b). No matter how brilliant a statesperson or how talented a military strategist a ruler is, he is still but one person with finite abilities and powers. Thus a wise ruler turns to those who can assist him. To ensure their loyalty, however, he must pay them their due in both monetary remuneration and respect:

As for one who does not accept a salary, even the son of heaven cannot make him a minister. One whose salary is low will not participate in the taking of great risks. (81:146b)

He who rules as the true king in the empire places little importance on the territory of his state and great importance on his officials.[69] Consequently, the state will be secure and his own person safe. (50:33b)

The relationship between the ruler and his ministers is one of mutual trust and respect. Each has his own duties, his own sphere of influence. For the government to function efficiently and the state to prosper, the ruler must work hand in hand with his subordinates. "Where the ruler is beneficent and the ministers loyal, the state is secure. Where the rulers rule and the ministers administer and those above and those below are not estranged, the state is strong. Where the ruler holds fast to the measures (*du*) and the ministers act according to principle (*li*), the state, reigning supreme among the various states, flourishes. Where the ruler occupies his position and the ministers attach to him like spokes, he will realize the kingly way" (49:27b).[70] While ruler and minister each has his unique role, they collectively constitute an integrated whole. When each mans his post and performs his proper function, the government whirls along like a well-oiled machine. The ruler may be the most important cog in that his is the most demanding task and hence he is the most difficult to adequately replace. But the others are equally necessary parts if the whole is to perform up to capacity or, for that matter, at all. Sometimes the most common and seemingly inconsequential part brings to a grinding halt the most sophisticated machine.

For this reason, the ruler must gain the support and loyalty of not only his ministers but of the masses as well. The author of the *Boshu* is aware that the secret to success lies in the ruler's love of the people.[71] To win their hearts, the ruler relies primarily on persuasion rather than terror. The author lays out a seven-year plan by which the wise leader slowly, steadfastly gains the support of the people. In the first year, he observes their customs; in the second, he demonstrates his good will by liberally distributing social resources; in the third, he cuts taxes so that the people show some gains; in the fourth and fifth, he begins to issue edicts and enforce penal laws to ensure social order and stability; in the sixth, the masses are won over so that by the seventh when the ruler issues the call to take up arms the people are willing to lay down their lives in response.[72]

The ruler, although paternalistic, is so in a parental, almost avuncular, way. Rather than a strict authoritarian demanding absolute obedience, the ruler is the well-intending parent who sincerely has the best interests of his offspring-subjects at heart. Instead of relying solely on the rod, the ruler encourages proper behavior in others by leading the way himself. "Without paternal conduct, the ruler does not attain filial service. Without maternal virtue, one cannot benefit fully from the strength of the masses. Where the conduct of the ruler is fully parental, this is the virtue of heaven and earth. Where these three are complete, affairs reach a successful conclusion" (47:21b).

In short, the state of Huang-Lao is a centralized bureaucracy with a well-developed hierarchy grounded in the natural order. It is a meritocracy where the able are appointed to positions commensurate with their abilities. And it is a unified state governed in accordance with natural law and presided over by a ruler who puts the interests of the people first. That the Huang-Lao state serves the people rather than the ruler is one of the main differences between Huang-Lao thought and Qin Legalism. Despite this, several commentators have argued that the philosophically significant differences between the *Boshu* and Legalism are negligible.[73] Though I offer a more extensive comparison in Chapter V, in the following section I lay the groundwork by substantiating in greater detail the claim that the Huang-Lao government of the *Boshu* is indeed government for the people and not for the ruler.

2.3   Government for the People

At the center of Huang-Lao political philosophy is the belief that the people constitute the raison d'être of the state. The government that does not improve the lives of its people fails in its primary function. In the world of Huang-Lao this is more than a political faux pas: it is a moral transgression. One is guilty of violating the moral order because to not benefit the people runs counter to the normative Way: "To bring it about that the masses share equally in the benefit and all rely on one is what is called righteousness" (76:129b). The ruler must either put the people first or lose them. Where one is tyrannical, he loses the support of the people (*shi min*). . . . When one loses the support of the people, he will suffer hardships" (51:36a). A common idea in Chinese political thought, *shi min* 失民 connotes more than loss of the people's support. Taken more literally, it suggests that the ruler loses the people themselves. The people vote with their feet by leaving the harsh conditions of a state commandeered by a tyrannical warlord to seek refuge in the more promising environs of a true practitioner of the kingly arts of rulership. In an age when the population density was considerably lower than it is today, this constituted a genuine threat to the survival of a state. Without sufficient numbers, one would not be able to defend oneself.

The ruler can ensure both his own personal safety and that of his state only if he is able to win the support of his subjects. For the people to be content with their lot they must feel fairly treated. All must believe they and everyone else have received their due. If so, no one will begrudge another's superior status. From the ruler on down to the peasant in the field, each will feel a part of a team and will experience the kind of affection that members of a team often have for each other. On the other hand, the state that fails at this is sure to be short lived. "Where the ministers do not have an abiding affection for the ruler, where those below do not have an abiding affection for their superiors, and where the clans do not have an abiding affection for their occupations, they run counter to domestic principle. Where there is this contrariness, it is called a dead state: engage military expeditions against it. As for the opposite, namely where there is compliance, it is called a living state: with a living state, nourish it" (54:55b).

The signs of a people-oriented Huang-Lao government are many. The legal system, for instance, is far from the draconian instrument of terror of the Qin Legalists Shang Yang and Han Fei. The latter have no qualms about the use of punishment for deterrence. In fact, Shang Yang even suggests that a ratio of nine punishments for every reward is about right.[74] The author of the *Boshu*, by contrast, insists that each punishment fit the crime. For punishments and rewards to miss the mark is to violate the normative order. Nor will it suffice to rely on punishments alone. The ruler is to offset punishments with rewards.[75]

Just as punishments must be offset by rewards so must the military side of the ledger be balanced by the counterweight of cultural achievement. As we have seen, the author acknowledges the need for military strength but gives equal place to the cultural dimension of civil rule. Any ruler who scales back on the costs of war would surely find favor with those hit most heavily by the incessant internecine feuding. And indeed the author promises that the ruler in this way will find himself with the people at his side. "Where there is civility, there is clarity; where there is martiality, there is strength. . . . Where there is clarity, one attains the natural order; where there is strength, one acts authoritatively. Where one aligns with heaven and earth, is in step with the hearts and minds of the people and implements both civility and martiality—this is called identifying with that above" (51:37b).

The limiting of wars to righteous ones is a further way in which the author tilts the scales in the direction of the people.[76] In addition to the obvious benefit of not losing their lives, the people gain economically in that they remain at home tilling their fields of grain rather than toiling abroad on the fields of war.

The economic well-being of the people is a primary concern of the author. He realizes that, although rich people are not necessarily happy, poor people are all too often unhappy—and unhappy people are a danger to the state. Consequently economic prosperity must be a top priority. The basics of Huang-Lao economic policy are summed up in the *Jing Fa*:

Where the ruler exercises moderation in his use of the strength of the masses, riches abound. Where taxes are levied with due measure, the masses prosper. (47:20a)

{To cut back on} over burdensome demands, to be restrained in levying taxes, and to not monopolize the time of the masses is to effect a stable sociopolitical order. (47:21a)[77]

To ensure the economic well-being of the people avoid war, promote agriculture, and cut taxes. Let the people find contentment in working the land and allow them to enjoy the fruits of their labors. The state will then be stable.

Of course taxes cannot be reduced if state expenditures go unchecked. And the biggest expense is often the lavish life-style of the ruler. Thus the author takes pains to warn the ruler of the dangers of profligacy.

He who realizes the kingly art of rulership, though he enjoys galloping about hunting, does not lose his head over it. He eats, drinks, and enjoys entertainment without becoming intoxicated with pleasure. He takes pleasure in his recreational diversions and in beautiful women but is not distracted by them. (49:30b)

Hoarding and amassing gold, pearls, and jade is the root of enmity. Chorus girls, recreational diversions, and roasted delicacies are the basis of chaos. Where one preserves the root of enmity and cultivates the basis of chaos, even were there a sage, he could not devise a way out for you. (52:46a)

Be it political, legal, military, or economic, Huang-Lao policy puts the interests of the people first. The people are the heart of the Huang-Lao state, the ruler is their servant. This represents not only a dramatic reversal of Qin Legalist policy but a sign that Huang-Lao thinkers are aware of the shortcomings of their intellectual predecessors and contemporaries and the need to respond to the historical and political realities of their era.

Constraints on the Ruler

To ensure that the state serves the people rather than the ruler, Huang-Lao imposes constraints on the ruler. The power of the ruler is curtailed in numerous ways: by the need to serve the people or lose them; by the requirement that punishments be offset by rewards; by the demand that he engage in only timely and righteous wars; by the limitation on his spending.

One of the most important mechanisms of constraint, however, is the natural law philosophy of Huang-Lao.[78] Most obviously, the ruler himself is bound by the laws. His actions are restricted. In the eyes of the law, he is to be treated like everyone else.

Yet the author's natural law theory constrains the ruler in other less apparent but more significant ways as well. For instance, laws cannot be altered to suit the fancy of the ruler. As observed earlier, the Yellow Emperor was known for the constancy of his laws. Like his mythical model, the Huang-Lao ruler respects the value of continuity: "One who holds fast to the Way, having generated the laws does not dare to violate them nor to abrogate them once they have been established" (43:1a). At the same time, the ruler is not to be fixated on the past. He is to learn from the past without becoming a slave to it: "When the myriad things arrive en masse there is none to which I cannot respond. I do not treasure precedents nor cling to the old. What has gone by is past. What is arriving is new. Not mixing up new and old, I have that which is universal" (79:141b).

Conditions change. The law must change accordingly. The ruler must remain flexible, always ready to adapt to new realities. Thus the author advises the ruler to keep a firm grasp on the six handles:

> The first is observation; the second is sorting things out; the third is action; the fourth is flexibility; the fifth is adaptability; and the sixth is transformability. Being observant, one will know the difference between a state that is to survive or perish. By sorting things out, one will know wherein lies survival or demise, prosperity or decline. Through action, one will be able to break down the powerful and elevate the weak. Remaining flexible, one will not digress from {the principle} of right and wrong.[79] Being adaptable, one will attack those who deserve to die and support those who deserve to live. Through transformation, one will be able to highlight the virtuous and eliminate the detrimental. Where the six handles are completely realized, there will be a true king. (53:53b)

The Huang-Lao universe is not static. Change is constant. The ruler must pay close attention to his changing environment, both natural and political, and respond accordingly. But objective reality, the Way itself, dictates change, not the whim of the ruler. The ruler is merely the medium through which the Way is translated into legislation. When change is required, the ruler should make sure it is carried out in an efficient and timely fashion. On the other hand, if the objective conditions do not merit change, the ruler is prohibited from acting on his own desires. "When one alters precedent and throws the constant into disorder, usurps control and changes enlightened ways, acts on one's heart's desires, puts one's person at risk and meets with misfortune, this is called going beyond the limits and missing the mark" (45:14a).

Although the natural law doctrine of Huang-Lao serves as a check on the power of the ruler, in the final analysis the Way itself reins him in. The author's foundational naturalism along with his correspondence epistemology and realist rectification theory of names limits the ruler's options. There is a preconfigured normative order with which even the ruler must comply.

That the author would seek through his foundational naturalism to provide a Way to constrain the ruler is readily understandable given the era. It matters little whether the author writes at the end of the Warring States period or at the beginning of the Han. Either way he would surely be aware of the tremendous suffering wrought by endless territorial struggles between the warlords. To restore order and bring peace to the people required a strong, Yellow Emperor type of ruler who would unify the empire—ironically, through military force if need be. At the same time, by reflecting on the lessons to be drawn from the despotic Legalist regime of Qin, the author would be equally aware of the dangers of a concentrating too much power in the hands of one person. One must strike a balance: the ruler must be strong but not too strong.

Huang-Lao philosophy is an outcome of this tug of war. There is to be one empire with one ruler but the power of the ruler is to be checked at every turn. The ruler is able to wage war but only when timely; he can implement laws but not interpret them; he may alter policy but only when objective conditions merit it. Though military strength is essential, it is to be counterbalanced by cultural refinement in the civil sector. Though punishments are necessary, they are to be offset by rewards. And most important, though the ruler is to lead the people, he is also to serve them.

IV. The Anthropocentric Pragmatism of Confucius

*

In the first two chapters, I sought to demonstrate how the various aspects of the *Boshu*'s Huang-Lao thought—metaphysics, epistemology, social and political theory, philosophy of language, and law—cohere with and are best understood in terms of the general hermeneutic of foundational naturalism. The demonstration was heavily textual.

Methodologically, however, an interpretation gains credibility by virtue of its scope. Interpretations, like scientific hypotheses, must account for the data; they must save the phenomena. The text, obviously, constitutes the most immediate data. To the extent that an interpretation cannot explain or reconcile passages in the text, it is a failure. Yet although a successful interpretation starts with the text, it does not end there. A theory that is able to tell a consistent and credible story of the emergence and place of the text within the larger intellectual, cultural, historical, and sociopolitical milieu is a better—a more powerful, more plausible, more believable—theory than one that cannot, all else being equal. In the following chapters, I show how interpreting Huang-Lao as foundational naturalism not only saves the immediate text but makes sense of and in the larger con*text*.

I begin by exploring in this chapter the relation between the foundational naturalism of Huang-Lao and the anthropocentric pragmatism of Confucius. This is not an obvious choice. Most commentators have concentrated on the relation between Huang-Lao and Daoism or Legalism—reasonably enough given the name Huang-*Lao* together with the importance invested in politics and law in the *Boshu*. To the extent that commentators have bothered with Confucianism at all, they usually do so on the basis of Sima Tan's statement that "[Huang-Lao] practice accords with the great order of the Yin Yang school, selects what is good from the doctrines of Confucians and Mohists, and combines with them the essential points of the School of Names and the Legalists."[1] They then proceed to list similar sounding passages and to catalogue the occurrence of key Confucian concepts. The argument is often of the form, x (ren, for instance) is central to Confucius; it occurs in the Boshu as well; therefore Huang-Lao thought is influenced by Confucianism. In some cases this may be illumining. In general, however, it sheds little light.

Classical Chinese philosophy is plagued by linguistic overlap. Different schools employ the same terminology: all use dao, de, fa; many use xing ming, ren, yi, and so forth. But what each makes of these varies according to the school. Of course, linguistic overlap is not peculiar to Chinese thought. As we have seen, both a Platonic correspondence theorist and a pragmatist like James may use 'truth' even though what each means by it differs dramatically. Nevertheless, the degree of overlap is perhaps greater in Chinese philosophy, due at least in part to respect for tradition and cultural continuity. As noted earlier, pre-Qin Chinese looked on arguments from authority much more favorably than most today. In classical China, to trace one's ideas back to a cultural icon gives them intellectual weight. Instead of claiming that I, of little cultural repute, believe such and such is so, I put the words in the mouth of a Yao, a Yellow Emperor, or even a Confucius. In contrast, Western philosophy since Aristotle has tended to value thinkers not for their ability to reinterpret someone else's ideas but for their novelty and uniqueness. This encourages one to develop vocabulary that will highlight differences from rather than similarities to one's intellectual predecessors.

At any rate, when faced with linguistic overlap, one first needs to appreciate the general character of the philosophy of the author and his or her school if one is to understand the meaning of a term in a particular text. One must examine how it is used in context, how it fits with the overall philosophical position of the text (author, school, tradition).[2]

For this reason, I open this section with a description of the general character of Confucius's philosophy as anthropocentric pragmatism. I clarify the pragmatic aspect of Confucius's thought by first explaining what I mean by pragmatism and then by examining the relation between pragmatism and an aesthetic order. To demonstrate that Confucius's thought is best characterized in terms of pragmatic coherence rather than foundational correspondence, as an aesthetic rather than a logical order, I examine his normative views about society, politics, ethics and law—much as I did for Huang-Lao.[3]

My aim in contrasting Confucius's Confucianism to the Boshu's Huang-Lao is not simply to prove that they use the same terms differently. Though interesting, this is to be expected. Nor is it to deny that Confucius has any influence on Huang-Lao thought. Quite the contrary. Many of

Confucius's ideas exert considerable influence on the author of the *Boshu*. The author's emphasis on moral virtue (as a complement to military strength) and on the interests of the people as the raison d'être of the state are central to Confucian thought. The intellectual debt is most manifest, however, not in the positive instances of conceptual borrowing. Rather, it is primarily as a reaction and response to the perceived failures of Confucianism that Confucius's influence on Huang-Lao thought is most apparent. To understand the place of Huang-Lao in the intellectual jigsaw puzzle of pre-Qin China, one must appreciate how it serves as a corrective to Confucianism, one of the dominant ideologies, perhaps the dominant ideology, of the period.

1. General Character of Confucius's Philosophy

Huang-Lao advances a foundational naturalism in which the natural order is privileged as the fundamental realm of value. As the cosmic natural order, dao is predetermined and transcendent. As the Way, dao is to be discovered and instantiated rather than created. The way of humans is implicate in the natural order, in the Way.

In the world of Confucius, however, the way is to be achieved. It emerges out of the particular context. It is dependent on and determined by the humans who create it. In sharp relief to the author of the *Boshu*, Confucius proclaims: "It is human beings who are capable of broadening the way. It is not the way that is capable of broadening human beings" (15:29). Rather than appeal to a fixed order or universal first principles, one is responsible for creating one's own world according to one's own standards. There is no predetermined pattern, no cosmic blueprint, against which to check one's progress. The measures of success are themselves determined by the concerned parties. One evaluates the world one lives in in light of one's own personal and communal interests, goals, needs, and beliefs. In this sense, Confucianism is more akin to the pragmatism of William James, John Dewey and Richard Rorty than to the foundationalism of Huang-Lao.

1.1 Pragmatic Coherence versus Foundational Correspondence

Pragmatism is another of those terms, like *naturalism*, that evokes a wide range of images. In everyday parlance, *pragmatic* is often used synonymously with *practical* and associated with a Machiavellian concern for results, for ends, rather than means. As a school of thought, pragmatism may be thought to refer to the ideas—convergent realism, will to believe, life as aesthetic experience, persons as social beings, holistic webs of belief, edifying conversation rather than rational debate, and so on—of philosophers such as Peirce, James, Dewey, Mead, Quine, and Rorty. Still more technically, it may signal a specific theory of knowledge, conception of truth, or methodology of normative discourse.

Obviously not every idea of every philosopher considered to be a pragmatist need be accepted as part of one's own theory of pragmatism. How consistent Peirce's convergent realism is with the contemporary pragmatic philosophy of science of Bas van Fraasen, for example, is debatable. Indeed, how consistent Peirce's convergent realism is with his own "pragmaticism" is debatable.[4]

Even more obviously, the pragmatism of Confucius differs in significant respects from its twentieth century American counterparts. Many issues that are of great concern to one go unmentioned by the other. For instance, Dewey's emphasis on science and technology as a means for curing social ills finds no analog in the *Analects*. Such differences are to be expected given the cultural and temporal as well as geographical distance that separates them. Yet despite the differences, Confucius's philosophy has enough in common with that of Dewey, James, Rorty, and company to merit the label *pragmatism*, though one must take care to state how that term is to be employed.

For purpose of contrast with the foundational naturalism of Huang-Lao, what I intend by Confucian pragmatism is a hybrid of the classical pragmatism, particularly the social and political beliefs, of Dewey and Mead with the neo-pragmatism, especially the epistemological critique of foundationalism, of Rorty.[5] It is Dewey's optimistic faith in Intelligence[6] and Mead's view of the person as inextricably social that most closely resonates with the social meliorism of Confucius's politics of harmony.[7] And it is Rorty's attack on correspondence epistemologies claiming to mirror nature that underwrites the postmodern and continental challenges to the notions of transcendence, determinacy of meaning, and the fact-value (subjective-objective, normative-positive) distinction that are equally anathema to the qualitative, aesthetic order of Confucius.[8]

Foundationalism for Rorty is "the search for some final vocabulary, which can somehow be known in advance to be the common core, the truth of, all the other vocabularies which might be advanced in its place."[9] Epistemologically, foundational philosophy seeks the Truth—*episteme* rather than *pistis* or *doxa*; metaphysically, it is concerned with Reality and correspondence to Reality whether this is understood rationally à la Plato, Kant, Russell, or empirically as with Hobbes, Locke, and Hume; ethically, it is the quest for Absolute Good rather than conditional good. It has been an attempt to ground philosophy in some fixed foundation, some transcendent source or realm of value. The individual is separated from the Forms, from God, from the Noumenal that represent ultimate value—be it Truth, the Good, or the Real. Correlate to this bifurcation is the generation of dualisms: theory, whether the contemplative life of the elite Greeks or the disinterested rational reflection of Descartes, takes precedence over practice; the body is subordinated to the mind; the subject is juxtaposed to the object; science reigns over and against aesthetics; fact is cut off from value; "is" wants connection to "ought." The result of this bifurcation of experience into discontinuous and static oppositions has been skepticism of one form of another: the solipsistic doubt of Descartes, the unknowable noumena of Kant, the Humean denial of causal connection.

Rorty's antifoundationalism entails the rejection of all forms of transcendence, be they correspondence theories of knowledge, semantic theories of truth, ethical systems that hold that normative judgments reflect or are derived from absolute moral principles, or natural law theories that ground law in divine commandments, pure reason, human nature, or the laws of nature. There is no way to leap outside of our skins—our cultural, linguistic, historical traditions in short, our human perspective—to gain direct access to a transcendent realm. Consequently, there is no way to verify that our ideas, theories, and beliefs match up with or correspond to the given standards.

Believing the view of knowledge as correspondence to be inherently self-defeating, pragmatists maintain that "the notion of knowledge as accurate representation, made possible by special mental processes, and intelligible through a general theory of representation, needs to be abandoned."[10] As Rorty sees it, "The idea of 'foundations of knowledge' is a product of metaphors. . . . We can think of knowledge as a relation to propositions, and thus of justification as a relation between the propositions in question and other propositions from which the former may be inferred. Or we may think of both knowledge and justification as privileged relations to the objects those propositions are about."[11]

I have referred to these two basic pictures of knowledge as the pragmatic coherence and foundational correspondence views, respectively.[12] On the former, justification consists of propositions brought forth in defense of other propositions. There is no single, privileged framework or standard to which one can appeal to settle the issue. One could continue to bring forth supporting reasons until agreement is reached or the parties agree to stop. On the latter view of knowledge, one hopes to bring the argument to a rational closure—a point where it is simply irrational to continue the debate—by getting behind the reasons to the absolute ground, by arriving at the point where "anyone gripped by the object in the required way will be *unable* to doubt or see an alternative."[13] One reaches, as it were, the privileged foundations of knowledge (truth, goodness, reality). When the Huang-Lao sage says he has discovered the Way and it entails a class distinction between the noble and lowly, the debate is over. Either one has oneself experienced the Way or one has not. If one has, then one knows what should be on the basis of one's direct experience of what is. A Confucian sage, on the other hand, could hope only to persuade others that such distinctions are justified by appeal to reasons relative to the participants. He would have to persuade them that in light of their own interests, beliefs, cultural traditions, and so forth a proclass society is better than a no class society.

The consequences of shifting from the foundational correspondence to the pragmatic coherence view are many. For starters, one no longer thinks of rationality as predicated on a special relation to certain objects. One does not somehow come face to face with the "foundations of knowledge" or "*the* principles of rationality" such that it is impossible in theory to continue a discussion. Gone is the belief in pure, "value-neutral" reason and with it the hope for "rational closure" in the Enlightenment-Kantian sense predicated on a single, universal rational order. Rather rationality for pragmatists has to do with the justificatory relation between persons and propositions; it exists in the "logical" space of reasons where one supports one's claims by appeal to one's current conceptual scheme, one's web of presently held aims and most warranted beliefs. What constitutes a rational argument depends on consensual agreement, on the social, epistemological, and moral practices of a particular community. The test of a rational argument, of a valid reason, is that, all things considered, those concerned take it to be so.

In assessing a normative theory, an epistemic claim or a scientific hypothesis, the question for the pragmatist becomes "Is it best, all things considered?" rather than "Is it right vis à vis some external standard?" Instead of absolute determinations of right or wrong, it fits the facts or it does not, one makes qualified judgments that admit of degrees of certainty. Because rationality is predicated on social consensus and conversation between persons rather than on interaction with nonhuman reality, rational certainty becomes fluid, changing as the beliefs of a community change. Rather than a final judgment on a subject, "rationally certain" means that for now no one has any telling counterarguments. It consists, therefore, "of the absence of a normal rejoinder in a normal conversation to a certain knowledge claim."[14] Given one's current aims, beliefs and so forth, there would simply be no further reason to dispute the claim. Of course, tomorrow could bring new data that would require one to reassess one's position. For this reason pragmatists' assertions are inherently comparative in nature: this is better than that; of these, this is best. For the pragmatists, there are no once and for all pronouncements.

In giving up the notions of transcendence, correspondence, and a single, universal rational order, one turns one's back on apodictic knowledge in empirical matters. Our knowledge of the world is fallible. As clarified by Peirce, the doctrine of fallibility does not "say that men cannot attain a sure knowledge of the creations of their own minds. It neither affirms nor denies that. It only says that people cannot attain absolute certainty concerning questions of fact."[15]

Pragmatists reject scientific realism and the belief that our theories cut at the joints of nature, that we speak with nature's own vocabulary, that we can finally rest assured that this time our theories have got it right. Knowledge, truth, rightness are relative to the standards of a particular community of inquirers. As inquirers, we are not disinterested spectators who passively experience reality as the "thing in itself" unmediated by our own perceptual, cognitive and hermeneutic biases. It is not the case that nature's images, immediate perceptions of objective reality as it were, directly imprint themselves on the blank slates of our minds. Nor do we have, for that matter, purely reasoning minds able to judge which ideas are clear and distinct, which mirror nature, and which are ipso facto true beyond all doubt. We are real people with real interests and real histories that affect how we experience, interpret, and evaluate the world. We inevitably view the world through the potentially distorting lens of our own interests, attitudes and beliefs. Further, and most important, there is no way to verify whether our lenses have indeed distorted nature's images and, if so, how. We cannot take off our glasses. We cannot escape our human perspective.

Thus a pragmatist would argue, *contra* Huang-Lao, that we cannot become purely unbiased, objective observers of the Way. It makes no sense to speak of totally overcoming subjectivity because we inevitably experience, interpret, and think from within and through our personal, communal, human perspectives. The view from nowhere is the view of nobody. Assuming, however, that one could somehow eliminate all subjectivity through a meditative process of emptying, there would still be no way to verify the experiential claim that one has objectively apprehended the normative order, the Way itself.[16]

Further, regardless of what the meditator may think, the meditative experience is just that: an experience. Any epistemic claims made on the basis of it exist not in personal meditative space but in the linguistic space, the philosophical space, the social space of our web of beliefs, attitudes, communal history. As a result, the felt immediacy, the perceived incorrigibility of experience that gives the practitioner her sense of certainty is lost. To those who have not had the experience, it is simply one more claim to have discovered Truth, God, or Enlightenment.

In insisting that all justification occur within the web of our beliefs, a pragmatic program like that of Confucius is internally regulating. There are no transcendent standards, no external benchmarks, no privileged foundations against which to judge one's theories or claims. To justify a claim, one never goes—indeed cannot go—outside of one's personal, communal and human perspective.[17]

The standard for pragmatists then is not correspondence to reality but how well an idea, claim, or theory "works" in light of one's interests, ends, and so forth. One tests a claim by its effects. Does it fulfill the purpose for which it is intended? Does it cohere with our other personal and communal beliefs, attitudes, and goals? Nothing counts as a justification unless one can make sense of it in light of one's other beliefs and attitudes. This is not merely an empirical indictment of human prejudice and narrow-mindedness. It is a necessary theoretical premise of pragmatic hermeneutics. If one is not able to reconcile a new piece of information in the form presented with older, more firmly embedded ideas and beliefs, there are three choices. Either one defuses the threat to the system by dismissing the new data or reinterpreting it in a way compatible with one's existing cognitive structure; or, alternatively, one adjusts one's cognitive structure to accommodate the new piece of information. The third possibility is merely a combination of the first two: one both reworks the data and adjusts one's system of beliefs. The goal is to achieve a coherent system, to attain and retain an equilibrium in one's web of beliefs, attitudes, interests.

While the goal is to render the system coherent, coherence is not logical consistency in the strict textbook sense. It may not be possible to reconcile all of the beliefs, attitudes, and goals that one has. One has to balance some against others. Some goals, for example, are more important. They are of greater weight. In a system that works, those goals will take precedence over and be realized before others. Similarly, some ideas or beliefs will not square with others. In purely logical terms, they are inconsistent. But one is committed to them to different degrees. Because one cannot be absolutely certain about most beliefs, one holds on to inconsistent ideas by placing them within different subsystems. One says in effect, if such and such is so, then this subsystem would be warranted; if not, however, that subsystem with those ideas would be more likely. One has to balance the likelihood of the various subsystems or branches within the overall system. Those subsystems and ideas that seem most warranted to us will be most firmly embedded in our overall web. To dislodge one of these would require significant adjustment to one's overall system.[18]

In the absence of a foundational standard, the assessment of coherence, of what constitutes equilibrium, requires qualitative judgment. The valuative process is more akin to the aesthetic appraisal of art work than to the solving of a mathematical problem. People will not always agree. Different persons will weight some of the criteria differently. Some may not even agree that a particular criterion is valid. After all, for the pragmatist the standards for judging rationality, truth, aesthetic, or moral value are part and parcel of our human perspective, of reality as we construe it. What counts as a valid criterion is, therefore, itself a valid topic of conversation.

Yet that there are no foundational standards and that all standards are themselves open to discussion does not entail that there are *no* standards. Far from it. We are bombarded by a plethora of standards, a booming, buzzing confusion of sometimes conflicting values, goals, beliefs, attitudes, desires, norms, and mores. For pragmatists from Confucius to James to Rorty, the void created by a lack of infallible, foundational criteria is filled by a host of contingent ones that arise out of our particular social, historical, political, philosophical, psychological, and religious circumstances and traditions.

Allowing this cornucopia of pragmatic criteria need not, however, commit one to anything-goes relativism or the dreaded cognitive egalitarianism: the absurd view that every theory is as well supported by any given body of evidence as any of its rivals.[19] There may be disagreement about which standards are valid or how they are to be weighted. Then again, there may not. Just as people often agree about art, so they may about normative issues or epistemic claims or scientific theories. When disagreements do arise, discussion—or edifying conversation, to use Rorty's terminology—will resolve some conflicts as one side becomes persuaded by the other. One comes to see the problem their way as it were. Alternatively, both sides may acquire a new view and reach consensus in that way.

Of course, not every issue will be resolvable. In some cases, people will continue to disagree about the standards. In others, even though there is agreement as to the standards, the criteria will underdetermine the choices: more than one theory may satisfy the standards.

While the possibility that reasonable people may not always be able to reach agreement on epistemic, aesthetic, or moral issues strikes fear in the heart of many, leading them to continue the quest for certainty and to posit in vain infallible, foundational standards, it hardly justifies such wildly counterintuitive and cataclysmic views as anything-goes relativism and cognitive egalitarianism. Were we all to become pragmatists, we would continue to do what we have always done: appeal to standards that appear reasonable in light of our web of beliefs and attempt to justify our claims with reasons we ourselves find persuasive. The only difference would be that one would not try to cloak one's discourse in a veil of universal truths, absolute standards, and first principles. Indeed, rather than occasioning despair and pessimism, the absence of philosophically tenable transcendent standards and foundational first principles allows the optimistic pragmatists the opportunity to test their own creativity in fashioning a world that suits their particular needs and tastes. The only limitation one faces is that the system as a whole work.

*

As a rough and ready way of summing up the distinction between pragmatic coherence and foundational correspondence theories, one could characterize the former as better understood in terms of postmodern hermeneutics rather than traditional epistemology in the Platonic-Enlightenment-Kantian sense. The latter attempts to reduce all rival claims to a single, privileged discourse and to postulate a neutral algorithm capable of adjudicating between all such claims. It is the hope that all theories may be "brought under a set of rules which will tell us how rational agreement can be reached on what would settle the issue . . . where statements seem to conflict. These rules tell us how to construct an ideal situation, in which all residual disagreement will be seen to be 'noncognitive' or merely verbal or else merely temporary. . . . Epistemology sees the hope of agreement as a token of the existence of common ground which, perhaps unbeknown to the speakers, unites them in a common rationality." Hermeneutics, on the other hand, "sees the relations between various discourses as those of strands in a possible conversation, a conversation which presupposes no disciplinary matrix which unites the speakers, but where hope of agreement is never lost so long as the conversation lasts."[20] As we have seen, epistemology thus understood conceives of rationality as rational closure, as determinate and conclusive. Hermeneutics, in contrast, thinks of rationality in terms of *rationales*; that is, of good reasons relative to a particular conceptual scheme and brought forth in conversation to support one's claim in an effort to move toward not rational closure but consensual agreement.

To understand rationality as a matter of conversation is to give up foundationalism and the search for certitude. But it is more than an injunction against seeking in one's scholarly battles to score logical points and carry the day by forcing the capitulation of one's opponent. Rather, by

calling attention to the politicohistorical factors involved in the institu-
tionalization of the conceptual or hermeneutic framework for a given community of inquirers, it suggests that we move away from this adversarial
winner-take-all conception of rational debate and focus on exploring areas
of commonality to see if agreement can be reached. Where such agreement
proves elusive, the call for continued conversation would encourage the
participants to develop new discourses and approaches to the problem that
would allow for consensual agreement. To this extent it guards against
dogmatism and promotes, rather than stifles, creativity and the exploration
of new avenues. It is this focus on the creative possibilities for interpersonal achievement that typifies the Confucian social and political project in
which exemplary persons strive to realize a humane state through the harmonizing of the disparate interests of the many members of society. Before
turning to Confucius's social and political thought, I further clarify the
pragmatic character of Confucian philosophy by examining pragmatism in
light of the aesthetic-logical distinction.

1.2 Pragmatic Coherence and the Logical-Aesthetic Distinction

In a major recent work, *Thinking Through Confucius*, Hall and
Ames argue at length and with considerable persuasive force that the world
of Confucius is best understood as having an aesthetic rather than a logical
order. The distinction between an aesthetic and logical order parallels in
many ways that between pragmatic coherence and foundational correspondence.

We have already had occasion to explore in detail the aesthetic-
logical distinction in respect to Huang-Lao thought that, I suggested, constitutes with minor qualifications a good example of a logical order.[21] Hall
and Ames summarize the important differences as follows:

> Two fundamental understandings of order are possible: one requires that
> order be achieved by application to a given situation of an antecedent pattern
> of relatedness. This we might call "rational" or "logical" order. A second
> meaning of order is fundamentally aesthetic. Aesthetic order is achieved by
> the creation of novel patterns. Logical order involves the act of closure; aes-
> thetic order is grounded in disclosure. Logical order may be realized by the
> instantiation of principles derived from the Mind of God, or the transcendent
> laws of nature, or the positive laws of a given society, or from a categorical
> imperative resident in one's conscience. Aesthetic order is a consequence of
> the contribution to a given context of a particular aspect, element, or event
> which both determines and is determined by the context.[22]

Logical order entails a preassigned pattern, be it defined in terms of transcendent principles, rules of pure reason, foundational ethical principles, or natural laws as with Huang-Lao. Order is a result of instantiation of this antecedent pattern rather than the product of a novel response to a particular context. By emphasizing closure—conformity to a universal standard—at the expense of individual disclosure, a logical order is typified by necessity rather than creativity.

Hall and Ames contend that, contrary to the traditional view, Confucius promotes an aesthetic order in which the way is created by humans rather than instantiated according to some predetermined format. Order emerges out of the particular context. It is the result of interaction between real persons in a historical context who fashion the way in light of their own beliefs, interests, or cultural heritage. What constitutes the right way is what is most appropriate in the particular context. It is a matter of aesthetic judgment rather than correspondence to an absolute standard.

The signals of the aesthetic character of Confucian order are many. The absence of a transcendent source of order becomes the immanence of the Confucian cosmos: heaven, earth, and humans are ontologically all of a piece. There is no divine creator who is ontologically distinct from and temporally prior to the world.[23] Similarly, the lack of transcendent regulative principles of order encourages conceptual polarities such as yin-yang instead of dualities like mind-body, theory-praxis, reality-appearance, being-becoming, knowledge-opinion, fact-value, self-other, or subject-object. In the former way of thinking, one component requires the other for its articulation: yin can be explained only by reference to yang. In dualistic thinking, one of the components is usually privileged over the other. The component that represents the transcendent realm, the realm not determined by humans but that serves as a foundational standard for humans, is held in higher esteem. As we have seen, reality takes precedence over appearance, noumena over phenomena, fact over value, and is over ought. Dualistic thinking, Hall and Ames assert, fosters cosmogonic theories in which a fundamentally undetermined creative source generates and disciplines its dependent object of creation. To illustrate, they point to the *creatio ex nihilo* origination myth of Genesis. They further contend cosmogonic thinking since the early Greeks has been characterized by linear cosmogonies in which one moves from chaos or multiple orders to a single order disciplined by some transcendent source or principle. In contrast, Confucius offers an anarchic (*an*: no + *arche*: regulative principle), self-generative cosmology where order is sui generis, a product of the local conditions.

Hall and Ames discuss several other indicators of aesthetic order:

Confucian tradition as context-specific interpretation rather than rational history; the interpretation of *xing* 性 as developmental character rather than a predetermined, innate human nature; the emphasis on knowledge as praxis (knowing how) rather than as theory (knowing that); the focus on personally inspirational *li* (禮—rites) rather than on externally imposed penal law; the concern for shame rather than guilt; the view of language as performative attunement of names rather than rectification of names and so on. Many of these points as well as others are discussed later. The more immediate concern, however, is to understand the relation between an aesthetic order and pragmatic coherence.

There are, obviously, many significant similarities between the two: the rejection of transcendence and the notion of correspondence to a preassigned pattern; the emphasis on human creativity, on novel responses to encountered difficulties; the value placed on the particular, on the individual person, as source, interpreter, and judge of what constitutes an appropriate order, a workable system; the view that order is contingent on and emerges out of the particular constituents; the belief that rightness is a matter of degree and relative to the standards of a specific community.

As for differences, the most striking is one of apparent emphasis. The pragmatic coherence versus foundational correspondence distinction is first and foremost an epistemological one that then ramifies through other branches. It is primarily concerned with the way in which we justify epistemic claims, be these scientific claims about matters of fact, metaphysical claims about the nature of the cosmos, religious claims about the existence of God, aesthetic claims about the value of a work of art, or moral claims about the normative permissibility of a particular action or practice. The logical versus aesthetic distinction, on the other hand, in centering on the nature of order, is at least at first blush more metaphysical or cosmological in orientation: either there is a preassigned pattern to the cosmos or there is not. Yet the claim that there is no predetermined order is not just a metaphysical claim about the nature of the cosmos. It is equally a claim that there is no predetermined order of any sort, be it social, political, legal, or whatever. Like the coherence-correspondence distinction, aesthetic-logical is applicable to other branches of thought from epistemology to social and political philosophy to jurisprudence.

More important, in the final analysis the fortunes of an aesthetic order as a viable and attractive philosophical position are closely intertwined with the tenability of the pragmatist's epistemological position. The denial of a transcendent pattern, of a predetermined order, that lies at the heart of an aesthetic world-view rests on and gains credence from the epistemological critique of foundationalism that constitutes the core of the pragmatic coherence view. Without it, the issue of aesthetic versus logical order is simply a matter of metaphysical speculation with little hope of resolution. Some favor a predetermined cosmos, others an aesthetic. At best, it rises to the level of a normative question: viewing the cosmos *as if it were* an aesthetic order (or logical order) would be better because it would have the following normatively superior consequences: *x, y, z* . . . With the antifoundationalist critique of transcendence and correspondence, however, one is compelled to assume an aesthetic rather than a logical approach to order quite irrespective of the metaphysical question of whether a predetermined pattern exists. One has no way to escape one's interpretive perspective to discover what the predetermined pattern, should there be one, would be. We are forced, as it were, to assume responsibility for the world we live in, the society we create, the normative standards we go by. In a nonfoundational world, "rightness" cannot help but be relative to the standards of a particular community.

In regard to both reasons for rejecting a logical order and practical approach to the problem of order, pragmatists and proponents of an aesthetic order share much in common. However, to the extent that the latter also make a radical positive assertion of speculative metaphysics, namely that the cosmic order is completely or largely plastic and undetermined, they go well beyond a position a *pragmatist* would feel comfortable assuming. Pragmatists on the whole are reluctant to engage in metaphysical speculation because there is no way to verify or support such claims. This is simply the converse of the denial of correspondence: one can no more escape one's interpretive perspective to verify that the cosmos is undetermined than one can to verify that it is predetermined.[24]

One of the central tenets of pragmatism is that an idea, belief, or concept is to be tested in terms of its practical consequences. In the extreme formulation of Peirce, if there is no difference in the practical effects of two ideas, then they are no different in meaning: "Consider what effects, that might conceivably have practical bearings, we conceive the object of our conception to have. Then, our conception of these effects is the whole of our conception of the object."[25] To the extent that one can test by its practical effects the metaphysical claim of proponents of an aesthetic order that order—cosmic and other—is plastic and undetermined, one must surely conclude that they have overstated their case. For all practical purposes, pun intended, there are constraints imposed on us. We are not totally free to fashion any world we choose. There are natural constraints: we need oxygen and clean air to live; we age according to a for-the-most-part all too predictable pattern; we have no choice but to adapt to seasonal patterns that regularly recur do what we may to stop them. In the human arena of politics and society, people have different abilities; some are bright, some are not. Some people are relatively altruistic, others more self-interested. Some people will tirelessly serve the state, others will be free riders.

To be sure, there is still much room for maneuvering. Many of the constraints, particularly those concerning humans, are not fixed forever. And even those constraints that are most resistant to change are largely underdetermining: we all need clean air to live, but how clean and how we are to organize our society to achieve this level of cleanliness allow for various possibilities.

The aesthetic order of Hall and Ames, however, entails complete openness, a total lack of foundational predetermination.[26] Anything that would impose a priori constraints on creativity, that would limit future possible orders, is inimical to an aesthetic order. Even the notion that the universe is just that, a *uni*-verse, is verboten.[27] They reject the more moderate view that there is one world but many interpretations for the dramatic if ill-defined position that there are multiple worlds for Confucius. For the contemporary pragmatist, there is little point to such speculation.[28] There is no way to test how many worlds there are by consideration of the practical effects. Nothing hinges on whether there *are* many worlds or whether we all interpret one world each in our own way such that we live in "different" worlds. There is no pragmatic difference, no difference that makes a difference. If anything, the stubbornness of sensation, the fact that we cannot make the world go away just by wishing it and that we all agree when looking at the Empire State Building we are indeed looking at *something*, suggests that there is but one world with many interpretations. Indeed, experience teaches us that there is a regularity to nature, to the world, that persists regardless of human interpretations or efforts to change it.[29]

In any event, the degree of overlap between the logical-aesthetic and pragmatic coherence-foundational correspondence views remains considerable. It is the epistemological implications of the latter that underscores and makes attractive the cosmological insights of the latter. At the same time, if the pragmatists' attack on transcendence and correspondence is persuasive, then it matters little whether metaphysically the world is predetermined or not, a universe or a multiverse. Either way, one is, like it or not, thrown into an aesthetic rather than a logical world where responsibility for the order generated, for the kind of world one lives in, is thrust squarely upon one's own shoulders and those of one's fellow human beings. For Confucius, this amounts to a call to realize a humane state that achieves the highest quality of social harmony possible.

2. Confucius's Social and Political Philosophy

As interpreters, we are caught in a hermeneutic circle. A particular aspect of someone's philosophy—the theory of names or law or politics—is evidence for the general character of that philosophy, and the general character of the philosophy provides evidence for reading a particular component a certain way. One is continually shifting back and forth, pulling oneself up by one's boostraps as it were, trying to attain the most coherent view all things considered. But one must begin somewhere. One gains an impression, even if only a first impression, of the overall character of a philosophy from one's initial encounters with the parts: with the words, the text. As one becomes more familiar with the text, one begins to see how the parts hang together.

The best way to appreciate the overall character of someone's philosophy is to start with an examination of the more sophisticated components. It is in these areas that one is likely to find the kind of data—statements on a given topic both more numerous and direct—that will allow for crucial experiments: those tests that enable one to eliminate or greatly reduce the likelihood of one or more competing theories.

The most well-developed area of Confucius's thought is not metaphysics. Confucius is first and foremost a social and political thinker. Hence it is in his social and political views, his ethics, his jurisprudence, that we can expect to find the most conclusive evidence for our reading of Confucius as an exponent of pragmatic coherence rather than correspondence foundationalism a la Huang-Lao.

2.1 Jurisprudence

The standard picture sketched in the writings of such prominent scholars as Needham, Duyvendak, and Bodde portrays Confucius as a natural law advocate.[30] In the first chapter, we observed that *natural law* covers a variety of sins. In coming to terms with this enigmatic concept, we found it helpful to contrast natural law with legal positivism, a key differentia being that the latter does not require law to display any necessary relation to morality to be valid. This was referred to as the minimum separation thesis. Natural law proponents deny the minimum separation thesis, asserting that "an unjust law is no law at all."

Unfortunately, to rely solely on the differentia of Hart's minimum separation thesis and the traditional distinction between natural and positive law does not allow one to appreciate fully the complexity of pre-Han philosophies of law. In examining the relation between morality and law, one must further distinguish between foundational and pragmatic coherence systems. Only then is it possible to capture the dramatic difference between a system like that of Huang-Lao and of Confucius.

Though Confucius believes there is a necessary linkage between law and morality—and hence rejects the minimum separation thesis and legal positivism—he is no foundationalist. My claim is that in regard to the relation between morals and the law, Confucius's legal theory is much closer to a Dworkinian coherence account of the law as constructive interpretation than to a foundational natural law system. The Confucian sage-judge makes his decision with an eye to the peculiarities of the particular situation rather than to transcendent and universal principles, be they divine, natural, rational, or ethical. In striving for an equilibrium among the conflicting interests that will reflect the highest possible degree of social harmony attainable given the particular constraints, the Confucian sage seeks to render the law consistent with a specific society's values, practices, goals, and needs. His goal, to emend the dictum of Dworkin, is to make both the law *and the world we live in* the best it can be.[31]

In Chapter I, I discussed four varieties of foundational natural law theories. The first, divine law, attempts to locate law in the sacred realm, in the word of God. The second hopes, as with Huang-Lao, to ground law in the normatively transcendent natural order. The third seeks to provide rational foundations for law and legal obligations by deriving them from self-evident first principles or from "truths" about human nature. The fourth and final type bases law on moral grounds that are themselves foundational in nature. Though these four varieties are far from exhaustive, they more than suffice for our purposes of assessing the assertion that Confucius's jurisprudence is best understood as one of natural law. In fact, only the last offers any real potential as a possible ground for reading Confucius's jurisprudence as natural law. Nevertheless, it will repay us to consider briefly the others as doing so will further attest to the pragmatic character of Confucius's philosophy.

Divine Law

Divine law is an unlikely foundation on which to build a case for Confucius's alleged natural law theory. In religious matters, Confucius is decidedly noncommittal:

"Sacrifice as if present" is taken to mean "sacrifice to the gods as if the gods were present." (3:12)

The Master did not talk about strange phenomena, feats of strength, disorderliness, or gods. (7:21)

Confucius was not one to wax eloquent about what cannot be known. His general advice was to cover all bases without becoming preoccupied with theological speculation.

> Keep a distance from the gods and spirits while showing them due reverence. . . . (6:22)

> Ji Lu asked about serving the gods and spirits of the dead, but the Master replied, "If you are not able to serve other people, how can you serve the spirits of the dead?" He then asked about death, but the Master replied, "If you do not yet understand life, how can you understand death?" (11:12)

To be sure *tian*, an anthropomorphic heaven, does play a role in Confucian ethics and politics, even legitimating political succession through the so-called mandate of heaven (*tian ming*).[32] Confucius himself, however, is disinclined to comment on the way of heaven. Further, to the extent that one can piece together a picture of *tian* by supplementing the meager mentions in the *Analects* with a broader survey of its occurrence in Confucian literature, one finds that the role of *tian* is not a foundational one. *Tian* is not some ontologically transcendent, independent source or dictator of moral standards as the Judeo-Christian God is generally taken to be. It is not even the normatively transcendent nonhuman nature of Huang-Lao. Rather than a dualism between transcendent moral principles cum laws and humans the obsequious followers, there is a polar continuum between immanent heaven and its human counterparts.[33] The relation is one of mutual interaction—as witnessed most clearly in the *Chun Qiu Fan Lu* ascribed to Dong Zhongshu.[34] Humans, particularly sages, contribute to the generation and definition of both the microcosmic human ethical realm and the larger "anthropocosmic" realm.[35] Thus the *Zhong Yong* states: "Great indeed is the way of the sage. Teeming, it spawns and nurtures the myriad things until they reach up to the heavens."[36] Confucius agrees that humans have the power, indeed the need, to take charge over their own physical and moral destinies, to chart their own ethical, political, and legal courses (*daos*). To the extent that *tian* refers to the order of the world, to cosmic order both human and non-, humans play a major role in its determination. Conversely, to the extent that *tian* refers only to what is nonhuman, to nature and all that which is beyond the control of humans, it is a topic best left alone. Confucius is more concerned with what we can do than with what we cannot do, with our opportunities for achievement and realization as a person, as a family, as a nation, as a world. Thus it is *tian* as a field of possibilities rather than as a limiting source of determination that most interests Confucius.

Laws of Nature and Natural Law

If the first source of natural law, divine law, is not a very likely candidate for the wellsprings of Confucius's alleged natural law, then the second, the laws of nature, is even less likely. Needham, based on his vast studies of science in China, claims that the ancient Chinese never conceive of nature in terms of the kind of laws necessary to give rise to a theory of natural law. Although we have found this to be somewhat overstated, it remains valid for Confucius. As just noted, *tian* is for Confucius an anthropomorphic heaven rather than an impersonal and amoral nature—as it is for Lao Zi, Xun Zi, and Huang-Lao—in conjunction with which a theory of the laws of nature, and ipso facto of natural law, might more easily emerge. Confucius evinces little interest in the fundamental laws of nature structuring the natural order. Indeed, he pays little heed to the animals and other elements that make up his more immediate environment. His ethical focus is trained on the human social realm, not the natural. "The stables caught fire. The Master, on returning from court, asked, 'Was anyone hurt?' He did not ask about the horses" (10:17).[37]

Consider also the story of Zi Lu who, having encountered a couple of recluses who advise him to abandon politics and retreat from society, asks Confucius about their suggestion. The Master replies, "One cannot associate with birds and beasts. Am I not a member of this human race? Who, then, is there for me to associate with? While the way is to be found in the Empire, I will not change place with them" (18:6).

As discussed in Chapter VI, this anthropocentric bias is one of the main differences between Confucius and his Daoist counterparts. Though the latter, in my reading, also reject rule ethics and foundational normative systems in favor of politics of harmony, they include in their domain of concern nonhuman nature.[38]

Reason, Human Nature, and the Law

Some natural law theorists attempt to justify both the law as an institution and specific laws on the grounds that they are rationally necessary. Some contend that pure reason alone can show us the rational necessity of the law and laws. Others proclaim the existence of special faculties that illumine God's commands, moral truths, and universal principles. Still others argue that the law is a rational byproduct of human nature or of our teleological purpose or ends as human beings.

A. C. Graham has found evidence that the later Mohists conceive of intelligence as a separate faculty through which one is able to ascertain necessary and immutable universal normative principles.[39] Others, Hansen among them, attribute to Mencius an innate moral sense by which one is able to evaluate ethical claims and that might serve as a ground for natural law: "The idealist wing of Confucianism. . . .claim[s] that the behavior dictated by the conventional code is, in fact, the natural inclination of humans—built into their hsin/hearts as innate dispositions to good (social) conduct. Thus it is the innatist, Mencius, who first makes the way truly metaphysical, prior to language, one, constant, absolute for all people and all times."[40]

Were Hansen's reading correct, this innate, immanent moral barometer would constitute a transcendent source of determinate order in the foundational sense. Although the kind of detailed treatment necessary to refute Hansen's claim lies beyond the boundaries of our current project, a few words may be in order.

A close study of the nature of human nature for Mencius and of the role of moral intuition or predisposition in the overall ethical reasoning process reveals Mencius to be more of a coherence pragmatist like his Master than the foundational innatist Hansen makes him out to be. Although one is born with an inchoate moral sensibility, it is by no means sufficient as a standard for ethical evaluation or as a source for natural law. Unless cultivated and developed, it is of little practical use. In fact, if not strengthened through repeated performance of good deeds, it withers away. In the wrong environment, Mencius is quick to warn, one's original predisposition toward goodness is soon lost. Ultimately, therefore, what we are born with is not as important as what we make of it. One must develop a moral sense over time. Only then will one have the ability to weigh the exigencies of the moment and decide what would be best in the given situation all things considered. As a consequence, it is the cultivated heart-mind of the sage with its intuitive sense of what is right that serves as the basis for normative assessments, not that of a newborn babe with its as yet undeveloped raw potentiality.

As noted in Chapter I, "intuition" is readily acknowledged to play a role in ethical and legal coherence theories. The goal is to reach an equilibrium between one's reflective judgments and one's intuitive sense of what is right. Further, in the absence of a foundational benchmark, the judgment as to what constitutes coherence-equilibrium is itself a product of the same process of balancing reflective judgments with intuitions.

That the ethical process is one of coherence requiring one to balance the particulars rather than appeal to universal principles is graphically illustrated in the following story. When asked whether it is permissible to lend a hand to one's drowning sister-in-law even though to do so violates the prescription of the rites against physical contact between members of the opposite sex, Mencius replies: "Not to lend a hand is to be a brute. It is prescribed by the *li* that male and female should not touch, but in lending a hand to one's drowning sister-in-law one uses discretion" (4a17). Significantly, the word used by Mencius to refer to this discretionary process is *quan* 權, which originally meant: (n) a scale, (v) to weigh. By extension, the word takes on the meaning of "authority." The one who is able to balance the various concerns is the person who has the authority, the power, to effect order. The pragmatic, coherence character of the project is brought out by an additional connotation of *quan*: exigency, as opposed to regularity (*jing* 經). In reaching a judgment that will restore ethical equilibrium, the sage responds to and weighs the exigencies, the particularities of the given situation. In the final word, the sage constitutes the authoritative source for order, be it ethical, legal or sociopolitical: "Goodness alone is insufficient to exercise government; the law unaided cannot implement itself (4a1). . . . The rites and judgments of what is right are derived from the person of superior character (1b16)."

Of course, one might ask why Mencius bothers proposing an inchoate moral sensibility tending toward the good if the real ethical work is done after birth. The answer, I believe, lies in the fact that Mencius is aware of opposition to the views of Confucius. This complicates his task as a wandering minstrel of philosophical wisdom in that he cannot simply parrot the Master. He must respond to critics such as Yang Zhu and Mo Zi. The former in particular threatens to undermine the basis of both Mohist and Confucian ethics by arguing that the way to comply with *tian* is to nurture one's own life:[41] the drive toward self-preservation is innate, given to us by *tian*; to seek one's own well-being, to attempt to live out the life span given to one by heaven is what is natural for humans; it is human nature—and it is sanctioned by heaven. Perhaps Mencius thought that by turning to heaven for a predisposition toward moral goodness he could circumvent Yang Zhu's criticisms without compromising the basic thrust of Confucius's coherence theory. If what counts is what happens after birth, not before, then to add the claim that human nature is good in the minimal sense that Mencius holds it to be provides, at little practical cost, a neat solution to the problem raised by the individualism of Yang Zhu: it is human nature, not to follow one's self-interested tendencies, but to be morally good, though one must develop these inchoate ethical propensities through moral education, training, and constant perseverance.[42]

At any rate, Confucius does not appeal to either a special faculty or to an innate sense for rational or ethical principles that could serve as the ground of a natural law theory. Nor does he appeal to the discovery of teleological features of a determinate human nature as a basis for his jurisprudence. Indeed, he is reluctant to speak of human nature. On those few occasions when he does, he emphasizes the fluid, developmental, potential-for-achievement aspect of human character rather than human nature as a static and predetermined end.[43] Confucius firmly believes in the power of moral suasion to shape human attitudes, behavior, and character, and champions the magic-like ability of the sage to foster through example and force of character an environment in which the members of society would be willing to put aside narrow self-interest and adapt themselves to the circumstances in creating a harmonious sociopolitical order. "In administering government, what need is there for you to kill? Just desire the good yourself and the common people will be good. The virtue (*de*—moral potency) of the exemplary person is like wind; the virtue of the small man is like grass. Let the wind blow over the grass and it is sure to bend" (12:19).

Ethics and the Law

The most promising source for Confucius's natural law would seem to be ethics. Indeed, both Needham and Bodde claim that Confucian law is grounded in universal ethical principles:[44] "[In the Han], law again became . . . firmly embedded in ethics, and successive emperors . . . justified their mandates by invoking natural law, i.e. norms of behavior universally considered moral—in fact, *li* [rites]—and not positive law."[45] Bodde adds, "The *li* [rites] derive their universal validity from the fact that they were created by the intelligent sages of antiquity in conformity with human nature and with the cosmic order. [Positive] law has no moral validity because it is merely the ad hoc creation of modern men who wish by means of it to generate political power."[46] If the *li* (禮—rites, not to be confused with another *li* [理] translated as principles for Huang-Lao) were indeed universal moral principles, we might very well have natural law in the strict foundationalist sense.[47] But are they? I suggest not.

To treat the *li* (rites) as universal principles is to render them static and determinate in a way that is incompatible not only with the spirit but the words of Confucius. To be sure the standard view takes Confucius to be "a prosaic and parochial moralizer," a conservative apologist for the Zhou dynasty who insists on rigid conformity to arcane ritual practices.[48] But Confucius, in sharp contrast to this unflattering portrayal, depicts himself as open-minded and tolerant. He claims that he is unlike others in that he is without fixed principles or presuppositions (18:8). And on numerous occasions in the *Analects*, we find Confucius not only evidencing considerable flexibility, but speaking out on its behalf.[49] In fact, he does so specifically with respect to the *li*: "A ceremonial cap of linen is what is prescribed by the rites. Today black silk is used instead. This is more frugal and hence I follow the general practice. To prostrate oneself before ascending the steps is what is prescribed by the rites. Nowadays, the practice is to bow after ascending the steps. This is presumptuous and hence I do not follow the majority but continue to bow before ascending" (9:3). Far from immutable, the *li* are to be changed when circumstances merit it. That does not mean they are to be altered at the drop of a ceremonial cap. Change must be justified. There must be good reasons. The normative force of the *li* is derived, after all, in part from their being the amassed wisdom of the ages: "there is no doubt that the ultimate solemnity of which rite is capable, the deep, archaic response it evokes in men's soul, are never present insofar as any pattern of conduct or gesture is felt to be new, invented, or utilitarian."[50]

But the *li* are important not merely because they are old or reflect the insights of the sages of yesteryear. Their main function is to serve in times of crisis as a common ground on which to reconstruct a harmonious social order. "Yu Zi said, 'As for the function of the rites, harmony is the most valuable. . . . If harmony is not modulated by the rites, it too will be impracticable'" (1:12). When there is a breakdown in the social order, we turn to the *li* as the communally owned treasury of shared meaning and value. We are inextricably a part of our tradition. However different we may be, there are still deep chords of affinity that bind us together as a result of our shared tradition. By tapping the areas of commonality, one may be able to find the ground on which to build a consensus, to forge a new harmony. It is the *li* that provide this common starting point for Confucius.

The *li* then are culture specific. As Needham and Bodde themselves, somewhat contradictorily, acknowledge, the *li* are customary: far from universally applicable principles, they are the particular mores, values and guidelines for human interaction of a particular society at a particular time.[51]

Because society is not a mere replaying of the records of the past, the *li* must be constantly interpreted and reappropriated to fit the changing situation. If the *li* are not invested with new meaning and value, if they are not reinterpreted in light of the current situations, they will degenerate into irrelevant and trivial formal rules of etiquette. Confucius is well aware of this: "Surely when one says, 'The rites, the rites,' it is not enough merely to mean presents of jade and silk. Surely when one says 'Music, music,' it is not enough merely to mean bells and drums" (17:11).

One must do more than mimic the forms; one must come to embody the qualitative excellence, the virtue, that they represent.[52] It is the authoritative—not authoritarian—person (*ren zhe* 仁者) who is able to appreciate the excellence and make it his own, to appropriate it and give expression to it in his own way and in light of his own particular circumstances. One must make the *li* significant, and in doing so, the authoritative person becomes a source of meaning and value for the society, authoring society through an ability to inspire others to participate in the realization of a higher quality of life and social harmony.

In short, Confucius is primarily interested, not in the predetermined constraints imposed on humankind, be they the laws of nature or human nature, but in the possibilities for achievement. He is not concerned with complying with a preestablished pattern, in constructing society according to some ethical blueprint, but in fostering the highest quality of harmony out of the particulars at hand. His is an emergent order that, in requiring interpretation and appropriation of the *li* in light of the particular circumstances, is incompatible with their construal as static, fixed principles that one need simply apply or mimic. As culture- and context-specific customary embodiments of shared value rather than universal and immutable principles, the *li* cannot be read in terms of or serve as the ground for foundational natural laws.

An examination of the normative reasoning process by which conflicts are resolved and order established will further substantiate this reading of *li* and verify that Confucius is indeed committed to a coherence approach to ethics and law.

2.2   Politics of Harmony

In *After Virtue*, Alasdair MacIntyre draws a distinction between moralities of virtue and moralities of law. The latter focuses on protecting the basic rights of individuals and prohibiting those actions that would destroy the bonds of the community. It is interested in guaranteeing a minimum standard below which society cannot sink and still function as a society. A morality of virtues, on the other hand, focuses on standards of excellence: "those qualities of mind and character which would contribute to the realization of the common good or goods."[53] Whereas a morality of law sets the minimum,[54] a morality of virtues aims at the maximum. The former tells you what is unacceptable, intolerable; the latter points to what is ideal, what is possible.

One of the primary motivations behind a morality of law is the belief that society consists of atomistic individuals in competition with each other. This is most apparent in the Hobbesian vision of society as a "war of all against all" with each person solely concerned with maximizing his or her own ends. But it also holds for the world of Rousseau where "noble savages" living free and independent lives enter into social relationships only when convenient to do so given their individual interests. Even the contemporary contractarian John Rawls makes it an explicit condition of his "original position."[55]

Given the assumption that society is an arena in which self-interested individuals compete for scarce goods and resources, what will be needed, it is asserted, is a set of principles, rules, or laws to adjudicate between conflicting claims plus some mechanism for enforcement. This will ensure that there is sufficient order for society to go about its business.

Furthermore, because individuals are considered to be solely interested in getting the biggest piece of pie possible, it becomes necessary to abstract away from their particular interests and circumstances to determine the laws or principles that, being agreeable to all rational agents, could provide the basis for adjudication between the conflicting ethical claims. One seeks a single, universal standard, a foundational principle, a base norm. This helps explain the exalted status of the virtue of justice within the Rawlsian ethical hierarchy.[56] It also accounts at least in part for other reductive theories such as Kant's deontic formalism in which one seeks rational consistency and the classical utilitarianism of Bentham and Mill in which the sole consideration becomes the maximization of some preferred consequence be it pleasure, "goods," or whatever. A further consequence is that such theories are radically ahistorical in their universalizability. Rawls, for instance, maintains that his principles of justice are operable in any social order. The principle of utility can similarly be applied anywhere at any time as can Kant's categorical imperative.

Edmund Pincoffs calls this tendency to reduce ethics to a kind of problem-solving activity *quandary ethics* and points out that this way of approaching ethics is of recent origin. Traditionally, from Plato through Aquinas to Hegel the concern was not so much with problematic situations as with virtues, standards of excellence, and ideals for humankind, and with what Pincoffs describes as "moral enlightenment, education, and the good for man."[57]

The shift from moralities of virtues to moralities of law is in part a response to a perceived collapse in the moral order. Moralities of virtue are predicated on a common sense of good and the sense of community that attends the feeling of shared values. With the increasing complexity of society and the influx of new peoples, alternative value systems spring up. Normative consensus begins to breaks down. Conflicting ethical claims arise. Resolution proves elusive because the conflicts are merely surface reflections of deeper disagreement as to basic values. The social fabric is torn. Disorder rears its ugly head. The community is fractured into rival factions. With the dissolution of the communal bonds provided by a shared vision of the ideal, moralities of law emerge to replace moralities of virtues in an effort to ensure the minimum standard of cooperation required to hold society together.[58] The result is the reduction of rich, highly textured, culture-specific virtue complexes to single criterion ethics, be it deontic formalisms, utilitarian principles, or social contract theories centered around inalienable rights, duties, and obligations.

Confucius, in contrast, offers an ethic of virtues,[59] of qualitative excellence in interpersonal relations (*ren* 仁) and harmony among social beings. Consequently he is not preoccupied, in the way his counterparts who advocate a morality of law are, with justice, rights, liberties, and the like. He calls not for legal justice, but for humanity, where humanity is understood to be the ultimate achievement, not something one inherits merely by reason of birth into a certain species. Moreover, where many contractarians and morality of law proponents see ahistorical individuals in competition with each other, Confucius sees persons bound together by deep historical roots grounded in the traditional *li* understood to include the full range of social customs, mores, and norms embodied in the complex relationships, organizations, and institutions of society. Whereas others emphasize the deontological ethics of universal laws and principles for rational agents, the pragmatic Confucius calls for discretionary judgments (*yi* 義) of coherence, of harmony, of qualities of life, and the establishment of inspirational models through the charismatic power (*de*) of exemplary persons (*jun zi*).

Humanity as an Achievement

The Enlightenment conception of justice begins with the assumption that individuals qua human beings are entitled to certain equal and inalienable rights. By virtue of being born into a particular biological species, we are automatically afforded a privileged status—and with it the benefits incumbent on that classification—not extended to beings of other species: humans have different rights than animals or plants.[60] Justice as the first virtue of social institutions entails safeguarding these basic rights conferred on individuals qua biological human beings: "Each person possesses an inviolability founded on justice that even the welfare of society as a whole cannot override."[61]

Confucius, however, draws a distinction between human beings qua members of a biological species and humans qua social beings. The well-publicized and much debated distinction between masses (*min* 民) and persons (*ren* 人) as well as that between the small person (*xiao ren* 小人) and the exemplary person (*jun zi* 君子) suggests that one must earn the benefits granted to one and guaranteed by society by achieving some minimal level of personhood, of humanity.[62] That is, to avail oneself of the privileges offered by society, one must first demonstrate one's credentials as a participating member of society; one makes one's claim to the goods provided by the social institutions as a human qua social being rather than simply as a human qua biological being.

> "A person is not entitled to political participation because he is born into an exclusive *ren* (human being) class. Rather, he becomes *ren* as a consequence of that personal cultivation and socialization that renders him particular. Being a person is something one does, not something that one is; it is an achievement rather than a given."[63]

The achievement, it should be emphasized, is a social one. For Confucius, one *becomes* a human being, a humane person, by virtue of participation in society; personhood and humanity are functions of socialization. At birth, before the process of enculturation, of becoming humane, we are not different than the other beasts.[64] If one does not or is not willing to participate in society, to enter into harmonious relations with others, one not only makes it more difficult for society to realize its potential by depriving the community of one's unique talents but one remains oneself at the level of a beast—of human qua member of a biological species. By turning one's back on society, the bestial person (literally "small person"—*xiao ren*) fails to utilize the cognitive, aesthetic, and spiritual powers that distinguish humans from other species.[65] It is just the engagement of these capacities in joining with others to shape a new world, to create a significantly different and better society, to overcome one's natural conditionality (*ming* 命) in achieving innovative resolutions to conflicts that is distinctive about humans. If one cannot overcome the passions, instincts, and desires that one shares with other beasts, if one wars against all and resorts to violence and brute strength to fulfill one's narcissistic wants, then one fails to become truly human, to achieve humanity.

Consequently, for society to aim at securing a minimum level of basic rights for alienated individuals unable or unwilling to participate cooperatively in collective living is to admit failure; it is to accept that there is no way to overcome the self-interested passions and desires of the animal world. If that is the case, then there is no hope for a humane society. Confucius realizes that laws cannot force people to be humane. "Lead the people with edicts, keep them in line with penal law, and they will avoid punishments but will have no sense of shame. Lead them with virtue, keep them in line with the rites, and they will not only have a sense of shame but will order themselves harmoniously" (2:3). For society to achieve collective humanity, the people that compose it must make it humane, and they can do this only if they are willing to put aside narrow self-interest and see themselves and hence their interests as inextricably tied to the interests of society at large.

The ethical focus, therefore, cannot be on determining and implementing a universal law or system of laws that establishes a minimum standard of basic rights for individuals alienated from each other and society. By their very nature laws in their impersonality violate the uniqueness of the particular person.[66] Instead the ethical orientation is to be directed toward the achievement of the highest quality of life made possible by the joint efforts of humans cooperating in collective living. For Confucius, the emphasis is on the realization of the kind of excellence in interpersonal relations for which the exemplary persons serve as inspirational models.[67] As A. S. Cua observes, "the concept of *ren* is the concept of an ideal of moral excellence. . . . The focus is on man himself and what he can morally accomplish in relation to others."[68]

Confucius is not unaware of the difficulties involved in achieving the ethical excellence of a humane society. As his disciple Zeng Zi reports, "a person of character must be strong and resolute, for his burden is heavy and the road is long. He takes *ren* as his burden" (8:7). Yet through the achievement of excellence in interpersonal relations one is transformed from the biological level of human qua beast to the higher levels of personhood in which the human qua social being is himself the determining factor in bringing about a harmonious social order. For Confucius this is the ultimate ethical challenge: to inspire in the many members of society the desire to achieve a humane society and to encourage them to direct their energies toward the attainment of a harmonious social order.

The Way of Harmony

Confucius rejects such limiting notions as rule ethics, pure procedural justice, and a normatively predetermined way.[69] That there are no hard and fast rules means that one must respond to the particular circumstances with an open mind, with a willingness to be flexible and to join in a cooperative search for a harmonious solution. Of course not everyone will make the effort or have the capacity to carry it out. There will always be a continuum from the bestial person (*xiao ren*) to the exemplary person (*jun zi*). Hence it will never be possible to completely do away with law. Nevertheless the goal is to foster an environment in which laws need be imposed as little as possible: "In hearing litigation I am much the same as anyone. If you insist on a difference, it is perhaps that I try to get the parties not to resort to litigation in the first place" (12:13).

What makes one an authoritative person deserving of respect and another a bestial person subject to penal law is not political or economic status but the ability to bring one's cognitive, aesthetic, and spiritual insights to bear on the situation in such a way as to inspire admiration and deference in others for one's vision of a high-quality way of living. This ability to look beyond the reductive scope of rules to weigh the intricacies of the particulars and draw the disparate pieces together in a vision of a harmonious social order is what is meant by discretionary or "aesthetic" judgment (*yi*) and is the defining trait of the *jun zi*. Thus the Master says, "The exemplary person, in his dealings with the empire, is without that which he is for or against. Rather it is with appropriateness (*yi*) that he stands shoulder to shoulder" (4:10). The sage takes not the formalistic application of rules as his task but the creative exploration of possibilities appropriate within the particular context.

The process conducive to social harmony is one of analogical projection (*shu* 恕).[70] One begins not with rational agents, but with real people in a historical, sociopolitical context who have goals, desires, values, and beliefs. For Confucius, as noted earlier, the *li* or traditional rites provide a common basis on which to build a new harmony. In the absence of a common tradition, one must start with whatever is at hand—the interests, attitudes, and so on of the particular peoples. One then tries to overcome the conflict, to move beyond the seemingly incommensurable claims of the participants, by projecting a vision of a new order that will be acceptable to all based on the particular characteristics of the concerned parties. Rather than trying to apply an abstract universal rule, or to adjudicate on the basis of a fixed law a decision such that one side wins and the other loses, one seeks to create a third vocabulary amenable to all concerned—the underlying assumption being that humans must ultimately be responsible for constructing their own just society.[71]

The advantage of placing the ball in the court of the members of society who must assume the responsibility for achieving or failing to achieve a humane society is that it fosters an environment in which compromise and innovative solutions can occur. In the absence of any fixed, external or privileged standards, the grounds for holding a dogmatic position are undermined. The final criterion is the quality of life within the society that would result from adopting the proposed alternative order.

In as much as the *li* cannot be understood as universal ethical principles and Confucius's ethical and legal system requires that "persons of superior character" balance the competing interests of the given particulars, Confucius's jurisprudence can be characterized as a "rule of man" (*ren zhi* 人治) as opposed to a "rule of law" (*fa zhi* 法治).[72] The *Yin Wen Zi* clarifies this distinction for us:[73]

Tian Zi, reading the *Shu Jing*, exclaimed, "The reign of Yao was one of great peace!" Sung Zi asked him, "Was this because of rule by sages or because of rule by sagacious laws?" Peng Meng, sitting off to one side, broke in, saying, "Because of rule by sagacious laws, not sages."

Sung Zi then asked, "What's the difference between the two?"

Peng Meng replied, "Your confusion of the terminology is extreme indeed! The administrative order of a sage emerges out of the sage himself; order by sagacious law emerges out of determinate principles. Determinate principles emerge from oneself, but one is not oneself the source of determinate principles. That is, one can give expression to determinate principles, but such principles are not simply determined by oneself. Thus on this score the rule of the sage is self-generating. When order is generated through rule of sagacious law, however, nothing is left unordered."

In a "rule of man," the sage is the source, expositor, and interpreter of social order and the law. To be sure the sage is the product of a social, political, cultural, and economic milieu. And he is not only shaped by but sensitive to the traditions of his community. Nevertheless, in the end, the sage determines what is best in a given situation based on his own judgment rather than by appeal to fixed laws or universal ethical principles. In the absence of any such principles, order is sui generis.

In *Yin Wen Zi*'s "rule of law," laws are based on determinate principles that transcend the individual opinion of a given person. One does not create the law but simply discovers it. When conflicts arise, a judge decides not what is best all things considered but what is right vis à vis the foundational laws. Order is not sui generis but constrained by transcendent principles.

Confucius's jurisprudence, in making the sage responsible for engineering and ensuring the smooth operation of a harmonious social order, constitutes "a rule of man." There are, of course, still laws. Hence Confucianism remains a rule of law broadly construed to entail the existence of the legal and enforcement mechanisms necessary to ensure the ability of society to function: it is not lawless anarchy; if need be, sanctions will be imposed. But similar to Dworkin's ideal judge Hercules, the sage is ultimately the one who must interpret the law and make it—and, in Confucius's view, society as well—the best they can be. In doing so, he is not precluded from taking ethical considerations into account. Indeed, it is incumbent upon him to do so. Confucianism is, therefore, not legal positivism.

Yet neither is it natural law in a strict foundational sense. Rather than trying to deduce the law from basic assumptions or universal principles,

Confucius's sage tries to harmonize the law with a particular society's ethical attitudes, goals, cultural practices, and so forth. He strives for an equilibrium that will allow the particular persons to realize their potential in and through cooperation with each other. Given this fundamental difference in methodology between Confucius's coherence approach and the correspondence approach of foundational natural law systems, we do well to avoid lumping him together with advocates of natural law.

2.3 A Huang-Lao Critique

As the grandfather of Chinese philosophy, Confucius was able to advance his optimistic vision of a harmonious humane society based on the attunement of names in an environment less hostile than that confronting subsequent thinkers. Although historical documentation is scant and dating always problematic, the standard story has it that the first rivals to Confucius did not enter the scene until after his exit at the close of the Spring and Autumn period. The following centuries witnessed increasingly bitter rivalry, both intellectually among the contending schools of thought and militarily among the turf-hungry warlords. Thus Confucius wrote in a time somewhat more conducive to the hopes of cooperative resolution to conflict than the chaotic and turbulent Warring States period of his successors. That the latter might question some of the underlying assumptions of Confucius's philosophy should come as no surprise. And indeed we find Legalists, Daoists, Mohists—even fellow Confucians—taking issue with his pragmatic politics of harmony.

The key to Confucius's ethical system is the possibility of harmonious resolution of normative conflicts. This entails at least three assumptions.

First, unlike many social contractarians from Hobbes to Rousseau to Rawls, Confucius assumes a positive rather than a zero-sum game.[74] He takes it for granted that a solution in which both sides come out ahead is possible. He does not allow that resources are so scarce that the gain of one is the loss of the other. In his view, there is enough or at least the possibility that there could be enough for each side to get—if not what it wants—then at minimum what it needs and can live with.

Xun Zi was one of the first to directly question whether it is possible to satisfy everybody. In his view, similar in many respects to that of Hobbes and his fellow contractarians, conflicts arise because desires are infinite while natural and social resources are finite. Regulations are needed to ensure an equitable distribution and to limit desire. "What is the origin of ritual? I reply: humans are born with desires. If one's desires are not satisfied, one cannot but seek some means to satisfy them. If there are no limits and degrees to one's seeking, then one will inevitably fall to wrangling with others. From wrangling comes disorder and from disorder comes exhaustion. The ancient kings hated such disorder, and therefore they established ritual practices in order to curb it, to train human desires and to provide for their satisfaction" (70/19/1, W89). For Xun Zi, there is one pie and everybody or most everybody wants as big a piece as possible. In contrast to Confucius, Xun Zi focuses less on making a bigger pie and more on the how and why of allocation.

Like Xun Zi, the author of the *Boshu* considers excessive desires for material wealth to be a major source of social disorder.[75] And though he never explicitly states that resources are limited, he does state that people have always contended and that penal laws are necessary to keep them in line. Even if the reason for their contention is not competition over scarce goods, the very fact that they always do contend undermines a second premise of Confucius's politics of harmony; namely, that people will be willing to seek a cooperative solution to their problems.

As we have seen, the ethical challenge for Confucius is to foster an environment in which people are willing to put aside narrowly defined self-interest to reach a solution that is acceptable to all concerned parties. If either side dogmatically insists on its own view, the most sagacious among them cannot mediate a compromise. For the author of the *Boshu*, writing as he does sometime during the Warring States to Han period, this assumption of open-minded, other-regarding people willing to cooperate in a search for novel solutions must have appeared to be if not hopelessly naive at least overly optimistic. Life is a struggle. All beings from insects to humans compete with each other and always have. Forget these utopian visions of harmonious societies populated by genuinely altruistic beings. We need a system that works. We need laws, punishments.

Third, it is not even clear that the author of the *Boshu* would allow that a harmonious society could be attained if people were willing to adopt an attitude of cooperation. To have any significant hope of reaching consensus, there must be in addition sufficient agreement as to standards, goals, and so forth. At the very least, there must be enough common ground to get the conversation started. Mo Zi, for one, challenges whether this is in fact the case. As he sees it, not only are people dogmatic and pig-headed, they also begin from radically different, even incommensurable, perspectives.

In ancient times, when mankind was first born and before there were any penal laws or government, it is said that every person's moral view was different. One person had one view, two persons had two views, ten persons had ten views. Moreover, each person believed that his own views were correct and disapproved of those of others so that people spent their time condemning one another. Within the family fathers and sons, older and younger brothers grew to hate each other and the family split up, unable to live in harmony, while throughout the world people all resorted to water, fire, poison in an effort to do each other injury. . . . The world was as chaotic as though it was inhabited by birds and beasts alone (14/11/1, W34).

Though the author of the *Boshu* never goes so far as to explicitly endorse incommensurability, he is obviously aware that people do not share the same value system. In fact, his positing a predetermined normative order grounded in foundational naturalism may be readily interpreted as an attempt to address this problem. A typical response to loss of a communal sense of the good and the ensuant breakdown of the normative order is the emergence of moralities of law in which highly textured or "thick" virtue complexes are replaced by a reductive or "thin" vision of the good. This is consistent with Huang-Lao thought: for the author of the *Boshu*, there is but one Way. One need not worry that ethical quandaries will prove unsolvable due to lack of common ground, of shared standards. In the world of Huang-Lao, we are all part of the one normative order. As a consequence, ethical conflicts are subject to univocal determinations. There is a right and a wrong and it the sage who discovers it.

The respective roles of the sage are then drastically different for Confucius and his Huang-Lao counterparts. Confucius's jurisprudential politics of harmony rests on the critical assumption that justice is best served by allowing the sage the discretion to determine what is best in the particular situation for all concerned. At heart, it remains a rule of man rather than a rule of law.

For Confucius the codification and public dissemination of laws sends the wrong kind of message. As noted previously, laws are designed to protect the minimum interests of the members of society and provide a mechanism for dealing with and removing those individuals who are not only unwilling to participate in fostering a harmonious social order, but whose behavior threatens the well-being of others and the ability of society to function. Making the laws public focuses attention not on the achievement of the highest quality of social harmony possible but on the lowest level of participation required by society. Consequently, it may encourage some persons to look only to manipulate the system for their own advantage.

Thus we find Confucius criticizing the state of Jin for publically promulgating laws: "Jin is going to ruin. It has lost its proper measures. . . . When those measures are abandoned and tripods with penal laws on them are cast instead, the people will study the tripods and not care to honor men of rank."[76] The proto-Confucian Shu Xiang adds: "In antiquity, the former kings considered the particular circumstances in regulating affairs. They did not make public general laws of punishments and penalties, fearing that this would foster a contentious attitude among the people which could not be stopped or controlled. For this reason, they used their discretionary judgment (*yi*) to keep the people in bounds . . . and guided them in their behavior through the rites (*li*)."[77]

As these passages suggest, the most important Confucian objection to the codification and publication of law may very well be that laws are too determinate, too gross, and inflexible.[78] They deprive the exemplary persons of the discretionary latitude—be this understood in terms of *yi* (aesthetic judgment), *shu* (analogical projection), or the *quan* (evaluative authority) of Mencius—necessary to weigh the intricacies of the situation and to balance the various interests in the most harmonious fashion.[79]

In contrast, followers of both Huang-Lao and Legalism view public law as a way of ensuring the smooth and effective operation of government.[80] As they see it, the Confucian system of *li*, by ceding to the nobles such wide discretionary powers, strengthens the hand of the elitist class. They question whether the sage-judge in actual practice will take into consideration the interests of not just a privileged few but of all concerned. Hence they take the limitation of the powers of the ruling noble class by law to be a praiseworthy way of undermining the dual class system in which "the *li* do not reach down to the common people; penal law does not reach up to the great officials."[81]

Although both the Legalists and the author of the *Boshu* assume that one is able to impartially interpret and apply the law, many today would challenge the very notion of impartial assessment. Even if one wanted to mediate fairly and justly, one cannot help but impart one's own normative beliefs as to what is fair and just into one's judgment of what is best all things considered.[82] Ironically, this is particularly worrisome in the case of Confucius in that his ethical gaze is so trained on the lofty heights achievable by humankind that he neglects to provide much of a minimal level of institutional protection for the individual over and against the state and fellow beings. One is simply left to trust in the upright character, fairmindedness, and good judgment of those in power. In making humanity so thoroughly a social and cultural achievement and then turning over to a few the power to decide what the standards for this achievement are to be and who has satisfied the criteria, Confucius opens the door to considerable abuse.

The replacement of Confucius's discretionary rule of man with a rule of impartial, publically promulgated law is one attempt to curb the abuse of those in power and provide some protection to even those at the bottom of the sociopolitical hierarchy.[83] As we have seen, the author of the *Boshu* seeks to limit the power of the ruler and ruling class by imposing a host of other constraints as well.[84] Indeed, that the ruler is restricted by the natural law doctrine of Huang-Lao and ultimately by the normatively predetermined Way of foundational naturalism not only differentiates Huang-Lao thought from Confucianism but from Legalism as well.

At any rate, the author of the *Boshu* is clearly much less sanguine about the benefits to be gained from, and the likelihood of, success of Confucius's politics of harmony. A product of an embattled age, he sees little hope for moral suasion and personal example alone to bring about harmony. On a national level, one needs a central government with the military strength to rein in the rival warlords. On a personal level, one needs to supplement the rhetoric of moral suasion with the practical incentives of rewards and punishments. One needs, in short, precisely the kind of synthesis of morality of virtues with rule of law that the author attempts to engineer in the *Boshu*.[85]

V. The Pragmatic Statesmanship of Han Fei

In the last chapter, I argued that during the Warring States and early Han periods one witnessed a breakdown in the moral order and with it the failure of Confucian politics of harmony. I further suggested that proponents of both Legalism and Huang-Lao responded to the social crisis and the theoretical inadequacies of Confucius's politics of harmony by endorsing a rule of law. Although I offered evidence that this is indeed the case for Huang-Lao, I have yet to do so for the Legalists. I rectify that deficiency in this chapter, arguing that Han Fei advanced a law–based rule, albeit one very different from that of Huang-Lao.

I concentrate on Han Fei's thought primarily for two reasons. First, he is generally acknowledged to be Legalism's most articulate and sophisticated spokesperson: he puts Legalism's best foot forward. Although the differences between Huang-Lao natural law and Legalist positive law are more obvious in the writings attributed to the extremist Shang Yang, if we are to give Legalism its best argument, we can do no better than to take Han Fei as its representative.

Second, some commentators have claimed that there are "striking and pervasive parallels" between the thought of Han Fei and Huang-Lao.[1] Indeed, they go so far as to assert that the writings of Han Fei and the *Boshu* are "intimately related in thought and content."[2]

"The main thrust [of the *Boshu*] is unmistakably Fa-chia [Legalism]...and remarkably analogous to Han Fei's synthesis of Fa-chia's divergent theoretical strains. More specifically, [Han Fei's] adept theoretical grounding of Fa-chia's politial thought on Lao Tzu's 'purposive' Taoism...is paralleled with a remarkable regularity in the four chapters of the *Huang-ti ssu-ching* [*Boshu*], although the four chapters are not as theoretically sophisticated and elaborately systematized as in Han Fei's five chapters."[3]

More concretely, Hsiao-po Wang and Leo S. Chang claim that, like Huang-Lao, Han Fei synthesizes Daoism and Legalism by basing *fa* (law) on dao; advances a holistic naturalism; and sponsors an epistemology in which one empties oneself of bias by becoming empty and tranquil (*xu jing*) so that one then objectively discovers the Way, understands the relation between names and reality, and knows how to *wu wei*.[4]

In this chapter, I challenge Wang and Chang's general thesis—that the philosophy of Huang-Lao is by and large the same as that of Han Fei— as well as many of their more specific claims. In section 1, I argue that Han Fei's philosophy, unlike that of the author of the *Boshu*, is not foundational, as a close study of his philosophy of language, epistemology, and jurisprudence reveals. This fundamental difference is especially apparent in the area of jurisprudence. Han Fei espouses not natural law grounded in a predetermined natural order but positive law where the ultimate authority is the word of the sovereign. In section 2, I argue that, although Wang and Chang are justified in taking exception to the widespread interpretation of Han Fei as a defender of despots and although there are, as they suggest, many similarities between the political philosophy of Huang-Lao and Legalism, there are also many differences, particularly in regard to the power of the ruler. Indeed, the Huang-Lao attempt to ground law in a predetermined order, to provide a single, unshakable foundation to normative issues, can be seen in part as an attempt to curtail the powers ceded a Legalist ruler.

1. Han Fei's Legal Positivism

1.1 Rule by Law

Unlike many of his contemporaries, Han Fei is explicit about law: "Law includes mandates and ordinances promulgated in the official bureaus, penalties certain in the minds of the people, rewards due to careful observers of laws, and punishments inflicted on offenders of orders. It is what the subjects and ministers take as their model" (304:6, L2:212). There can be little doubt as to the central role of law in Han Fei's political machinery. Han Fei maintains that without law social disorder is all but inevitable: "To discard the law and trust to wisdom is the road to bewilderment and confusion" (92:8, L1:165). Law is and has long been the basis of a well-governed and stable state: "The early kings took dao as the constant standard and law as the basis of government" (92:4, L1:164). Hence, "whoever clarifies the law is strong; whoever neglects the law is weak" (91:11, L1:163).

In sharp contrast to his Confucian and Daoist counterparts—though in keeping with the author of the *Boshu*—Han Fei insisted that the law be made public. "Law is codified in books, established in government offices and promulgated among the hundred surnames. Technique is hidden in the bosom and useful in comparing diverse motivating factors of human conduct and in manipulating the body of officials secretly. Therefore law wants nothing more than publicity; technique abhors visibility" (290:13, L2:188). Han Fei worried that people will take advantage of ill-defined laws to pursue their own ends. For his system of impartial rewards and punishments based on obedience to law and performance of stipulated duties (*xing ming*) to function, each person must be clear as to what exactly is expected. Making the law public vitiates ignorance as an excuse. In addition, it has the further benefit of undermining the power base of, and potential for abuse by, officials in that discretion is virtually eliminated.[5]

Government, for Han Fei, is government for the average person by the average ruler.[6] Hence the law should be what everybody can understand and follow. It should not be so abstruse that only the literati can make sense of it; nor should it be so demanding that only exemplary sages can live up to it. "What can be understood only by bright scholars should not be made an order because the people are not all bright. What can be practiced only by persons of superior character should not be made a law because the people are not all of superior character" (325:15, L2:250).

The laws are meant to eliminate, not to generate, confusion; they are to serve as constant standards for regulating social interactions. Han Fei, like the author of the *Boshu*, often compares the law to reliable and exact mechanical instruments such as the compass, L-square, or scales: "The way and the law are absolutely reliable, wisdom and ability are liable to errors. Similarly, to hang up the balance and know the plane, to turn round the compass and know the circle, is an absolutely reliable way. . . . To discard the compass and trust to skillfulness, to discard the law and trust to wisdom is the road to bewilderment and confusion" (92:6, L1:165).

Once established, laws are changed only if necessary. To be sure, Han Fei, well known for his "rejection of the ancients," demands that laws fit the circumstances. As times change, so must laws. "There are no absolute constants in the governing of the masses. The law alone leads to political order. Where laws are adjusted to the time, there is good government. . . . Therefore the sage in governing the masses makes laws move with the times and prohibitions change with abilities" (366:2, L2:328). Although laws must keep pace with political realities, they are not to be changed willy nilly: "If the ruler . . . alters laws and prohibitions readily and issues commands and orders frequently, ruin is possible" (79:14, L1:138). If laws are abrogated at the drop of a hat, the lives of the people and hence the order of society will be disrupted: "If when governing a big state you alter laws frequently, the masses will suffer hardships" (104:3, L1:185).

One key to the success of the law as a means of political control is impartial enforcement. Han Fei repeatedly cautions the ruler that he must resist the temptation to tamper with the scales of justice: "If the ruler is fond of twisting laws by virtue of his wisdom, continually mixing private with public affairs . . . then ruin is possible" (79:14, L1:138). On the other hand, "Where one is able to put an end to private scheming and bring about impartial public law, the masses are secure and the state well ordered. Where one is able to put an end to selfish pursuits and implement impartial public law, the military will be strong and one's enemies weak" (22:3, L1:38, W4).

Han Fei objects to the Confucian system in which "the *li* do not reach down to the common people; penal law does not reach up to the great officials."[7] His law has no regard for social status: "The law does not fawn on the noble; the plumb-line does not bend to accommodate the crooked" (26:4, L1:45). The ruler's highest officials, his female companions, even members of his family must all obey the law or suffer the consequences: "The intelligent ruler, as regards women, may enjoy their beauty but ought not to follow their entreaties and comply with their personal requests. As regards those near him, though he enjoys their presence, he must call their words to account and never let them utter any uncalled-for opinions. As regards uncles, brothers and high level ministers, the ruler, on adopting their words, ought to hold them liable to penalties in case of failure and appoint them to office in case of success but never grant them any arbitrary promotion" (38:5, L1:66). The only exception is the ruler himself: as the ultimate authority for the law, he is in effect beyond its reach. This is one indication that law for Han Fei is positive rather than natural law.

1.2   Rule by Positive Law

Of the various theories that fall under the label *legal positivism*, one of the more well known is the sovereign command theory of John Austin, which holds that laws are the general orders backed by threat of sanction given by the sovereign[8] or subordinates in obedience to the sovereign.[9] Although this theory has been criticized by H. L. A. Hart and others, it will suffice as a departure point for elucidating the positivist character of Han Fei's law.[10]

In the Legalist system of Han Fei, there is to be but one sovereign with ultimate authority over the law: "As laws are the means to forbid extra-judicial action and exterminate selfish motives and severe penalties the means to execute decrees and censure inferiors, legal authority should not be delegated to anybody and legal control should not be open to common use. Should legal authority and control be held in common, all manners of abuse will appear" (25:9, L1:44). In the final word, law is what the ruler says it is; it is what pleases the ruler. As Hart points out, there could be for Austin no *legal* limitations to the sovereign's power. By definition, he need answer to none. Similarly, Han Fei confers on the ruler ultimate authority to determine what the laws will be, how they ought to be applied, and whether or not they should be changed.

Morality and Law

In recent years, however, the yardstick of legal positivism has not been the ultimate authority of the sovereign, but Hart's minimum separation thesis. Those theories that deny that there need be any *necessary* relation between law and morality—or for that matter particular laws and morality—are labeled *positivist*. Hart's formulation of the law in terms of primary and secondary rules is a good example.[11]

Whereas Han Fei favors a system more similar to Austin's command theory of law than to Hart's, he does share the latter's belief that morality and the law need not coincide. Indeed, Han Fei not only tolerates but condones the subordination of morality to the practical demands of political realities. He is interested above all in protecting the state. He ridiculed, for instance, Duke Xiang of Song for delaying his attack until the forces of Chu could align themselves. When the Duke was subsequently defeated, Han Fei lamented that this "is the calamity of yearning after benevolence and righteousness" (212:2, L2:56). And he is not above spreading rumors or telling lies to weaken another state and gain the upper hand: "Regarding matters of confusion and suspicion and of dismissal and appointment, the intelligent ruler exterminates them at home but propagates them abroad. Financing the poor and supporting the weak [in the enemy states] is called 'inter-palatial assaults'" (181:11, L2:5). Han Fei even suggests that the ruler lie in an effort to trick his own ministers into revealing their hand. "Give ministers false encouragements and thereby extirpate their attempts to infringe on the ruler's jurisdiction. Invert your words and thereby put suspects to the test. Establish the system of espionage and thereby rectify the fraudulent people. . . . Create quarrels among adherents and partisans and thereby disperse them. . . . Divulge false ideas and thereby make the inferiors think matters over (335:1, L2:266).

Han Fei is wholly unimpressed with virtue for virtue's sake. He deprecates scholars and intellectuals: "Erudite, learned, eloquent, and wise as Confucius and Mo Zi were, if they never till and farm the land, what could they contribute to the state" (326:6, L2:251). And he belittles exemplars of Confucian virtue such as Yu Ran who chopped off his nose to avenge the death of his lord. Practical man that he is, Han Fei takes this to be a literal example of cutting off your nose to spite your face. Similarly, he finds the conduct of Bo Yi and Shu Qi—who, not wanting to compromise their ethical standards, decline office in a corrupt state and flee to a distant mountain where they starve to death—censurable rather than laudable. Han Fei mocks these martyrs, saying that they suffered and died for no practical reason—better had they instructed their superiors in law and the arts of rulership.

More specifically in regard to the law, Han Fei favors the ethically suspect doctrine of heavy punishments for minor infractions. "In inflicting punishments, light offenses should be punished severely. If light offenses do not appear, heavy offenses will not come. This is called to abolish punishments by means of punishments" (365:1, L2:325). To be sure heavy punishments are meant as a deterrent: "Heavy penalties are not for the sole purpose of punishing criminals. . . . While the heavily punished are robbers, the terrified and trembling are good people" (321:13, L2:243). Though one could argue that Han Fei's policy of heavy punishments for minor crimes is ethical on utilitarian grounds, two points merit mention. First, whether ethical or not, his (utilitarian?)[12] deterrence theory of punishments contrasts sharply with Huang-Lao's (retributive) penal theory, which requires that penalties match the crime. Not only does one violate the normative order on the latter's view by meting out excessively harsh punishments, but one runs the risk of having calamity redound upon one's own head.

Second, one might be sympathetic to heavy punishments for those guilty of violating the law or failing to live up to their duties. But it is more difficult to accept that even those who go *beyond* their duties to perform supererogatory acts of moral heroism are to be severely punished, even executed, as Han Fei proposes in the following story:

Once in by-gone days, Marquis Zhao of Han was drunk and fell into a nap. The crown-keeper, seeing the ruler exposed to the cold, put a coat over him. When the Marquis awoke, he was glad and asked the attendants, "Who put more clothes on my body?"

"The crown-keeper did," they replied. The Marquis then fined the coat-keeper and put the crown-keeper to death. He punished the coat-keeper for neglect of his duty, and the crown-keeper for overriding his post. (28:5, L1:49)

Supererogatory acts by definition entail going beyond one's stipulated duties and hence violate the Legalist policy of accountability (*xing ming*). One could, I suppose, argue that punishment for supererogatory acts is morally justified on utilitarian grounds in that such acts threaten the basic principle of accountability on which the Legalist system and a fortiori hope for social order is based. Yet it is not at all clear how the argument would proceed: it would seem that supererogatory acts enhance rather than diminish the quality of social life and hence both directly and indirectly increase utility—however that is to be measured.[13]

More important, however, if we allow that Han Fei's system does on utilitarian grounds reflect a necessary relation between law and morality, then Hart's minimum separation thesis is rendered obsolete as a workable differentia of positive and natural law: any system, no matter how immoral by any other than utilitarian standards, can claim moral legitimacy and a necessary relation between law and morality simply by claiming that it is the only way to prevent social chaos and realize the greatest good.[14] But the natural law claim that there must be a necessary relation between law and morality is a stronger one than this kind of general rule-utilitarian rationalization. It entails that specific *laws*, not just the general institution of *law*, be moral in light of our ethical principles, judgments, and intuitions. Moreover, natural law advocates tend to assume that humans have certain rights based on fundamental ethical considerations that even the good of society as a whole cannot override. Each individual possesses a right to life, a dignity as a human being, an inviolability that prohibits his execution regardless of any amount of deterrence to be gained by society. To be sure, only the most extreme utilitarian would allow that execution is justifiable punishment for an act of kindness, or that lying and scheming are ethically appropriate behaviors for the sovereign in all but the most unusual of circumstances. Yet that there remains for utilitarians even the remotest possibility of such circumstances indicates that natural law theorists are seeking more than a necessary utilitarian link between law and morality. Therefore, to the extent that Hart's minimum separation thesis is an operable criterion for differentiating natural law and legal positivism, Han Fei's system, utilitarian justifications notwithstanding, merits the label.[15]

Pragmatic Positive Law versus Foundational Natural Law

Hsiao-po Wang and Leo Chang provide perhaps the most thoroughgoing account of Han Fei as something more than a legal positivist. They not only argue that for both Legalism and Confucianism "ethics and politics constituted an integrated whole,"[16] but portray Han Fei in much the same way I depict the author of the *Boshu*, contending that he supports natural law grounded in the objective laws of nature.[17]

> Han Fei sees the natural world and the human world in one continuum. The very same Tao and principle (*li*) pervade both worlds, and it is by being informed by the objective Tao and *li* that the ruler is able to conform to the truly natural order of things and realize the fullness of his inborn potentiality. (Wang and Chang, p. 7)

> Thus from surveying the patterns of nature, we can not only deduce the regularity that is discernible vis-a-vis the unpredictable and unknown, but also can identify Tao's objective principle and its corollary regulatory standards as manifested in the way both the natural and the human world function. (ibid., p. 9)

> For Han Fei, the objective principle that regulates the human society is law. It is law that establishes order and suppresses chaos, for it is patterned after 'acknowledged principles' and 'self-existent standards'. (ibid., p. 10)

Wang and Chang base their reading of Han Fei's Legalism as Huang-Lao thought grounded in Lao Zi's Daoism primarily on five chapters: "Yu Lao," "Jie Lao," "Zhu Dao," "Yang Quan," "Da Ti." The authenticity of these chapters, particularly the first four, has long been questioned by many scholars.[18] However, as it is always difficult to prove conclusively what is spurious and what is not, I take a different tack in arguing against Wang and Chang's interpretation. While acknowledging that these chapters may represent Han Fei's sincere effort to adopt Daoism and Huang-Lao thought as the cosmological basis on which to erect his Legalist political edifice,[19] I contend that Han Fei at best is only partially successful. Han Fei never fills in the rough outline sketched in these few chapters. Further, and more important, because the Legalist, Daoist, and Huang-Lao systems are in many ways incompatible, Han Fei is forced to reinterpret Daoist and Huang-Lao thought to render them consistent with his Legalist tenets. One must take care not to be misled by linguistic overlap into reading Han Fei as if he were a Daoist or Huang-Lao exponent: although the language is similar, the terms are put to different uses. Han Fei gives a Legalist twist to key Daoist and Huang-Lao concepts: *wu wei, xu jing, xing ming*, and so on. Thus, even in these five contested chapters, Han Fei differs significantly from the author of the *Boshu* on issues ranging from philosophy of language to epistemology, indicating that he is a legal positivist and not a natural law theorist. Consequently, while Daoism and Huang-Lao thought may have provided the initial inspiration, they do not upon further analysis constitute the basis of Han Fei's Legalism.

The Pragmatism of Han Fei

Han Fei is, above all, a practical man. He is not given to metaphysical musing. The vast majority of what has come down to us as the writings of Han Fei focus on the concrete issues of how to run a state. They reveal the thoughts of a tough-minded pragmatist[20] more concerned with devising a system of political techniques that will work in the real world than with theoretical issues of legitimacy or utopian visions of ideal governments for make-believe perfect beings. This spirit of down-to-earth practicality infuses and is manifest in every area of Han Fei's thought, be it politics, epistemology, jurisprudence, or aesthetics.

Han Fei is not one to wax eloquent over the virtues of "museum art." He has no time for useless things. Recalling the artisan who painted a whip that when held up to the light revealed dragons and serpents, Han Fei matter of factly comments, "the work done to this whip was certainly delicate and difficult. Even so its utility is the same as that of any plainly varnished whip" (202:8, L2:40).

Renowned for his scathing criticisms of Confucians scholars and gentlemen of letters, Han Fei is not so much against formal education as opposed to learning without cash value. He criticizes Confucius and Mo Zi, not for being erudite, knowledgeable, and wise, but for neglecting to till the fields.[21] Whether in times of peace or war, scholars are of little use to the ruler: "Private scholars, pursuing studies when the state is at peace, never exert their physical strength, and, once an emergency comes, never don armor. If revered, they neglect the work of farming and fighting; if not revered, they injure the law of the sovereign. When the state is secure, they are ennobled and celebrated; when the state is in danger, they are as cowardly as Qu Gong. Such being the case, what can the ruler gain out of private scholars pursuing studies" (197:7, L2:30).

The pedantic Logicians or Dialecticians (*ming jia* 名家) represent all that Han Fei finds most despicable about the literati. Famous for word games and sophistry, they delight in turning common sense on its head with paradoxes such as "I go to Yue today yet arrived yesterday." Han Fei pokes fun at them in the story of Ni Yue, a skillful dialectician from Song who had stumped his learned rivals of the prestigious Jixia Academy with the argument that "a white horse is not a horse." Reaching a border pass, Ni Yue, riding a white horse, is obliged to pay the horse tax. Han Fei

147

condescendingly concludes, "in playing with empty words he could triumph over the whole country, but on investigating facts and examining the shape of things he could deceive no one" (201:3, L2:38).

Han Fei's political philosophy is similarly practical. Responding to those who maintain statecraft to be nothing more than compliance with the dictums of the ancient kings, Han Fei counters that the true art of rulership is to match today's political policies with today's political realities. The ultimate standard of one's policies is that they meet the demands of the time; the ultimate measure of one's government is a well-ordered state. As Han Fei puts it, "Whoever does not suit means of political control to actual state affairs but takes advice solely from the words of the early kings is like the man going home from the shoe market to get the measurements of his feet" (196:12, L2:29). Just as our own feet are the standards for choosing shoes, so are our own attitudes, beliefs, and goals about justice, fairness, equity, and so on the standards for assessing government. In this sense, Han Fei is a pragmatist rather than an a Huang-Lao foundationalist: unlike the author of the *Boshu*, he does not look to a transcendent, normatively predetermined natural order as the standard for political order.

Philosophy of Language

The difference between the pragmatic philosophy of Han Fei and the foundational philosophy of Huang-Lao is apparent in their respective views on language. As observed in Chapter II, Huang-Lao sponsors a semantic or realist correspondence theory of language where names pick out objects and reflect distinctions that exist in objective reality. Each thing in the Huang-Lao universe comes into existence with a form and name attached.

Although realist in the everyday sense of that term—that is, a down-to-earth practical person as opposed to a utopian dreamer—Han Fei is no realist in the philosophy of language sense.[22] The ultimate standard by which to judge names and language is utility: they must work; speakers must be able to use them to realize their chosen communicative ends. In keeping with his practical bent, Han Fei insists that words be judged for their functional value rather than eloquence:

> If the ruler, in listening to words, does not take achievement and utility as objective, dialecticians will present such absurd discussions as the Stories of the Bramble Thorn and the White Horse. . . . Therefore, words that are too minute to be scrutinized and too ineffable to be carried out are not in need of honor. Thus, for instance, Ji Liang, Hui Shi, Song Xing and Mo Di were like the painter of the whip in that their theories, being roundabout, profound,

magnificent and exaggerated, were not practical. . . . For this reason, to seek for authenticity one must revert to practical means. (195:7, L2:26–27)

As for Han Fei's theory of *xing ming*, it is more of a technique for political control than a theory of correspondence between word and a predetermined natural order. "If the ruler wishes to put an end to evil-doing, he must be careful to ensure stipulations and performances, words and deeds, correspond. The ministers come forward to present their proposals; the ruler assigns them tasks on the basis of their words, and then concentrates on demanding the accomplishment of the task. If the accomplishment fits the task, and the task fits the words, then he bestows reward; but if they do not match, he doles out punishment" (27:15, W24).

Ames sums up Han Fei's theory of *xing ming* as follows:

> [An] important system is the establishment of a bureaucratic organization kept in check by a political application of the "name and form" theory: "accountability." The bureaucracy, like society at large, is regulated by being held constantly and unconditionally responsible for its conduct. The theory behind accountability is straightforward. The duties and obligations of each office are clearly defined (hence the "name" *ming*). At given intervals, the performance (hence the "form" *xing*) of officeholders is compared with their prescribed duties. Where performance is congruent with the objective definition of the office, rewards and promotions are both generous and constant; where discrepancies occur, however, the axe falls both swiftly and decisively. The important point is that the officeholder, before embarking on any course of action, is wholly aware of the consequence of that action.[23]

To keep his ministers in line, the ruler assigns them specific duties or approves their own proposals. He then verifies that they have in fact done what they were supposed to do. The only "reality" that Han Fei is concerned with is everyday political reality. "The ruler will decide between right and wrong according to the relationship between name and reality and scrutinize words and phrases by means of comparative examination and verification (*can yan* 參驗)" (70:5, L1:120).

Even Wang and Chang admit that Han Fei's theory of *xing ming* is a practical, political one:[24] "Han Fei's discrimination between what is apparent and what is intrinsically real is not epistemological in nature; rather, his search for what is intrinsically real has everything to do with the reality of effective performance. Comparative verification (*can yan*) is clearly performance-oriented." As they see it, "Han Fei's ultimate goal is to insure an effective performance of the tasks assigned through a system of inevitable accountability. In short, [*xing ming* and its corollary, *can yan*] constitute the sovereign's technique of controlling his subordinates."[25] Han Fei's theory of accountability is one pragmatic art of rulership in the Legalist ruler's bag of tricks.

Epistemology

Han Fei's practical mind puts its stamp on his epistemology as well. He will have no part of prognosticators, diviners, nor anyone else who claims knowledge of what lies beyond our ability to test and verify via its practical effects: "If the ruler believes in astrological date-selecting, worships ghosts and spirits, believes in divination and lot-casting, and likes sacrifices and celebrations, ruin is possible" (78:6, L1:135). Like Peirce and James, Han Fei implores us to stick to the "facts": "To be sure of anything that has no corroborating empirical evidence (*can yan*) is stupid; to abide by anything that one cannot be sure of is self-deceptive (351:11, L2:299).

At times Han Fei employs language similar to that of Huang-Lao: "Dao is the beginning of the myriad things, the guideline of right and wrong. For this reason the intelligent ruler, by holding fast to the beginning, knows the source of everything and, by effecting order according to the guideline, knows the origin of good and evil. Therefore, by virtue of resting empty and reposed, he awaits for his orders to enforce themself so that names will be defined of themselves and all affairs will be settled of themselves" (17:16, L1:30). Confronting this passage by itself, out of context, one would be hard pressed to deny that it might very well have been penned by the author of the *Boshu*. Many of the key elements of Huang-Lao epistemology are present: the need to empty oneself of bias and become tranquil; the notion that one will thereby discover the Way, the source of all things and the standard of right and wrong; the assertion that names will name themselves and affairs sort themselves out.

Yet again one must be wary of the dangers of linguistic overlap. Revealing his true Legalist colors, Han Fei continues the preceding passage: "Who utters a word creates himself a name; who undertakes an affair creates himself a form. Compare forms and names and see if they are identical. Then the ruler will have nothing to take up as everything is reduced to its reality. Hence the saying, 'The ruler must not reveal his wants.' For if he reveals his wants the ministers will polish their manners accordingly" (18:3, L1:30). Han Fei is advocating a political technique: *xu* (emptiness) and *jing* (tranquility) are not preparatory stages for discovering the Way but simply means for drawing out the intentions of the ministers; by remaining at ease and allowing the ministers to make the first move, the ruler conceals his weaknesses and forces the ministers to state their positions. Hence names are generated not by the Way itself but by the ministers; the ruler matches up the proposals of the ministers with their actual performance, not names with a normatively predetermined order.

In fact, Han Fei is straightforward in his disdain for Huang-Lao's jargon-laden cant about "emptiness" and direct intuition of some mysterious Way:[26] "I think the philosophy of calmness and quietude is a useless notion and the doctrine of indistinctness and mysteriousness a lawless theory. . . ."(360:3, L2:315). Han Fei believes that we are inevitably bound to our human perspectives, we can never truly be "empty." The more one tries to become "empty," the more fixated and the less empty one becomes.

> Those who make much of non-impositional action (*wu wei*) and the avoidance of reflective thought as constituting emptiness say it is because their intentions are in this way not controlled by anything. For this reason, those who lack techniques take *wu wei* and avoidance of reflective thought to be emptiness. But to be sure those who think of emptiness in this way never forget emptiness and are thus controlled by the whole process of becoming empty. 'Emptiness' means that one's intentions are not controlled by anything. Now, to be controlled by the whole business about becoming empty is not emptiness. The *wu wei*ing of one who is empty does not make of *wu wei* a constant norm. Where one does not turn *wu wei* into a constant norm, one is empty. (95:10, L1:170)

The words are similar, but the purposes to which they are put differ like night from day. For Han Fei, one does not discover the Way but fashions it through an array of practical techniques of political control. He takes Huang-Lao's mysterious foundational epistemology and gives it a pragmatic Legalist spin. *Xu jing* (emptiness and tranquility) is a political expedient, not some dubious process of meditative self-negation and enlightenment: by holding back and refraining from taking a personal stand, the ruler conceals his weaknesses and forces the ministers to take the initiative. *Wu si* (impartiality) is another art of rulership: although one cannot entirely eliminate bias, one can be more "objective" in the Rortean postmodern sense discussed earlier[27]—one can, for instance, appoint on the basis of merit rather than personal connections. *Wu wei* is a third tool: it consists, for Han Fei, of hands off management by the ruler who assigns the details of the daily operations of government to his ministers,[28] not in compliance with a predetermined natural order as with Huang-Lao.

In short, the epistemology of the five contested chapters, far from confirming the similarity of Han Fei and the author of the *Boshu*, attests to their differences.

Positive Law

Law for Han Fei is simply one more pragmatic technique of political control. The rationale for law is that it is the best means of maintaining power and ensuring social order. "If laws are clearly defined, superiors will be honored and not encroached upon. Where they are honored and not encroached upon, the ruler is strong and able to hold on to what is essential. Such was the reason that the Former Kings held law in high esteem and passed it down to posterity" (26:9, L1:46).

The Yellow Emperor, it is to be remembered, is associated with constant and regular laws. The author of the *Boshu*, for whom laws are grounded in the constant and reliable natural order, is likewise reluctant to change laws and will do so only if dictated by the Way itself. Han Fei, although also wary of randomly tampering with the laws, allows alteration when doing so is calculated by the ruler to be advantageous: "The law regulates what one does. What one does dictates what one gains. When laws once promulgated are found to be problematic, one must estimate their costs. If one finds what is to be done can be accomplished, one enacts them. If one finds the accomplishment involves losses, one estimates the losses. If one finds gain will exceed losses, one goes ahead with them. For there are in this world neither laws without drawbacks nor gains without losses" (327:8, L2:252). Ultimately the ruler decides if, when, and how the laws are to be changed, not by overcoming all bias and directly apprehending the Way, but by observing political realities and making up his mind as best he can. "Those who do not know how to effect sociopolitical order adamantly declare, 'Never alter ancient precedent, never remove existing norms.' Change or no change, the sage does not mind. For he aims only at rectification of government. Whether or not ancient precedents should be altered, whether or not existing norms should be removed, all depends upon the question whether or not such precedents and norms are still useful for present-day political purposes" (87:6, L1:154).

In sum, though Han Fei advocates a rule of law, (or perhaps more accurately, a rule by law), it is rule of (by) positive law designed not to accord with the natural order but to serve the interests of the ruler and the state. To be sure many have gone so far as to interpret Han Fei's pragmatic Legalist arts of rulership as tools for furthering the cause of the ruler at the expense of the people. Yet this is unfair to Han Fei, who, though no

Huang-Lao exponent, does, like the author of the *Boshu*, maintain that the raison d'être of government is to serve the people.

2. Han Fei's Pragmatic Arts of Rulership

History has not been kind to Han Fei. He is generally held responsible for the brutal and boorish Qin, of which the Han philosopher, Jia Yi, says:

> Qin, beginning with an insignificant amount of territory, reached the power of a great state and for a hundred years made all the other great lords pay homage to it. Yet after it had become master of the whole empire and established itself with the fastness of the Pass, a single commoner opposed it and its ancestral temples toppled, its ruler died by the hands of men, and it became the laughing stock of the world. Why? Because it failed to rule with humanity and righteousness and to realize that the power to attack and the power to retain what one has thereby won are not the same.[29]

Han Fei, with his links to the harsh Qin regime,[30] is guilty by association: "Qin Shi Huang Di's burning of books and burying alive Confucian scholars cannot be said but to be an unleashing of Han Fei's 'Lonely Indignation' [a chapter of the *Han Fei*]. Pre-Qin thought was backed up by the rear guard of Han Fei's thought, and that is a dark shadow as well as undeletable dirty speck in the history of Chinese thought."[31] The typical textbook portrait of Han Fei and his fellow Legalists is anything but flattering: "Technicians of power [Legalists] . . . in fact glorified power for its own sake and looked upon the human being as having no worth apart from his possible use to the state."[32]

Han Fei is looked on as a Chinese Machiavelli,[33] one who designs, perhaps as a means to curry favor, a system whose primary purpose is to serve and protect the interests of the ruler: "Legalist political philosophy might be described as 'government of the ruler, by the ruler, and for the ruler.' In other words, the end served by this kind of government is first and foremost the interests of the ruler. These interests involve total control over the lives and actions of his subjects to serve the ends of absolute power, stability, personal safety, military strength, wealth and luxury, and freedom to enjoy the privileges due his position."[34]

There is, however, as I have suggested, a rival, more charitable, view. One might argue, as Wang and Chang do, that Han Fei is not a political opportunist but a down-to-earth practitioner of realpolitik. "Un-

153

doubtedly, Han Fei was a political realist who called for harsh measures—given the chaotic political situation of his time—as the most efficacious means of 'saving the present age.'"[35] Consequently, "it would be unfair," Bodde and Morris add, "to regard [Legalists] merely as unscrupulous power-hungry politicians, for they sincerely believed that only through total methods could eventual peace and unity be brought to their war torn world."[36]

Han Fei, the story goes, lived in an embattled age: the moral order had all but collapsed; warlords carried on incessant internecine feuding; traditional thought systems offered little in the way of real solutions. Drastic times call for drastic measures. Legalist policies, though harsh, promised an end to the warring and a restoration of social order.

In the following two sections, I argue for the more charitable reading of Han Fei. I contend that to construe Han Fei's Legalism as "government of the ruler, by the ruler and for the ruler" does a disservice to Han Fei and violence to the text. In making my case, I allow Han Fei to speak for himself (as much as this is possible) by amply citing the text. Too often those who denigrate Han Fei fail to reconcile their interpretation—based on isolated passages quoted out of context and extra-textual matters such as the failure of Qin—with the text itself.[37]

Arguing that Han Fei is not the enfant terrible that many make him out to be and that his Legalist system is designed to serve the people narrows the distance between his political philosophy and that of Huang-Lao. Yet significant differences remain. Most important, Han Fei grants the ruler more and greater powers than does the author of the *Boshu*.

2.1 The Practical Way of Han Fei

Han Fei is like Machiavelli in at least one respect: he articulates a political philosophy meant for the real rather than ideal world. He would, one suspects, wholeheartedly concur with the following sentiments of his Italian counterpart:

> Because I want to write what will be useful to anyone who understands, it seems to me better to concentrate on what really happens rather than on theories or speculations. . . . How men live is so different from how men should live that a ruler who does not do what is generally done, but persists in doing what ought to be done, will undermine his power rather than maintain it. If a ruler who wants always to act honorably is surrounded by many unscrupulous men his downfall is inevitable. Therefore, a ruler who wishes to maintain his power must be prepared to act immorally when this becomes necessary.[38]

Han Fei is interested in a government that works: and a government that works must adapt to the changing times. "People of antiquity strove to be known as moral and virtuous; those of the middle age struggled to be known as wise and resourceful; now people fight for the reputation of being vigorous and powerful" (341:12, L2:279). The policies of Yao or Shun or Confucius may have been sufficient to realize sociopolitical order in the gentler, kinder days of yesteryear. Today, however, the world is a tougher place: "People of yore made light of goods, not because they were benevolent, but because goods were abundant; people of today quarrel and pillage, not because they are brutish, but because goods are scarce" (340:16, L2:278). Han Fei, like his teacher Xun Zi and the author of the *Boshu*, challenges one of the key assumptions of Confucius's politics of harmony: that there are ample resources to allow for positive sum solutions. Although there may have been in the past, there are not now. Governmental policies must reflect the new realities.

Confronting a scarcity of goods, most individuals, Han Fei believes, seek to fulfill self-interests. As a rational being, each calculates costs and benefits in light of his or her individual ends and responds accordingly.[39]

> In the case of workmen selling their services in sowing deeds and tilling farms, the master would at the expense of his housekeeping give them delicious food and by appropriating cash and cloth make payments for their services. Not that they love the hired workmen, but that, they say, by so doing they can make the workmen till the land deeper and pick the weed more carefully. The hired workmen, by exerting their physical strength, speedily pick the weed and till the land. . . . Not that they love their master, but that, they say, by their so doing the soup will be delicious and both cash and cloth paid to them. Thus the master's provisions and the workmen's services supplement each other as if between them were the compassion of father and son. However, their minds are disposed to act for each other because they cherish self-seeking motives respectively. (204:15, L2:43–44)

The world is not, Han Fei reminds us, populated by exemplary other-regarding beings of the likes of Confucius, nor by hard-working and egalitarian heroes of the stature of Shen Nung. Most people are not even capable of avoiding the pitfalls of rampant materialism. Rather than resting content with adequate if humble shelter, food, and clothing, people demand ever more.

> People as a whole, while living, if they have enough money to spend, do not apply themselves; if the superior's rule is weak, they indulge in wrong-doing.

One who has enough money to spend and yet still exerts himself strenuously can be nobody but Shen Nung. . . . Clearly enough, the masses of people cannot live up to the level of Shen Nung. . . . Who on account of vitiation and humiliation seeks nothing other than contentment can be nobody but Lao Zi. To think that order can be effected by making the masses content is to assume everybody to be like Lao Zi. (323:6, L245–246)

Han Fei does not believe that *all* people are narrowly self-interested, materialistic free riders. There are your Yaos, your Shuns, and so on. But one cannot devise policies as if all were Yaos and Shuns. Nor can one devise policies as if all were the treacherous lechers Jie and Zhou. For a political system to function, it must take as its basis the characteristics of the majority of people. "Government is to govern the ordinary persons; its way is to lead the ordinary persons. . . . The highest person of the world cannot be encouraged with reward; nor can the lowest person of the world be restrained by penalty. However, if on account of the highest person reward is not established, and on account of the lowest person punishment is not established, the way to govern the state and employ the masses will be missed" (361:5, L2:317).

Just as Han Fei's Legalist policies are aimed at the average person, so is his advice intended for the typical ruler. "Yao and Shun as well as Jie and Zhou appear once in a thousand generations whereas the opposite types are born shoulder to shoulder and on the heels of one another. As a matter of fact, most rulers in the world form a continuous line of average men. It is for the average rulers that I speak about political purchase (*shi* 勢)" (300:5, L2:204).

The goal is to design a system that will work even with—or, rather, despite—a ruler who is neither exceptionally bright, morally good, nor politically adept.

The first step is to conceal the weaknesses of the ruler. "Who can prevent others from seeing the limits of his own affairs can keep the safety of his person and have possession of the state. Hence the saying, 'If no one knows his limits, he can have possession of the state'" (103:1, L1:183). The ruler who reveals his hand, so to speak, will find himself manipulated by his subordinates: "The ruler must not reveal his wants. For, if he reveals his wants, the ministers will polish their manners accordingly" (18:4, L1:31).

One conceals the shortcomings of the sovereign by erecting a screen of institutional mechanisms, political strategies, and techniques or "arts" of rulership (*shu* 術). The Legalist government is to be as self-regulating as possible. The ruler, once he approves the various policies or mechanisms, assumes a low profile. He allows the system to proceed without interference.

No where is this hands-off policy more important than in regard to the law. As noted earlier, for the law to operate in a proper, machine-like way, personal bias must be eliminated as far as possible. Those who are guilty must be punished without exception. The ruler is not to issue pardons. He is not to interfere on behalf of his family or friends. Legalist law is publicly promulgated, simple enough to be understood by all, and applicable to everyone—everyone, that is, but the ruler himself.

Were the ruler to abandon the law and rely on his own abilities, the overwhelming odds are that disorder would result. "Where rulers uphold the law and make use of the power of their position, order obtains; where they turn their backs on the law and relinquish their position, chaos prevails. Now suppose you abandon your position, turn your back on the law and wait for Yao and Shun to appear. And suppose order obtains after the arrival of Yao and Shun. This will lead to order in one out of a thousand generations of continuous chaos" (300:6, L2:204).[40] Laws are necessary because most rulers do not have the ability, intelligence, or moral power to persuade other people to put aside narrow self-interest and pursue a harmonious resolution to problems. In the judgment of Han Fei, Confucian politics of harmony—in addition to being out of step with the contemporary era of scarce goods—simply asks too much of an average ruler. To be sure, in those instances when the state is governed by a Yao or Shun, the quality of justice will be superior to that attainable under a rule of impartial law. Laws are too gross to adequately reflect every possible contingency. The Confucian system, in granting such wide discretionary powers to the sage-judge, is sufficiently flexible to take into account the relevant concerns and mitigating factors of the particular parties.

Han Fei need not question that meliorisms such as Confucianism, in striving for ethical excellence, hold out the possibility that each and every one will realize his or her maximum potential. Practical man that he is, Han Fei bases his objection on the empirical claim that all too often the idealistic vision of politics of harmony shows itself in the harsh light of reality politics to be nothing but empty promise. Appealing in theory, it is unrealizable in practice.

Nowadays there are not more than ten truly credible and trustworthy persons in this country, whereas there are hundreds of official posts. So if only credible and trustworthy persons are selected for public service, the candidates will not be sufficient to fill all the official posts. In that case, those who maintain order would be few while those who disrupt order would abound. There-fore, the way of the enlightened ruler is to unify laws instead of seeking the wise, to shore up techniques instead of yearning after trustworthy servants. (346:10, L2:289)

Further, utopian dreams of political harmony exact a real-life toll. When those in power fall short of the exemplary standards set by Con-fucius, for instance, the costs to particular individuals and to society as a whole are often great. As we have seen, Confucius fails to provide ade-quate institutional protections for the average person. By allowing those in power to resolve conflicts in light of their best judgment all things con-sidered, Confucius opens the door to a wide range of abuse from nepotism to bribery to class bigotry. Han Fei, setting his ethical sights consider-ably lower, is willing to secure greater protection for the average person at the cost of a potentially more finely tuned justice meted out by a once-in-a-thousand-generations true sage. His is a government of average rulers for average people.

Yet Han Fei advises the ruler to hide behind the veil of institutional mechanisms not simply because he is likely to be inept. Even were the ruler a Yao or a Shun, he would still be better served by depending on the law rather than his own abilities. He is, after all, but one person. No matter how brilliant and capable, a single person cannot oversee every operational detail of a highly complex political empire. "If the ruler tries to keep a personal check on all the various offices of his government, he will find the day too short and his energies insufficient. . . . The former kings . . . accordingly set aside their own abilities; instead they relied upon law and techniques" (24:12, L1:43). The ruler who tries to do it all himself fails to appreciate his proper role. Han Fei compares him to a foolish fire chief who by attempting more accomplishes less. "In putting out a fire, were the fire chief to grab pots and jugs and run to the fire, he would have the use of only one person. If, on the other hand, picking up a whip and taking com-mand he superintends the others, he will have legions under his control. Therefore the sage does not join the rabble or personally undertake mat-ters of little consequence" (258:13; L2:133).

The ruler must take advantage of his position, his political purchase (*shi*):

As a special Legalist term, *shih* can be rendered "political purchase". . . . Whereas the ruler as individual is limited in his capacity to regulate the con-duct of others, from the strategically advantageous position of the throne he can use his political status as *ruler* to amplify his influence over others. It is this political status and its application as a fulcrum for increasing the ruler's capacity to influence others that constitute his *shih*. . . . The concept of *shih* thus expressed in its political application indicates the relationship between the position of the ruler and other elements of the state, a relationship which can be described in terms of political differential or "purchase".[41]

Having studied the historical records, Han Fei is keenly aware that without the power of position even a great sage will find himself thwarted: "Lacking the purchase afforded by the dignity and respect of the position and without laws governing rewards and punishments, even a Yao or Shun would be unable to establish proper order" (74:13, L2:205). On the other hand, as recent history demonstrates, with the power that falls to the leader of a great state, even a person of modest intelligence like Ronald Reagan can dramatically shape the course of world events.

Taking advantage of one's strategic position at the top of the hierarchy, the ruler overcomes the limitations inherent in being a single (average) person by doling out responsibilities to his ministers. As observed, *xing ming* is for Han Fei a political technique whereby the ruler assigns each person specific duties and then verifies that performances match up with stipulated duties.

The practice of *xing ming* allows the ruler to transfer the creative burden of charting the empire's course to his ministers. They, not the ruler, must generate proposals and devise strategies. If their plans succeed, they are rewarded, the government whirls along smoothly, and the ruler is praised. When things go awry, the ruler distances himself from the policies by blaming his ministers. The masses, for their part, gain some comfort if not recompense by knowing that those responsible are invariably punished.

Han Fei invests great importance in reliable and constant rewards and punishments: "The enlightened ruler controls his ministers by means of two handles alone: punishments and rewards" (26:12, W20). Ironically, that human beings are self-interested, far from being a cause for concern, is for Han Fei the very reason for the success of his impartial governing system: "It is the masses' nature to abhor toil and enjoy ease. Where they pursue ease, the land will waste; where the land wastes, the state will not be in order. Where the state is not in order, it will be chaotic. Where reward and punishment take no effect among the inferiors, there is to sure to be a deadlock" (365:14, L2:327). Because people are self-interested, they will respond in a predictable way and hence can be manipulated to achieve a harmonious order. "When people deal with each other in carrying out tasks and rendering services, if their motive is hope for gain, then even with a native from Yue, it will be easy to attain harmony" (205:4, L2:45). It is the existence of those beyond the pale of reward and punishment—be they the great sages Shen Nung and Lao Zi or the despicable villains Jie and Zhou—that most threatens the machinelike regularity of Han Fei's system. Fortunately, such persons are rare.

Han Fei's practical arts of rulership culminate in the technique of *wu wei*. *Wu wei* means different things to different thinkers. For Lao Zi and Zhuang Zi, it is a nonimpositional, creative response to the contingencies of a particular situation. For Huang-Lao, it is compliance with an objective, predetermined natural order, particularly, though not exclusively, on the part of the ruler. Interpreted more narrowly as a political doctrine, it refers to the burden-sharing and hands-off management style of the ruler who designates responsibilities to his ministers. It is this narrow interpretation of *wu wei* as a political technique that Han Fei favors.

> The ruler, though wise, does not thereby deliberate, forcing all to understand their own place. Though of superior character, he does not thereby act, observing closely what motivates his ministers. Though courageous, he does not thereby vent anger, forcing every minister to display his martial prowess. So, leave aside [the ruler's] wisdom and there will be [the ministers'] clarity; leave aside superior character and there will be achievements; leave aside courage and there will be strength. . . . Thus, the intelligent ruler does nothing, but his ministers tremble all the more. (18:8, L1:31–32)

By remaining aloof, the ruler is able to derive the maximum benefit from his subordinates. The latter, not knowing the opinions and biases of the ruler, are forced to make proposals on the basis of what would be good for the state rather than for the ruler. The technique of *wu wei*, of remaining behind the scenes as a hands-off manager, dovetails with Han Fei's desire to conceal the weaknesses of the common ruler: "If it is apparent that you are informed, others will hide things from you. If your ignorance is apparent, others will size you up. . . . Therefore it is said, 'Only in doing nothing can I keep and eye on them'" (238:12, L2:100).

In sum, having sized up the political realities of his day, Han Fei realizes that the body politic is gravely ill. People are no longer benevolent, righteous, other-regarding beings, if they ever were. Nowadays self-interested people compete for scarce goods. If given the opportunity, they will turn the weaknesses of the ruler to their own advantage. Consequently, the ruler must arm himself with an arsenal of techniques. By capitalizing on the self-interestedness of people and the power of his position, he is able to manipulate others through rewards and punishments and strict application of the law. In the eyes of the tough-minded Han Fei, Legalist arts of rulership, though they may be unpalatable, are the bitter medicine needed to cure the social disorders of the Warring States period. To accuse Han Fei of designing a system for the sole purpose of protecting the interests of the ruler is to blame the doctor for the disease. That Han Fei seeks to construct a practical system that will measure up to political realities as well as serve the interests of the people becomes all the more apparent when one considers his conception of the state and the relation between the ruler, ministers, and people.

2.2 Han Fei's Legalist State

In Chapter III, I argued that the Huang-Lao state is a centralized, bureaucratic meritocracy. In this section, I argue that, although this depiction fits Han Fei's Legalist state as well, there are nevertheless significant differences, most notably with respect to the role of the ruler.

Bureaucatic Meritocracy

We have already observed in passing the bureaucratic character of Han Fei's state. Each person is to be assigned a post and incumbent duties. Whoever performs the duties to the letter is rewarded; whoever does not is punished. The system is merit based in two respects. First, one is to be appointed solely for one's abilities: "When selecting for inner court posts, one does not neglect relatives; when selecting for external posts, one does not neglect enemies. Whoever is right for it is raised, whoever is wrong for it is punished" (310:3, L2:222). Han Fei is adamant that all personal considerations be set aside. He relates with approval the story of Jie Hu who recommended his enemy Xing Bailiu to Lord Jian for premiership. When Xing, surprised, comes to thank him, Jie Hu replies: "Recommending you is an impartial public matter. I recommended you because I regarded your ability equal to the post. To have hatred for you is my private feud with you. I have never on account of my feud with you kept you from my superior. Hence the saying: 'No private feud should go through the public gates'" (229:5, L2:83).

Merit, of course, plays a second role: after appointment, one's performance constitutes the grounds for reward and punishment. When people are given their just deserts, differences in wealth and status follow: "To bestow ranks and emoluments, flags and badges, is to differentiate between achievements as well as to distinguish between the worthy and unworthy" (227:6, L2:80). Thus Han Fei, though loath to accept a noble class privileged by inheritance or birthright, is himself no Shen Nung egalitarian. The Legalist state is very much a hierarchical bureaucracy that demands proper behavior in keeping with one's station. "'Righteousness' refers to the manners of ruler and minister, superior and inferior, the distinction between father and son, high and low. . . . The minister serves the ruler properly; the inferior comforts the superior properly; the son serves the father properly. . . ." (96:3, L1:171). Han Fei, like the author of the *Boshu*, believes that people will not begrudge others their success if it is earned: "High and low do not trespass against each other; the fool and wise keep the scale and stand in perfect balance" (24:2, L1:41).

Yet unlike the author of the *Boshu*, Han Fei does not ground the social order in the natural order or claim that the particular class distinctions and sociopolitical hierarchy is inherent in nature or somehow "natural." In fact, Han Fei maintains that many orders are possible depending on the mix of rewards and punishments. If one alters the structure of costs and benefits, people, as rational self-interested calculators, will reassess their plans and adjust their behavioral responses accordingly. "If the ruler is fond of celebrating scholar-recluses from rocky caves and employs them in the court, then warriors will neglect their duties at the camps; if the superior esteems learned men, with country scholars residing at court, then farmers will relax their efforts in the fields" (210:4, 2:53). As noted earlier, Han Fei cautions the ruler that should his preferences become known, sycophants will modify their actions and speech to please the ruler. To make his point, Han Fei tells the amusing story of a king whose penchant for purple clothes led to so many people wearing them that the price of purple material exceeded that of white by five times. Following the advice of one of his ministers, the king issued a statement that he found purple clothes offensive. Within three days, no one in the state was found wearing purple.[42]

Therefore, although both Huang-Lao and Legalism favor bureaucratic meritocracies, the underlying justification and motivation for their respective systems differs dramatically. Whereas Huang-Lao grounds its social order in the predetermined natural order, Han Fei relies on the self-interest of humans and the behavioral technique of rewards and punishments to bring about a desired order.

The Ruler and the State

In the Huang-Lao system, there can be but one ruler. With this, Han Fei emphatically concurs: "Without a sovereign, it is not possible to effect sociopolitical order" (272:8, L2:155). Further, in light of the historical realities of the Warring States, neither the author of the *Boshu* nor Han Fei believes that multiple, independent sovereign states will exist peacefully side by side. War is sure to break out. Like his Huang-Lao counterpart,

Han Fei maintains that the only way to put an end to the constant feuding of the warlords and restore peace and order is to unify the empire, if need be by military means. "If the people attend to duties and officials are in good order, the state will be rich; if the state is rich, the army will be strong. In consequence, the enterprise of hegemonic ruler will be realized. To be a hegomonic ruler is the greatest benefit of a ruler of men" (319:16, L2:240).

Passages such as this might lead one to conclude along with one commentator that "the business of the Legalist state, at its fullest development by Han Fei, is primarily war."[43] Yet although if left no alternative Han Fei will resort to military might to unify the empire, this is clearly not his first choice. Han Fei states in no uncertain terms that where the ruler is overly fond of war and seeks to advance his personal cause at the expense of his people and neighboring well-governed states, he puts his own person and his state in danger. "If the sovereign is often angered and fond of resorting to arms, gives short shrift to basic teachings and ventures warfare and invasion heedlessly, then ruin is possible" (80:5, L1:138).

Much to be preferred is for the ruler to rely on Legalist arts of rulership. Having set in motion the interlocking system of laws, rewards, punishments, and accountability, where the ruler refrains from interfering the state will be well-ordered, the officials kept in check, and the people satisfied. Such a state is bound to prevail over its competitors. In peace, members of other states, pursuing self-interest, will come in search of a better life. In war, it is sure to be victorious because people will lay down their lives in defense—if not out of loyalty, then for the sake of reward. Indicative of his preference for political techniques rather than military might, Han Fei concludes the preceding passage calling for a unified empire by declaring that "if the ruler is not benevolent and the ministers loyal, hegemony cannot be attained" (320:4, L2:240).

Although no warmonger, Han Fei does not limit the ruler's ability to deploy troops as severely as does the author of the *Boshu*. In the end, it is for Han Fei the ruler who determines what is and what is not a just war. He is advised to give due weight to his ministers' advice. But ultimately he makes the decision in light of his own best judgment as to what would be best for the state—or so Han Fei hopes. A Huang-Lao ruler, on the other hand, at least in theory is constrained by the objective natural order. Having eliminated personal considerations, he directly discovers the course to be followed, waging war only when sanctioned by the Way.

The Legalist ruler, not bound by a predetermined natural order, has far greater powers than does his Huang-Lao counterpart. He has the final say on such matters as whether and when to declare war, change a law, or issue a pardon. To explain why it is absolutely essential that there be but one ruler with ultimate authority, Han Fei provides the following analogy: "If the taste, whether sour or sweet, salty or bland, is not judged by the mouth of the sovereign but determined by the chef, then all the cooks will slight the ruler and revere the chef. . . . Similarly, if the government of the state, whether right or wrong, is not judged by the sovereign's own techniques but determined by his favorites, then the ministers and inferiors will slight the ruler and revere the favorites" (329:11, L2:256). In the absence of any foundational standards, it is the one with the power that defines the rules of the game. Han Fei is for this reason unyielding in his conviction that power not be shared. The ruler, moreover, must take care to zealously guard his power because others are more than willing to take full advantage of every little opportunity to advance their own cause: "Authority and position should not be lent to anybody. If the sovereign loses one, the ministers would turn that one into a hundred" (179:5, L2:1). As soon as power is split, disorder results as people cater to the whims of the different power brokers. If left unattended, factions will continue to develop their respective power bases until they become strong enough to challenge the ruler. Herein lies the seeds of chaos.

Indeed, one senses in Han Fei the intense dread of civil war felt so acutely by Hobbes. Both men personally experienced the misery of social disorder and internal strife. And both responded by calling for a sovereign with extraordinary powers who would have the political authority and military strength to quash rebellion, impose order, and ensure stability. The danger, as their intellectual heirs are quick to point out, is that one exchanges the misery of civil war for the horrors of despotism.[44] Much as it is left to Locke and others to rein in the Hobbesian leviathan, so does it fall to disciples of Huang-Lao to impose constraints on Han Fei's Legalist ruler.

The Ruler and His Ministers

One of the most obvious differences between the political philosophies of Huang-Lao and Han Fei centers on the relation of ruler to his ministers. As observed earlier, the Huang-Lao ruler is ever eager to consult his advisers. He is portrayed as an open-minded, sympathetic listener willing to work with his subordinates. Together, ruler and officials chart a course that accords with the Way and wins the hearts of the people.

In stark contrast, Han Fei speaks of the ruler-minister relation as a constant battle. "The Yellow Emperor had a saying: 'Superior and inferior wage one hundred battles a day.' The inferior conceals his self-interested tricks which he uses to test the superior; the superior manipulates rules and measures to control the inferiors. . . . If the superior loses one or two inches, the inferior will gain eight or sixteen feet" (34:10, L1:60). In addition to the graphic image of ruler and minister locked in hand to hand combat, this passage is significant in that it contains one of Han Fei's few substantive references to the Yellow Emperor, and reveals his attempt to recast the Yellow Emperor in a Legalist mold. Not only is the Yellow Emperor, contrary to the standard depiction, the spokesperson for an adversary relation between ruler and minister. It is even suggested that his underlying motivation for establishing a system of rules and measures is not compliance with the normative Way but to ward off challenges to one's power base: as a purely practical matter, given the different agendas of ruler and ministers, the former must keep the latter in line by holding them to the law and demanding performance of stipulated duties.

That Han Fei sees the relation between ruler and minister as one of diametrically opposed short-term interests is beyond question. "The interests of rulers and ministers mutually differ. . . . The sovereign's interests lie in having able persons appointed to office, the minister's in securing employment without any abilities; the ruler's in awarding rank and salary for work done, the minister's in obtaining wealth and honor without any achievements; the ruler's in having heroic men exerting their abilities, the minister's in having their friends and partisans serve self-seeking purposes" (59:6, L1:104).

It is tempting to interpret the Legalist relationship between ruler and minister as totally one-sided. In fact, many commentators, as we have seen, do so. Power after all, is concentrated in the hands of the ruler. And Han Fei does on occasion speak as if the ministers were simply the ruler's tools to be used in service of his own personal rather than the state's interests: "It is the ministers who do the toil; it is the ruler who gets the spoil. This is the everlasting principle of the worthy sovereign" (18:16, L1:31).

Yet to read Han Fei as an apologist for a despotic sovereign would be a mistake. Han Fei's policy of nonintervention by the ruler (*wu wei*) while the ministers actively carry out the day-to-day business of the government (*you wei* 有為) is designed not primarily to further the personal interests of the ruler but to hide his weaknesses; it is to prevent the ministers from exploiting the ineptness of an average ruler.

No doubt the Legalist ruler-minister relation is based not on loyalty but on the more mundane and practical consideration of maximization of one's ends: the ruler wants more from his ministers; the ministers want more from their ruler. As a result, there is on-going negotiation and jockeying for position as both sides continually calculate costs and benefits.

The ruler employs his ministers with a calculating mind; the minister serves the ruler with a calculating mind. Their interaction is one of mutual calculation. The minister does not harm his person to benefit the state; the ruler does not harm the state to benefit the minister. The reality of the minister is to see harm to himself as unbeneficial; the reality of the ruler is to see harm to the state as something other than the parental-like conduct expected of the ruler. The ruler and minister, through rational calculation, work together. (93:14, L1:168)

The point to be underscored, however, is that out of the conflict of interests emerges a predictable and mutually beneficial working relationship between ruler and ministers. The ruler's desire to further the interest of the state coupled with the self-interestedness of the ministers makes rational assessment of behavior and ipso facto a stable social organization possible. All parties—the ruler, ministers, and people—enjoy the benefits of peace and stability. In addition, because the rules are stipulated in advance, both ministers and ordinary persons alike gain the psychological comfort of knowing what to expect. They can plan their lives without fear that the rules will be changed in mid-game depending on the whims of whomever happens to be in charge.

Thus the Legalist ruler and minister in their own antagonistic way form a symbiotic relationship: the ruler is dependent on his ministers for advice; the ministers are dependent on their ruler for rewards. Each wanting what the other has to offer, they cooperate. "To bring the empire under one rule and call nine conferences of the feudal lords was a brilliant achievement. However, it was neither entirely due to the ability of the ruler nor entirely due to the abilities of the ministers" (275:16, L2:161). In the end, the behind-the-scenes management style of the Legalist ruler in conjunction with the system of automatic rewards and punishments enhances the prospects for good government by stimulating competition among the ministers. Each minister hopes to further his own self-interest by being rewarded for policies that the ruler believes will further the interests of the state. The ruler need but sit back and allow his ministers to make and debate proposals. If no plan emerges as clearly superior, the ruler makes the final determination as to the best of the available alternatives.

Of course, the system will serve the interests of the people only if the ruler himself seeks to serve those interests. If he is interested in his own rather than the people's ends, then he will choose and his ministers devise plans to meet those ends. For all of Han Fei's political acumen and insight into the less than ideal character of human beings, he seriously overestimates the willingness of the average ruler to serve the public. As the example of Qin Shi Huang Di demonstrates, not all rulers will put the interests of the people first—and when they do not the results can be tragic. Yet Han Fei nevertheless intends the ruler and the Legalist system as whole to serve the people.

The Ruler and the People

One would suspect in light of the virulent attacks on Han Fei that it would be all but impossible to produce textual evidence reflecting the ruler's concern for the people or the notion that government is to serve the people. But on surprisingly numerous occasions, Han Fei voices precisely such views.[45] For instance, he explicitly states that a ruler is sure to fail unless he wins the hearts of the masses: "The factors in the intelligent ruler's success are four: the first is said to be 'natural timeliness'; the second, 'the hearts of the people'; the third, 'technical ability;' the fourth, 'power of position'. . . . When the ruler wins the hearts of the people, he elevates himself without being raised. . . . Because he is upheld by the masses with united hearts, he is glorious . . ." (154:16, L1:276). Further, Han Fei declares that to be a morally good ruler, one must look after the needs of his people: "Who takes no notice of the welfare of the masses cannot be called benevolent or righteous" (270:9, L2:151). In fact, Han Fei insists that to be a virtuous ruler one must pursue the benefit of the people rather than one's own interests: "If the sovereign neither has to apply penalties at home nor to work to the advantage of his own investments abroad, the masses will multiply and prosper. When the masses multiply and prosper, their savings and stockpiles will swell. To have the masses multiply and prosper and savings and stockpiles swell is called to possess virtue" (105:3, L1:186).

Han Fei, ever the realist, realizes that people are self-interested. Thus he cannot simply ask them to work for the good of the state out of sheer altruism. "As to why the masses work for me, it is not because of my love that they work for me, but because of my power of position. Suppose I discard my position and attempt to win their hearts with love. Then, as soon as I happen to slacken my love, they will no longer work for me. Therefore, I chuck away the policy of love" (254:4, L2:126).

Rather than cajoling the people with kindness or beseeching them with impassioned rhetoric, the Legalist ruler holds fast to the twin handles of reward and punishment. But he does so not to exploit the people for his own ends. On the contrary. The ruler strictly enforces the law and reliably doles out punishment and reward because to do so is in the best interest of the people. "The sage in governing the masses considers the basics, does not acquiesce to their desires, but seeks their benefit and nothing more. Therefore, the penalty he inflicts is not due to any hatred for the masses but based on his love of them. . . . The triumph of punishments is the harbinger of order. The abundance of rewards is the basis of chaos" (365:5, 2:326).

The truly benevolent ruler, the one who sincerely has the interests of his people at heart, is not afraid to spare the rod lest he spoil the child. As the father of the people, the ruler must perform the unenviable but necessary role of disciplinarian.

A mother's love of her child is twice that of a father's but the father enforces orders among children ten times better than a mother does. Officials have no love for the masses but they enforce orders among them ten thousand times better than parents do. Parents heap up their love but their orders come to naught. Officials rely on authority and strictness and the masses listen and obey. Thus, you can easily make the choice between strictness and love. . . . The ruler neither loves nor benefits the masses but demands their death and toil and that his orders be carried out. The intelligent ruler knows this. Thus he does not cultivate a heart of mercy and love but augments his position of authority and strictness. (320:9, L2:241)

In the long run, the establishment of an orderly state benefits the people the most—though their short-term interests might blind them to this. Consequently, the enlightened ruler must have the farsightedness, self-confidence, and wherewithal to withstand immediate pleas for leniency and special favors. "The ruler must be intelligent enough to know how to effect sociopolitical order and severe enough to ensure it comes about. Therefore, even if he has to act contrary to the hearts and minds of the masses, he will establish an orderly government" (87:11, L1:154).

Of course, one could always claim that Han Fei is simply spinning an elaborate ruse to conceal his true intent of advancing the cause of the ruler: winning the hearts of the people is merely a means to the ruler's own end; the ruler rewards the people and is frugal in the use of their labor to keep them from rebelling;[46] laws and punishments, far from being a necessary response to the failure of politics of harmony, are tools for manipulating the people to the benefit of the ruler . . . No amount of textual evidence to the contrary can refute such a cynical claim. However, when given a charitable reading, Han Fei comes across as a sincere if hard-nosed political theorist who has the interests of the people at heart. His Legalist government is first and foremost a government for the people, not the ruler.

Why then have so many interpreted Han Fei as an champion of

tyrants? One reason may be that most commentators lump Han Fei together with Shang Yang and discuss both simultaneously under the rubric *Legalist*. The political philosophy of Shang Yang does in fact subordinate the interests of the people to the ruler: "In government if you introduce policies people hate, the people are weakened; if policies they enjoy, they are strengthened. The people being weak, the state is strong, the people being strong, the state is weak."[47]

A second explanation is that in practice Han Fei's policies do come to serve the despotic ends of the tyrant Qin Shi Huang Di. Given Han Fei's historical connections to the Qin ruler, some have apparently concluded, his writings to the contrary, that he supports Qin Shi Huang Di's policies and actions. Yet surely it is often the case that rulers ignore their advisers' counsel. One can hardly hold Han Fei responsible for all of the excesses of Qin.

A final possible reason for the unflattering portrait of Han Fei is that he favors a morality of, and a rule by, law. In contrast to the impassioned rhetoric and utopian visions of his predecessors' morality of virtues and politics of harmony, Han Fei's down-to-earth call for strict laws and reliable punishments comes across as hopelessly mundane and uninspiring. But had Han Fei's Legalist policies worked, their matter of fact practicality would have been a plus rather than a fatal drawback.

This is not to say that there are no valid criticisms of Han Fei's philosophy or that those who have taken Han Fei to task are completely without basis. Far from it. Han Fei can be criticized on many grounds. But that his is a system designed primarily to protect the paramount interests of the ruler is not one of them.

From the Huang-Lao perspective, however, that a tyrant like Qin Shi Huang Di is able to turn Han Fei's Legalist system to his own despotic ends, although not making Han Fei a Qin loyalist, does attest to the theoretical flaws of Legalism. By allowing the ruler the final word, Legalism lends theoretical legitimacy to the excesses of a Qin Shi Huang. As sovereign, he has the powers to declare war, establish harsh laws, and impose draconian penalties. The failure to build into the system sufficient safeguards against the possibility of tyrants is for Huang-Lao exponents the most egregious shortcoming of Legalism.

Han Fei could argue in his own defense that his policy of *wu wei* by the ruler while the ministers *you wei* effectively reduces the ruler's role. It is the ministers who run the government; they make the day-to-day decisions. More figurehead than policy maker, the ruler simply follows the advice of his ministers, verifies that performances match stipulated duties, and refrains from disrupting the self-regulating governmental institutions with his personal views. Granted, Han Fei would allow, even the Legalist system, designed to be as foolproof as possible, cannot withstand a "fool" the likes of Qin Shi Huang Di. He is a contemporary Jie and Zhou. But surely one should not judge Legalism on the basis of a single extreme case. Legalist policies, after all, are intended for average rulers, not a once-in-a-blue-moon sage or villain.

Were the failures of Legalism as rare as a Jie or a Zhou, one might be able to accept the argument that the technique of *wu wei* is a sufficient check on the power of the ruler. But for Han Fei's *wu wei* technique to work, the ruler must be willing and able to remain behind the scenes. How many rulers will be able to resist imposing their own views on the course of political events? Those who battle their way through the mine field of Warring States politics to reach the lofty position of ruler are not likely to be timid wallflowers. Rulers in general tend to be decisive, strong-willed, self-confident, opinionated individuals. On the other hand, they are still mere mortals and, like the overwhelming majority of mortals, in Han Fei's view, all too often more interested in advancing their private ends than serving the state.

When all is said and done, Han Fei's Legalism fails for much the same reason as does Confucianism: there are no checks on the power of those in charge. If anything, by concentrating all of the power in the hands of the ruler, Han Fei exacerbates rather than alleviates the problem—the intent of his rule by law and practical arts of rulership notwithstanding.[48] The Huang-Lao response is to constrain the power of the ruler and provide a theoretical and moral foundation for a rule of law by grounding the sociopolitical order in the normatively predetermined natural order. Ultimate authority lies not with the ruler but with the Way. The ruler is merely the medium through which the Way becomes articulated and enacted. To understand the origins of Huang-Lao's Way, however, one must turn to the *Dao De Jing* of Lao Zi.

VI. The Daoist Ways of Lao Zi and Zhuang Zi

In Chapters II and III, I examined Huang-Lao philosophy as presented in the *Boshu*. I then began to support my reading by expanding the scope, demonstrating how Huang-Lao interpreted as foundational naturalism fits the broader intellectual context. I did so by first comparing it to one of the leading ideologies of the time, Confucianism. I argued that Confucius influenced Huang-Lao in a positive sense through his emphasis on a moral government of virtuous rulers who serve the interests of the people. Confucius's greatest influence, however, is negative. Huang-Lao rejects as inadequate Confucius's philosophical pragmatism, politics of harmony, ethical coherence theory, and jurisprudential rule of man. Rather than pragmatism, Huang-Lao favors foundational naturalism; to offset the inability of Confucius's politics of harmony and ethical coherence systems to provide univocal, universally acceptable solutions to conflicts, Huang-Lao opts for a moral order grounded in a predetermined natural order; to curtail the discretionary latitude of and potential for abuse of power by sage-judges in Confucius's legal system, Huang-Lao sides with Legalists such as Han Fei in advancing a law–based rule.

However, as argued in the last chapter, Huang-Lao's rule of law differs in fundamental ways from Han Fei's rule by law. Huang-Lao takes exception to the sweeping powers ceded the Legalist sovereign. As a result, the author rejects Han Fei's legal positivism in favor of a natural law system that acts as a theoretical constraint on the ruler. Law is not what the ruler says it is. Rather, it is discovered in and determined by the Way. Whereas Legalist centralism challenges hereditary powers of the aristocrats, Huang-Lao foundational naturalism serves to curtail both aristocratic and imperial powers by subjugating everyone to an objective natural standard.

In this chapter, I examine the relation between Huang-Lao and the classical Daoism of Lao Zi and Zhuang Zi. Many have noted that there are obvious and important differences between them in regards to politics, law, and ethics. I argue that these differences grow out of disparities in their respective epistemologies and conceptions of dao. Nevertheless, Huang-Lao's understanding of dao as the natural Way is an interpretation and development of Lao Zi's dao, and its correspondence epistemology based on overcoming self-bias owes much to Lao Zi's meditative epistemology in which one *discovers* dao, albeit dao understood as an emergent rather than a predetermined order.

As with Lao Zi and Confucius and *contra* Huang-Lao, Zhuang Zi takes dao to be emergent rather than predetermined. Nevertheless, in not allowing that one directly discovers the way, he does not privilege the meditative or epistemological experience as do Lao Zi and Huang-Lao. Though he does allow that meditation can bring about a pure consciousness experience in which the ego-self and indeed all distinctions are eliminated, he does not believe that this experience automatically culminates in a harmonious order in practice. The way the sage advances as a result of the meditative experience is but one more way—one more "*this* that goes by circumstance." This is not to say that in practice any theory or any way is as good as any other. I will take exception to the reading that takes Zhuang Zi to be an "anything-goes" relativist. Whereas Zhuang Zi does not want to privilege any particular standards, epistemic experiences, or ways (daos) as a priori or infallibly correct, he does allow that some ways are pragmatically better in light of our social and personal practices, attitudes, ends, and so forth. At any rate, his epistemology—his antifoundationalism and the belief that dao is realized rather than discovered—makes his position less attractive to Huang-Lao than that of Lao Zi, explaining in part perhaps why Huang-Lao is 'Huang-Lao' and not 'Huang-Zhuang.'

1. Lao Zi's Way

Examining the issue of what it means to *zhi dao* (知道—to "know" dao) is one way to illumine fundamental differences in the philosophies of Huang-Lao, Lao Zi, Zhuang Zi, and for that matter, Confucius. Roughly, the four positions can be summarized as follows:

- For Huang-Lao, *zhi dao* is to discover a predetermined, natural order.
- For Lao Zi, *zhi dao* is to discover an emergent order.
- For Zhuang Zi, *zhi dao* is to realize an emergent order.
- For Confucius, *zhi* (*ren* 人/仁) *dao* is to realize an emergent (human) order.

Several points merit comment. First, to present the positions in this way is to oversimplify. Each of these summary statements stands in need of both qualification and elaboration. Nevertheless, this overview may serve as a heuristic guide to the ensuing discussion. Further, laying out the respective positions in this way reveals, as one would expect, that the position of Lao Zi shares more in common with that of Huang-Lao than does either that of Zhuang Zi or Confucius. What may be surprising to some, given the historical tendency to portray Confucianism and Daoism in starkly contrastive hues,[1] is the similarity between Confucius and Lao Zi and, to an even greater extent, between Confucius and Zhuang Zi. I shall argue that, although perhaps surprising, this reading is justified on further reflection and that the differences between Confucius and his Daoist counterparts have tended to be overstated. Finally, and perhaps least surprisingly, with respect to epistemology Huang-Lao and Confucius represent opposite ends of the philosophical continuum. As limiting cases, their positions constitute benchmarks for comparison and hence will be clarified before turning to Lao Zi and Zhuang Zi.

Confucius: Realizing an Emergent Human Way

As observed, dao for Confucius represents an order that emerges out of the particular context. That humans must create their own way rather than simply replicate a predetermined order is succinctly captured in Confucius's dictum, "it is human beings who extend the way, not the way which extends human beings" (15:29). For Confucius, dao is primarily the human way (*ren dao*). It is the achievement of interpersonal and sociopolitical harmony. The achievement, or realization, of harmony involves the *li* (rites)—broadly construed to include the normative standards and institutions of society. The *li*, together with the context-specific goals, attitudes, and beliefs of the particular parties, are subject to the discretionary judgment (*yi*) of the sage. In reflecting on how best to realize harmony, the sage employs the method of *shu*, or "analogical projection," whereby one puts oneself in the other person's shoes, as it were, and then reasons on the basis of one's past experiences and accumulated wisdom what would be the best in this instance. The sage, having applied his refined sense of what is appropriate to the *li* and the particulars of the given situation, then relies on his *de*—the moral credibility and respect gained from being a virtuous, cultivated person—to inspire in people the willingness to pursue a harmonious resolution to the conflict. The sage's *de* is, in effect, his storehouse of moral credit, earned over the years through repeated demonstration of wisdom and perceived excellence, which he draws on in times of conflict to persuade people and win them over to his own vision of how best to balance the various concerns to achieve the highest quality harmony possible.

Given this process and the notion of dao as an emergent way rather than a predetermined order, to *zhi dao* or "know the way" for Confucius cannot but entail an epistemology that differs radically from that of Huang-Lao and from that of many Western philosophers. Roger Ames has examined the differences between knowing in a Confucian sense and knowing as understood by many within the Western tradition. In highlighting the following six points, I draw on his insights.[2]

First, *zhi* is best understood as performative presentation, as a constructive making of the world, rather than as re-presentation of ontologically privileged objects that our mind copies. We are interested participants in the process rather than disinterested spectators. We participate in bringing the world into existence by carving up the flux of reality according to our traditions, experiences, goals and so forth. In short, we realize the world rather than simply discover it ready-made. We make the world real, not only in the sense that the world in which we live—the world we experience and take to be real—is the one we construct out of the flux, but also in the sense that how we construct the world actually affects the world that comes into existence. We are instrumental in bringing about the world in which we live.

Second, and correlated to the first, *zhi* is better understood in terms of images rather than ideas or conceptions. For the purposes of this distinction, an idea is a representation of the essential structure of the object in the mind of the subject. By contrast, imaging in this view is the act of generating meaning by circumscribing, isolating, and positioning things. The Confucian world of images is one of fluid boundaries where the thing known is defined, distinguished, or carved from the continuous flux of which it is a part according to the context-specific particulars of the perceiver-imager-knower.[3] Things are defined, and known, relationally. Knowing is not having an idea in the mind that captures the defining trait of a discrete object, that which makes that thing *that* thing and nothing else.[4] In Confucian epistemology, what a thing is depends on the perspective from which it is known or imaged.

Third, *zhi* is historical. Knowledge for Confucius is not the result of an operation of a privileged faculty of an individual mind. Knowledge is culturally and historically constructed, emerging out of the social and cultural dynamics of experience in the world. Our traditions and past experiences affect not only what we image, what we realize, but how we assess those epistemic experiences. What constitutes knowledge in a Confucian world depends on the traditions that inform it and serve as epistemic standards by which to judge new claims to knowledge.

There is, then, a social as well as a historical dimension to knowledge in the Confucian world. How we image the world is influenced by social practices, by the distinctions made in our language, for example. Further, for Confucius, the pursuit of "knowledge for its own sake" gives way to knowledge to serve the ends of society and the persons that make up society. To know is not so much to *know that* as to *know how*. The valuative standards are implicit in performance. The status and value of knowledge is a function of its ability to foster social cohesiveness. From Confucius's perspective, the utmost *zhi* is knowing how to realize social harmony, how to balance competing interests and resolve conflicts harmoniously.

There is, fifth, a moral dimension to *zhi*. Knowing how to promote harmony is a moral end, a moral project. Confucian *zhi* is knowing what is appropriate in a particular context. It is not the discovery of external, value-neutral, objective truths. Standards, be they moral or epistemic, are for Confucius relative to a particular community.

Finally, Confucian *zhi* draws on both the cognitive and the affective. This distinction comes in many guises: thinking-feeling, reason-passion, mentality-sentimentality, thought-emotion, fact-value, logic-rhetoric, rational-irrational. Many epistemologies tend to privilege the cognitive over the affective, the mind over the heart. Significantly, *xin* 心 in Chinese is the heart-mind, the locus of both the cognitive and the affective. There is for Confucius no clear separation between thinking and feeling: thinking is a modality of feeling; feeling is a modality of thinking. As noted previously, we are not disinterested spectators pursuing knowledge for its own sake (knowledge that). Rather, we are real people with real interests and needs pursuing knowledge as a way to meet those needs.

Huang-Lao: Discovering a Predetermined Way

In contrast to the emergent way of Confucius, the dao of Huang-Lao is the predetermined Way. Dao refers to a constant, though not static, rule governed natural order. The social order is implicate in the natural order. Rather than being realized contextually, it simply needs to be discovered and instantiated.

Epistemologically, *zhi* entails then not a process of realization but discovery of an antecedent order. As discussed earlier,[5] one proceeds from *xu jing* to *wu si* to *shen ming* to *jian zhi bu huo*; that is, the "emptying" or overcoming of subjective bias leads to tranquility, which ensures impartiality, which in turn gives rise to intuitive clarity, which results in apprehension and understanding/discovery of the Way without confusion. In short, one discovers the objective order by eliminating all subjectivity. The historical, social, and affective dimensions of knowing that play such an influential and constructive role in the Confucian process of realizing the world are eviscerated, if not eradicated, in the Huang-Lao process of discovery of dao cum natural order.

In contrast to Confucius's *zhi* as performative presentation of a way that emerges in and through the process of realization, Huang-Lao *zhi* is representation of a predetermined order. As we have seen, for the author of the *Boshu*, each discrete thing comes into existence replete with a form and name. It is the task of the individual to ascertain the correct form and name and to order society accordingly. Huang-Lao *zhi* is, consequently, more of a knowing that than a knowing how. Huang-Lao deemphasizes the performative aspect of knowing in that performance—that is, replication of the predetermined order—is determined by knowledge, by what one discovers. Replication or instantiation is a unidirectional process. Realization is bidirectional: how one interacts with the world affects one's understanding of the world, which at the same time affects how one performs in the world—which affects the world that is created, and so on.[6]

One point which Huang-Lao and Confucian epistemologies share is that both allow for a moral dimension. If anything, there is a stronger sense of moral order in that for Huang-Lao to discover the Way is to discover the normatively correct order. Indeed, the attainment of moral certainty through the epistemological process explains much of its appeal to the author who is seeking something more in the way of standards than the cultivated moral judgment of the sage.

Yet, although there is a moral component to both epistemologies, the nature and role of morality differs dramatically. The different natures of the moral systems has been discussed at length. Suffice it to say that for Huang-Lao, the moral order is predetermined whereas, for Confucius, it is something that is achieved contextually. As for the respective roles of morality in the epistemological process, they reflect the difference between unidirectionality and bidirectionality just mentioned. Huang-Lao discovery and instantiation of the moral order is unidirectional—hence the label *transcendent*.[7] Realization, on the other hand, is bidirectional: one's moral beliefs affect one's understanding of the world and one's understanding of the world informs and shapes one's moral beliefs about what constitutes a harmonious order.

Having sketched briefly the limiting cases, I will argue in section 1 that Lao Zi's position is a hybrid of the Confucian and Huang-Lao position. That is, the sage discovers a way to harmonize the various interests through a process of emptying and tranquility similar to that of the author of the *Boshu*. However, whereas Huang-Lao epistemology entails a direct discovery of a predetermined order, in the classical Daoist system, dao is not a predetermined single order. Rather, dao, as for Confucius, is a constantly changing, harmonious order that allows for various forms of expression depending on the particular circumstances. Lao Zi, in effect, seeks to attain the openness of the Confucian order while at the same time securing the certainty of Huang-Lao. He does so by modifying Confucius's pragmatic, coherence epistemology. The sage does not rely on fallible judgment of what is best all things considered to bring about a harmonious order, but by engaging in the (meditative) process of emptying, directly intuits the best way to proceed.

Normatively, Lao Zi, taking dao as emergent, sides with Confucius and *contra* Huang-Lao in favoring politics of harmony. He rejects rule ethics, codified laws, absolute values in favor of a context-specific solution agreeable to all. However, unlike Confucius's politics of harmony, that of Lao Zi is wider in scope, embracing within its domain of concern all the myriad things of the universe.

In section 2, I argue that Zhuang Zi also sides with Confucius and Lao Zi on normative issues in preferring politics of harmony to a rule of codified laws and a morally predetermined order. Further, like Lao Zi, his domain of concern extends beyond the narrow anthropocentrism of Confucius.

However, while Zhuang Zi agrees with Lao Zi that dao-order is emergent rather than predetermined, he does not believe that the meditative process of emptying leading to a pure consciousness experience in which there are no images and a fortiori no distinctions automatically informs one how to proceed. At best, it clears the mind of preconceived, limiting ideas, attitudes, distinctions—opening the way for "insight." But in realizing a harmonious order in practice, one inevitably makes distinctions. Any course of action one takes is fallible and, more important, action from a particular perspective may not be compatible, at least initially, with the daos or ways of others. Thus, as for Confucius, a harmonious order remains something to be achieved or realized rather than simply discovered, and hence it cannot be presumed to follow "spontaneously" or "naturally" from the epistemological process.

1.1 Zhi *as Discovery*

Although the *Dao De Jing* has been translated, interpreted, and commented on in more ways by more scholars than any other Chinese work, the role of meditation in Lao Zi's epistemology by and large has been neglected.[8] One reason for this is the inherent obscurity, both of the passages and of the meditative process itself. Consider, for instance, the following:

> Uniting the spiritual and sentient souls and embracing the one, can you not depart from it?
> Concentrating the breath and attaining softness, can you be like a newborn babe?
> Wiping clean the mysterious mirror, can you leave no blemish?
> Loving the people and governing the state, can you not act?
> The gates of heaven opening and closing, can you keep to the role of the female?
> Clear-mindedly penetrating the four quarters, can you be without knowledge?
> It engenders them and rears them.
> It engenders them and yet does not possess them.
> It benefits them yet exacts no retribution.
> It is the elder yet exercises no authority—this is mysterious potency.
> (10)

Assuming the translation to be reasonable, what are we to make of the one? the mysterious mirror? the gates of heaven and earth? What does it mean to not depart from the one? to wipe clean the mysterious mirror? to clear-mindedly penetrate the four quarters and yet be without knowledge? Such murky waters are not for the scholarly faint of heart.

A second possible explanation for the scant attention paid meditation is that it is not clear that it is a necessary condition for discovering dao. Although meditation may be necessary to stop the mind so that all distinctions are eliminated and one returns to the uncarved block, embraces the one, cleanses the mysterious mirror, and so on, it may not be necessary to achieve harmony in praxis. Some people may be able to overcome egoistic desire (*wu yu* 無欲) and to *wu wei* (act nonimpositionally) without having first gone through a meditative process. Indeed, even for those who meditate, for daily living itself to become a form of meditation is often a goal. While the meditative experience of returning to the uncarved block (the pure consciousness event) might continue to be valuable intrinsically, it would not be necessary as a prelude to life as egoless harmony.[9]

Finally, it may also be that Western philosophers have avoided the topic of meditation because it lies beyond the conventional boundary lines of their discipline: meditation is the stuff of religion departments, not of tough-minded philosophers. Of course, the boundary between philosophy and religion is drawn differently in Eastern thought. Meditation is and has historically been a subject of serious philosophical discussion, particularly in the Buddhist tradition. As a Westerner examining Chinese philosophy, one does well to take seriously Chinese sensibilities. Thus, despite the obscurity of the material and the risk of professional marginalization, I will explore rather than ignore the meditation passages in *Lao Zi* and *Zhuang Zi*.

Apophatic Meditation

For Lao Zi, dao is discovered through an *apophatic* as opposed to a *kataphatic* meditative process—that is, one of emptying of all images (thoughts, feelings, and so on) rather than concentration on or filling the mind with images.[10] Others, speaking of *nirodhasamāpatti*—a Buddhist meditation of *śūnyatā* (emptiness)—have referred to this process as "cessation meditation."[11] Lao Zi offers various descriptions:[12]

> In pursuit of learning, one expands daily; in the pursuit of the way, one decreases daily. Decrease it and decrease it again until one arrives at *wu wei* (literally, "nonaction"). One does nothing and nothing is left undone. (48)

> Block the openings, shut the doors, blunt the sharpness, untangle the knots, harmonize the radiance, identify with the common: this is called mysterious sameness. (56)

The immediate goal[13] or end of the meditative process is *xu*: emptiness, vacuity. Lao Zi instructs one to "attain the highest level of emptiness (*xu*); preserve the most profound tranquility (*jing*)" (16). The result is that one discovers the way, described as embracing the one (10), or returning to the uncarved block (1, 37), the mysterious sameness (56), or the infinite (28). The uncarved block, one, mysterious sameness, and infinite are, I suggest, metaphors for what Robert Forman calls the "pure consciousness event," an event or experience "in which one is awake and alert but devoid of any and all objects of consciousness. One entertains therein no feeling, sensation, thought, perception, or even the realization, 'Oh, now I am having an unusual experience.'"[14] It is the state of pure, undifferentiatedness (*wu* 無) as opposed to awareness of and in the distinction-laden phenomenal world (*you* 有).

In this state, one is literally without desires (*wu yu*). To be sure, Lao Zi's notion of *wu yu* allows for various interpretations. On a commonsense level, it refers to moderation rather than complete elimination of desire. There are, generally speaking, two ways to be happy: one is to set high goals and achieve them; the other to lower one's expectations and be content with less, to be satisfied with the simple pleasures of life. Lao Zi favors the latter.

> The five colors make one's eyes blind.
> The five sounds make one's ears deaf.
> The five tastes injure one's palate.
> Riding and hunting make one's mind go wild with excitement.
> Goods hard to come by serve to hinder one's progress.
> Hence the sage is for the belly and not the eye. (12)

For Lao Zi, fame and fortune are cause for concern in that once accustomed to them, one lives in fear of losing them. A cautious person, Lao Zi would appreciate the Japanese proverb that the nail that sticks out gets hammered down. Indeed, he warns that "where gold and jade fill the hall, none of it can be preserved; where one is wealthy, honored, and arrogant, one brings calamity on oneself" (9). Thus he concludes, "he who overcomes others has force; he who overcomes himself is strong; he who knows contentment is rich" (33).

Wu yu connotes not only moderation of desire but also "objectless desire." As David Hall explains, "*wu yu*, as objectless desire, permits enjoyment without attachment—i.e., that kind of feeling in and through another which does not depend upon the objectification of the other and need not lead, therefore, to the desire to manipulate, dominate or control. Such detached emotion is the ground of deference and mutuality which, when combined with *wu-chih* [無知—unprincipled knowing] and *wu-wei* [nonimpositional action], maximizes the possibility of harmonious relationships."[15] Thus interpreted, *wu yu* entails, first, nonegoity: one is not attached to past experiences, conceptions, perceptions—fixed ways of discriminating, of making sense of the booming, buzzing flux of reality—which collectively constitute one's "self." One retains, as it were, an open mind. Second, as *objectless* desire, *wu yu* reflects the Daoist sensibility wherein one does not see other persons or things as mere objects for the exercise of one's power, as means to one's ends. Rather than imposing one's will on a resistant object, one seeks a harmonious order that incorporates, and is defined by, the interests of all concerned parties such that the oppositional self that stands over and against others becomes a collective "we."

I elaborate on this aspect of *wu yu* when I discuss Lao Zi's politics of harmony later. I now want to suggest, however, a third reading of *wu yu*, one that takes seriously the literal rendering, "without desires." Given Lao Zi's apophatic meditative process in which one attains the highest emptiness in returning to dao, the nameless uncarved block,[16] one does well to take Lao Zi at his word when he says one is to be without desires. By eliminating desires, one discovers dao: "The nameless is the beginning of heaven and earth. . . . Constantly without desires one observes thereby its mysteries" (1). In fact, dao as the uncarved block is itself said to be without desires: "The nameless uncarved block is but freedom from desire; being without desire and thereby tranquil (*jing*), the empire will be securely settled of its own accord" (37).

The state of emptiness is not only one of *wu yu* understood literally as absence of all desires but of *wu wei* and *wu zhi*, also to be taken in their literal sense of absence of action and knowledge respectively.[17] To be sure, *wu wei* and *wu zhi*, like *wu yu*, can be variously interpreted. The former is often characterized as "nonimpositional" or "nonassertive action," capturing the way in which the interpersonal and sociopolitical goal of harmony involves accounting for the interests of each of the concerned parties so that all become willing participants in a collective action. *Wu wei* is not the imposition of a given form of behavior but rather behavior that emerges from the creative activities of persons cooperating in the pursuit of a common goal. As for *wu zhi*, Hall suggests that it be read as "unprincipled knowing," "the sort of knowing that does not have recourse to principles as external, determining sources of order."[18] That Lao Zi wishes to avoid understanding *zhi dao* as knowledge of a predetermined order disciplined by constant and universal principles is, I believe, correct. For Lao Zi, *zhi dao* is knowledge of a way that is emerging in the process of being discovered and enacted. It is therefore more context specific and ad hoc than the kind of "principled knowing" to which Hall objects.

Nevertheless, to regard *wu yu* as objectless desire, *wu wei* as nonimpositional action, and *wu zhi* as unprincipled knowing is to focus on the postmeditative praxis aspect of the way. Thusly interpreted, they refer to a way of being, a way of living that one assumes as a result of the meditative process of emptying. Of course, one need not consciously set out to develop an attitude of objectless desire, nonimpositional action, and unprincipled knowing. One is, rather, transformed by the meditative experience.

Before turning to postmeditative praxis, however, it bears underscoring that in terms of the transformative meditative process itself, *wu zhi* is to be understood literally as the absence of knowing: in the state of pure consciousness, there is no knower and nothing known. Hence to talk of

181

one discovering dao is, strictly speaking, inappropriate. There is no "one" to discover, and dao is not a differentiated object of consciousness but rather undifferentiated consciousness itself. That dao is nameless from the standpoint of the meditator in the state of pure consciousness is easily understood: a name is an object of consciousness—were one cognizant of the name *dao*, one would by definition not be in a state of pure consciousness. Of course, one could later refer to undifferentiated consciousness as *dao*. And Lao Zi does so (25). Therefore the issue is not whether dao can *ever* be named but in what sense it is nameless (*wu ming* 無名). This need not be as mysterious as some make it out to be if one recalls that for Lao Zi, to name something is to differentiate it from others things: to name is to carve the uncarved block (32).[19] But dao as the uncarved block is pure undifferentiated consciousness, and hence is name*less* (*wu ming*), though name*able* (*ke ming* 可名) from our everyday, non-pure consciousness, perspective.[20] Lao Zi does not contend that one is to remain permanently in the meditative state of pure consciousness. One inevitably returns to the world. One will then not only be able to give the name *dao* to undifferentiated pure consciousness,[21] but be able to, if not set the empire aright, at least live out one's years.[22]

Dao of Praxis

For Lao Zi, to discover dao is to discover how to live in practice, how to effect harmony. Dao is not only *wu*, the undifferentiated world of pure consciousness, but also *you*, the phenomenal world of differentiated things. The sage experiences both:

> The nameless is the beginning of heaven and earth.
> The named is the mother of the myriad things.
> Hence by constantly having no desires observe its mysteries;
> constantly having desires observe its manifestations.
> These two have different names but the same origin. (1)

One cannot and is not encouraged to remain constantly without desires in a state of pure consciousness. One must also explore dao in the phenomenal world of praxis. "The world has its origins which can be taken as the mother of the world. When you get the mother, use this to know the offspring. When you know the offspring, go back to holding fast to the mother, and to the end of your days you will meet with no danger" (52). The sage uses the meditative state of pure consciousness to inform his practice. Transformed by the meditative process, he encounters no obstacles in his experiences in the everyday world. Should some difficulty arise, or perhaps simply as a matter of habitual practice, he resumes his meditation and returns to the state of pure consciousness. At some point during the meditation, he discovers or becomes aware of an appropriate response to the difficulty confronted in the realm of praxis. He has an insight, as it were; he intuits what to do.

Lao Zi, like the author of the *Boshu*, conflates the attainment of emptiness with the discovery of how to proceed in the world. The sage, through meditation, discovers dao.

> Without going beyond his doors, he knows (*zhi*) the world.
> Without looking out his windows, he sees the heavenly way.
> The further one goes, the less one knows.
> Therefore the sage knows without having to stir,
> is clear without having to see,
> and accomplishes without having to act. (47)

When one "attains the highest levels of emptiness," then one "knows constancy" (16). What does it mean to know constancy? "Knowing harmony is called constancy. And knowing constancy is called clarity (*ming* 明—sometimes translated "enlightenment").[23]

Lao Zi does not clearly distinguish between the attainment of emptiness as a pure consciousness event (*wu*) and as an illuminative event in which one discovers or intuits how to effect harmony in the phenomenal world (*you*). In contrast to Zhuang Zi, the transition from the state of pure consciousness to unprincipled knowledge of how to effect a harmonious order is automatic. For Lao Zi, harmony is, in effect, the default position. If one attains emptiness through the elimination of desires, one discovers harmony.

Once empty, one can effect harmony "spontaneously," "naturally." That is, there is no need for further reflection, cognitive assessment, balancing of alternatives, or generation of new alternatives as there often is for Confucius and, though perhaps to a lesser extent, for Zhuang Zi.[24] The attainment of emptiness is sufficient to know the way. As A. C. Graham says, "[Lao Zi's] Taoism loses all point unless when distinctions cease you do find yourself drawn in the direction which is the Way."[25] At the point of utmost emptiness, one becomes aware of the harmonious way: it then becomes a matter of enacting it.

There is a measure of inevitability, of certainty, to the program that comes from privileging the meditative experience that is absent in the realization of harmony for Confucius and Zhuang Zi. The latter two, given their antifoundational epistemologies, view the process of achieving harmony more as a matter of pulling oneself up by one's bootstraps. There is no infallible mode of experience—meditative or otherwise—in which to ground one's behavior, one's way, one's claim to have discovered the most harmonious order possible. The only certainty that one has that harmony has been attained at all comes from the expressed consensus among the concerned parties that the chosen way does in fact meet their standards.

Significantly, the certainty of Lao Zi's epistemology, although absent in that of Confucius and Zhuang Zi, is characteristic of Huang-Lao epistemology. In both, one discovers or intuits dao and does so as a result of becoming empty (*xu*) and tranquil (*jing*). There is even a passage in the *Shiliu Jing* section of the *Boshu* that evokes the image of meditation. The Yellow Emperor, fretting that he has not yet gained personal knowledge, asks his assistant Ran Yan what he should do. Ran replies, "dive deeply into the abyss in order to seek your inner form" (65:92a).

For the author of the *Boshu*, however, the result of becoming *xu* is the direct discovery or intuition of the Way, not as undifferentiated pure consciousness, but already differentiated in terms of *xing ming* (forms and names), *fa* (laws), and *li* (principles). This is a difference in emphasis: the pure consciousness experience of the *Lao Zi* in which one is empty of all images receives little, if any, attention in the *Boshu*.[26] But it also signals a more fundamental difference in the respective positions. Huang-Lao stresses the illuminative character of the emptying process because that is where the importance lies: in the discovery of a predetermined order. It is primarily concerned with getting the sociopolitical order right, with discovering the Way. By contrast, although the emptying process is illuminative for Lao Zi, he gives considerable weight to the meditative, pure consciousness aspect to call attention to the need to be open minded in a world that is open ended. It is during the pure consciousness event that one is most open minded, and hence most able to respond appropriately to an ever-changing world.[27]

Further, for the author of the *Boshu*, although one discovers the way by emptying oneself of subjective bias, one is not necessarily transformed as a person in the process. In fact, the author of the *Boshu* states: "one who sees beyond the standards acts but cannot be transformed" (58:70b).[28] For Lao Zi, on the other hand, the emptying process is both illuminative and transformative. That it is illuminative means that the foundational epistemological experience of pure consciousness will infallibly inform one as to what is needed to effect harmony: in the emptying process, one discovers not just dao as undifferentiatedness (*wu*) but dao as harmony in praxis (*you*). But knowing what to do is not to do it: to go from discovery of dao as harmony in praxis to the actual effecting of harmony is another step. It is the transformative aspect of the process that ensures that one will effect the discovered way to harmony.

Transformation may, however, be a more gradual process than the sudden illumination-discovery of what to do in the particular circumstances.[29] As a result, performance may lag behind. This explains in part why Lao Zi devotes such attention to politics of harmony and the attitudes—*wu yu* (nonegoic, objectless desire), *wu wei* (nonimpositional action), *wu zhi* (unprincipled knowing), *bu zheng* (不爭—noncontention), *bu xian* (不先—not taking the lead), and so on—most conducive to effecting harmony in postmeditative praxis.[30]

The Politics of Harmony

For Lao Zi, meditation in one's room must give way to and inform one's return to the everyday world. When one both discovers what to do and is transformed by the process, harmony follows in due course. Therefore the sage says,

I *wu wei* and the people are transformed of themselves.
I prefer tranquility (*jing*) and the people put themselves in proper order.
I do not intervene and the people prosper of themselves.
I am without desires (*wu yu*) and the people themselves become simple like the uncarved block. (57)

One who is transformed in and by the process of attaining emptiness gains a potency (*de*) that ensures that, at minimum, one's own life will be harmonious.

One who possesses *de* in abundance is comparable to a newborn babe:
    poisonous insects will not sting him;
    ferocious beasts will not maul him;
    predatory birds will not snatch him up . . .
He howls all day long but does not become hoarse,
this is the utmost of harmony. (55)[31]

One derives from the experience an almost magic-like power, a mysterious potency (*xuan de* 玄德).[32] One who accumulates this potency will be able to overcome all of life's obstacles (59), even avoid premature death (50). Further, such a person possesses a kind of charisma that draws others to him: "Hold fast to the great form and all the world will throng to you. Thronging to you and yet meeting no harm, all find contentment in concord and equanimity" (35). The greater his *de*, the more people he is able to bring together, and consequently the larger the domain in which he is able to effect harmony:

> Cultivating it in his person, his *de* will be genuine.
> Cultivating it in his family, his *de* will be ample.
> Cultivating it in his neighborhood, his *de* will be enduring.
> Cultivating it in his state, his *de* will be abundant.
> Cultivating it in the world, his *de* will be pervasive. (54)

The possessor of *de* is able to attract others to him because of his ability to effect harmony. Yet his role in the process is that of a facilitator as opposed to a director or dictator. He acts in a nonimpositional (*wu wei*) fashion. He does not seek to force or compel others to obey, but rather hopes to induce them to participate willingly. It bears noting that, while the Confucian sage shares this goal, his approach differs slightly. Confucius places greater faith in the ability of the sage to persuade others of the merits of his vision through reasoned discussion, whereas Lao Zi relies more on the force of the sage's character—his mysterious *de*—and the intrinsic appeal of his vision to bring about a voluntary and active involvement in the creation of the emerging harmony. In the world of Lao Zi, "one who knows does not speak; one who speaks does not know" (56). Thus the Daoist sage "practices the teaching that uses no words" (2), leading more by example and force of character than verbal instruction.

Lao Zi compares such a person to the emptiness at the hub of wheel where the many individual spokes meet: "Thirty spokes share one hub; from the nothing therein comes the use of the cart" (11). The sage is like the empty hub in that he is *wu yu*. In the meditative process, *wu yu* refers to the elimination of all desire. In postmeditation practice, it refers to moderation of desire and to nonegoic or objectless desire. The sage is able to attract others to him and to win them over to his vision of harmony because, transformed by the meditative experience, he does not pursue selfish desires or define self-interest in a narrow way.[33] He seeks his own fulfillment in and through that of others. Because he seeks not to contend with but to benefit others, no one contends with him.

He does not show himself, and thus is illustrious.
He does not assert himself and thus is distinguished.
He does not brag, and thus has achievements.
He does not wallow in self-conceit, and thus endures.
It is only because he does not contend (*bu zheng*) that no one in the empire contends with him. (22)

Ironically, the sage's nonegoic pursuit of harmony allows him to develop personal interests and to attain personal goals. One of the assumptions of Lao Zi's politics of harmony—and of Confucius's—is that conflicts can be resolved in a positive rather than a zero-sum fashion: that is, in such a manner that all parties gain. That in interpersonal transactions the gain of one need not entail the loss of another leads Lao Zi to conclude, "the more one does for others, the more one gains for oneself. The more one bestows on others, the more one has for oneself" (81).[34]

Another factor in the sage's success is his ability to remain flexible and without knowledge (*wu zhi*). As noted previously, in terms of the meditative process itself, *wu zhi* is to be understood literally as no knowledge. In terms of postmeditation experience in the world and the actuation of harmony, however, it connotes unprincipled knowing. Lao Zi is critical of knowledge and erudition—whether derived from books or from past experiences. Knowledge binds one to fixed perspectives. One becomes dogmatic, unable to respond to the exigencies of situation. The more certain one is of what one knows, the less likely one is to entertain alternatives. Rather than approaching a situation with an open mind, one seeks to impose one's conceptual framework on it. In reducing the data to fit one's own theory, however, something is lost, left out. Violence is done to the particular when order is attained through the application of antecedently determined laws, rules, and principles.

Harmony for Lao Zi is context specific. He, like Confucius, rejects rule ethics and rule of codified law. True moral virtue cannot be reduced to rules. One's response must be appropriate in light of the particular circumstances. The ability to respond appropriately and effectively is what makes the sage such a magnet for others.

Ironically, despite Confucius's own writings to the contrary, Confucian morality is for Lao Zi the epitome of dogmatic rule ethics. This may be due to the way in which later disciples interpreted Confucius's words. Or it may be due to the way his views became institutionalized in the Chinese tradition. It may even be nothing more than an uncharitable reading of a

Confucian by a Daoist: whereas the author of the *Boshu* appears to have written in the late Warring States to early Han, during the period of rapprochement when "the one hundred schools flowed together," the *Lao Zi* is a product of an earlier era when the various schools contended stridently—Confucians criticized Daoists and Mohists who in turn criticized Confucians and each other. That the author of the *Lao Zi* would deliberately cast Confucius's views in their least favorable light is possible, though to do so would be to run counter to his own professed ethic of tolerance. Whatever the cause, the *Lao Zi* portrays Confucian *li, ren, yi,* and *de* as part of the problem rather the solution: the *li* are rigid moral codes; *ren* is a calculating, artificial benevolence;[35] *yi* is not moral appropriateness or discretionary judgment but fixed duties; and Confucian or lowly *de* is not virtue in the Daoist sense of power or ability to bring about harmony but virtue in a pedantic, schoolmarmish sense.[36]

Where there is harmony and people work out their differences in a mutually satisfactory way, there is no need to emphasize benevolence, righteousness, moral codes, and so forth. Only when the way is lost, when things are bad, do we call for rules to define the good.

> When the great way is abandoned, there is benevolence and
> righteousness.
> When erudition and wisdom emerge, there is great pretense.
> When the six relations are not harmonious, there is filial piety and
> parental commiseration.
> When the state is disrupted and disordered, there are loyal ministers.
> (18)

But rules actually cause things to get worse as people plot and connive to circumvent them:

> The more restrictions and prohibitions in the empire, the more
> destitute the people . . .
> The more overt laws and ordinances, the more thieves and robbers
> there are. (57)

Thus Lao Zi, in stark contrast to Huang-Lao, rejects rule of law as a means to social order. Although this has been often noted, that it follows from Lao Zi's politics of harmony and his view of the way as emergent rather than predetermined and absolute has drawn little, if any, comment. This is not surprising given the pervasive reading of Lao Zi's dao as an absolute, predetermined metaphysical entity or order. That the tradition has tended to interpret Lao Zi in such terms—terms more appropriate to a reading of Huang-Lao's dao—has obscured the uniqueness of Huang-Lao and the extent to which it constitutes an aberration within the intellectual tradition of ancient China.

In any event, for the sage to effect harmony he must proceed in a case-by-case fashion, guided not by determinate principles of an absolute order but by a clear-minded appreciation of the various components that constitute the particular situation. Not feeling the need to impose his own conceptual framework, he is free to entertain the views of others: "The sage is without a fixed heart-mind. He takes the heart-mind of the people as his own" (49). In effecting harmony, the sage works with whatever is at hand. He starts from the specific beliefs, attitudes, and interests of the particular parties. He then acts as a catalyst to bring about an order in which all benefit. For the sage, there are no useless things:

> If something is deformed then it can be made whole.
> If something is warped then it can be made straight.
> If something is hollow then it can be made full.
> If something is worn out then it can be made new (recycled).
> If something is few then it can receive.
> If something is many then it can become confused. (22)

The challenge is to discover an order in which each thing finds a place. No thing or no one can be left out: "the sage is always adept at saving others, thus there are no discarded people. He is always good at saving things, and thus there are no discarded things" (27).[27] Lao Zi's politics of harmony do not allow for utilitarian compromises where the well-being of one is sacrificed to the overall utility of the rest. Each person and each thing possesses an inviolability, an integrity, that must be accounted for in the resulting sociopolitical and cosmic order.[38]

Lao Zi's expansion of the sage's domain of concern to nonhuman elements in one's environment differentiates his position from the anthropocentric concerns of Confucius. There are other differences. As noted earlier, Confucius places greater faith in the ability of the sage to persuade others as to the wisdom of his particular vision through reasoned discourse.[39] Lao Zi, for his part, relies on the intrinsic appeal of the sage's vision of harmony discovered in the meditative process together with force of character (*de*) gained from that process to win people over. He is, therefore, less dependent on others being predisposed to willingly and open-mindedly participate in generating harmony in that his "non-verbal teachings" (*wu yan zhi jiao* 无言之教) are transmitted on a more subliminal or direct level, as it were, than Confucius's reasoned persuasion.[40]

Further, Confucius is more ambitious than Lao Zi. Both see harmony as a matter of degree, radiating out in ever-increasing concentric circles: self, family, neighborhood, state, empire, cosmos. For Confucius, however, the failure to achieve harmony within the human social order as a whole is a personal failure. Confucius cannot rest content until the human order is set right. Lao Zi, on the other hand, believes one does better to find contentment in whatever level of harmony one is able to effect. If one has the ability, the *de*, to effect harmony on a cosmic level, so much the better. If one only has the *de* to effect harmony on a personal level, that will do as well.

In fact, Lao Zi realized that the more interests involved—the greater the domain of one's concern—the more difficult it is to effect harmony. This is one reason why he advocates small communities (80). It also helps explain why so much of the *Lao Zi* is addressed to the ruler. He is the one person who has the power attendant to the position to effect harmony on the grandest scale.

But not all will be rulers. Not everyone will be in a position to directly alter the course of events beyond the relatively small sphere of one's personal acquaintances. For Lao Zi, this is not cause for despair. By effecting harmony within one's relatively modest sphere, one is able to gain personal contentment. There is no need to travel about seeking an audience with the political powers that be, nor to lament, as Confucius and his disciples do, that their advice is being ignored. Contentment is not a matter of fame and fortune, of success in the eyes of others, of triumph as defined by society. It may be found in the harmony of one person's life.

That one may find contentment on a personal level makes Lao Zi's assertion that harmony will automatically result from the meditative process more plausible. If one is indeed transformed by the process into a person who interacts with others in terms of *wu yu* (nonegoic objectless desire), *wu zhi* (unprincipled knowing), and *wu wei* (nonimpositional action), one may very well be able to find contentment in whatever one encounters in life. Not only will such a person find that good things tend to come one's way because of one's attitude, but even when they do not, one will be able to respond accordingly. One will, in short, be able to adjust to the vicissitudes of life without losing one's inner harmony and contentment.

Whatever their differences, Lao Zi and Confucius share in common one notion that sets them apart from Huang-Lao: the view that the way emerges contextually, in the realm of praxis, rather than existing predetermined in the realm of theory or metaphysics.

1.2   Dao as Emergent Order

Many commentators have argued that Huang-Lao's dao is based on, if not the same as, that of Lao Zi. As Ge Rongjin, Jan Yun-hua, and others have pointed out, the author's description of dao in the *Dao Yuan* section parallels that of Lao Zi not only in content but in language. Ge notes the following similarities: dao is described as *xu* (empty) and *wu* (undifferentiated), as the totality, oneness, as "timeless," as predating heaven and earth, as the source of all things, that from which all things arose and that by which all things are sustained, as omnipresent.[41] Jan concludes his study by claiming that "the descriptions of Tao [in the *Boshu*] as beginningless, unnameable, uncaused, vacuous, unfathomable, independent, unchanging, the One and the originator of all phenomena are all in agreement with other Taoist texts."[42]

I contend that, although there are many similarities between Huang-Lao's conception of dao and that of Lao Zi, there are also important differences. Mainland Chinese scholars, as discussed previously, have attempted to elucidate the differences largely in terms of the materialistic-idealistic distinction—unfortunately, this has been less than completely effective.[43] I will take a different tack, arguing that what differentiates Lao Zi's dao from that of Huang-Lao is that Lao Zi's is to be understood as emergent, as dependent on and responsive to context and to the particulars that collectively constitute the totality, rather than as a predetermined single order. In this sense, it shares more with the way of Confucius and Zhuang Zi than it does with Huang-Lao.

At the same time, there is admittedly more of a metaphysical or cosmological color to Lao Zi's dao than to that of either Confucius or Zhuang Zi. As we have seen, Confucius is reluctant to engage in metaphysical speculation. His dao is *ren* dao—the way in which we as individuals and as a society live. Zhuang Zi, although does not conceive of the way as anthropocentrically as Confucius, does understand dao as the way(s) in which we as individuals, as society, and as an ecosystem live. As Hansen has argued, rather than an absolute, metaphysical object, Zhuang Zi's dao may be more profitably understood as "a scheme of classifications which generates a pattern of behavior via its influence on affective attitudes."[44]

Central to an understanding of the open-ended, emergent character of Lao Zi's dao is the notion of *zi ran* 自然, variously translated as "nature", "naturally," "spontaneously," "action-discrimination from a particular perspective," and, most literally, "self-so" or "so of itself."[45] Chapter ⌐5 of the *Dao De Jing* reads,

> Humans take as their standard earth;
> earth takes as its standard heaven;
> heaven takes as its standard dao;
> dao takes as its standard what is so of itself (*zi ran*).

Contrary to what some have argued, dao is not predicated on or subordinate to an antecedent pattern or predetermined, transcendent laws—of nature or any other sort. As what is so of itself, dao is sui generis. Dao, the self-so one or totality, is defined by the particulars that constitute it. As the particulars change, so does dao—both in a descriptive sense and a normative sense.[46] Normatively, dao entails for Lao Zi the actuation of harmony. But a signal feature of harmony is that it allows for various forms of expression as opposed to requiring instantiation or replication of a single correct order.[47]

The absence of an antecedent pattern is further reflected in Lao Zi's cosmogony. As *zi ran*, dao, the cosmic order, is so of itself in the sense of *self*-generating.[48]

> Dao begets one;
> one begets two;
> two begets three
> and three begets the myriad creatures. (42)

> Dao engenders them;
> *de* (potency) rears them;
> things form them;
> circumstances complete them. (51)

So accustomed are many of us to the Judeo-Christian cosmogonic myths in which a transcendent God creates the world ex nihilo that it is difficult to avoid reading the *Lao Zi* in a similar fashion. Yet to do so would be a mistake. As Needham and others argue, there is no notion of an ontologically transcendent deity in ancient China who creates the world of substance out of nothing.

Further, to think of substantial something or being as generated out of nothing is inappropriate in the Daoist context. The issue in Daoist cosmogony is not how one gets something from nothing—how could there ever have been nothing?—but how one gets from primal undifferentiatedness (*wu*) to the differentiated phenomenal world (*you*) that we live in. Rather than understanding reality in terms of substances and essences, one does well to think of it in terms of regularity, of habitual processes and fixed ways of carving up the uncarved block.[49] What is most real is what is least susceptible to alternative ways of perceiving, of construing, of imaging. There is a persistence to reality.

This idea finds its Western analog in the writings of Peirce, who turns Lao Zi's observation inside out, arguing that reality *is* persistence. "If all things are continuous, the universe must be undergoing a continuous growth from nonexistence to existence. There is no difficulty in conceiving existence as a matter of degree. The reality of things consists in their persistent forcing themselves upon our recognition. Reality, then, is persistence, is regularity."[50] Peirce's doctrine of continuity entails the rejection of nominalism, of atomism, of discrete entities prior to the formation of habits.[51] Like Lao Zi, Peirce conceives of the primal origins as an undifferentiated state of chaos, a period before the formation of habitual ways of cutting up the undifferentiated flux. "In the original chaos, where there was no regularity, there was no existence. . . . This we may suppose was in the infinitely distant past. . . . Uniformities in the modes of action of things have come about by their taking habits. . . . We look back toward a point in the infinitely distant past when there was no law but mere indeterminacy."[52]

Lao Zi, for his part, states:

Dao is vacuous . . .
Deep, like the ancestor of the myriad things . . .
I do not know whose son it is—
it seems to be prior to the gods. (4)

There was something confusedly formed, engendered before heaven and earth.
Soundless, formless, it stands alone and does not change . . .
It is capable of constituting the mother of the universe.
I do not know its name.
So, compelled to attach a word to it,
I call it "dao." (25)

Within the undifferentiatedness (*wu*) from which the phenomenal world of the myriad things (*you*) arose (40), there already existed the potential for generation and growth. There is no need for a transcendent deity to initiate the process.

Peirce explains the cosmological process as the result of the tendency of all things to assume habits.[53] "All things have a tendency to take habits. For atoms and their parts, molecules and groups of molecules, and in short every conceivable real object, there is a greater probability of acting as on a former like occasion than otherwise."[54] The process of generation, of moving from undifferentiatedness to differentiatedness, is not, it is to be noted, initially a linguistic one. Long before there are life forms, things are already beginning to take on habits, form, regularity. That things do assume habits, that reality does have a certain persistence, encourages people to cut up the flux in certain ways, both perceptually and linguistically. In fact, Peirce argues that the inherent tendency to take on habits will in the infinitely long run lead to a closed, determinate universe reducible to laws: "Uniformities in the modes of action of things have come about by their taking habits. At present, the course of events is approximately defined by law. In the past that approximation was less perfect; in the future it will be more perfect. . . . We look forward to a point in the infinitely distant future when there will be no indeterminacy or chance but a complete reign of law."[55] Many of Peirce's critics make much of statements such as this as well as his notion that scientific theories will in the long run converge on reality, on the truth. Yet in fairness to Peirce, he does hasten to add that "at any assignable date in the future there will always be some slight aberrancy from law."[56] Peirce—who labels this doctrine *tychism*—explains: "Try to verify any law of nature, and you will find that the more precise your observations, the more certain they will be to show irregular departures from the law. . . . Trace their causes back far enough and you will be forced to admit they are always due to arbitrary determination, chance."[57]

There is no reason to suspect that Lao Zi would agree with Peirce that even in the infinitely long run the universe will become determinate and reducible to law without error. Yet if Peirce's critics tend to overstate the determinacy of his position, Lao Zi's commentators err in the opposite direction, attributing to him a radically open, anarchic cosmology.[58] Lao Zi, however, does allow that nature has taken on a habitual pattern.[59] There is a regularity to the natural order and to the myriad things: "Each thing returns to its root . . . this is called returning to one's natural conditions. Returning to one's natural conditions is called constancy. Discovering constancy is called clarity" (16). One must have respect for the integrity of the particular that is defined at least in part by its natural conditions (*ming* 命). The natural conditions are the most determinate features of a thing, its regularity: in Peircean terms, the most entrenched habits. This regularity cannot be explained completely in terms of human practices, linguistic or otherwise. In the earliest stages, the way is sui generis, self-generating: distinctions/habits arise from within, from probabilities, potentialities, or tendencies implicate in the undifferentiated qi (often translated "ether") itself. What probabilities or tendencies were inherent in the original undifferentiatedness, and hence to what extent nature is preprogrammed, is an open and almost assuredly unanswerable question. It may be that in the infinitely distant past some random event occurred that led to the formation of this particular regularity. Given the *zi ran* (sui generis) character of dao, Lao Zi would most likely find appealing the notion that there was and continues to be an element of spontaneity, of randomness, to the particular habits that constitute the natural order and the natural conditions of a particular person. That the universe could have been, and someday will be, other than it is now violates neither the letter nor the spirit of the *Lao Zi*.

In the present moment, however, there is a given regularity to the universe and to the myriad things that populate it. Yet the regularity comes not from nature alone, but from nurture as well. Lao Zi is, moreover, more concerned with the regularity we attribute to things through our conventional practices than he is with the regularity derived from nature. He believes that the process of moving from the primal undifferentiatedness to the present phenomenal world of differentiated things is largely if not primarily the result of social practices, the most important being language. It is by assigning names to things that one begins to carve the uncarved block: "Dao is the constantly nameless uncarved block. . . . Beginning to systematize, there were names" (32). In learning a language, we acquire certain habits: when we see a cow, we call it *cow* rather than *horse*. We learn how to see the world, how to cut up the flux. Not only do we learn in the process how to perceive, name, behave, and think, we learn how to value as well. We learn what is "beautiful" and what is "ugly" (2). It is this conventional regularity, this socially acquired habit, that Lao Zi seeks to overcome through the meditative process whereby one regains the ability to approach life with an open, creative mind.

By placing greater weight on the less determinate habits generated by social convention, Lao Zi calls attention to the ability of humans to shape and alter the world in which they live. Humans are an integral component in shaping the emergent way: "Dao is great; heaven is great; earth is great; and humans are also great" (25). That humans contribute to the formation of the way in both a normative and descriptive sense indicates not only that the way is emergent rather than predetermined, but that there is an ineradicable element of contingency to Lao Zi's dao.

Dao, sui generis and self-so, is not then the product of predetermined laws. Nor, moreover, can dao be reduced to or explicated in terms of mechanical, determinate rules or laws. In the Daoist cosmos, there is always an element of spontaneity, a potential for novelty, that is negligible if not completely lacking in the world of Huang-Lao. This spontaneity militates against the prospect that one could ever capture once and for all the emerging dao.[60]

In Peirce's *tychism*, the ineradicable element of spontaneity and the subsequent impossibility of reducing the cosmos to mechanical laws attests to the livingness of the cosmos. Allowing that the universe is living—that is, spontaneously and continually evolving in novel ways—permits Peirce to explain the phenomenon of diversification, of generation of new and unpredictable forms of life.

> By thus admitting pure spontaneity or life as a character of the universe, acting always and everywhere though restrained within narrow bounds by law, producing infinitesimal departures from law continually, and great ones with infinite infrequency, I account for all the variety and diversity, in the only sense in which the really *sui generis* and new can be said to be accounted for. The ordinary view has to admit the inexhaustible multitudinous variety of the world, has to admit that his mechanical law cannot account for this in the least, that variety can spring only from spontaneity . . .[61]

That there is an element of contingency and spontaneity to dao as an emergent order not only allows Lao Zi to account for variety, but encourages him to adopt the kind of tolerant, creative approach to life that characterizes his politics of harmony. As Richard Bernstein points out, the cosmology and metaphysics of the pragmatists influence their social and political philosophy:

> The insistence on the inescapability of chance and contingency—on what Dewey called the "precariousness of existence" where the "world is a scene of risk" and is "uncannily unstable"—conditioned [the pragmatists] understanding of experience and philosophy itself. We can never hope to "master" unforeseen and unexpected contingencies. We live in an "open" universe which is always at once threatening and a source of tragedy and opportunity. This is why the pragmatists placed so much emphasis on how we are to

respond to contingencies—on developing the complex of dispositions and critical habits that Dewey called "reflective intelligence."[62]

Although Dewey's reflective intelligence may share more in common with Confucius's epistemology than with Lao Zi's emptiness-based epistemology, Bernstein's general point remains valid: namely, that the openness of the cosmos contributes to both Dewey's and Lao Zi's rejection of rule ethics, absolute principles, and all forms of dogmatism in favor of an open-minded approach to problems. In fact, a pragmatist would do well to adopt the *wu yu* (nonegoic, objectless desire), *wu zhi* (unprincipled knowing), *wu wei* (nonimpositional action) approach of the Daoist sage.

2. Zhuang Zi's Way

That the *Lao Zi* influences Huang-Lao and the author of the *Boshu* is readily apparent. The influence of Zhuang Zi, on the other hand, seems negligible. Many argue that Zhuang Zi is a political recluse who advocates withdrawal from politics and society, and for this reason is ignored by the politically active and sophisticated Huang-Lao school.[63] I disagree.

I maintain that Zhuang Zi is not as apolitical as many make him out to be. In any event, he is ignored by Huang-Lao for (at least) two other reasons. First, he conceives of the way as emergent rather than predetermined, as something to be realized rather than discovered. Second, he deconstructs on the basis of his antifoundational epistemology the human-nature distinction, arguing that there is no way for humans to escape from their human perspectives to directly access nature. Hence, it is impossible to know (discover) what the natural order is, undermining the essence of the Huang-Lao position.

2.1 Zhi Dao: *Realizing an Emergent Order*

To understand Zhuang Zi's epistemology requires reference to the meditation passages in the text, as it did for Lao Zi.[64] The nature of the meditation described in *Zhuang Zi* is by and large the same as that in *Lao Zi*. Both advocate apophatic or cessation meditation in which one empties oneself of all thoughts, images, feelings: in short, of all objects of consciousness.[65]

One of the terms Zhuang Zi uses to describe apophatic meditation is *zuo wang* 坐忘: sitting and forgetting. This process is explained in a delightful story in which Zhuang Zi mischievously employs Confucius and his disciple Yan Hui as spokespersons for his views. Yan, reporting on his practice to Confucius, states that, he has forgotten about morality and duty, and later, that he has forgotten about music and rites. Confucius cautions that, although this represents progress, he still has some way to go. Finally, Yan reports that he just "sits and forgets." Confucius, taken aback, asks what he means by "just sit and forget." Yan replies, "I let the organs and members drop away, dismiss eyesight and hearing, part from the body and expel knowledge, and go along with the great thoroughfare." To which Confucius declares, "if you go along with it, you have no preferences; if you let yourself transform, you have no constant norms. Has it really turned out that you are the better of us? Oblige me by taking me as your disciple" (19/6/89, G92).

The apophatic nature of the process is evident. One does away with sense perceptions, with all forms of cognition (thoughts, knowledge, conceptions, ideas, images), with all valuations (preferences, norms, mores). Cognate to and a variant of *wang* (忘 —to forget) is *wang* (亡 —to destroy, perish, disappear, not exist). In the apophatic meditative process, all distinctions and ways of distinguishing are "forgotten" in the sense of eliminated: they cease to exist.

On another occasion, Zhuang Zi again has Confucius advising his disciple Yan Hui. He is admonishing Yan for being too organized, too tied down to fixed perspectives: as he puts it, for taking the heart-mind as one's authority. Confucius advises him to fast. But he is to fast the heart-mind (*xin zhai* 心齋), not the body: "Unify your attention. Rather than listen with the ear, listen with the heart-mind. Rather than listen with the heart-mind, listen with your energies (*qi*). Listening stops at the ear, the heart-mind at what tallies with thought. As for 'energy,' it is empty (*xu*) and waits to be roused by other things. Only the way brings together emptiness. The emptying is the fasting of the heart-mind" (9/4/26, G68). *Xin zhai*, literally fasting of the heart-mind, is the apophatic process of emptying oneself of all objects of consciousness. The heart-mind is the locus of the cognitive and affective that, along with sense perceptions, are to be eliminated. In the process of emptying, one overcomes the encapsulated self, the ego-self, that stands opposed to objects of consciousness as the conscious subject. Thus Yan continues the conversation with Confucius by saying, "when Hui has never yet succeeded in being an agent, a deed derives from Hui. When he does succeed in being its agent, there has never yet begun to be a Hui. Would that be what you call emptying?" "Perfect!" answers Confucius.

The overcoming of the ego-self through meditation is most clearly expressed in the story of Zi Qi of Nan Guo who, "reclining elbow on armrest, looked up at the sky and exhaled, in a trance as though he had lost the counterpart of himself. Yan Cheng Ziyou, standing in wait before him, says, 'What is this? Can the frame really be made like withered wood, the heart-mind like dead ashes? The reclining man here now is not the reclining man of yesterday.' Zi Qi replies, 'You do well to ask that, Ziyou. This time I had lost my own self (*sang wo* 喪我)'" (3/2/1, G48).

That apophatic meditation leads to an overcoming of the ego-self is a point shared by both Lao Zi and Zhuang Zi. Indeed, Zhuang Zi even allows that the emptying process may lead to a pure consciousness event in which all distinctions are eliminated. One returns, in the language of Lao Zi, to the uncarved block. Zhuang Zi, for his part, refers to this state not as the uncarved block but as the limitless (*wu jing* 無境): "forget the years, forget duty, be shaken into motion by the limitless, and so find things their lodging-places in the limitless" (7/2/93, G60). The limitless is the place where there are no things, no borders, no differentiation of the undifferentiated consciousness: "The men of old, their knowledge had arrived at something; at what had it arrived? There were some who thought there had not yet begun to be things—the utmost, the exhaustive, there is no more to add. The next thought that there were things but there had not yet begun to be borders. The next thought there were borders to them but there had not yet begun to be 'that's it, that's not' (*shi fei* 是非). The manifesting of 'that's it, that's not' is the reason the way is flawed" (5/2/40, G54). The utmost men of old did not carve up the undifferentiated to form things.[66] The next thought that there is more to life than the pure consciousness experience. While they dwell in the phenomenal world of differentiated objects, they do not believe that there is any inherent or fixed ways of cutting up the flux. How one draws borders around things is relative to the goals, backgrounds and so forth of the person and the community. It is when people begin to believe they have captured the truth—that their theories cut at the joints of nature, that their valuations correspond to moral reality—that dao becomes construed as a single, predetermined order and the emergent way is lost.

For Zhuang Zi, every way of differentiating, every way of assigning value, every "that's it" (*shi*) is relative to a particular perspective: each is a *yin shi* 因是, a "that's it" that goes by circumstance. It is only during the pure consciousness event, in the state of *wu jing* (the limitless), that *yin shi* stops. As soon as one returns to the phenomenal world, the instant an object of consciousness enters one's heart-mind, the moment the undifferentiated is differentiated, one has taken a step back into the phenomenal world of *yin shi*. Thus Zhuang Zi says, "take no step at all, and the 'that's it' that goes by circumstance will come to an end" (5/2/55, G56).

Unlike Lao Zi, however, Zhuang Zi does not privilege the meditative

experience. He does not allow that the pure consciousness event, the return to the limitless, the cessation of all *yin shi*, necessarily leads to either
the discovery or the realization of harmony in praxis. In and of itself, the
pure consciousness event is just empty. It may allow one to overcome the
ego-self and fixed ways of perceiving, imaging, and valuing, thereby opening the mind to new insights. But when one gains the insight, one is no
longer in the state of pure consciousness. In the return to everyday life, to
dao in praxis, one must inevitably interpret or apply the experience: one
must take a step. Thus Zhuang Zi maintains that "a way comes about as we
walk it" (4/2/33, G53). Dao is a product of our *shi*ing and *fei*ing. For
Zhuang Zi to *shi* something is not only to differentiate *this* (the literal
meaning of *shi*) from *that* (*fei*), but to affirm that which one *shi*s—to
assign it positive value, as opposed to *fei* as negative. It is to say, "this is it,
(better, best, most appropriate), that is not." Moreover, to *shi* something
is to act in an appropriate fashion. There is a performative aspect to *shi* and
fei: if one *shi*s team A over team B, one hopes team A wins, cheers them
on, and so forth.[67]

Dao then emerges from our *shi*ing and *fei*ing. But every *shi* is a *yin
shi*, a way of judging, interpreting, differentiating that arises from a particular perspective, from the heart-mind of a particular person. As Zhuang
Zi puts it, "For there to be a 'that's it, that's not' before they are formed in
the heart-mind would be to go to Yue today and have arrived yesterday"
(4/2/22, G51). Even the way of the sage is but one more *yin shi*: one more
affirmation that goes by circumstance, one more constructed, perspectival
course of action or way (4/2/29, G52).

Thus Zhuang Zi, in contrast to Lao Zi, draws a distinction between
the emptying and the illuminative aspects of the meditation process, between the pure consciousness event and the discovery of dao. One does not
simply discover dao through meditation. Nor does one, as with Huang-
Lao, directly apprehend dao as the objective way delineated in terms of *fa*
(laws), *li* (principles), and *xing ming* (forms and names). Rather, dao is
realized in the phenomenal world of practice, in the subjective world of
perspectival *yin shi*.

Zhuang Zi's Antifoundationalism

Zhuang Zi's perspectivism is itself an implicit rebuke of foundational
epistemologies claiming to have discovered objective truth. There is no
way to escape from one's perspective to verify that one's theories, ideas,
intuitions, or experiences correspond to nature, to moral reality, or to any
other transcendent realm of value. One might suspect that to attribute to
Zhuang Zi such a postmodern, antifoundationalist sensibility is to read him

anachronistically. If so, one need only consider Zhuang Zi's own explicit critique of foundational naturalism.

> 'Knowing that which nature does and that which man does is the utmost in knowledge. Whoever knows what nature does lives the life generated by nature . . .'
> Still, there's a difficulty. Knowing depends on something with which it is later matched; however, what it depends on is never fixed. How do I know that which I deem 'nature' is not 'man?' How do I know that which I deem 'man' is not 'nature?' (15/6/1, G84).

With this Rortean challenge, Zhuang Zi undermines any attempt such as that of Huang-Lao to conceive of the epistemological process as one of discovery of the way understood as a predetermined metaphysical entity. How could one know what is dao, the predetermined natural order, and what is human interpretation? One cannot escape from one's human perspective to some "objective" Archimedean point to verify one's metaphysical hypothesis—to gain access to, as it were, Nature's Own Vocabulary.

Knowledge is not a matter of discovery, of coming face to face with reality, of directly confronting, intuiting, or experiencing privileged objects of consciousness or experience. Rather, it depends, as Zhuang Zi puts it, on something with which it is later matched; namely, our personal and social standards, attitudes, goals, and so forth. We take something to be known if it coheres with the rest of our web of beliefs or, perhaps failing that, if it allows us to realize our ends.

Yet the fact that it coheres with our beliefs, that it makes sense to us individually and as a society, even that it serves our personal and collective ends, does not mean that it is true in an absolute or apodictic sense. Zhuang Zi's perspectivism and antifoundationalism entail the rejection of certainty, of rational closure of the Enlightenment-Kantian type predicated on a single, universal rational order. In theory, there is no way to prove once and for all that one view is correct and another wrong; both sides could continue to insist that they are right.[68] In practice, the conversation could continue until agreement is reached, until both sides agree to disagree, or until they retire.

> You and I have been made to argue over alternatives, if it is you not I that wins, is it really you who are on to it, I who am not? If it is not you that wins, is it really I who am on to it, you who are not? Is one of us on to it and the other of us not? Or are both of us on to it and both of us not? If you and I are unable to know where we stand, others will surely be in the dark because of

us. Whom shall I call in to decide it? If I get someone of your party to decide it, being already of your party how can he decide it? If I get someone of my party to decide it, being already of my party how can he decide it? If I get someone of a party different from either of us to decide it, being already of a party different from either of us how can he decide it? If I get someone of the same party as both of us to decide it, being already of the same party as both of us how can he decide it? Consequently you and I and he are all unable to know where we stand, and shall we find someone else to depend on? (7/2/84, G60).

Zhuang Zi refuses to privilege interpersonal or social standards for adjudicating epistemic claims. There is always the possibility that the individual might be right and the rest of society wrong.[69] History provides more than enough instances of this to lend credibility to Zhuang Zi's fallibilist position.

So thoroughgoing a fallibilist is Zhuang Zi that he even turns his antifoundationalist sights on the pragmatists' position. He deconstructs their distinction of knowledge-ignorance as what works/does not work in practice given one's own personal ends by challenging the view that one knows what constitutes benefit and harm. He begins with a general attack on the knowledge/ignorance distinction (6/2/64, G58):

Gaptooth put a question to Wang Ni, "Would you know something of which all things agreed 'that's it?'"
How would I know that?
Would you know what you did not know?
How would I know that?
Then does no thing know anything?
How would I know that? However, let me try to say it—How do I know that what I call knowing is not ignorance? How do I know that what I call ignorance is not knowing?

Wang Ni then goes on to point out that when humans sleep in damp places their bodies ache, but not so for a loach. Zhuang Zi is again making the point that we all assess epistemic claims from a particular perspective, and that there is no value neutral or Archimedean perspective.

Gaptooth, however, is not quite finished. Surely, he reasons, one can know what constitutes benefit and harm for one's own self: "If you do not know benefit from harm, would you deny that the utmost person knows benefit from harm?" Zhuang Zi, slipping into rhapsodic prose, manages the weak reply that "the utmost person is daemonic . . . death and life alter nothing in him, still less the principle of benefit and harm."

Later, however, Zhuang Zi readdresses the issue. He relates the story of a young woman who wept and wailed at the prospects of living with the King of Jin. But once she experienced the benefits of the royal lifestyle, she regretted her tears. The moral of the story: who is to say what is benefit and what is harm? Even that considered to be the greatest harm—death—may turn out to be more desirable than life: as Zhuang Zi puts it, "how do I know that to take pleasure in life is not a delusion? How do I know that we who hate death are not exiles since childhood who have forgotten the way home?" (6/2/80, G59).

Unfortunately, Zhuang Zi does not consider the objection that, although one may be mistaken about what constitutes harm or benefit, one cannot be similarly mistaken about pain and pleasure. The only hint of a potential response is that for Zhuang Zi the realized person is able to take all in stride: "Death and life, survival and ruin, success and failure, poverty and riches, competence and incompetence, slander and praise, hunger and thirst, these are the mutations of affairs, the course of destiny. . . . There is no point in letting them disturb one's harmony. . . . *De* (potency) is the wholly at peace with itself on the course which is harmony" (14/2/43, G80-81). Yet to argue that one may be able to overcome or ignore pain does not refute the claim that one can know one's own pain: in fact, one would have to be able to "know" one was in pain to make an effort to overcome it.[70]

In any event, Zhuang Zi's perspectivism and antifoundationalism put him at odds with the epistemologies of Huang-Lao and Lao Zi in which one discovers dao through the emptying process: no particular experience or state of consciousness is to be privileged as infallibly and apodicticly correct. His perspectivism and antifoundationalism do not, however, commit him to radical subjectivism and anything-goes relativism, as many commentators contend.

Hansen, for instance, declares: "Chuang-tzu's conventionalism shades into pure subjectivism. Our use of language distinctions is not even fixed within a linguistic community but varies for each speaker. . . . There is no sense in which we can hope to settle disputes that arise at any level because they rest on adopting arbitrary beginning points."[71] At times, Hansen portrays people almost as if they were atomistic individuals, incommensurable linguistic monads trapped in private language systems. "Language is a system of distinguishing and evaluating that is perspective-bound—that is, each person in using the language creates his own conceptual and valuative perspective. Conflicting judgments or disputes are therefore inevitable and irreconcilable."[72]

Graham too claims that there is for Zhuang Zi no way to settle disputes. Having examined the passage cited earlier in which Zhuang Zi contends that bringing in third parties to settle disputes cannot produce rational closure, Graham concludes, "We cannot break out of deadlock unless we can find an independent standpoint from which to judge whether the righteous is appropriate or beneficial, but there is none."[73]

Although it is true that for Zhuang Zi there is no independent, Archimedean point for adjudication, that does not entail that we have no way to resolve conflicts. It simply means that there is no way to prove one side is correct once and for all. That is to be expected given Zhuang Zi's fallibilism. But that we cannot prove apodicticly a claim to be correct does not conflate to the impossibility of resolving any and all disputes. One does not need an independent standard to resolve conflicts. One only needs an *accepted* standard, an *agreed upon* standard. One's own pragmatic ends can provide such standards. Although one might be wrong about the actual benefit and value of what one wants, one knows one's wants at this point in time. One can resolve a conflict by pointing out to someone that her position is inconsistent even by her own lights, that her way will not allow her to achieve her own professed goals.

Further, one can resolve conflicts by starting with common ground, with shared goals, interests, values and so forth, and then building a consensus. By achieving a harmonious solution that is amenable to all parties, one dissolves the deadlock: Zhuang Zi calls this letting both alternatives proceed.[74]

Where does one find this common ground? One of the main sources is tradition, as discussed earlier in regards to Confucius's politics of harmony. That we are all humans living on one earth is another. A third is language. The fact is we are not linguistic monads, each trapped in incommensurable worlds of *shi* and *fei*. Language is a social practice. To be sure each party brings a different background, linguistic and otherwise, to the conversation. As a consequence, there is often, perhaps always, a degree of miscommunication, a slight difference in what each makes of a word, phrase, sentence, and so on. Nevertheless, there is also considerable agreement. By and large, those who speak English, for instance, do understand each other. One can use this area of commonality, this shared language and mutual understanding, to persuade, to negotiate, to explain—either to settle on one of the original positions or to create a new one acceptable to both. For Zhuang Zi, it is the latter option that holds the most promise. Rather than trying to win the other over to one's own side, he believes it best to attempt to forge a new way, to achieve a new harmony that allows both alternatives to proceed.

2.2 Zhuang Zi's Politics of Harmony

Traditionally, the tendency has been to portray Daoism and Confucianism in sharply contrastive terms. The following passage of Richard J. Smith is a good example:

> For the elite, at least, the *yang* of Confucian social responsibility was balanced by the *yin* of Taoist escape into nature. . . . It provided an emotional and intellectual escape valve for world-weary Confucians, trammeled by social responsibility. . . . The Taoist impulse was to defy authority, question conventional wisdom, admire the weak, and accept the relativity of things. . . . Taoism was preeminently a philosophy of individual liberation. Where Confucianism stressed others, Taoism stressed self. Where Confucians sought wisdom, Taoists sought blissful ignorance. Where Confucians esteemed ritual and self-control, Taoists valued spontaneity. Where Confucians stressed hierarchy, Taoists emphasized equality, and where Confucians valued refinement, Taoists prized primitivity. What to Confucians were cosmic virtues were to Taoists simply arbitrary labels. . . . The former gave Chinese life structure and purpose, while the latter encouraged freedom of expression and artistic creativity.[75]

Ames has pointed out three reasons for this tendency to dichotomize.[76] First, early representatives of Daoism and Confucianism characterized each other in contrastive terms. As noted earlier, the early to mid-Warring States period was a time of contention among the various schools, with each attacking the others in an often less than charitable fashion. Not until the rapprochement of the late Warring States did the schools begin to emphasize commonalities rather than differences. Second, the disparate roles of Confucianism and Daoism in the Chinese tradition has heightened sensitivity to their distinctness. Confucianism has played a more central role in Chinese politics: in the Han, the Confucian classics became the basis of educational system and the state ideology.[77] Daoism, in contrast, was more often the choice of the artistic community and the apolitical. Third, failure to distinguish between the writings of the seminal philosophers and what is made of their writings by later disciples further exacerbates the perceived differences. Confucius, for example, is much less of a conservative and universal moralist than many of his commentators, particularly those influenced by Neo-Confucianism, make him out to be.

There is, I believe, another reason. When elaborating on the differences between Confucianism and Daoism, it is common practice to draw on Confucius, Mencius, and Xun Zi, on the one hand, and on Lao Zi and

Zhuang Zi, on the other, without distinguishing the many differences among the Confucians and Daoists themselves. Choosing the most extreme positions within the respective schools as representative of the school as a whole, although effective rhetorically, exaggerates the degree of difference.[78] For instance, I have argued that in regard to the epistemological issue of what it means to *zhi dao*, the position of Zhuang Zi is closer to that of Confucius than is that of Lao Zi. To appeal only to Lao Zi for one's statement of the "Daoist" position, while allowing one to highlight the differences, would be misleading.[79]

Although the tendency among sinologues has been to read the relationship between Confucianism and Daoism dichotomously, some have argued that the differences are overstated. Although acknowledging some truth to the traditional contrasts, Ames and A. S. Cua, for instance, suggest that, on closer examination, there is considerable commonality between the two schools. Ames points out that both see life as art rather than as a science; both express a this-worldly concern for the concrete details of immediate existence rather than pursuing grand abstractions and ideals; both acknowledge the uniqueness and importance of the particular person; both see the person as organismically related to context. And, most important, both are proponents of an aesthetic rather than a logical order.[80]

Cua notes that Zhuang Zi, far from rejecting morality, emphasizes, as does Confucius, the moral theme of harmony. And like Confucius, he turns to the beliefs, attitudes, and interests of the particular persons-in-context rather than to dogmatic, absolute, or universal rules or principles for direction in dissolving ethical conflict.[81] This rejection of rule ethics is one of the key features of Zhuang Zi's politics of harmony.

Like Lao Zi, Zhuang Zi not only rejects rule ethics, but attributes to Confucius precisely such a moral view, despite Confucius's own writings to the contrary. Consider the story of Xu Yu, who asks Yier Zi,

> What riches did you get from Yao (an ideal Confucian sage)?
> Yao told me, "Be sure to devote yourself to morality and duty and say plainly, 'that's it, that's not.'"
> Then what do you think you are doing here? When Yao has already branded your hide with morality (*ren*) and duty (*yi*), and snipped off your nose with his 'that's it, that's not,' how are you going to roam that free and easy take-any-turn-you-please path? (18/2/82, G91).

For Zhuang Zi, Confucian *ren* and *yi* are prescribed ethical codes, fixed moral duties. They are dogmatic statements of what is right and what is wrong. He reprimands Confucians—and Mohists as well—for obscuring the emerging way, for preventing the realization of a harmonious order, with their militant cant as to what and who is right: "Dao is hidden by formation of the lesser. . . . And so we have the 'that's it, that's not' of Confucians and Mohists, by which what is it for one of them for the other is not, what is not for one of them for the other is" (4/2/25, G52).

Zhuang Zi points out that in the absence of foundational standards, one can always deny what the other affirms and affirm what the other denies from some perspective: "If going by circumstance that's it then going by circumstance that's not [and vice versa]. This is why the sage does not take this course, but illumines things by heaven" (4/2/23, G52). Lest anyone be fooled into taking the sage's illumination by heaven as some foundational benchmark, Zhuang Zi hastens to add that "the sage's course too is a "'that's it' that goes by circumstance."

But what then does it mean to illumine things by heaven? It means, I believe, that one is to find common ground on which to build a way that is amenable to all parties, a way that reconciles differences and allows both parties to move beyond the conflict. The illumination is the insight or clarity (*ming*), perhaps gained as a result of the emptying process, that allows one to overcome the conflict, to see a new way, a new approach to the problem.[82] To gain this insight, one must be open minded. One cannot cling to preconceived notions. That is why Zhuang Zi values the meditative process even though he does not believe that one directly discovers a predetermined dao. It also explains why he is so critical of the Confucian and Mohists who insist on their particular *shi-fei*, their particular view as to what is right and wrong.

> What is It is also Other, what is Other is also It. There they say "that's it, that's not" from one point of view, here we say "that's it, that's not" from another point of view. Are there really It and Other? Or really no It an Other? Where neither It nor Other finds its opposite is called the axis of dao (*dao shu* 道樞). When once the axis is found at the center of the circle there is no limit to responding with either, on the one hand no limit to what is it, on the other no limit to what is not. Therefore I say: "The best means is clarity (*ming*)." (4/2/29, G52)

In everyday life, conflicts arise. One is unable to proceed: one is stuck. To become unstuck, one needs to find a solution, to move beyond adversary and seemingly incommensurable points of view. One way to resolve, or rather dissolve, the conflict is to find the axis of daos, the place where the seemingly incompatible *shi*s and *fei*s are rendered compatible.[83]

Rendering initially antithetical *shi*s and *fei*s compatible is called "smoothing them out on the whetstone of heaven." Having pointed out the futility of appealing to third parties in the passage cited previously, Zhuang Zi continues:

> It makes no difference whether the voices in their transformations have each other to depend on or not. Smooth them out on the whetstone of heaven, use them to go by and let the stream find its own channels; this is the way to live out your years. Forget the years, forget duty, be shaken into motion by the limitless, and so find things their lodging-places in the limitless. What is meant by "smooth things out on the whetstone of heaven?" Treat as "it" even what is not, treat as "so" even what is not. (7/2/89, G60)

Confronting conflicting voices in the conversation, Zhuang Zi does not throw his hands up in despair, abandoning all hope of resolution. Instead, he advises one to look for ways to incorporate rather than dismiss the other's perspective, to treat as "so" what is not. To take as so what is not so is to render compatible (*tong* 通) the disparate positions. It begins by starting with the particulars at hand. One then attempts to assume that perspective, to see it from the other's persons side as it were. Graham's translation of *tong* as interchange captures this part of the program. But *tong* implies more than role reversal. It also connotes penetration. Like a string that penetrates a series of ancient coins, one hopes to connect the disparate perspectives together into a single strand.

> It is inherent in a thing that from somewhere that's so of it, from somewhere that's allowable of it; of no thing is it not so, of no thing is it unallowable. Therefore when a 'That's it' which deems (*wei shi* 為是) picks out a stalk from a pillar, a hag from the beautiful Xi Shi, things however peculiar or incongruous, dao interchanges (*tong*) them and deems them one. . . . Only the person who sees right through things knows how to interchange and deem them one; the "That's it" which deems he does not use, but finds for them lodging-places in the usual. The "usual" is the usable, the "usable" is the interchangeable, to see as "interchangeable" is to grasp; and once you grasp them you are almost there. (4/2/34, G52)

This passage is important in that it attests to the pragmatic character of Zhuang Zi's politics of harmony. One is not trying to ascertain who is right according to some fixed standard. The benchmark for success is the everyday one of meeting one's ends. The goal is simply to move beyond the conflict, to resume life, to restore harmony.

Perhaps the best illustration of this process in actual practice is the story of the monkey-keeper:

A monkey keeper handing out nuts said, "three every morning and four every evening." The monkeys were all in a rage. "All right then," he said, "four every morning and three every evening."

The monkeys were all delighted. Without anything being missed out either in name or substance, their pleasure and anger were put to use; his too was a "that's it" which goes by circumstance. This is why the sage smooths things out with his "That's it, that's not," and stays at the point of rest on the potter's wheel of heaven. It is this that is called "Letting both alternatives proceed." (5/2/38, G54)

This story serves well as a reminder that conflicts are often based on trivial concerns. Sometimes they are more a matter of appearance than substance. At other times, conflicts emerge because of the feelings and egos of those involved. The sage, free from ego-attachment himself, is able to respond freely to these concerns. He is flexible, open minded. His way is still a *yin shi*, but one that seeks to reconcile differences. His is a way that lets both alternatives proceed by building a mutually acceptable solution on common ground.

Politics of Harmony: Zhuang Zi and Confucius

I have argued that Zhuang Zi, like Confucius, understands *zhi dao* as realizing an emergent way, and promotes politics of harmony. Nevertheless, there are several differences in their positions. Confucius's domain of concern is primarily the human social order. In contrast, Zhuang Zi, like Lao Zi, expands the scope of his harmonious order to include nonhuman nature as well: "There can be no genuine realization until there are Realized Persons. . . . Someone in whom neither nature nor man is victor over the other, this is what is meant by a Realized Person" (15/6/4-20, G85).

Second, although Confucius and Zhuang Zi advance nonfoundational theories aimed at harmony, Confucius is the more Apollonian, Zhuang Zi the more Dionysian—with these Nietzschean classifications understood as ends of a continuum rather than exclusive either-or categories. That is, Confucius's approach to achieving harmony is more cognitive; it is more of a reasoned process than for Zhuang Zi who emphasizes the aesthetic and noncognitive or arational factors in achieving harmony. Confucius is optimistic about the ability of sage to persuade others as to the wisdom of his vision of harmony. He is confident that people will be sufficiently open minded to come to a reasoned agreement as to what is best all things considered—moral views, contextual rationales, personal feelings, cultural attitudes, spiritual beliefs, and so on.

Further, in assessing what is best in a given context, Confucius is more concerned with overall coherence than either Lao Zi or Zhuang Zi. That is, Confucius, like Rawls, wishes to bring into coherence intuitions, reflective judgments, *and* the rationales or justifications for the resultant coherence. In contrast, Lao Zi and Zhuang Zi are concerned primarily with the practical result of coherence; namely, that it produce harmony; that it let both alternatives proceed. They are less concerned with providing a rationale or justifying as reasonable a given way as long as it works. Indeed, for Lao Zi the "justification" of a particular way is simply that it was discovered or directly intuited in meditation.

To put the point slightly differently, Confucius's politics of harmony seeks not only to bring into reflective equilibrium one's present beliefs, attitudes, goals, and so on but to render them consistent with previous beliefs, attitudes, and goals. One seeks a coherence that reconciles past with present—hence Confucius's greater emphasis on tradition. In contrast, the Daoist approach does not privilege overall coherence. Of course, consistency with past decisions and with one's other beliefs and so on would be a factor in favor of a proposed way. However, although cross-temporal coherence is something to be desired, the main emphasis is on finding a workable solution, on reaching consensus, in the particular case. A Daoist is more interested in synchronic as opposed to diachronic coherence. That is, a Daoist, given his *wu zhi* (unprincipled knowing) sensibility, is more willing to accept what would be unpalatable ad hoc solutions to those seeking a more robust coherence.

The willingness to settle for a workable solution in the given moment may reflect different assessments not only of the extent to which the process is arational and aesthetic as opposed to reasoned but of the likelihood of attaining coherent solutions to social problems. Zhuang Zi is less sanguine about the chances of realizing harmony than Confucius. For Zhuang Zi, a harmonious order is more like a work of art. There may be great divergence of opinion as to its merit. Even those brought up in the same tradition, sharing similar values and tastes, may disagree about a particular piece. When it comes to harmony on an interpersonal and social level, agreement is all the more elusive due to the sheer number of divergent perspectives involved.

For Zhuang Zi, there is no guarantee that harmony will be realized even if all members of society are transformed through the meditative process. Social harmony is more of a theoretical ideal than a realizable practical goal. This reservation about the likelihood of realizing harmony helps explain two distinctive features of Zhuang Zi: his relative lack of concern with politics and, conversely, his emphasis on personal transformation, creativity, and freedom.

Before elaborating, a word of caution. One must take care not to overstate the "hermit" aspect of Zhuang Zi. He is not as apolitical as many suggest. The attention he pays to politics of harmony attests to his interest in interpersonal interactions. And his proclamation that the realized person is one in whom the interests of humans and nonhuman nature are reconciled indicates that he takes himself to be related to the other elements in his environment and the cosmos at large.

Indeed, there is a story in the *Zhuang Zi* that Graham suggests "may well record [Zhuang Zi's] crisis of conversion" from individualistic Yangism to a more other-oriented philosophy in which the person is seen as inextricably interrelated to other persons and things. One day Zhuang Zi is poaching in the game reserve at Tiaoling. He is taking aim at a huge magpie that does not see him because it is tracking a mantis that itself is concentrating on a cicada resting in the shade. "Hmmm!", said Zhuang Zi uneasily, "it is inherent in things that they are ties to each other, that one kind calls up another." He throws down his crossbow and, as he is running away, notices that he in turn has been observed by the gamekeeper (54/20/61, G118).[84]

Of course, Zhuang Zi may never have had such an experience. Nevertheless, the story captures an appreciation for the interrelations of things that lies at the heart of his politics of harmony, and of politics and social responsibility in general.

Though not indifferent to the well-being of society, Zhuang Zi was fully aware that given the excessive material orientation and egocentricism of most people, harmony on a societal level is not likely. Personal harmony, however, may be. If one were able to overcome the ego-self and be open minded, one was perhaps realize harmony in one's daily interactions.

To be sure even on a personal level, life may not work out as one wishes. For Lao Zi, the transformative meditative process inevitably leads to a harmonious life in which one lives out one's days in peaceful contentment. For Zhuang Zi, the road may be considerably bumpier. His writings are filled with death and deformity, with story after story of colorful figures who, despite their personal attainment, are physically crippled and maimed. Ironically, these misshapen few, filled with potency (*de*), continue to attract others and to serve as exemplars and leaders despite their disfigurement.

Zhuang Zi invests great importance in the ability to reconcile oneself to whatever one confronts—perhaps because self-cultivation, through meditation or any other means, is no guarantee that all will go well. The authentically realized person is able to *xiao yao you* 逍遙遊: to transform along with his environment, to adapt and respond to the changing circumstances. Such a person "lets his heart roam in the flavorless, blends his energies with the featureless, accords with the sui generis emergent order of things while allowing no room for ego attachment" (20/7/10, G95). "They roam beyond the guidelines. They think of life as an obstinate wart or a dangling wen, of death as bursting the boil or letting out the pus. . . . Heedlessly they go roving beyond the dust and grime, go rambling through the lore in which there is nothing to do. How could they be finicky about the rites of common custom, on watch for inquisitive eyes and ears of the vulgar?" (18/6/66, G89). The person of *xiao yao you* is transformed. Sensitive to particularities, he gives up absolutes. He is always prepared to dispense with conventional rules, to abandon ideas, concepts, and beliefs gained from past experience in order to respond to new circumstances. Although he is not so passive as to simply allow circumstances to determine his course, he is ready to affirm whatever comes his way.

But one should not let Zhuang Zi's enraptured prose obscure his philosophical position. Although more of an antirationalist than Confucius in that he does not believe everybody will be won over to the sage's vision of harmony through reasoned persuasion, he is not the arch antirationalist some contend. Graham, for instance, asserts that "what logic there is in *Chuang-tzu* is directed against reason itself, in particular against rational choice between one course of action and another."[85] One would do well, however, to distinguish between "rational" in the Kantian-Enlightenment sense and in a pragmatic sense. Although Zhuang Zi rejects foundational rationality, he does allow that one can provide rationales and give reasons for one's actions and beliefs, albeit rationales and reasons relative to one's particular context, tradition and so forth.

In contrast, in Graham's view, Zhuang Zi advocates one dispense with all reasoning and simply respond "spontaneously," "with awareness (of what is objectively so)."[86] Meditation leads not simply to the emptiness of the pure consciousness event but to the infusion of an illuminative "daimonic power from outside."

> The stilling of passions and clarification of senses and heart leading to the coming and going of the daimon is assumed to orient one in the direction of the benevolent and the right. . . . [This assumption] is supported by the experience that spontaneity in meditation leads rather to loss of self (Chuang-tzu's 'the utmost man has no self') than to selfishness. . . . However, this

spontaneity is also a liberation from fixed standards. It is surrender to daimonic power from outside which being independent of man is by definition from Heaven, and may collide with instead of confirming accepted morality. In such conflict the spontaneous preference in heightened awareness carries with it a self-evident authority which is not merely a matter of subjective conviction.[87]

Elsewhere, Graham compares the mind of Zhuang Zi's sage to a mirror that "reflect[s] the situation as it objectively is."[88] The sage "keeps his heart empty and lets the external scene fill it, sort itself out in its objective relations, and then 'move' him."[89] He goes so far as to speak of the process in the language of behavioral psychology, of Pavlovian stimulus and response, arguing that the sage's actions derive "not from man but from Heaven working through him."[90]

We are in agreement on several points: that meditation leads to a loss of ego-self, to an abandonment of fixed standards; that one responds to the conditions in which one finds oneself; that one's response may conflict with conventional morality. I do not agree, however, that Zhuang Zi privileges the meditative experience or the state of "spontaneous" awareness. The result of meditation, of the emptying process, is not that our minds mirror nature. Zhuang Zi's antifoundationalism militates against any such reading.[91] While the state of pure consciousness is one of emptiness and arguably transcends subjectivity, once one becomes aware of "objective reality," one is already interpreting, making distinctions, constructing experience. One is back in the subjective world of perspectival *yin shi*. The way of the sage is one more *yin shi*, one more that's it that goes by circumstance.

The view that one "surrenders" to some "daimonic force" that infallibly leads to "the Way" is also problematic. First, Zhuang Zi does not allow that the meditative process will infallibly lead to *the* Way. At best, one may gain an insight as to *a* way to proceed. But that way will not necessarily lead to harmony and contentment even on a personal level.[92] Second, to speak of surrender to a daimonic force from outside is to make the process too passive. One is not only conditioned by one's environment. One is as well a constituting factor in one's environment. One both conditions and is conditioned by one's world. The goal is not passive submission to nature, but a world in which neither nature nor man is victor over the other.

Further, to describe the process as "spontaneous" is somewhat misleading. Although the initial insight that comes to one in the meditative process may be instantaneous, one is not necessarily to act simply on that insight. The insight might be, if not misguided, at least insufficient in and of itself to solve the problem. There is considerably more reflection and sorting out prior to the initiation of action than "spontaneity" would allow. Indeed, Graham acknowledges that "a lot of hard thinking" might be needed before a person responds with awareness: "the Taoist art of living is supremely intelligent responsiveness."[93] He points out, moreover, that Zhuang Zi does speak favorably of one kind of thinking and distinction making: *lun* (論 —sorting out).[94]

> Dao has never had borders, speaking has never had constant norms. It is by a "That's it" which deems that a boundary is marked. Let me say something about the marking of boundaries. You can locate as there and enclose by a line, sort out (*lun*) and assess, divide up and discriminate between alternatives, compete over and fight over: these I call the Eight Powers. What is outside the cosmos the sage locates (*cun* 存) as there but does not sort out (*lun*). What is within the cosmos the sage sorts out as there but does not assess (*yi* 議). The records of the former kings in the successive reigns in the Annals the sage assesses, but he does not argue over alternatives (*bian* 辯) (5/2/55, G57).

Even in the "knack stories" that Graham points to as illustrations of spontaneity, there is more reflection and thinking than one would expect. For instance, Cook Ding, the famous butcher who after several years has become so adept at carving oxen that he need "not look with the eye" because he "knows with the senses where to stop," must at times pause and reflect on how to proceed: "whenever I come to something intricate, I see where it will be hard to handle, and cautiously prepare myself, my gaze settles on it, action slows down for it . . . and at one stroke the tangle has been unravelled" (8/3/10, G63).

Of course, when one does finally act, it may be "spontaneous" in the sense that it is instantaneous and not the result of a conscious directive from the mind. Further, Graham is right, I believe, that at bottom of all rationality—be it of the Enlightenment-Kantian sort or that of coherence theories—there is an element of spontaneity, of intuition.[95] That is a key insight of antifoundationalism. Every system rests on some unsupported assumption. Coherence theorists simply give up the pretense to have built a system of rationality from the ground up. They openly acknowledge that at some point reasons may run out and we will be left with our intuitions as to what constitutes a coherent system, a best response, all things considered.

Nevertheless, that one cannot ultimately ground one's decisions in an unshakable foundation of reason need not prevent one from engaging in reasoned assessment of the most appropriate way to proceed in the particular context. In seeking a way that will allow one to respond to the exigencies of one's own life, and that will in the event of interpersonal conflict allow both alternatives to proceed, one may discuss or sort out (*lun*) the situation with the other parties. For one party to insist on a particular course of action on the grounds that it is one's spontaneous preference would be anathema to Zhuang Zi. One must always maintain an open mind.

Indeed, as Graham admits, there are differences in levels of awareness. How then does one determine that one has responded with awareness rather than from paranoia or delusion? Graham suggests that one must put one's argument into "a coherent and publicly testable form," for this is "the only assurance even for himself that he is illuminated and not deluded."[96] Granted, the concurrence of others cannot prove apodicticly that one is right or wrong. Nevertheless, one must be at least willing to entertain their arguments that one has not responded appropriately, that one's spontaneous act does not reflect the highest level of awareness possible in the situation.

There is, then, room for fallible, perspectival reasoning in Zhuang Zi's realization of a way that works for the parties concerned. In fact, that dao does emerge out of fallible judgments (*yin shi*) distinguishes Zhuang Zi from Huang-Lao. The privileging of the spontaneous discovery of the objective Way is characteristic not of the antifoundational epistemology of Zhuang Zi, but of the foundational naturalism of Huang-Lao.

VII. The Evolution of Huang-Lao Thought

✳

I have argued that the Huang-Lao thought of the *Boshu* is best understood as a foundational naturalism in which the human social order is based on and implicate in the natural order. As a naturalism, the natural order is normatively privileged. As a foundational naturalism, it is predetermined. That the human social order—encompassing personal behavior as well as social institutions—is grounded in, justified by, and judged against the natural order is evidenced in various ways. Jurisprudentially, the author advances a natural law theory in that laws arise from dao, the natural order. In terms of philosophy of language, he sponsors a realist, correspondence theory of names in which names and forms (*xing ming*) are a direct manifestation of dao. Sociopolitically, he favors a hierarchy where social classes are held to be "natural," a constant and given feature of the preconfigured natural order. These aspects of Huang-Lao philosophy are predicated on a foundational, correspondence epistemology in which one discovers dao, the objective natural order articulated in terms of *li* (principles), *fa* (laws), and *xing ming* (forms and names), by eliminating subjective bias through the attainment of emptiness and tranquility (*xu jing*).

But Huang-Lao thought did not spring fully bloomed from the mind of the author of the *Boshu* alone. Rather, the author melded into a single system ideas of diverse thinkers and schools. In Chapters IV to VI, I presented Huang-Lao thought as a development of and response to several major thinkers, primarily Confucius, Han Fei Zi, Lao Zi, and Zhuang Zi. Yet there are many more who contributed important pieces to the Huang-Lao intellectual synthesis: some conceived of dao-nature as predetermined; others predicated law on dao; still others explicated *xing ming* as objective forms and names. Although no one person may have combined these ideas into the Huang-Lao system of the *Boshu*, each furnished one or more of the key building blocks. In section 1, I examine these antecedents of Huang-Lao thought. I begin with the rise of naturalism, and then turn to

217

the philosophers of the Jixia Academy whose views foreshadow most if not all of the individual components of Huang-Lao thought.

As a school of thought, Huang-Lao's sphere of influence extends well beyond the intellectual circles of the Jixia Academy. For a period of time, arguably from the collapse of Qin in 206 B.C. to the enthronement of Han Wu Di in 140 B.C., it was the dominant court ideology. In sections 2 and 3, I chart the rise and fall of Huang-Lao in the early Han. I first suggest reasons for the popularity of Huang-Lao among early Han political leaders. Then, having documented the number of politicians reported to be proponents of Huang-Lao, I offer evidence from the historical records that the policies of early Han leaders do in fact square with Huang-Lao tenets. In sections 3, I examine the political and philosophical reasons underlying the downfall of Huang-Lao during the reign of Emperor Wu.

Finally, in section 4, I trace Huang-Lao after its fall from power and expulsion from court. It is sometimes suggested that after its banishment by Wu Di, Huang-Lao as a political philosophy rapidly withers away, no longer to exert an influence on Han politics. Yet careful scrutiny of the historical records reveals that this simply is not so. Many political figures continue to espouse Huang-Lao ideas and implement Huang-Lao policies during the late Han.

Nevertheless, Huang-Lao's influence as a political philosophy diminishes drastically and continually in the late Han. Indeed, Huang-Lao exerts its greatest influence during this period not through its political philosophy but through its reemergence in conjunction with religious Daoism and immortality practices associated with the Yellow Emperor. As Holmes Welch has demonstrated, the tributaries flowing into religious Daoism are many.[1] One of these is the pursuit of immortality and the practices developed for that end by the *fang shi* (方士—so-called magicians) of Qi and others. In section 4, I reconstruct one of the bridges connecting Huang-Lao to religious Daoism by sketching the role of naturalism in the development of early Han immortality practices.[2]

1. Antecedents

1.1 Emergence of Naturalism

The interpretation of classical Daoism as naturalism is long standing. By the end of the Warring States period, Xun Zi was already characterizing Daoists as naturalists, and criticizing them for neglecting the significant role of humans in shaping the world one lives in.

You glorify nature and meditate on her;
Why not domesticate her and regulate her?
You obey nature and sing her praises;
Why not control her course and use it?
You look on the seasons with reverence and await them;
Why not respond to them by seasonal activities? . . .
To neglect man and speculate about nature
is to misunderstand the facts of the universe. (64/17/44, W86)

Two points merit comment. First, Xun Zi attributes to Daoism a view of nature similar to the predetermined natural order of Huang-Lao. Nature is a transcendent realm of value: it constitutes a normatively privileged order to which the personal behavior and social institutions of humans must conform. Therefore the second point: the "Daoist" understanding of the natural order as predetermined and normatively privileged creates a separation between humans and normative authority. For Xun Zi, this places humans in too deferential a position and ignores their capacity to effect change in the sociocosmic order. Xun Zi, insisting on a greater role for humans in shaping the cosmos, refuses to privilege the natural order to the extent Daoists do—in his reading.[3]

One might suspect that Xun Zi had Huang-Lao Daoists in mind when he offered his critique.[4] Yet he specifically criticizes Lao Zi and Zhuang Zi along similar lines, verifying that his remarks apply to their positions. He admonishes Zhuang Zi for privileging nature, saying, "Zhuang Zi was obsessed by thoughts on nature . . . and did not understand the importance of man. . . . He who thinks only of nature will take the way to be wholly a matter of harmonizing with the natural forces" (79/21/23, W126). In light of Zhuang Zi's deconstruction of the nature-human dichotomy, Xun Zi's criticism is misdirected. As discussed in the last chapter, Zhuang Zi refuses to privilege nature over humans, arguing for a balance in which "neither nature nor man is victor over the other."[5] That he does so militates against interpretations of his Daoism as naturalism as defined in Chapter II and intended in Huang-Lao thought.

Given the name Huang-*Lao*, one might assume Lao Zi to be the more likely source for "Daoist" or Huang-Lao naturalism. Indeed, it is difficult to find interpretations of the *Dao De Jing*, whether ancient or modern, that do not at some point appeal to some version of naturalism. Xun Zi, for instance, disagreeing with what he considers to be an excessively acquiescent attitude toward nature, castigates Lao Zi as one who "had insight about bending but not about expansion" (64/17/51, C123). Chen Guying, on the other hand, speaks for many modern scholars when he asserts that "Lao Zi's philosophy is fundamentally a simple naturalism."[6]

Of course, what the commentators mean by *naturalism* often differs widely. Some take natural to refer to that which is spontaneous, unforced, nonpurposive. Duyvendak champions this view: "The Taoist Saint . . . keeps to the weak and lowly, and refrains from any conspicuous effort, any striving after a set purpose. In a sense therefore he may be said to have a purpose. His *wu wei* is practiced with a conscious design; he chooses this attitude in the conviction that only by so doing the 'natural' development of things will favor him."[7]

A second understanding of *natural* is that which is in keeping with one's inner nature. Feng Yu-lan, for instance, suggests that to act naturally is to act in accordance with one's inherent self-nature, one's *de*—"what individual objects obtain from Tao and thereby become what they are." "*Wu Wei* can be translated literally as 'having-no-activity' or 'non-action'. . . . According to the theory of 'having-no-activity,' a man should restrict his activities to what is necessary and what is natural. 'Necessary' means necessary for a certain purpose, and never over-doing. 'Natural' means following one's [*de*] with no arbitrary effort."[8]

A third sense of *natural* is that which is not artificial. Burton Watson is one advocate of this ubiquitous view. In ascribing to Zhuang Zi a naturalism in which one achieves spontaneous union with nature, he states "Nature . . . pertains to the natural as opposed to the artificial."[9]

I have offered a critique of these three positions elsewhere.[10] These interpretations rest on senses of *natural* that differ from those intended by Huang-Lao. For Huang-Lao, *natural* refers to (a) human behavior or social practices that imitate or are modeled on nonhuman nature and (b) human behavior or social practices that instantiate a predetermined role in the cosmic natural order.[11] Because the senses of natural differ from those of Huang-Lao, I will not consider these three views further.

There are, however, other interpretations of Lao Zi's naturalism that although not identical to Huang-Lao naturalism, nevertheless merit attention. Needham, for instance, argues that Lao Zi's dao is the logos of the natural order, the underlying structure of the cosmos:

For the Taoists the Tao or Way was not the right way of life within human society, but the way in which the universe worked; in other words the Order of Nature. . . . Tao as the Order of Nature, which brought all things into existence and governs their very action, not so much by force as by a kind of natural curvature in space and time, reminds us of the *logos* of Heracleitus of Ephesus, controlling the orderly process of change. . . . The Tao was thought of not only as vaguely informing all things, but as being the naturalness, the very structure, of particular and individual things.[12]

In this reading, dao is what Feng Yu-lan calls "the all-embracing first principle of things."[13] The *logos* of the universe, dao determines the cosmos and all that is in it.[14] The universe is an a priori organic whole in that all the myriad things that collectively constitute the totality, including humans, are part of the natural order. As such, they are all subject to dao as the governing principle–the natural laws: "Tao as the Order of Nature . . . governs their very action."

Yet this view is problematic. If humans are part of dao the natural order—as is the case for Needham and all naturalists who attribute all-inclusiveness to dao—the normative exhortation to comply with dao (to obey the laws of nature, to act naturally) is unnecessary. What else could one do? Dao is the logos of the natural order, the laws of nature governing the universe, and everything in it. Humans are part of the universe. Therefore dao governs humans.

Humans must inevitably conform to laws of nature and the natural order; they cannot *not* obey them. It is just as impossible for humans to avoid undergoing the physical, chemical, and biological processes governed by natural laws as it is for any nonhuman thing in the universe. To instruct one that he "has to" obey in a normative sense is therefore useless advice: one need not tell a person jumping off the Empire State Building to obey the law of gravity.[15]

Proponents of this interpretation could salvage their theory by drawing a distinction between dao the descriptive and dao the normative natural order. Dao as the descriptive totality, the cosmic order that does in fact attain at any given moment, is all-embracing. However, there is also a normative dao, a normative natural order, that is not necessarily attained. To *wu wei* is to comply with dao the normative natural order.[16]

This is the route taken by the author of the *Boshu*. It is also the route taken by Chan in his interpretation of Lao Zi's alleged naturalism. He rejects the notion that the cosmos is a priori a normative organic whole. Rather this is something that humans must achieve: "It is not an exaggeration to say that Tao operates according to certain laws which are constant and regular. One may even say there is an element of necessity in these laws, for Tao by its very nature behaves in this way and all things in order to achieve their full realization, have to obey them. Tao, after all, is *the* Way. . . . When things obey its laws, all parts of the universe will form a harmonious whole and the universe will become an integrated organism."[17] In this view, dao is a rule governed, normatively predetermined natural order. Although so of itself (*zi ran*) in the sense that the laws that govern the Way are not the product of an ontologically distinct source such as God, dao is nevertheless predetermined: as Chan puts it, there is a necessity to the laws which govern the Way.

In the last chapter, I argued that such a reading, though appropriate for the Huang-Lao thought of the *Boshu*, does not square with the spontaneous, open-ended, and nonteleological evolutionary character of Lao Zi's emergent order. Although Lao Zi favors an understanding of *tian* that is naturalistic and nonanthropomorphic, and although he does encourage humans to model nonhuman nature in a general sense,[18] he does not believe in a rule governed, predetermined, fixed natural order.

The source of the misreading would appear to be Chapter 25 where Lao Zi declares that "man takes earth as the standard; earth takes heaven (*tian*) as the standard; heaven takes dao as the standard; and dao takes what is so of itself (*zi ran*) as standard." Chan tellingly translates the last phrase, "and Tao models itself after Nature," taking *zi ran* in the modern sense of *da zi ran*: (great) nature.[19] I have argued for a more literal reading of *zi ran* as so of itself. On a cosmological or metaphysical level, dao is *zi ran*—so of itself in the sense that the natural order is emergent. That is, dao is not disciplined by a transcendent, determinant source of order but arises contextually out of the conditions that constitute it. Although there is some regularity to the natural order, it is not completely determinate, closed off as it were to the possibility of evolving novel patterns. On the contrary. There is an ineradicable element of spontaneity to the cosmos that undermines any attempt to reduce it to mechanical and infallible rules.

Further, because the world one lives in is open to unforseen and unforeseeable change, one must maintain an open mind, constantly ridding oneself of bias through the apopathic "return to the root." Thus the normative dao-order discovered on a personal level and manifested in personal and interpersonal behavior is also *zi ran*, so of itself. For this reason, it cannot be conceived in terms of or reduced to predetermined laws—hence Lao Zi's rejection of rule ethics. Normatively appropriate (*wu wei*) behavior is so of itself, *zi ran*, in two ways. First, there are no external principles, no foundational realms of value, to which one must or even might appeal as determinate guides to one's behavior. Rather, the only standards for determining appropriate behavior are internal: they arise out of the concerns, values, and so forth of the parties themselves—they are self-so, self-generated. Second, in seeking a harmonious order in which the interests of all are given due consideration and no one is left out, there are no others to be acted against. If not other, then all are in some sense "self": as a harmonious community, the many individuals comprise a collective self.

For both Lao Zi and Zhuang Zi, dao-the way consists of an appropriate relation of humans to the universe, a certain orientation of the individual person to his or her environment of other particulars that, conceived of in the broadest sense, includes all of the myriad things—human and nonhuman—forming the cosmos. Lao Zi refers to this way as *tian dao* (the way of heaven) as opposed to *ren dao* (the way of man). As discussed in the last chapter, the latter is based on self-interest arising from the perception of one's environment as consisting of discrete objects in opposition to one another. The former results from an understanding of one's environment as a harmony of interrelated particulars. It is through *de* (potency) that one, acknowledging one's interrelation to others, integrates harmoniously into one's world. As Zhuang Zi says, "this person, this potency (*de*) that is in him, would merge the myriad creatures and make them one" (2/1/31, G46). The result is that one *wu wei*s (acts nonimpositionally) so that nothing is left undone.[20]

Thus *wu wei* and *you wei* refer to a qualitative distinction in behavior originating from two contrasting perspectives. In *you wei*, the individual acts from the perspective of a discrete individual in opposition to other individuals in his environment. Seeking self-benefit, one creates conflict. *You wei* is the way of most humans most of the time, *ren dao*. *Wu wei*, by contrast, results from the apprehension of one's environment as a sphere of interrelated persons and things so that there are no extrinsically opposed others. One realizes one's potential with and through others. Acknowledging and incorporating the intrinsic uniqueness, value, and interests of the others in one's behavior, one does not contend but harmonizes. To *wu wei* is the way of heaven, *tian dao*, and the way of the sage.

In sum, the normative order for Lao Zi results from *wu wei* behavior that does not conform to predetermined rules and that arises out of and incorporates the interests, concerns, and attitudes of particular parties. As such, the normative order, like the descriptive natural order, is *zi ran*, so of itself. Thus Lao Zi does not privilege the (predetermined) natural order as the normative basis of the human social order. Rejecting the notion of a rule governed natural order and rule ethics along with it, he takes dao in both its descriptive and normative senses to be emergent.

Why then do so many learned scholars interpret the *Lao Zi* as naturalism? There are, in addition to the tendency to read *zi ran* as *da zi ran* (nature), several reasons. First, some take the censure of Confucianism by Lao Zi and Zhuang Zi to be a rejection of anthropocentrism *and* conversely an endorsement of naturalism. It is thought to be a condemnation of the human realm in deference to the supremacy of the natural: "We can see a major difference between the Taoist and Confucian schools. Whereas Confucius lays great stress on 'ornamentation' in the form of rites, cere-monies, and moral standards, Lao Tzu condemns them as an obstruction to the expression of man's natural spontaneity."[21] Yet while Lao Zi and Zhuang Zi object to the primacy of the human realm in the Confucian tradition, this does not mean that they subscribe to naturalism. On the contrary. They are against the excessive limitations of Confucian anthro-pocentricism. They favor, not the *exclusion* of humans in a radical dualism with nature, but the *inclusion* of nonhumans with humans in an organic whole. The ideal, as Zhuang Zi states, is a balance between the two, a harmony in which neither is subjugated to the other.

A second reason for the pervasiveness of naturalist readings is that "natural" means many things to many people. Some naturalist interpreta-tions may prove helpful in elucidating aspects of Lao Zi's thought. It may be possible, for example, to interpret the injunction to act naturally rather than artificially in a way that accounts for Lao Zi's advocacy of a simple, "primitive" life-style that calls into question the value of technology.[22]

A third potential explanation is that commentators from Xun Zi to Chan have tended to elide Lao Zi's position with that of Huang-Lao. That they would do so is understandable. By the late Warring States period, Huang-Lao had gained considerable influence; by the early Han, it had become the dominant court ideology. Given the high degree of linguistic overlap characteristic of Chinese philosophy in general and even more pre-valent between the *Lao Zi* and the Huang-Lao thought of the *Boshu*, that later Warring States and early Han commentators would read Lao Zi in terms of the then dominant Huang-Lao school is certainly possible. Mod-ern commentators, for their part, brought up on a scientific understanding of nature—not to mention a steady diet of foundational epistemologies, correspondence theories of truth, and universalizable ethical rules—may have found it hard to resist recasting Lao Zi's impersonal but emergent natural order in terms of their own determinate and rule governed under-standing of nature.

Whatever the explanation, many have attributed to Lao Zi a natural-ist world-view that belongs more appropriately to Huang-Lao. Yet if the author of the *Boshu* did not get the idea of a predetermined, rule governed natural order from Lao Zi, where did he get it? The answer may very well lie with Zou Yan and his fellow Jixia philosophers.

1.2   Jixia Academy

In the first chapter, I discussed the political background of the Jixia Academy and its relation to Huang-Lao. To recapitulate, the Tian family of Qi usurped power from the legitimate ruling house. Needing to justify their takeover, they appealed to the symbol of the Yellow Emperor, a mythic warrior who unified the empire through military conquest. In addition, they sponsored many intellectuals who gathered together at what has become known as the Jixia Academy. Some have argued that the Tian clan patronized these philosophers in an attempt to emulate earlier noble houses, and to regain thereby support of the people. Others have suggested that they sought an ideology to justify political unification and hoped the philosophers of Jixia would provide it. Whatever their intentions, the result, it is argued, is the emergence of a new, eclectic school of thought known as Huang-Lao.

In support of this view, many have noted that the first dated reference to the Yellow Emperor is a bronze inscription in which the Tian clan claims the Yellow Emperor as ancient ancestor.[23] There are, moreover, numerous other ties between the Huang-Lao school and the Jixia Academy. For instance, several thinkers linked to Huang-Lao in the historical records, most notably Zou Yan and Shen Dao, are reported to have spent time at Jixia.[24] And the *Guan Zi*, a multi-author work that contains many of the central ideas of the *Boshu*, is believed to have been compiled at the academy.[25] In this section, I explore the close relation between Huang-Lao and the Jixia Academy by examining the writings of Jixia philosophers as potential sources for the Huang-Lao thought of the *Boshu*.

Zou Yan and the Yin Yang *Wu Xing* (Five Phases) School

Zou Yan (350?–270?)[26] of Qi is the alleged founder of the Yin Yang Five Phases school of Jixia, and one of the first to conceive of nature as rule governed. Sima Qian summarizes his importance as follows:

> The state of Qi had three scholars named Zou. . . . Zou Yan was the second. . . . He saw that rulers were becoming more dissolute and were incapable of valuing virtue. . . . So he examined deeply into the phenomena of the increase and decrease of yin and yang and wrote essays totalling more than 100,000 words about their strange permutations, and about the cycles of the great sages from beginning to end. His sayings were vast and far-reaching and not in accord with the accepted beliefs of the classics. He began by examining small objects, and from these he drew conclusions about large ones, until he reached what was without limit. He spoke about modern times, and from this went back to the time of Huang Di. The scholars all studied his arts. . . . He began by classifying China's notable mountains, great rivers and connecting valleys; its birds and beasts; the fruitfulness of its waters and soils, and its rare products; and from this extended his survey to what is beyond the seas, and men are unable to observe. . . . Kings, dukes and great officials,

when they first witnessed his arts, fearfully transformed themselves. . . . Thus Master Zou was highly regarded in Qi. (74.2344, F(1), 1:159)

Zou Yan is an influential figure not only at the Jixia Academy but throughout the state of Qi and beyond.[27] He appears to have been held in particularly high regard by the politicians of his day. This is understandable in that his intellectual contribution lies in the establishment of natural foundations for the moral and sociopolitical order. Confronting the Warring States breakdown in the normative order, Zou Yan turns to the regular cycles of the natural order as the basis for human social order. He claims that by investigating the natural processes, one is able to determine the underlying principles of the way and to model human society accordingly. For Zou Yan, the underlying principles structuring the natural order are yin and yang and the five phases (*wu xing*).

The original meaning of yin and yang is unclear. Etymologically the words are associated with the shady and sunny sides of mountains or valleys, darkness and light, heat and cold.[28] Although the terms occur in works as early as the *Shu Ching* and *Zuo Zhuan*, many scholars believe these early mentions to be later interpolations,[29] with yin yang first assuming philosophical meaning as the primary cyclical cosmological forces in the third or fourth century B.C.[30] As for *wu xing*, Graham contends that they "were imposed on an older system of fives coordinated with the six *ch'i*, causing some rearrangements."[31]

Zou Yan is generally credited as the first to fuse the originally independent yin yang and five phases into a single system. His theory is an example of correlative thinking, "a kind of anthropocosmology in which entities, processes and classes of phenomena found in nature correspond to or 'go together' with various entities, processes and classes of phenomena in the human world."[32]

The essence of Zou Yan's correlative cosmology is that the cosmos consists of two or five forces which sequentially succeed each other in a constant, reliable cycle. The Han philosopher Dong Zhongshu summarizes yin yang theory as follows: "The constant cause of heaven is that forces in opposition to each other cannot both arise simultaneously. . . . The yin and yang are these mutually opposite forces. Therefore when one expands outward, the other retracts inward. . . . (51/12/5, F(1), 2:23).

Having postulated a theory delineating the principles structuring nature, Zou Yan and the Yin Yang school then extend their correlative theory into the human realm. Thus Dong Zhongshu contends, "the relationships between ruler and subject, father and son, husband and wife, are all derived from the principles of yin and yang. The ruler is yang, the subject yin, the father yang, the son yin, the husband yang, the wife yin" (53/12.8, F(1), 2:42).[33]

One sees in yin-yang five phases theory the beginnings of Huang-Lao foundational naturalism: the natural order is rule governed, with the rules that apply to nonhuman nature applying equally to the human social realm. Further, although the yin-yang five phases correlative paradigm may have existed long before Zou Yan, only from about the time of Zou in the late Warring States and then continuing on into the Han—the time of the rise of the Yellow Emperor and Huang-Lao, and the writing of the *Boshu*—are correlative cosmologies such as yin yang and the five phases considered as the *causal* forces behind the natural processes.[34]

As Graham cautions, "one should not think of [early] Chinese correlative thinking as the application of metaphysical theories about Yin Yang and the Five Phases."[35] That is, prior to Zou Yan, yin yang and the five phases serve as classification paradigms but do not provide causal explanations of the natural order. Consider the following schema:

Yang-A	*Yin-B*
heaven	earth
sun	moon
male	female
hot	cold

As Graham explains, "the cosmologist is not applying a *theory* about yin and yang; for purposes of explanation and inference, 'yang' and 'yin' function like our 'A' and 'B', they mark the series with which something connects and the opposite series with a member of which it contrasts."[36]

With Zou Yan, however, a shift occurs in the nature of correlative thinking. Yin-yang and the five phases are now understood as causal cosmological principles, as forces determining the natural order.[37] The incorporation of yin and yang into various cosmogonical schemata, generally similar to that found in the *Huai Nan Zi*, attests to this development:

The Great Beginning produced an empty extensiveness, and this empty extensiveness produced the cosmos. The cosmos produced the primal qi, which had its limits. That which was clear and light (yang) collected to form Heaven. That which was heavy and turbid (yin) congealed to form Earth . . .
    The essence of Heaven and Earth formed the yin and yang, and the concentrated essence of yin and yang formed the four seasons. The scattered essences of the yin and yang formed the myriad things. The hot force (qi) of yang . . . produced fire, and the essence of fire formed the sun. The cold force (qi) of yin . . . produced water and the essence of water formed the

moon . . . [and so on until the whole natural cosmos is formed]. (3/35/3, F(1), 1:396–397)

The shift from descriptive to causal correlative cosmologies—from classification schemes to a theory accounting for the actual mechanism by which things are correlated and exert influence on each other—is made possible by a conception of the cosmos as a constant, rule governed natural order. This conception lies at the heart of Huang-Lao foundational naturalism where the human social order is grounded in the predetermined natural order.

Zou Yan's theory parallels that of Huang-Lao in two other respects. For both, humans are part of the cosmic natural order and, as such, are governed by the same laws that govern nonhuman nature. Second, and correlate to the first, humans are to follow nature and the natural order. In the early causal correlative cosmology of Zou Yan and even more clearly in the foundational naturalism of the *Boshu*, humans simply conform to the normatively given natural order. By contrast, among Han causal correlative cosmologists and immortality seekers, humans are able to interact with and effect change in nonhuman nature and the natural order. Because humans and the human social order are linked to nature and the natural order through the medium of qi underlying the yin yang five phases cosmological forces, humans can effect change in nature and the natural order by manipulating qi and hence the cosmic forces of yin yang five phases. As a result, determination of the descriptive and normative order becomes truly *co*-relative, a result of the negotiation and interaction of humans with their natural environment. As will be discussed later, this understanding of order as bidirectional plays a pivotal role in the development of numerous Han immortality practices eventually adopted by religious Daoism.

The task at hand, however, is to document the shift in the *Boshu* from yin yang understood as descriptive categories to yin yang as cosmological forces.

Where in seasons of plenty there is inadequate effort, the yin elements will reassert themselves and the qi of earth will repeat the harvest.[38] Unless one practices punishment consistent with the designated season, the hibernating creatures will not come out. Becoming cold again, it will snow and frost and the grain will wither in its first month of growth. With these calamities befalling them, those who go about their affairs in such a manner will not succeed. Where in seasons of scarcity one is overzealous, the yang elements will reassert themselves and the qi of the earth will not induce the harvest. Unless one relaxes punishments consistent with the designated season, the hibernating creatures will start to sound forth and the grasses will once again flourish. With yang adding to yang, and seasons repeating themselves without luster, those who go about their affairs in such a manner will not continue on. Once the way of heaven is fulfilled, the earthly phenomena will find their completion. (62:88a)

Yin and yang are described as forces (qi) that effect changes in nature. If humans do not conform to the predetermined natural order, to the regular cycles of yin and yang, then there will be a physical reaction: snow will fall in summer and so on. Further, although human behavior affects the natural order, the proper order is taken as given. When humans do not comply with the proper proper natural order, cosmic harmony is lost and disorder ensues. It is the job of the sage-ruler to discover the natural order and to make sure humans do not deviate from it.

Zou Yan's causal correlative cosmology delineating the natural order in terms of determinate forces may have been one of the inspirations for the foundational naturalism of the *Boshu*. Of course, given the problems of dating both Zou Yan and the *Boshu*, it is impossible to determine who preceded, and hence might have influenced, whom. Indeed, the *Boshu* in many ways appears to predate the full development of yin-yang five phases as a causal correlative cosmology. The text makes no mention of the five phases. And while yin yang are used in a causal correlative way,[39] they are also often used in their earlier senses, as lightness versus darkness,[40] and as descriptive categories.[41] Although one cannot conclude from this that the *Boshu* necessarily predated Zou Yan, it does favor a late Warring States as opposed to a Han dating: by the Han, five phases theory is so widespread and closely linked to yin-yang that one would expect the author to take note of, if not incorporate, the five phases into his own yin yang naturalism.[42]

Of one thing one can be certain. There existed in the Jixia Academy naturalist world-views similar to that of the author of the *Boshu*. If one is seeking a source for the author's ideas, the Academy would seem a more likely birthplace for his conception of nature than the *Lao Zi*. In any event, the existence of similar naturalist world-views strengthens the claim that the Huang-Lao school arose at—or at least in conjunction with the ideas of—the Jixia Academy. Examination of the thought of other Jixia philosophers such as Shen Dao further supports this view.

Shen Dao

Shen Dao's association with Jixia is recorded in the *Shi Ji* (46.1895). Because his writings are no longer available except in collected fragments, it is difficult to determine his exact position. He has been variously described as a Legalist, a Daoist, both Legalist and Daoist, an eclectic (*za jia* 雜家), and as an early proponent of Huang-Lao.[43] With respect to the last, Sima Qian reports that Shen Dao "studied the techniques of Huang-Lao Daoism" (74.2347).

Taking their cue from Sima Qian, several modern scholars have compared Shen Dao to the author of the *Boshu*. As pertains to my thesis, the main points of comparison are twofold: Shen Dao synthesizes dao and law (*fa*); and he grounds law in dao understood as the natural order, thus advancing a natural law theory similar to that of the *Boshu*.[44]

I accept the first claim: that there is role for both dao and law in Shen Dao's philosophy. I reject, however, the second claim: that Shen Dao offers a natural law theory similar to that of the *Boshu*. To sort these claims out requires an examination of Shen Dao's view of nature.

In a passage that occurs with only minor variations in the *Boshu*, Shen Dao depicts nature as impersonal, with heaven and earth offering their bounty without the least regard for the needs of humans.[45] He contends, moreover, that humans are to follow nature in some sense: "It is the way of nature that the results of accommodation are great and that the results of alteration are small. By 'accommodation' is meant accommodation to human reality" (28). Jiang Ronghai concludes that Shen Dao is advising humans to take the natural order (*tian dao*) as the standard by which to measure human affairs.[46]

Gao Yinxiu and Zhang Zhihua add that the "Tianxia" chapter of *Zhuang Zi* supports the view that humans, according to Shen Dao, are to follow dao the natural order. The "Tianxia" chapter portrays Shen as an antirationalist urging the abandonment of knowledge: "Simply attain to being like a thing without knowledge. Have no use for excellence or sagehood; a clump of soil does not miss the Way" (92/33/50, G280). Shen Dao, apparently confusing the descriptive way with the prescriptive or normative way, seems to be advocating that one abandon knowledge, cease arguing over who is right (*shi*) and who wrong (*fei*), and simply follow nature. There is but one way, the natural one. No matter what one does, one is part of the cosmic natural order; as a consequence, one inevitably conforms to its laws. Thus there is no need for knowledge, no cause for dispute.[47]

Assembling the disparate strands, the argument is that Shen Dao's assertion that humans are to follow the natural order coupled with his rejection of knowledge in favor of the natural way provides the basis for a natural law theory in which (a) rule of law as a general social institution or practice is rationally justified and (b) specific laws are grounded in the natural order. Thus Gao Yinxiu and Zhang Zhihua claim that "the theoretical basis of Shen Dao's rule of law thought is the Daoist philosophy of following nature. His goal lies in proving the natural (*tian ran*) rationality of a rule of law . . . Shen Dao, taking what nature produces as the perfect standard for the movements of the world, demands that social regulations be compared with, emulate and model nature."[48] Jiang Ronghai, for his part, claims that "dao produces laws; laws are a manifestation of dao. . . . The intimate relation between dao and law is a definitive feature of the Huang-Lao school."[49]

There are several problems with this argument. First, one must take with a grain of salt the *Zhuang Zi* passages. They attribute to Shen Dao a much more antirationalist leaning than is consistent with his predominantly legalist orientation evinced in the attested fragments.[50] Indeed, the *Zhuang Zi* ascribes to Shen Dao views which contradict his expressed position in other works. For instance, the Shen Dao of the fragments contends that "in these present times, the state lacks a constant way and officials constant laws. This is why the state is daily enmeshed in greater error" (19). That the state is enmeshed in error because it deviates from the constant dao is at odds with the view ascribed to him in the *Zhuang Zi*, where even a clod follows dao. Further, if even a clod follows dao, why worry about juristic laws in the first place? Were Shen Dao as confused about the difference between dao the descriptive natural order and dao the normative natural order as the *Zhuang Zi* would have one believe, he would have no reason to fret over which policies and social institutions are most efficacious for attaining social order. His concern for such matters indicates that he is not the simple-minded naturalist that many make him out to be.

Second, although Shen Dao does contend that humans are in some sense to follow the way of nature (*tian dao*), this need not commit him to a natural law theory where juristic laws are grounded in the natural order; nor need it commit him to the project of proving the natural rationality of a rule of law, as Gao and Zhang assert. In fact, even if committed to the latter project, this need not commit him to the first. One could argue that law as an institution is rationally justified in light of certain features of human nature, for example, and still not believe particular laws to be rationally justified. This is roughly the position of Hobbes. Given his view of humans as radically self-interested, atomistic individuals in competition over scarce goods, laws are necessary to protect one and one's property from others. For this reason, the argument goes, rule of law as a social practice or institution is rationally justified.[51] However, whether any particular law is valid or legitimate depends not on its rationality but rather on whether or not it was decreed or sanctioned by the sovereign. In taking what pleases the sovereign as the criterion of validity, Hobbes reveals his positivist colors.[52]

Shen Dao, like Hobbes, believes there are sufficient reasons to justify a rule of law: people are self-interested (29);[53] rulers are often of limited intelligence, and even if brilliant they are only one person and hence cannot personally hear every case; without impartial laws people are subject to the whims of those in power. But this acceptance of rule of law does not commit him to a natural law theory in which specific laws are rationally justified or grounded in the natural order.

Although Shen Dao holds the view that one is to follow nature, and perhaps that dao is the natural way, and although he surely advocates a rule of law, he does not ground particular laws in the natural order. His law is not natural law but positive law, though to demonstrate this will require closer scrutiny not only of his jurisprudence but of his epistemology as well.

There are many similarities between Shen Dao's jurisprudence—indeed his social and political philosophy more generally—and that of the *Boshu*. In regard to jurisprudence, both maintain that the state is to be ordered through rule of law (78–79);[54] laws are to be impartial (25, 26, 61–67, 75–77); laws are constant standards comparable to scales and balances (18, 102, 107, 120, 121); laws are to be held constant and changed only if necessary and in accordance with the way (19, 78). In terms of administrative policy and political philosophy, there also many points of agreement: appointments are made on the basis of ability rather than personal relations (25, 26, 27); duties are to be clear and not to overlap so that one person is responsible for one post (17, 26, 57–60); ruler and minister have their own duties and yet still cooperate (16, 53–56); government is for the sake of the people rather than the ruler alone (21, 22). It bears mention that the cooperative attitude of the ruler and ministers is a point shared in common by Shen Dao and Huang-Lao and denied by Han Fei, and that that attitude as well as the belief that government is for the sake of the people distances Shen Dao from Shang Yang.

Yet although Shen Dao may share much in common with the Huang-Lao philosophy of the *Boshu*, his law remains positive law; that of the *Boshu*, natural law. The primary motivation in advocating a rule of law for Shen Dao seems to be his distrust of a rule of man. He believes law will ensure impartiality: "Of the accomplishments of law, none is greater than the inhibition of private interests" (75). So concerned is he with possible abuses of power that he argues "even if the laws are not good, they are still preferable to no laws at all" (23).[55] This runs counter to a fundamental tenet of natural law theory: that an unjust law is no law at all. Shen Dao seems to be accepting the single most definitive characteristic of positivism, the by-now familiar minimum separation thesis: "the simple contention that it is in no sense a necessary truth that laws reproduce or satisfy certain demands of morality."

At the very least, Shen Dao's position is out of step with the Huang-Lao view that law is an expression of the normative natural order objectively discovered by the sage. But then Shen Dao flatly denies that discovery of the objective natural order is even possible: "Laws do not come down from heaven; they do not rise up out of the earth. They come from humans and simply coincide with their intentions."[56] With this, Shen Dao rejects the foundational, correspondence epistemology of the *Boshu*.[57] There is no way to read juristic laws off the face of the discovered natural order. Indeed, there is no discovered natural order, only human interpretations of the natural order. Thus, in the pivotal passage on which Jiang, Gao, and Zhang base much of their argument, Shen Dao declares not only that "it is the way of nature that the results of accommodation are great and that the results of alteration are small," but that "by 'accommodation' is meant accommodation to *human* reality" (28). Humans cannot escape their historical, cultural, and linguistic perspectives to gain access to the natural order and to discover therein the proper laws for society.

Particular laws and indeed the social institution of law itself are the products of human invention designed to serve human ends. Shen Dao sponsors a rule of law because it is the best way to promote social order. Not only does it encourage impartiality, thus serving the interests of the people, but it protects the ruler as well. Shen Dao believes, like Han Fei, that the average ruler is not likely to possess the intelligence of a sage (42). Even were he to, he would still be but one person (43). So the ruler must set up a mechanical process of impartial laws and then not interfere (*wu wei*), allowing his ministers to implement the system (*you wei*) (38–41, 45). Of utmost importance is that the ruler maintain complete control over the power of his position (44)[58] and not put his trust in the loyalty of his ministers (46–55). He is to rely on his *shi*—his political purchase, the power of his position—to govern.[59]

This reliance by the ruler on *shi* points to a third indicator—in addition to the acceptance of the minimum separation thesis and the rejection of Huang-Lao epistemology—of the difference between Shen Dao's positive law and the *Boshu*'s natural law. For Shen Dao as for Han Fei, the standard for changing laws is the judgment of the ruler.[60] Gao and Zhang call attention to the potential for abuse in this arrangement: the ruler's interests may conflict with the stated law; because the ruler relies on the power of his position (*shi*) to govern as he sees fit, the law is held hostage to the interests and integrity of the ruler. There are no institutional checks on his power. One can merely hope that he will appreciate the wisdom of not interfering (*wu wei*) and possess the moral character to maintain the interests of the people foremost in mind. Unfortunately, history has shown that one can rely on neither the wisdom nor the virtue of those with absolute power.

In the end, one can understand Xun Zi's summary assessment that "Shen Dao exalted *fa* (law) but had no *fa*"—no law or method—as saying that law for Shen Dao had no foundations.[61] While many of the elements of Huang-Lao natural law theory are present—most notably government as a rule of law, and dao as the natural order—Shen Dao does not ground the former in the latter via an epistemology of discovery of dao the natural order manifest in objective laws, principles (*li*) and forms and names (*xing ming*). Indeed, he rejects such an epistemology. Yet an epistemology very similar to that of the *Boshu* is to be found in another Jixia work, the *Guan Zi*.

Guan Zi

The *Guan Zi* is an eclectic text consisting of well over a hundred thousand characters and more than seventy chapters. Although dating and authorship problems are formidable, it is highly unlikely that any of the chapters are the work of Guan Zhong, the renowned statesman who died in 645 B.C., and after whom the book is titled.[62]

Whoever its authors, the *Guan Zi* constitutes an important treasury of Huang-Lao ideas. In fact, Hu Jiacong, the contemporary scholar most responsible for explicating the relation of Huang-Lao to Jixia and the *Guan Zi*, contends that one can find within its many chapters virtually all of the essential elements of the Huang-Lao synthesis achieved in the *Boshu*.

Beginning with the nature of nature, the *Boshu*'s notion that the natural order is governed by constant and objective principles originates, Hu suggests, at the Jixia Academy where heaven and earth are construed as an impersonal natural order rather than anthropomorphically.[63] Hu goes so far as to claim that in several chapters of the *Guan Zi*, dao is to be understood as an objective natural order, and that the human social order is to be based on and modeled after the discovered natural order, just as it is for Huang-Lao.[64]

As for the epistemology of Huang-Lao in which one discovers dao manifest as objective names and principles by emptying oneself of all subjective bias, this, he suggests, is directly inherited from the *Guan Zi*'s "Xinshu shang and xia" and "Neiye" chapters.[65] Further, Huang-Lao develops on the basis of its epistemology a philosophy of language which combines *ming* (names) with *li* (principles), *shi* (實—reality, actuality), *fa* (law), and dao. This philosophy of language is, Hu argues, also present in the Jixia Daoist chapters of the *Guan Zi*.[66]

Even the military theory of Huang-Lao is to be found in the *Guan Zi*. As discussed previously, the *Boshu* insists that one must complement military strength (*wu*) with moral suasion and cultural refinement (*wen*). *Wen* and *wu* are, moreover, grounded in the natural order in that one must engage in the behavior proper to the season. Hu points out the occurrence of similar ideas in the *Guan Zi*'s "Mumin," "Renfa" and "Quanxiu" chapters.[67]

In regard to philosophy of law, one finds in the *Guan Zi* several of the most important tenets of Huang-Lao jurisprudence: the state is to be governed through rule of impartial law, not according to the discretion of those in power; laws are to be predicated on dao; the ruler must obey the law, and so on. Significantly, that the ruler must respect the law is a key differentia between the natural law of Huang-Lao and the positive law of Han Fei.

Taking note of this difference, Kanaya Osamu argues that one must distinguish the Li Kui-Shang Yang-Han Fei line of Legalism associated with Qin Shihuang Di and the San Jin-Qin area from the Dao-Fa Jia scholars of the Jixia academy and the state of Qi.[68] The latter includes the works of Shen Dao, Shen Buhai, parts of the Guan Zi, four contested chapters of the *Han Fei Zi*, and Huang-Lao.[69] Although there is room for discussion of which chapters of which text belong where, I certainly agree that this basic distinction is necessary. I would merely add that more work needs to be done to further distinguish the various legal philosophies, particularly, though not exclusively, those of the latter group.

Fortunately, Hu, who also advocates differentiating Qin Legalism from Tian Qi or Jixia Legalism,[70] has begun this project by subdividing the Jixia scholars of Qi into Jixia Daoists[71] and Jixia Legalists.[72] Although both contend that law is generated by dao and synthesize dao, *fa* (law), and Confucian *li yi* (rites and morality), the Jixia Daoists take dao as the basis for *li* and *yi* whereas the Legalists turn to *fa*.[73] A second differentia is that, although both advocate that the ruler *wu wei* (not intervene) while the ministers *you wei* (carry out the daily business of government), Jixia Legalists, according to Hu, invest considerable importance in *shi* (political purchase), *shu* (術—techniques), and *quan* (authority) while paying relatively little attention to *xing ming* (forms and names–titles and performances). Jixia Daoists, on the other hand, attend to the relation between *xing ming* and *wu wei* as arts of rulership: the ruler is able to *wu wei*, to delegate responsibility, because of the *xing ming* system of accountability in which the ministers are impartially and reliably rewarded or punished according to their performance of previously stipulated duties.[74]

Whatever their differences, both Jixia Daoists and Jixia Legalists are for Hu part of the Huang-Lao school, or at least precursors to it. For Hu, the defining feature of Huang-Lao is the synthesis of dao and *fa* and the grounding of *fa* in dao.[75] This synthesis is achieved, he argues, in the *Guan Zi*.

In comparing the *Guan Zi* to Huang-Lao, Hu draws freely on many chapters belonging to different branches of Jixia thought. This is of course reasonable given his purpose: to demonstrate the extent to which the ideas of the *Boshu* are present in the *Guan Zi*. Yet there are drawbacks to this approach. Many different sects are represented within *Guan Zi*. To appreciate the uniqueness of the *Boshu*, one needs to make more detailed comparisons of the various thought systems.[76]

For instance, Hu's willingness to include under the rubric of Huang-Lao both Jixia Daoism and Jixia Legalism conceals the extent to which they differ not only from each other but from the Huang-Lao philosophy of the *Boshu*. When one compares the Huang-Lao thought of the *Boshu* to either Jixia Daoism or Legalism, or to any given chapter of the *Guan Zi*, then the extent to which Huang-Lao represents a unique system of thought becomes apparent. This is not to deny that the author of the *Boshu* may have drawn heavily on the *Guan Zi* and the ideas of Jixia thinkers. Nevertheless, his system appears to be unique in that he assimilates in one work elements of many different chapters and sects. In so doing, he incorporates ideas from various authors in a way that any one author might find objectionable. Conversely, he selects ideas from chapters in the *Guan Zi* that contain other ideas at odds with or at least different in emphasis from his own thought.

To illustrate, the author of *Boshu* grounds his objective epistemology, theory of names, and philosophy of law in dao the natural order understood as predetermined rather than emergent. Although some *Guan Zi* authors conceive of the natural order as predetermined,[77] and others ground the social order (*fa*, *li*, *xing ming*) in dao the discovered objective order,[78] no one appears to have put them together.

The extent to which the *Boshu* constitutes a unique system can be demonstrated by examining the chapters to which it is most often compared—"Neiye" (內業—Inward training), "Xinshu shang" and "xia" (心術上下—Techniques of the heart-mind A and B)—on an issue of considerable importance to both the *Boshu* and the Jixia authors of the *Guan Zi*: epistemology.[79]

"Neiye"

The epistemology of the "Neiye"[80] can be summarized as follows: by controlling the breath (*qi*, 1a), expelling all emotions (joy, anger, desire, self-interestedness, 1b), and quieting the mind's thoughts (3b), one becomes tranquil (*jing*, 2a).[81] This tranquility leads to a refined state of breathing and concentration (*jing*, 2b) and to a state of intuitive clarity (*shen*, 3b) in which one gains a kind of charismatic, persuasive potency (*de*, 1b, 3a). One also discovers dao understood both as oneness (*yi*, 3a) and as the way of harmony (*he zhi dao*, 5b). The result is that "one changes with the times yet is not transformed, accords with things yet is not moved" (2b); one is able to "exhaust the limits of heaven and earth and reach all within the four seas; if within there are no doubts, there will be no calamities without" (4a). As a consequence, the empire will be well ordered (4b), and one will achieve long life (5b).

That this epistemology is similar to that of both the *Boshu* and the *Lao Zi* is readily apparent: through control and moderation of thoughts and emotions one becomes tranquil, thereby discovering dao and gaining a comprehensive knowledge on the basis of which the empire is set aright. In keeping with the *Boshu* and *Lao Zi*, and *contra* Zhuang Zi, the Neiye elides attainment of tranquility with discovery of dao, the way of harmony in praxis.

In one sense, the "Neiye" is more similar to the *Boshu* than to the *Lao Zi*: it emphasizes the illuminative aspect of the discovery of dao as opposed to the state of pure consciousness. Indeed, the "Neiye" never mentions *xu* (emptiness). Although it does declare that one should cleanse the heart-mind of thoughts, it seems to be promoting primarily a kataphatic meditation in which one concentrates on the breath to settle the mind. For instance, in the "Neiye," the notion of "holding fast to the one" (*shou yi* 守一) appears to indicate a kind of focusing exercise by which one clears the mind.[82] Concentration on breath and mind-focusing exercises, strictly speaking kataphatic techniques, may of course be considered preparatory for the pure consciousness event wherein one no longer attempts to focus the mind or concentrate on the breath, but relinquishes all such acts of cognition and objects of consciousness. On the other hand, concentration on breath and mind focusing may be ends in themselves: through these techniques one is able to relax, to move beyond the concerns that dominate one's everyday consciousness, and thereby gain a new perspective on and a new attitude to one's daily life. This latter understanding seems to be the intent of the "Neiye," judging by the absence of *xu*—present in the "Xinshu shang" chapter—together with the outward orientation of its meditation that culminates in the illumination of dao as harmony in praxis.

At any rate, even allowing this similarity to Huang-Lao, the "Neiye" is aligned with Lao Zi and against the *Boshu* in one important respect: the way discovered through the meditative process is an emergent social one, not a preconfigured natural order. As the text states, dao, rather than being predetermined, "is born together with me" (2a). Consequently, humans participate in the creation of the way. The "Neiye" exhorts one to clear the mind of biases and preconceptions so that one will be able to respond to a situation with an open mind and an awareness of the concerns of others. The call is to transform with the changing context, to respond to one's world as it is rather than as one would want it to be given one's own interests alone. To be sure, the author states that "dao is the means to cultivate the heart-mind so as to rectify forms (*xing*)," and that "forms are filled by the way."[83] Yet these forms are not predetermined as in the *Boshu*, but contingent, constantly changing, open ended. They are the realities of the moment that must be taken into consideration in effecting the way, in forging a new harmony.

In the "Neiye," when one becomes tranquil, one gains not only the clarity of mind and purpose required to effect order, but the ability to do so as well. As with Confucius, the primary task is to rectify one's own person. Having done so, the empire can then be put aright in due course. Revealingly, no mention is made of the need for standards or laws. Indeed, the text states, "rewards are not enough to encourage goodness; punishments are not enough to discipline errors" (4b). The notion that one is to rely primarily on the self-cultivation of those in power, on their virtuous potency (*de*), to determine and implement sociopolitical order is a Confucian and, with qualifications, Daoist idea. By contrast, both Huang-Lao and the Legalists contend it is folly to rely solely on personal character and the normative discretion of individuals. Rather, one must implement an impartial rule of law with reliable and, in the case of Huang-Lao, just rewards and punishments.

The influence of Confucianism is further manifested in the Neiye's sponsoring of poetry, music and the rites as means to ensure proper order (6a). The Confucian orientation is informative: as discussed in chapter IV, the way for Confucius is the realization of an emergent harmony, not the instantiation of a predetermined natural order as for Huang-Lao. When all is said and done, the philosophy of Neiye, while sharing an epistemology similar in many respects to that of the *Boshu*, nevertheless differs dramatically in its understanding of the nature of the way discovered.

"Xinshu xia"

Although the epistemology of the "Xinshu xia" chapter is by and large the same as that of the "Neiye,"[84] it does take two more steps in the direction of the *Boshu*. First, it calls attention to the objective character of the process by making explicit the need to overcome partiality and subjective bias (*wu si*, 6a). Second, it introduces names (*ming*): things are said to come bearing names; the sage, by overcoming bias, becoming tranquil and so on, discovers the proper names of things; he then responds accordingly, and as a result the empire is well regulated.

Yet despite these overtures toward Huang-Lao, several of the points distinguishing the "Neiye" from the *Boshu* are also present in the "Xinshu xia": no mention is made of *xu* (emptiness);[85] once more the reliance is on the charismatic potency derived from self-cultivation and the Confucian methods of poetry, music, and the rites as means to effect sociopolitical order; conversely, the use of laws for promoting order is ignored, and the value of punishments and rewards questioned. Again, it would seem the author is maintaining that by overcoming biases and attaining tranquility, one is able to discover and respond to the way as it emerges. To be sure it is difficult to determine conclusively whether or not the author of "Xinshu xia" conceives of dao as emergent or predetermined. But in any event there is no indication that he takes dao to be the predetermined natural order of the *Boshu*.

"Xinshu shang"

The "Xinshu shang" chapter consists of original text and a commentary, the latter probably not written until much later.[86] Because the original is most likely an earlier work by a different author, I discuss it first. It is worth noting at the outset, however, that, of the three chapters, the "Xinshu shang" (both in the original and commentary) is closest in its epistemology to that of the *Boshu*. At the same time, it too parts company with the *Boshu* over the nature of dao.

Of the three chapters, the "Xinshu shang" is the only one to explicitly introduce *xu* (emptiness) into the process: one is to empty oneself of desires (1b4), knowledge (1b5), preferences (2a5), and sense perceptions (2a5). Having attained emptiness and tranquility (*xu jing*, 3a9, 1b4), one is able to be impartial (*wu si*, 2a5). This leads to intuitive clarity (*shen*, 3a10, 2a5, 4b4) and discovery of dao (2a9). As a result, one is able to act non-impositionally (*wu wei*, 2a9), to respond to things in an "unprincipled" (*wu zhi*) fashion (2b3), and to match names to forms (2a9).

In addition to the use of the term *xu*, other novel features include the explicit endorsement of *wu wei* and the acceptance of a role for *fa* (law) in the establishment of sociopolitical order (1b11). This latter point aligns the Xinshu shang with the *Boshu* and against the *Lao Zi*. However, in regard to the crucial issue of the nature of dao, the text sides with the *Lao Zi* against the *Boshu* in understanding dao as an emergent order.

The task of the sage is to respond appropriately to the particular circumstances (2a1). He is to do so by ridding himself of all preconceptions: "When things become confused and as if in turmoil, remain tranquil toward them and they will put themselves in order. . . . Wisdom cannot exhaustively plan for every exigency" (2a7). For the author, the open-ended cosmos cannot be reduced to fixed and infallible rules. One must always be willing to abandon what one thinks one knows, and to reassess the situation unencumbered by previously held ideas.

To be sure, there is some regularity to the world: "things certainly have forms; forms certainly have names. He who makes names correspond is the sage" (2a9). But as in the Neiye chapter, the forms are emerging forms, not something fixed and grounded in a predetermined natural order. The goal is to respond appropriately to the ever changing circumstances. That this is so is all the more obvious in the commentary.

As one would expect, the commentary adheres closely to the epistemology of the original.[87] One difference is that it explicitly grounds *fa* (law) in dao: "laws arise from *quan* (authority, discretion, expediency); *quan* arises from dao" (4a6). As noted earlier, *quan* originally meant a balance, a scale. A scale constitutes the means by which order is maintained; it serves as a standard for adjudicating conflict. By extension, *quan* comes to denote authority. The person who has the power to adjudicate conflict, to determine what constitutes proper order, possesses authority. In the case of Mencius, it refers to the discretionary judgment of the sage that allows him to balance the particular elements defining a situation. The emergent character of Mencian order is reflected in the contrast between *quan* (contingency, exigency) and *jing* (經 —regularity). The ruler who goes by *quan* relies on his discretionary judgment to assess what is most appropriate given the exigencies of the particular context.

By grounding *fa* (law) in *quan* (discretion), which is in turn based on dao, the author reveals that he favors an understanding of dao as emergent and context specific rather than predetermined and rule governed. The way ultimately consists of what is most appropriate in particular circumstance (4a2): "Morality (*yi* 義) refers to each thing finding its appropriate (*yi*) place. As for the rites (*li*), they are predicated on the way humans are. . . . Thus rites refer to there being principles (*li*). Principles clarify (social) distinctions in order to make known the meaning of morality (*yi*). Thus the rites are derived from morality (*yi*), morality is derived from principles (*li*), and principles are predicated on appropriateness (*yi*)." In the end, though the author of the "Xinshu shang" moves closer to the *Boshu*, employing much of the same vocabulary and grounding *fa* in dao, his is not the predetermined natural order of the *Boshu* but the emergent order of Lao Zi.

Despite the differences, the *Guan Zi* is an important text for Huang-Lao studies. A rich source of pre-Qin jurisprudence, it attests to the need to distinguish between the harsh Legalism of Qin and Jixia philosophies of law. For those interested in the history of the Huang-Lao school and the origins of the *Boshu*, the *Guan Zi* represents a common intellectual heritage. Many of the most salient ideas of the *Boshu* are to be found within its wide covers: nature as an impersonal, objective, rule-governed order; *fa* (law) and *xing ming* (forms and names) predicated on dao; an epistemology of discovery through emptiness and tranquility of the objective way, and so on. Yet these ideas, scattered among diverse sects, remain isolated pieces of an intellectual puzzle. The task of assembling the fragments into a unified, coherent system of thought is accomplished by the author of the *Boshu*, and therein lies his singular importance within the history of Chinese philosophy.

Shen Buhai

Although not a member of the Jixia Academy, Shen Buhai is associated with the Huang-Lao school in the *Shi Ji*, where Sima Qian claims that the doctrines of Shen Buhai are "based on Huang-Lao and give prominence to *xing ming* (forms and names; performance and stipulated duties)" (63.2146). Thus his views merit at least brief comment.

Most of the scholarly attention paid to Shen Buhai since the Mawang-dui discovery has focused on his theory of *xing ming*.[88] However, Shen Buhai, like the legal theorists of Jixia, shares many traits with Huang-Lao, one of the most important being that he distances himself from Shang Yang and Han Fei in not construing the relationship of the ruler to his ministers and people as antagonistic. Moreover, he must be considered, even acknowledging Creel's point that he does not emphasize *fa* (law), an advocate of a rule of law as opposed to a rule of man. He repeatedly warns against the display of discretionary powers on the part of the ruler, advising him to hide behind the technique of an impartial matching of his officials' titles or stipulated duties (*xing*) with their actual performances (*ming*).[89]

Yet in contrast to the author of the *Boshu*, Shen Buhai comes across in the last word, as Creel insightfully observes, as a pragmatic administrator. He never attempts to delineate the ethical or natural foundations for law but simply offers it as a useful means for ensuring a smooth-running government serving the interests of the people as well as the ruler. His technique of *xing ming* is not tied to metaphysical grounds via an epistemological project like that of the *Boshu*, but rather is much more limited in scope, constituting one more political tool for the ruler.

Once again, it appears the author of the *Boshu* has taken an idea current in the intellectual world of his day—the notion of *xing ming*—reworked it in light of his own philosophical beliefs, and created in the process a unique system of thought. This is consistent with Sima Tan's statement that Huang-Lao "accords with the great order of the Yin Yang school, selects what is good from the doctrines of Confucians and Mohists, and combines with them the essential points of the School of Names and the Legalists" (*SJ* 130.3289). As documented in this section and throughout this work, many of the ideas central to the *Boshu* are found in other pre-Qin works:

1. Nature as an impersonal, nonanthropomorphic order: *Lao Zi, Xun Zi, Shen Dao Fragments.*
2. Nature as an impersonal, predetermined, and rule-governed order: Zou Yan, *Guan Zi* ("Banfa," "Xingshi").
3. The eliding of *fa* (law) and dao: *Shen Dao Fragments, Guan Zi* ("Xinshu shang," "Fafa," "Renfa").
4. The grounding of *xing ming* (forms and names) in dao: *Shen Buhai Fragments*; *Guan Zi* ("Xinshu shang" and "xia").
5. The epistemology of discovery of an objective dao: *Lao Zi, Guan Zi* ("Neiye," "Xinshu shang" and "xia").[90]

Yet it is only at the hands of the author of the *Boshu* that these disparate elements are synthesized into a single, coherent philosophical system. Of course, given the problems of dating, we may never know whether the *Boshu* was composed before or after many of these works. It may turn out that some of them, far from being antecedents of the author's thought, are a response to and development of Huang-Lao philosophy as presented in the *Boshu*.

2. Ascendence in the Early Han

2.1 Huang-Lao: A Response to the Times

China was devastated by the ravishes of Qin. The economy was ruined, famine widespread. The same attitude that perpetuated the infamous burning of the books stifled the intellectual flourishing of the War-ring States period. Harsh laws and excessive use of conscripted labor in-stilled in the hearts of the people hatred of the government. With the inevitable collapse of the despotic Qin regime, the state stood in dire need of a more people oriented ideology, one capable of rebuilding the devastated economy, restoring the debilitated political structures, and regaining the lost support of the masses. Huang-Lao was just such an ideology.[91]

According to Huang-Lao, government exists to serve the interests of the people. For this reason, the author of the *Boshu* called for a more balanced approach to effecting social order than employed by Qin. The draconian Qin laws were to be eliminated, replaced by fewer and more just laws. The ruler was to lead by moral example and suasion, not through restrictions and fear of the rod alone. Punishments were to be offset by rewards, military strength by cultural refinement. To be sure military strength remained necessary in light of the power vacuum created by the downfall of Qin. A strong central government was required to hold the nascent Han empire together, to prevent it from splintering into competing factions and thus returning to the chaotic and turbulent conditions of the pre-Qin Warring States period. Yet Huang-Lao rulership was to be gov-ernment with a human face.

The state was to tend not only to the spiritual and cultural conditions of the people, but to their economic health as well. One would restore the material well-being of the people through lower taxes, reductions in con-scripted labor, and restrictions on the use of government funds to support the lavish life-styles of those in power.

Most important, Huang-Lao addressed the inadequacies of Qin Legalism by imposing constraints on the power of the ruler. Although it did support an empire unified under a single ruler, he was not to be a despotic tyrant like Qin Shihuang or even an all-powerful Confucian sage-ruler who relies on his discretion to determine what constitutes socio-political order in the given context. The Huang-Lao ruler was to be con-strained by the need to serve the people, by the belief that he is to mini-mize material possessions and government expenditures, by the injunction that military force may be deployed only for righteous causes and at the right time and by the natural law theory where the ruler is obligated to obey the law—not only in his application of the law to others, but in his own personal conduct as well. Yet in the end, the biggest constraint, at least in theory, was the notion of foundational naturalism itself: the ruler must follow the way, dao, articulated in terms of *fa* (law), *li* (principles), and *xing ming* (forms and names). He must act in accordance with the objectively discovered normative way, with the natural order defined by the forces of yin and yang and the regular cycles of the seasons.

2.2 Huang-Lao Policies and Early Han Politics

A survey of the historical records reveals that many of the most prominent political figures of the early Han favored, studied, or followed Huang-Lao philosophy, including the Emperors Wen and Jing, the Empress Dowager Dou, and the ministers, officials and court personages Gai Gong, Cao Can, Chen Ping, Tian Shu, Sima Li Zhu, Ji An, Zheng Dangshi, Wang Sheng, Huang Sheng, Sima Tan, Sima Qian, Liu De, Yang Wangsun, Deng Zhang, and An Qisheng.[92] Others, though not on record as having explicitly endorsed Huang-Lao thought, implemented Huang-Lao policies.[93] One such person is the first ruler of the Han, Liu Bang— originally Liu Ji, and also referred to as Gao Zu, the "First Emperor."

Liu Bang

One of Liu Bang's first acts as future ruler foreshadows the Huang-Lao character of his reign. After the surrender of Qin, he gathered the leaders of the region and proclaimed:

> Fathers and Elders, you have suffered long enough from the cruel laws of Qin: those who spoke ill or criticized the government have been cruelly executed with their relatives, those who talked in private have been publicly executed in the marketplace. . . . I am merely going to agree with you, Fathers and Elders, upon a code of laws in three articles: he who kills anyone will be put to death; he who wounds anyone or robs will be punished according to his offense; as to the remainder, I am repealing and doing away with all the laws of Qin. You, the officials and people, should all live quietly and undisturbed as before. All that I have come for is to deliver you, Elders, from harm. I do not have any intention of exploiting or tyrannizing over you. (*HS* 1a:20b, Ds1:58)

It is significant that one of Liu Bang's first steps to restore confidence in the government was to relax the excessively restrictive laws of Qin. His doing so in conjunction with the leading forces of the area not only reflects political acumen but the Huang-Lao policy that the ruler is to seek and heed the advice of his subordinates. Liu is reported, moreover, to have remained true to his word not to exploit the people by refusing to accept their food and by prohibiting looting and taking advantage of the conquered city's women (*HS* 1a:20b).

History has giving high marks to Liu's rule. One noted historian, H. Dubs, summarizes his reign thusly:

> While Kao-tsu adopted many of the Ch'in practises, he nevertheless . . .carefully avoided any semblance of such absolutism. . . . He consciously adopted the policy of always considering the interests of the people and the requirements of justice and righteousness. . . . At the surrender of the Ch'in king, he was careful to be generous and indulgent and to avoid plundering the people. . . . He exempted from taxes those people who had been too heavily burdened in furnishing the armies with supplies, and granted his soldiers various and increasing exemptions. He continued the practise of giving the representatives of the people the position of *San-lao*, and had them advise with the officials so that the people would have a direct voice in government. He granted general amnesties on all appropriate occasions. He had his soldiers who had died in battle enshrouded and encoffined and sent home to be buried at official expense. He appointed caretakers for the graves of the great kings, in order that their hungry manes might not disturb the country. He waited to assume the title of Emperor until it was formally offered him by his followers, and then accepted it because 'the vassal kings would be favored by it and they considered it to be an advantage to all the people in the world.' At his accession he freed all slaves and restored to civil rights all refugees and exiles. He granted aristocratic ranks to all his soldiers. He fixed the amount of military tax so that the people would not be oppressed by exactions. More important still, soon after his accession he adopted the practise of not taking initiative in appointing any of his relatives or sons to any kingdoms or nobilities, but acting only at the suggestion of his followers. . . . This custom, that the ruler acts at the suggestion of his important subordinates, was a real and often effective limitation upon the imperial power.[94]

I cite this lengthy passage because it captures the essence of Huang-Lao political philosophy and the reasons for its popularity in post-Qin Han: regain the confidence of people by being a magnanimous and just ruler; rebuild the economy through lower taxes; govern through rule of law, but one more humane than that of Qin; take into consideration the concerns, needs, and views of both the ministers and people; check the ruler's power by having him confer with and act on the advice of his ministers.

Granted, Liu Bang may not have set out to follow Huang-Lao policies. Although he did sacrifice to the Yellow Emperor (*HS* 1a.9a), by the Han the Yellow Emperor was embraced by numerous philosophical schools, religious sects, and the popular culture at large. Further, Liu Bang himself was not a highly literate fellow. In keeping with his humble origins, he was known to squat in the manner of fieldhands and use colorful, rough speech. He is reported to have shown his disdain for men of letters by removing the ceremonial cap of one Confucian literati and urinating in it.[95] And when Lu Jia, another esteemed Confucian pedant,[96] cited the *Book of Odes*, Gao Zu remarked sarcastically, "I got the empire on horseback, why should I bother with the *Book of Odes*."[97]

Nevertheless, Liu would have been familiar with Huang-Lao thought, if not through study of the original texts, then through discussion with his ministers, several of whom are reported to have studied Huang-Lao.[98] Indeed, Huang-Lao, with its politically practical philosophy—evinced in its acceptance of punishments, laws, and a strong military—may have appealed to this rough-hewn ruler more than overly refined and idealistic Confucianism.[99] At any rate, Liu Bang, despite his disdain for the literati, did govern in a way consistent with Huang-Lao thought. Not only did he combine military strength with a beneficent government that served the people, he repealed the harsh laws of Qin, rebuilt the economy and appointed ministers who favored Huang-Lao polices. One such minister was Cao Can.[100]

Cao Can

Cao Can, under the threat of execution by the magistrate of Pei, joined forces with Liu Bang when Liu was first beginning his rise to power (*HS* 1a:8b, Ds1:40). He was, therefore, a trusted friend of long standing when Liu appointed him prime minister of Qi.

Cao Can was a disciple of Gai Gong, a proponent of Huang-Lao who instructed Cao to "value pure tranquility and the masses will settle themselves" (*SJ* 54.2029, W1:422). Cao, heeding his advice, was renowned for his relaxed laws and hands-off style of governing.[101] Indeed, he is almost a caricature of a *wu wei* administrator. He is said to have given himself to drinking day and night. When people visited on official business, he would give them wine before they could begin and more wine when they seemed about to reopen their business. When he visited the office of his subordinates, all of whom were drinking, he not only drank along, but sang and shouted louder than anyone. He is reported, moreover, to have "shielded those who committed small crimes so that there was no business done in his office" (*HS* 39:11b, Ds1:186).[102]

Further, the historical records state that Cao Can "uniformly respected the bonds of Xiao He," Liu Bang's famous minister of justice.[103] On this basis, many claim that Cao Can simply adopted the legal practices of Xiao He, who had relaxed the strict laws of Qin and added three sections of his own to the six sections of the *Fa Jing* by Li Kui.[104] Indeed, Cao Can, arguing that he was no match for the wise Xiao He, is reported to have admitted as much.[105]

A colorful picture of a *wu wei* administrator, this portrait is unfortunately not entirely accurate. Although Xiao He had begun the process of reforming the law, some of the harsh Qin codes were still in effect at the time of his death. The job of reform fell to Cao Can. Therefore the *Han Shu* reports that after the death of Xiao and under the watch of Cao, changes were made: the number of crimes punishable by mutilation was reduced (2:3a), and the Qin law against possession of books repealed (2:5a). Furthermore, Cao Can replaced several of Xiao He's subordinates who continued to enforce the draconian laws of Qin with his own like-minded supporters, thereby circumventing any threat of reversion to Qin-style rule, and furthering the realization of a more humane Huang-Lao state.[106]

Cao Can's lenient rule gained great favor among the people who expressed their gratitude in a song composed in his honor.

> Xiao He made us laws,
> as plain as a straight line.
> Cao Can took his place
> And upheld them without fault.
> He governed with purity and stillness
> and the people were at peace. (*SJ* 54.2031, W1:425)

Yet neither Cao Can nor Huang-Lao philosophy advocated anarchy and complete eradication of laws. Although the times called for a government less intrusive in the daily life of the people than the tyrannical rule of Qin and for relaxation of its despotic laws, the need for a strong centralized government based on rule of law remained. The increasing stature of Huang-Lao among subsequent Han rulers from Emperor Hui through Jing is due to its ability to provide the requisite ideology to underwrite such a government.

The Political Influence of Huang-Lao: Emperors Hui to Jing

The reign of Emperor Hui, enthroned at the age of sixteen, was dominated by the Empress Dowager Lu who assumed power upon Hui's death some seven years later. During her tenure at the helm, Empress Dowager Lu schemed and plotted to secure power for the Lu clan. Yet despite the court intrigue, government policies continued to favor the interests of the people: taxes were reduced, punishments lightened, and so forth. Empress Dowager Lu may have realized that for her plans to consolidate power to succeed, she could not afford to alienate the masses. Whatever her motivation, she continued the policies of the first emperor, Liu Bang.

Of all the Han rulers, perhaps Lu's successor, Emperor Wen, best exemplified the positive features of Huang-Lao both in personal conduct and state policies.[107] He not only promoted agriculture, reduced taxes, cut back on government expenditures, established old-age pensions, ameliorated severities in the law, and abolished mutilating punishments. He also encouraged criticism from his ministers. In an era when few were willing to jeopardize their salaries by challenging the ruler, this policy must have lifted a heavy burden from well-intending but timid officials.[108]

In contrast to the rule of Emperor Wen, that of Emperor Jing has been disparaged by many historians, one of the first being Sima Qian. Yet, although Sima fails to find many redeeming features to Jing, the Han historian Ban Gu praises him as a good ruler. Dubs, siding with Ban Gu, points out that Jing did benefit the people by "limiting severities, punishing wrong-doing, and improving the administration."[109] Thus, despite the emperor's personal shortcomings and indulgence of petty whims, the reign of Jing was primarily a time of peace. The economy prospered and the empire flourished. With the renewed strength came the desire to flex the state's muscles, issuing in an era of military expansion and with it a period of extravagance and luxury that would lead to economic collapse under Emperor Wu.

Huang-Lao had reached its apogee. A succession of political leaders espousing Huang-Lao ideas and implementing Huang-Lao policies had nursed the sick state back to health. To be sure, the seeds of future difficulties were already sown: the court was riddled with intrigue between Confucians and devotees of other schools, each seeking to gain the emperor's favor and have his rivals expelled; the government policy instituted by Emperor Wen of reclaiming power from the local potentates by dividing up the great fiefs had already led to rebellion. Further, no ruler had remained completely faithful to the letter of Huang-Lao ideas. Each had personal deficiencies. Confronting the day-to-day demands of realpolitik, they often acted in ways inconsistent with Huang-Lao tenets, setting dangerous precedents for future rulers.

Yet by and large, the early Han was dominated by a series of rulers who remained true to Huang-Lao philosophy. This was all to change with the ascendence to the throne of Han Wu Di.

3. The Fall from Power

3.1 Court Intrigue

Throughout much of Chinese history Confucians and Daoists, later joined at court by Buddhists, competed for the favor of those in power. In the early Han, from the time of Liu Bang to the enthronement of Emperor Wu and the death of Empress Dowager Dou, Huang-Lao constituted a powerful and at times dominant court ideology. By the end of the reign of Emperor Wu, the school's fortunes had reversed, with Huang-Lao expelled from court and Confucianism institutionalized as the curriculum of state universities. However, as Dubs points out, that Confucianism won a sudden and lasting victory with the ascendancy of Emperor Wu is overly simplistic. The process began with Liu Bang and was not completed until the reign of King Yuan more than a century and a half later.[110]

Although disdainful of intellectuals, Liu Bang was adept at recognizing talent. As a military and political leader, he was able to take advantage of the strengths of others to further his own ends. He rewarded those who performed well, regardless of background or intellectual affiliation. As a result, among his advisers were proponents not only of Huang-Lao but of various schools, including Confucianism. In fact, one of Liu Bang's longest and closest counselors was his brother, Liu Zhao, a renowned Confucian. And, as observed previously, Liu Bang is reported to have solicited a political treatise from Lu Jia, an eclectic Confucian. Thus in the early years of the Han, both Huang-Lao and Confucian voices were heard at court.

The nadir of Confucianism corresponds to the zenith of power of Empress Dowager Dou, an ardent supporter of Huang-Lao. Her attacks on Confucian officials are legendary. When the Confucian Yuan Gusheng declared the *Lao Zi* to be nothing more than menial aphorisms, Dou ordered Yuan thrown into a pigpen (*SJ* 121.3123, W2:405). Zhao Wan and Wang Zang, two Confucians who tried to undermine Dou by having matters of state forwarded directly to the emperor, were tried and sent to prison where they committed suicide. Two other prominent Confucian officials, Dou Ying and Tian Fen, were also dismissed from office at that time.[111]

The anti-Confucian attitude of Empress Dowager Dou set the tone for the reign of Emperors Wen and Jing, both of whom were educated in Huang-Lao thought. Although Emperor Wen favored proponents of Huang-Lao and Legalism, he did not exclude from court representatives of other schools. One of his most prominent advisors, Jia Yi, was a Confucian. Emperor Jing, on the other hand, appears not to have appointed Confucian scholars.[112]

The ascension of Emperor Wu brought with it many changes, both in government policies and court ideology. From the beginning Wu looked kindly on Confucians: "When Emperor Wu had newly ascended the throne, the Marquises of Wei Qi (Dou Ying) and Wu An (Tian Fen) became his chancellors, and made Confucianism flourish" (HS 56:20b, Ds2:341). Soon after, following the advice of his minister, the Confucian Wei Wan, Emperor Wu dismissed all the officials and candidates who specialized in or advocated the thought of Shen Buhai, Shang Yang, Han Fei, Su Qi, and Zhang Yi (HS 6:1b). Although these thinkers are primarily associated with Legalism, the intent was, as Ban Gu states, to eliminate all non-Confucians from government service (HS 6:39a).

With Empress Dowager Dou protecting proponents of Huang-Lao and Daoism, Wu could not purge all of the rivals to Confucianism in one fell swoop. However, when the empress died shortly thereafter, Wu seized the opportunity to reappoint the Confucian Tian Fen, previously dismissed by the empress dowager. Tian in turn appointed several hundred Confucians and demoted or dismissed the followers of Huang-Lao and Daoism (HS 88:3b).

A year later, Dong Zhongshu proposed a ban on non-Confucian schools of thought:

> The teachers of today have diverse ways, men have diverse doctrines, and each of the philosophic schools has its own particular position, and differs in the ideas it teaches. Hence it is that the rulers possess nothing whereby they may effect general unification, the government statutes having often been changed, while the ruled know not what to cling to. I, your ignorant servitor, hold that all not within the field of the Six Disciplines [*Chun Qiu*, *I Jing*, books of *Poetry*, *History*, *Rites*, and *Music*] or the arts of Confucius should be cut short and not allowed to progress further. Evil and licentious talk should be put to a stop. Only after this, can there be general unification, and can laws be made distinct, so that people may know what to follow. (HS 56:20, F(1), 1:16)

When Emperor Wu, following Dong Zhongshu's advice, established the Imperial University and examination system with the Confucian classics as core curriculum, the eventual victory of Confucianism was assured.[113]

Yet Han Wu Di was in no way a prototypical Confucian. He was preoccupied with immortality and the supernatural.[114] Further, in contrast to his predecessors, he was a more active ruler who like the authoritarian Qin Shihuang personally executed state affairs rather than delegating responsibility to his subordinates. Chafing at the restrictions on his power, he continued the strategy of Emperor Wen, diminishing the power of the nobles and ministers by continually finding reasons to dismiss potential threats and then replacing them with his own fresh, and hence less well-connected and powerful, supporters.[115]

Wu also adopted a more severe rule of law than his predecessors. He then used the new laws to eliminate powerful officials. For this reason, there were often more than a hundred officials in prison. In fact, over a thousand cases concerning commandery officials were tried in one year. Emperor Wen, by contrast, is said to have heard only 400 cases during his entire reign.[116]

In addition, Wu overturned many policies favored by Confucianism and Huang-Lao alike. He greatly increased the amount of conscripted labor to build luxurious palaces and carry out his ambitious projects. He raised taxes to finance military expeditions. He nationalized profitable industries, making government monopolies of salt, iron, and liquor. All these measures represented a reversion to the totalitarian practices of Qin Shihuang Di and signaled the end of Huang-Lao's reign as the dominant ideology.

3.2 Explaining the Fall

Several scholars have proposed explanations for the demise of Huang-Lao during the reign of Emperor Wu. Ironically, most contend that the success of Huang-Lao was its own undoing. Huang-Lao policies were so successful, the story goes, that they created the conditions permitting, if not necessitating, a more active central government.[117] Relaxation of the draconian laws of Qin and restoration of the economy through tax cuts, reductions in state expenditures, and so forth won back the support of the people. The central government, economically and politically fortified, was ready to reclaim some of the power that Liu Bang, debilitated by the arduous campaign against Qin, had been forced to cede to local authorities. Although this process began during the reign of Emperor Wen, Emperor Wu, eager to secure his own dominance, accelerated the pace.

Huang-Lao political philosophy, designed to ensure that government serve the interests of the people through an array of constraints on the power of the ruler, was out of step with the activist central government of Emperor Wu. A new ideology was needed to support Wu's authoritarian inclinations and expansionist policies. Dong Zhongshu, New Text Confucianism in hand, was ready to respond to the call.

A second though compatible thesis is put forth by Nishikawa Yasuji. Nishikawa concurs that Huang-Lao fell from power in part because a more activist political ideology was needed. However, he proposes an additional reason: an inherent and unresolvable contradiction between Huang-Lao individualism aimed at self-attainment, implicit in the doctrine of *qing jing wu wei* (清靜無为 —pure tranquility and nonaction), and Huang-Lao political philosophy that purports to provide an ideological basis for large-scale politics. As he sees it, classical Daoism was given over primarily to self-cultivation. Its individualist and apolitical character is manifest most clearly in the large number of stories about Daoist hermits and recluses who withdraw from society to pursue inner development. To the extent that Daoists did offer a political philosophy, it was based on the notion of minimum interference by a self-cultivated ruler who led by example and force of character rather than law: the ideal being that one does nothing and yet nothing is left undone (*wu wei er wu bu wei*). This ideology was appropriate for a small state only. To rule a large state, laws were needed.

The proponents of both Legalism and Huang-Lao realized that a unified empire could not be run without the use of laws. Qin Legalists, however, implemented a severe legal code that did not take into consideration local conditions or the concerns of the people. The laws of the people-oriented Huang-Lao government, by contrast, reflected a sensitivity to both local conditions and the needs of the people. As noted previously, one of the first acts of both Liu Bang and Cao Can was to convene a meeting with the local authorities to negotiate an appropriate code of laws.

Although Huang-Lao was able to overcome the inadequacies of Qin Legalism, it was not, Nishikawa contends, able to reconcile completely its own two wings: the outward-looking political wing (adopted from Legalism) and the inward-looking individualist wing (of classical Daoism). Han supporters of Huang-Lao attempted to conceal their political agenda under the Daoist doctrine of *qing jing wu wei*. They did so by reinterpreting this notion. Pure tranquility became the Huang-Lao epistemology of emptiness and tranquility (*xu jing*) through which one discovered dao understood in terms of objective laws regulating the natural, including the human-social, order.[118] Thus self-cultivation led to political order, much as it did for classical Daoists. However, it did not lead to personal freedom. The individual discovered himself or herself to be part of a social and cosmic order that was rule governed and predetermined. Rather than being a coauthor of an as yet unscripted play, one was, if not a bit player, an actor whose creativity was checked at every turn by a heavy-handed director.

There is considerable merit to both of these explanations. There are also considerable difficulties. It is not obvious that Huang-Lao did not have the conceptual resources needed to meet the new age's demand for a strong and activist centralized government presided over by a single ruler.

Huang-Lao clearly sponsors an empire unified under a single ruler, even sanctioning military conquest as an appropriate means to that end.

Further, one of the most often-noted points of distinction between the political views of Huang-Lao and the classical Daoists Lao Zi and Zhuang Zi is that the former promotes a more active role for government in effecting sociopolitical order. This is evidenced not only by its call for political unification, but in its sponsoring of a rule of law and its reinterpretation of *wu wei*. It is often claimed, as for instance by Nishikawa, that Lao Zi and Zhuang Zi are more individualistic and less political than Huang-Lao, and that *wu wei* is a doctrine of political passivity. Although I have challenged this view, arguing that Lao Zi and Zhuang Zi are not as apolitical as some contend and that *wu wei* understood as nonimpositional action lies at the heart of classical Daoist politics of harmony, I nevertheless agree that Huang-Lao is politically more "active" in its pursuit of a unified empire ruled by law.[119] But then this argues *for* the view that Huang-Lao thought has the resources to support the possibility of active government.

Indeed, many scholars contend that the *Boshu*'s epistemology, in which one discovers dao the objective natural order manifest in impartial laws, is simply a means to legitimate the interests of the ruling class and conceal from the masses the fact that the ruler is still relying on his own best judgment and discretion to determine the law.[120] By claiming the discovered laws to be grounded in the normative natural order, those in power portray law as both universally applicable and ethically justified. Further, because there is no way to verify the ruler's epistemic claim to have discovered the correct laws, the ruler's power remains as unchecked in practice as that of either the Confucian or Legalist ruler.[121] If anything, the privileging of the epistemic state of emptiness and tranquility in an individual prevents remonstration by others, precluding criticism of the ruler's policies by his officials—an important means for reining in the ruler in the Confucian system.

Therefore it would seem Huang-Lao has the conceptual tools necessary to support a strong centralized government controlled by an activist, authoritarian ruler. Why then did it lose out to Confucianism? There are several possible explanations.

The downfall of Huang-Lao may of course be due to something as mundane as the rhetorical deficiencies of its advocates at court: the Confucians may simply have been more persuasive in extolling the merits of their position to Emperor Wu, and thus able to convince him not only to adopt their policies but to banish Huang-Lao from court.

A more intellectually satisfying explanation attributes the demise of Huang-Lao to the failure of foundational naturalism as a philosophy. There is simply no way to verify that one has directly discovered reality. Far from putting an end to all disagreements by providing a universal standard, the claim of Huang-Lao epistemology to have discovered the Way simply gives rise to new disputes as to whether the way has really been discovered and, if so, by whom. The masses, for their part, would soon realize that the attempt to naturalize the current social order is simply a guise to conceal the will to power of the ruling class. For this reason, they would be inclined to reject Huang-Lao in favor of a new ideology.

One shortcoming of this theory that Huang-Lao lost out to Confucianism because of the inadequacies of its foundational philosophy is that it explains why the people, ministers, or other philosophers would reject Huang-Lao, but not why the emperor would. To understand Emperor Wu's reasons, one does well to draw upon the kernel of truth in the original two theories: Huang-Lao thought, even allowing that a ruler could turn its foundational epistemology to his own end, imposed too many restrictions on a ruler's power to satisfy Emperor Wu. Although the ruler could claim to have discovered the way and hence determine what the law would be, once he did so, he himself had to follow it.[122] Further, he remained bound by Huang-Lao economic policies mandating low taxes, minimal government expenditures, and frugality on the part of the ruler.

To escape from these political shackles, Emperor Wu turned to Confucianism. As we have seen, Confucianism gives authority to the wise and benevolent ruler who, though encouraged to remain within the bounds of the li (rites), determines what is best for the state in light of his own cultivated judgment. Although he may wish to consider the advice of his ministers, he is in no way obligated to do so.[123] In short, Confucianism, even in its classical expression by Confucius, is more readily turned to the advantage of an authoritarian ruler than is Huang-Lao. As a consequence, Emperor Wu, not wanting to hide his true authority behind the veil of Huang-Lao foundational epistemology, adopted Confucianism as the state ideology.

Further, and perhaps even more important, whereas classical Confucianism offered Emperor Wu political control not to be had with Huang-Lao, the New Text yin yang five phases Confucianism of Dong Zhongshu promised a wholly new dimension of control: control over nature and the natural processes, including, when taken to its logical extension, control over death itself. Although the Boshu's yin yang correlative cosmology entailed a relation between humans and the natural order, the natural order remained the determinant source of order. Humans were to comply with the natural order, at pain of disaster. Dong Zhongshu, thinking through the implications of *co-relative* cosmology, proposed that humans are not only determined by but also determining of the natural order. By manipulating the forces of yin and yang and the five phases that relate the human body and the social order to nonhuman nature and the natural order, one is able to effect change in nature and the cosmos at large. Most important, by controlling, manipulating, and cultivating the (yang) forces of life, one is able to hold off the (yin) forces of death. Thus the world-view implicit in Dong's Confucianism underwrites what is of utmost concern to Emperor Wu: the attainment of immortality.[124]

Emperor Wu's preoccupation with immortality is well documented. Dubs notes that Wu enlarged imperial sacrifices, introduced a new deity, established the Feng and Shan sacrifices and recreated the Ming Tang as a hall for sacrifices.[125] Like Qin Shihuang before him, Wu sent out expeditions in search of the isle of immortals and magical herbs and mushrooms.[126] He also practiced alchemy[127] and provided government support for *fang shi* (magicians) and other immortality seekers.

> With the rise of the Han, Xin Yuanping of Zhao, Shao Wen, Gongsung Qin, Luan Da and others of Qi all received honors and favors from Emperor Wu on account of their acquaintanceship with immortals, alchemy, sacrificial offerings, serving and controlling spirits, and going to sea to search for immortals and drugs. Gifts bestowed on them measured to thousands of measures of gold. Luan Da was particularly honored and even married a princess. Titles and positions were heaped on him to such an extent that all within the four seas were shocked. Therefore [during the time of Emperor Wu] there were thousands of *fang shi* in the areas of Qi and Yan . . . who claimed to know such arts as achieving immortality, of sacrificial offerings and of obtaining blessings. (*HS* 25b.7a)

So preoccupied did Emperor Wu become with everlasting life that his pursuits of immortality influenced his policies.[128] It is not surprising then that a philosophy such as Dong's New Text Confucianism, which allowed for control of natural processes and consequently the possibility of overcoming death, would have appealed to Emperor Wu. By contrast, the foundational naturalism of Huang-Lao, in which humans simply sought to comply with a predetermined natural order, had nothing to offer the obsessed emperor but sure death. This, perhaps as much as any political deficiency, may have been the fatal flaw of Huang-Lao responsible for its sudden demise under Emperor Wu.

4. Dénouement

One might suspect that after its banishment from court, Huang-Lao thought would have disappeared from the Han political scene. Yet Zhong Zhaopeng has shown that many Eastern Han political figures continued to study Huang-Lao thought and promote Huang-Lao policies.[129] Nevertheless, despite its enduring appeal to some politicians, Huang-Lao's heyday as a political force had come to an end. To the extent that Huang-Lao continued to play a significant role in the intellectual events of the later Han, it did so through its influence on immortality practices and religious Daoism.

4.1 Huang-Lao and Religious Daoism

The Yellow Emperor is an important figure in Han immortality beliefs and practices. Of ten works classified under the school of immortals in the Han bibliography, the "Yi Wen Zhi," four mention the Yellow Emperor in the title. In addition, the Yellow Emperor is associated with astrology, divination, Yin Yang, Five Phases, alchemy, medicine, and sexual yoga, all of which figure in Han immortality practices.[130] Daoists texts locate the Yellow Emperor at Kun Lun, mountain residence of immortals.[131] The inner chapters of the *Zhuang Zi* describe the Yellow Emperor's ascent into the cloudy heavens and tie him to Xi Wang Mu, the immortal Queen Mother of the West.[132] And in the *Shi Ji*, the alchemist Li Shaojun informed Emperor Wu that he could attain immortality like the Yellow Emperor by performing the Feng and Shan sacrifice and by turning cinnabar into gold.[133]

That there exists an intimate relation between the Yellow Emperor and Han immortality circles is apparent; that Huang-Lao stands in a similar relation is less obvious. To be sure, *Huang-Lao Jun* eventually referred to an immortal deity of Daoist religion.[134] Further, the *Shi Ji* traces the origins of Huang-Lao thought back to the mysterious He Shang Zhang Ren, who is said to be an immortal.[135] His disciple, An Qisheng is reported to have been made immortal by the *fang shi* (magicians) of Qi.[136] In fact, some suggest that An Qisheng was himself a *fang shi*.[137] Another *fang shi*, Zhe Xiang, was fond of the tenets of Huang-Lao.[138] It is, moreover, the *fang shi* who are largely responsible for propagating the story of the Yellow Emperor as an immortal.[139] Further, they are known to have populated the Jixia Academy, where they would have had the opportunity to steep themselves in Huang-Lao thought.[140] Not surprising, several scholars have suggested that the link between Huang-Lao, Han immortality practices, and Daoist religion runs through the *fang shi*.[141]

Yet there is little, if any, direct support for immortality practices to be found in the Huang-Lao thought of the *Boshu*. Nor, for that matter, is such support to be found in the classical Daoism of Lao Zi and Zhuang Zi. Zhuang Zi, far from wishing to avoid death, seems enraptured by the notion. And while the terseness of the *Lao Zi* allows for a wide range of interpretations, the consensus among scholars is that the text does not espouse eternal life.[142] Indeed, several passages declare as much: "life commences in birth and culminates in death" (50); "the myriad things all return to their roots" (16).

What, then, is the connection between Huang-Lao, the *fang shi* of Qi and the immortality practices of religious Daoism? One connection lies, I believe, in the naturalist world-view—especially the notion of causal correlative cosmology—of Zou Yan, present in rudimentary form in the Huang-Lao thought of the *Boshu* and developed by Dong Zhongshu. The *fang shi* appropriated the idea of causal correlative cosmology and turned it to their ends, using it as a theoretical basis for many of their immortality practices.[143]

4.2 Naturalism and Immortality

Many ancient Chinese, including Confucius, conceived of *tian* as an anthropomorphic heaven cum natural order. In contrast, one finds in the classical Daoist writings of Lao Zi and Zhuang Zi a conception of *tian* as an impersonal natural order. This view of nature became increasingly popular among late Warring States and Han philosophers. It was adopted by Huang-Lao disciples such as the author of the *Boshu*, by Jixia thinkers such as Zou Yan, even by Confucians such as Xun Zi.

Despite the broadly shared conception of nature, differences remain. Whereas Lao Zi and Zhuang Zi thought of nature as emergent, the author of the *Boshu* and Zou Yan thought it to be rule governed and predetermined. One of the ways in which the latter two articulated the rule governed character of the natural order was in terms of yin and yang, and, in the case of Zou Yan, yin yang five phases. Yin yang and five phases theories are examples of correlative thinking, an attempt to bring order to one's world by organizing into a coherent system the diverse phenomena of the cosmos—both human and nonhuman—on the basis of perceived correspondences.

Although the correspondence of the human order to the natural order is present in the yin yang theory of the *Boshu* (83:164b), it reached its fullest development in the Han notion of the human body as a physical microcosm of the macrocosmic natural universe. Although the motif of man as replica in miniature of macrocosmic nature is common in Han works, I cite the *Chun Qiu Fan Lu* attributed to Dong Zhongshu because of Dong's pivotal role in conquest of Confucianism over Huang-Lao at the court of the immortality seeking Emperor Wu.

> In the physical form of man. . . . his head is large and round, like heaven's countenance. His hair is like the stars and constellations. His ears and eyes, with their brilliance, are like the sun and moon. His nostrils. . . are like the wind. . . . His abdomen and womb. . . are like the hundred creatures. . . . The symbols of heaven and earth are ever established in the human body. The body is like heaven, and its numerical categories correspond with those of the latter, so that life is linked with the latter. With the number of days that fills a year heaven gives form to man's body. Thus the 366 lesser joints of the body correspond to the number of days in a year, and the twelve divisions of the larger joints correspond to the number of months. Within the body their are five viscera, which correspond in number to the five phases. Externally there are the four limbs, which correspond in number to the four seasons. . . . In what may be numbered, there is a correspondences in number. In what may not be numbered, there is a correspondence in kind. There is an identity in both cases and a single correspondence of man with heaven. (56/13/13, F(1), 2:31)

The notion that the human body is correlated to the natural order comes to play an important role in Han immortality practices. By controlling and manipulating the human body, one can control and manipulate nature. This ability to effect actual change in the cosmos, however, is predicated on the existence of a causal mechanism underlying the various correspondences between the human body and the natural order. It requires, in short, precisely the shift outlined previously from correlative systems as descriptive schemes to correlative systems understood as causal correlative cosmologies.

Again, it is Dong Zhongshu who gives clearest expression to this development in naturalist theory with his notion of *tian ren gan ying*: mutual response between humans and nature.[144] "Heaven possesses yin and yang and man also possesses yin and yang. When the yin *qi* of the universe arises, man's yin *qi* likewise rises in response. And vice versa. . . . Their course is one. He who understands this, when he wishes to bring rain, activates the human yin in order to arouse the yin of the universe; when he wishes to stop the rain, he activates the human yang in order to arouse the yang of the universe" (57/13/10, F(1), 2:56). Two points bear notice. First, it is via the mechanism of *qi* that one sphere is able to influence the other related sphere. Second, influence is bidirectional. The individual controls through his or her actions the macrocosmic natural processes such as rain by manipulating the cosmological forces of yin and yang inherent within oneself. As a result, one is no longer in a position of mere acquiescence and subjugation to the forces of nature. Rather, as Xun Zi had hoped earlier, one is at long last capable of determining and effecting the natural order that most suits one's needs: one has attained control over the universe.[145]

In contrast, though the author of the *Boshu* does at times espouse a causal correlative yin yang theory in which change is effected through the medium of *qi*, he continues to privilege the normatively predetermined natural order. Human behavior can effect change in the natural order, thus instantiating or not instantiating the predetermined normative order. Either way, however, the normative order itself remains the same.

Huang-Lao's positing of a normative order independent of humans, an order to be discovered and instantiated by humans rather than realized and created by humans, represents an aberration within the Chinese tradition. Confucius, for instance, places the responsibility for determining what constitutes a proper social order squarely on the shoulders of the sage, who, having taken into account the traditional wisdom embodied in the rites and having considered the contingencies of the particular situation, proceeds on the basis of his cultivated judgment. Even Lao Zi, who like Huang-Lao maintains the way is discovered, assigns a more determinative role to humans as participants in the generation of order. Dong Zhongshu, by emphasizing the mutual determination of sociocosmic order, overcomes the separation generated by Huang-Lao between humans and the normative and cosmological source of order. Humans once again become responsible for the world, both human-social and natural, in which they live. Dong remains, in this sense, true to the spirit of Confucius.

In any event, what has become the conceptual framework of the period—the correspondence between the human microcosm and natural macrocosm with its implicit corollary of the individual's power to control the cosmological forces—comes also to serve as a theoretical foundation for many Han immortality seekers. Because the physical body itself embodies the cosmological forces responsible for the natural processes, one can therefore control the very processes of nature, including death, by controlling one's own body and the cosmological forces within one's body.

Han Naturalism-Based Immortality Practices

The search for immortality in the Han, supported financially and politically by Emperor Wu, made popular a wide variety of theories and methods aimed at long life. Many of the methods—breath circulation, abstinence from cereals, herbal drugs—had existed before. Others, the Feng and Shan sacrifices, for example, have theoretical foundations in traditions other than naturalism. Nevertheless, many new theories and practices emerge that build upon the developments in naturalist thought discussed previously.

Given the body as a microcosm, if one wants to overcome the natural processes of life and death and achieve immortality, one must maintain the forces of life within oneself by taking care of one's body. Many texts emphasize the need for moderation to maintain one's health. The *Yellow Emperor's Classic of Internal Medicine* declares that those who understood dao "patterned themselves on yin and yang. . . there was temperance in eating and drinking. Their hours of rising were regular. . . . By these means the ancients kept their bodies united with their souls."[146] Similar passages in praise of abstemious living to preserve the forces of health in the body are also found in the *Guan Zi* and the *Huai Nan Zi*.[147]

Several techniques rely explicitly on causal correlative cosmology as their theoretical foundation. For instance, there arises during the Han a logical, if peculiar, means of strengthening the yin and yang of the body. Because yang is the principle of the sun, males—also yang—lie in the sun to "absorb its rays." Similarly, females "moon bathe," yin being the force of females and the moon. With their essential forces periodically vivified, they are able to live forever.[148]

Interestingly, although through the bathing process one seeks to increase the force corresponding to one's gender, in some sexual practices aimed at immortality one seeks to acquire the opposing force. Thus the man attempts to extract the yin essence from the woman. More rarely, the woman is the initiator, trying to sap the man's yang energy. This is reportedly the way in which the Queen Mother of the West attained her immortality.[149]

The cosmological basis for sexual practices as a means to immortality is presented in this passage: "The union with man and woman. . . is like the mating of heaven and earth. It is because they have the art that they last forever. . . . If a man could learn. . . to keep away all ills by the art of yin and yang, he too would last forever."[150] In essence, one gains control over one's mortality by manipulating sexually the macrocosmic forces of yin and yang within the body.[151]

As to be expected, five phases theory also plays a role in the cultivation of the body to attain immortality. The *Yellow Emperor's Classic of Internal Medicine* provides many explicit techniques to stimulate a particular organ to maintain or restore the balance required to enjoy a life "as long as heaven and earth." "Grass and herbs bring forth the five colors

. . . and also produce the five flavors. . . . Humans receive the five qi as food from heaven and the five flavors as food from earth. The five qi enter the nostrils and are stored by the heart and lungs. . . . The five colors restore brightness and light. The five musical sounds are manifestations of talent and ability. The five flavors enter the mouth and are stored by the stomach. . . . Together, all these influences help to perfect the mind, which then begins to function spontaneously."[152] By controlling the musical notes one hears, the colors one sees, and the flavors one tastes, one strengthens the influence of a particular force to attain the optimal proportion and ensure the proper functioning of an organ. The general theory remains the same—by stimulating certain forces within the human body, one is able to overcome the processes leading to death.

In sum, the development of elaborate systematic correspondences of natural phenomena, the correlating of the natural and human order through these systems of correspondences, the propagation of the theory of the human body as a miniature replica of the macrocosm, the positing of qi as the medium underlying mutual response between like things—all are incorporated by, and constitute the theoretical foundations for, many Han immortality practices later adopted by religious Daoism.[153]

No doubt much remains to be said. What I have been referring to as *religious Daoism* is by no means a monolithic entity. Rather, it encompasses a wide variety of sects, movements, and beliefs. The role of immortality practices on particular sects deserves further exploration, as does the compatibility of Huang-Lao and classical Daoist philosophy with the central tenets of the various movements. Yet this is neither the time nor the place to embark on such a study.[154]

The limited project of this section has been to demonstrate that Huang-Lao did resurface in the Han in conjunction with immortality practices and religious Daoism and to suggest one possible connection. While the historical, political, philosophical, and religious ties between Huang-Lao and religious Daoism are surely many, at least one runs through the *fang shi* and immortality seekers of the late Warring States and Han who make use of Huang-Lao's rule governed naturalist world-view as a stepping stone for the development of causal correlative cosmologies and microcosm-macrocosm theories that underwrite numerous immortality practices incorporated into religious Daoism.

VIII. Epilogue

✳

Huang-Lao studies are just beginning. This work constitutes an initial foray into what has been, particularly for the English-speaking world, largely uncharted philosophical territory. Much remains to be said, not only in regard to Huang-Lao's role in the development of Chinese philosophy, but with respect to its influence on the historical, political, and religious traditions of ancient China.

Histories written prior to the Mawangdui discovery tend to portray Legalists and Confucians as the main contestants in the struggle for Han political power, with Daoists considered too apolitical to dirty their hands with court intrigue.[1] When Daoists are acknowledged to have joined the fray, they are presented as spokespersons for the views of Lao Zi and Zhuang Zi. The failure of many historians to distinguish between classical Daoism and Huang-Lao is of course attributable in part to insufficient resources prior to Mawangdui to draw a convincing distinction. It also reflects, however, the tendency to take Sima Tan, the first historian to elide classical Daoism and Huang-Lao, at his word.

The discovery of the *Boshu* has made it apparent that there are significant differences between Huang-Lao and classical Daoism. Although the most obvious differences may be their respective legal philosophies, the most philosophically fundamental may be their views on the nature of order, both social and cosmological. In any event, these differences furnish historians with a new challenge: to sort out Huang-Lao from Lao-Zhuang supporters in early Han politics and to assess their respective impacts on government policies.[2]

The debate as to the relationship between philosophical Daoism and religious Daoism also stands to gain from further study of Huang-Lao. Although I have argued that certain immortality practices adopted by religious Daoism are based on a naturalist world-view that may be traced back to Huang-Lao and ultimately to classical Daoism, there are many other potential links. More research needs to be done to uncover the occurrences, uses, and meanings of Yellow Emperor images in religious Daoism, to clarify the relation between Daoist religion, Huang-Lao thought, Han politics, and so on.

Philosophically, the relation of Huang-Lao to the thought of the Jixia Academy philosophers—including Zou Yan, Shen Dao, Tian Pian, Huan Yuan, Jie Zi, Song Xing, and the authors of the *Guan Zi*—requires a more detailed examination than could be provided in this work. To be sure, initial steps have been taken, and the scarcity of extant texts bodes ill for further progress. Unless new works are discovered, it may be unrealistic to expect great advancement in this area. Yet progress has been unnecessarily impeded by the tendency to lump all Jixia works under the heading "Huang-Lao." Paying greater heed to the differences between the various thinkers will enhance our appreciation of the complexities of pre-Qin philosophy and the uniqueness of the Huang-Lao school.

The "three schools of thought" approach,[3] although perhaps still useful didactically, is now overly restrictive and hermeneutically misleading. No where is this more true than in regard to the late Warring States and Han eclectic texts—the *Boshu, He Guan Zi, Guan Zi, Huai Nan Zi*, and *Lu Shi Chun Qiu*—of which at least the last four are multiple-author works reflecting divergent philosophical positions. To make full use of these texts as treasuries of classical Chinese thought requires chapter-by-chapter analysis. To argue that the *Huai Nan Zi*, for example, is a "Daoist" rather than "Huang-Lao" text, or vice versa, is as much to obfuscate as to illumine.

Huang-Lao studies will also shed light on the works of other philosophers. I have made only passing reference to two major intellectual figures, Mencius and Xun Zi. The latter in particular merits attention from Huang-Lao scholars because of his naturalist world-view, his sophisticated synthesis of *li* (rites), *yi* (moral appropriateness), and *fa* (law), and his association with the Jixia Academy and the Legalists Han Fei and Li Si. When all is said and done, Xun Zi remains, I believe, firmly rooted in the pragmatic Confucian tradition.[4] However, living as he did centuries after Confucius, he was aware of some of the limitations of Confucius's system. Most important, he realized the value of law as a central means of social control and as a way of checking the power of the ruler. Yet, like Confucius, he ultimately grounded law not in the discovered natural order but in the discretion of the sage. To what extent he succeeded where Confucius failed must await another forum.

The influence both direct and indirect of Huang-Lao thought on Chinese philosophy after the early Han merits study as well. For instance, *li* (principle) assumes central importance in Neo-Confucianism. The *Boshu* is one of the primary classical sources for this term. Indeed, other texts or parts of texts in which the term occurs—certain chapters of *Han Fei*, the *Guan Zi*, the outer chapters of the *Zhuang Zi*—often reflect if not Huang-Lao influence at least a world-view in many ways compatible with that of the *Boshu*. The indirect influence of Huang-Lao may be most prominent, however, in the way one interprets classical Daoism. Many of the developments believed to be predicated on the philosophy of Lao Zi and Zhuang Zi may in fact have their roots in Huang-Lao thought.

The Mawangdui discovery will assuredly make possible great advancement in the understanding of the intellectual history of China. Yet one cannot help but wonder if Huang-Lao thought has the resources to contribute to contemporary philosophical debates.

1. Huang-Lao and Contemporary Philosophy

The value of the study of ancient Chinese philosophy is greatly enhanced in my view if it can be made relevant to today's world and the contemporary philosophical scene. Unfortunately, I do not believe the *Boshu* has much to offer a comparative philosopher from the West. To be sure its foundational naturalism is unique in many respects. Yet, although one may not find in the annals of Western philosophy an exact equivalent, one does find a more than ample and varied supply of foundationalisms. Ironically, whereas the *Boshu* represents an aberration within the Chinese intellectual tradition and may be of considerable interest for that reason alone, it is in its broad contours all too common within the Western.

The *Boshu* is, moreover, a victim of bad timing. How unfortunate to lie buried and neglected for 2000 years only to be unearthed in the era of postmodernism, perhaps in the history of Western philosophy the intellectual milieu least hospitable to epistemological foundationalisms, correspondence theories of truth, natural law doctrines, and the like. The quest for certainty in normative or empirical matters has been attacked so relentlessly for so long, it has been all but abandoned. Foundational epistemologies in which the mind mirrors nature have been out of vogue for some time, the victim of sustained critique by Sellars, Rorty, and an army of others. The myth of the naturally given has been exposed. The prevailing ethos favors instead epistemic and normative claims made in the reasoned space of social and personal beliefs and evaluated according to the values, attitudes, ideas of the concerned parties. Value neutrality has given way to theory ladenness, universality to context specificity, ahistoricicty to historicity.

As for Huang-Lao jurisprudence, theories of natural law and natural rights have been viewed with skepticism if not disdain ever since Bentham declared them to be nothing more than nonsense on stilts.[5] To be sure there are still defenders of modified versions of natural law. And many would agree with the assessment of one commentator that, although foundational "natural law theory is too implausible to merit serious study as a philosophical theory on the nature of law . . . the motivations of the theory were important and . . . it was groping, however confusedly, toward genuinely profound insights."[6] Yet the ability of Dworkin's interpretive theory to incorporate ethical concerns into the judicial decision-making process seems to capture the main insights and concerns of classical natural theories without falling prey to the myth of the naturally given and other assorted evils of foundationalism. Dworkin's avoidance of such pitfalls is not surprising given that his theory of law as integrity owes much to postmodernism, particularly Continental literary theory.

This is not to suggest that the debate is over. Dworkin's theory has drawn criticism from all quarters: positivists, natural law theorists, and members of the critical legal studies movement alike have all raised objections. And the concerns that gave rise to Huang-Lao—the need to impose limits on those in power, to create institutional obstacles to potential abuses by the ruling class, and to rein in judicial discretion—are as pressing today as they were in the time of Huang-Lao. That not only Western but Eastern jurisprudes continue to grapple with these and other tough issues—how to justify law; the nature of law; the proper role of judges; the status and philosophical defense of rights—is apparent in a recent article published in the *Beijing Review*, an official weekly of the People's Republic of China.[7]

2. Huang-Lao and Contemporary Jurisprudence in the PRC

The PRC's attempt to design and implement a new legal system has met with considerable difficulties, as the title of Li Maoguan's article, "Why 'Laws Go Unenforced,'" suggests. Some are practical in nature. Since the end of the "Cultural Revolution" and the opening to the West, many new laws have been formulated. Nevertheless, the need for further legislation, particularly economic and administrative, remains. In addition, more efforts must be made to educate the people about the new laws and more people trained if the system is to be successfully implemented.[9]

Apart from these practical concerns, however, there are problems more fundamental, more theoretical, in nature. Li identifies three: law is overshadowed by power; the relationship between the Communist Party and the law is out of kilter; the negative influence of China's traditional legal culture persists. As for the first, many politically powerful people believe they are above the law. The law is only for the "rank and filers, while they themselves stand high above the law, far out of its reach, and do not need to be limited by it. Some power-holders even regard the power in their hands as a means for law violation."[10]

In regard to the relationship between the party and the law, the constitution states that the party is subject to and bound by the laws of the state. In the past, however, the party was the most powerful, sovereign body.[11] Its policies took precedence over the law. As a result, "some leading cadres still take it for granted that Party organizations are free from legal restrictions and have the right to control everything and meddle in everything. In some places, for example, Party committees invalidate the election results of the people's congresses, deliberately dismiss leaders from government and judicial departments without going through the proper procedures, and interfere in or take over the work of judicial departments."[12]

The negative affects of China's traditional legal culture and attitudes about law are manifold. People fear the legal system as a means to solve problems.[13] This explains in part why most have traditionally preferred and continue to prefer to settle their disputes outside of courts, often turning to personal contacts to act as mediators.[14] The reliance on personal connections (*guan xi* 関係) favors the powerful, however, reinforcing the belief among the people that laws and the legal system as a whole serve the interests of the ruling class.[15]

In addition, moral principles continue to be given pride of place over laws. Many will not press for legal entitlements if doing so conflicts with ethical beliefs. To illustrate, Li Maoguan tells of one rape victim who reportedly refused to prosecute for fear of shaming herself and family.

Even when there is no ethical conflict, many are still reluctant to insist on their rights granted by the constitution.[16] As Louis Henkin and others have noted, the Chinese constitution provides most of the same rights as its American counterpart: freedom of speech, press, assembly, association, procession, demonstration, religious belief and practice; inviolability of the person, protection from arrest except by proper authority; prohibition of unlawful detention or search of person; and so on.[17] Yet because of "centuries of feudal rule," wherein "ordinary Chinese citizens had the duty to abide by the law but little [access] to legal protection of their rights," a passive attitude developed towards obedience to the law.[18] Of course, articles such as number 51 of the 1982 constitution prohibiting anything deemed not in the interests of the state may also explain in part why citizens are reluctant to actively pursue their rights "granted" by law.[19]

For example, students who attempted to exercise their constitutional right to demonstrate in the spring of 1989 were informed that they would have to attain approval from local authorities, approval that of course was not forthcoming. The fact that there have been twelve officially promulgated constitutions and numerous drafts since the turn of the century may also give a would-be rights claimer pause.[20]

These problems—the use of social status and political power to circumvent, distort, and ultimately undermine the law; questions of sovereignty; conflict between law and ethical customs; fear of a legal system that works more on the basis of *guan xi* (connections) than pure justice—not only existed in the classical era but led to the doctrinal differences discussed previously.

As noted, Confucius rejected codified and publicly promulgated laws because they tie the hands of those seeking to create new and mutually acceptable solutions to conflicts. Hard and fast laws rob one of the flexibility, the discretion, to generate solutions sensitive to the particulars of the given case. For this reason, Confucius maintained that law as a means of social control is intended to ensure, and only capable of achieving, a minimum level of socially acceptable behavior. One cannot legislate humanity; one cannot legally require people to do their best to resolve conflicts in a way that allows all concerned to most fully realize their potential. In fact, promulgating laws has just the opposite effect. Instead of seeking cooperative solutions to problems, people take advantage of the laws to pursue their own interests, demanding through lawsuits that the court grant them that to which they are strictly entitled by law, regardless of larger moral concerns of justice and fairness.

No doubt the influence of Confucianism on the legal culture of China has been great. As remarked, people continue to turn to morality rather than the law for guidance in interpersonal interactions. It is a commonplace that when conflicts arise, one is well advised to begin with *qing* 情: appeal to the other's feelings, emotions, sense of humanity, or common decency. Only when all such avenues are exhausted does one turn to *li* 理: discursive reasoning, rational principles, logical arguments, and the like. If this too proves unavailing, one is then forced as a last resort to invoke *fa*: the law. By way of contrast, it is often suggested that Westerners, particularly Americans, invert the process, opening discussions by citing the letter of the law. Only when the law is not clear on the particular point does one attempt to be reasonable. If reasoned persuasion cannot resolve the impasse, one then, perhaps somewhat shamefacedly, assumes the role of supplicant, beseeching the other party with emotional appeals. Although this sketch may exaggerate the eagerness of Americans to turn to law, there can be little doubt that most feel more comfortable persuading others as to the merits of their view through reasoned discourse rather than emotional appeal.

A second enduring influence of Confucius's legal legacy is the reliance on out-of-court settlements, often mediated by a community elder who acts the part of the sage in determining according to his or her cultivated ethical sense what is appropriate in the particular case. This approach has the advantage of speed—one need not wait for an overburdened court system to resolve one's disputes. It also allows both sides to forgo the possible loss of esteem associated with a negative court decision.[21]

Yet this method also evidences the deficiencies inherent in Confucius's legal system. Confucius assumed that a mutually acceptable solution could be reached. His positive-sum assumption is not only denied by Western philosophers from Hobbes to Rawls but by his own disciple Xun Zi. Confucius further assumed that people would be willing to cooperate in finding a mutually acceptable solution. Again both Hobbes and Xun Zi would disagree: people are too self-interested for this method to be realizable in practice. Those with the most power will put their interests first, and those without power will have little choice but to acquiesce. As the Legalists pointed out, this system, by giving such wide discretionary authority to those in power, fosters a dual class system in which the law falls heavily on those below while not reaching up to the nobles above.

Nowadays, the *gan bu* (幹部—political cadres) are the noble elite of China. They are the powerful ones exempt in many instances from the law that governs the lives of the masses. As Li Maoguan has observed, given their powerful positions and personal connections, they are often able to circumvent and distort the legal process.[22]

To address these problems, many thinkers from the late Warring States to the present have called for a rule of law rather than rule of man.[23] What is needed, it is argued, are publicly promulgated, impartially applied laws—a central tenet of Huang-Lao and Legalist jurisprudence.

Legalism's rule by law remedied some of the inadequacies of Confucius's rule of man. Yet it had difficulties of its own. Although it promoted a rule by law, it was rule by positive law. In the final word, law was whatever the ruler declared it to be. As a consequence, the all-powerful Legalist sovereign remained above the law. Today, a similar problem exists: the party remains above the law. There is a need for real constraints on party power. Simply declaring the constitution to be the ultimate authority is not sufficient.[24]

A second problem shared by both Legalism and the contemporary legal system is the failure of laws to reflect the moral beliefs and traditions of the people. The result, as observed, is that people often act in accordance with what they think is right, not with what the law dictates.

On the surface, it appears that what is needed nowadays is what was needed two millennia ago. To diminish the excessive influence of powerful individuals, the rule of man must give way to the rule of law. Yet it must be a rule of law that reflects the moral concerns of the people. In addition, it must impose legal and institutional constraints on those with the power to create, interpret, and alter the law.

Huang-Lao represents an attempt to design and implement such a system. It is a rule of law wherein even the ruler has to obey the law. It addresses the ethical deficiencies of positivist rule of law by relaxing the draconian laws of Qin Legalism in favor of more moderate and just regulations complemented by a Confucian emphasis on moral suasion and benevolent government. It seeks to simultaneously justify laws and curb the power of the ruler by grounding the legal and sociopolitical order in a predetermined natural order.

The intentions of Huang-Lao's natural law theory are laudable. Individuals need some protection against the state and against the "best judgments" of those in power. Yet the Huang-Lao system ultimately suffers from shortcomings of its own. The philosophical validity of its foundational naturalism and natural law doctrines is tenuous at best. Perhaps even more important, the Huang-Lao system fails in practice to impose real constraints on the sovereign. In the absence of institutional checks on his power, the ruler continues to have the final word as to what constitutes proper order, be it social, political, ethical, or legal.

Given the many failed attempts by Westerners and Easterners alike to design a system that is both philosophically justifiable and practically workable, one wonders if the project is not hopeless. It may be that there are fundamental conflicts that no system can resolve consistently. There may be no systematic way to balance the interests of the individual against those of the collective, the state. While any impartial rule of law may be too gross to produce normatively appropriate judgments in specific cases, any system that allows for sufficient flexibility and discretion to adequately reflect particularities may fall prey to abuse by those in power and disadvantage those who are not. Further, given the different historical, ethical, political, philosophical, and legal traditions of China and Western countries, there is little reason to suspect that what would work best for one would necessarily work for the other.

That said, it does seem possible to identify certain general features that all philosophically justifiable and workable systems must possess: institutional checks on those in power, particularly the sovereign; commitment to similar treatment of similar cases; mechanisms for generating and publicizing laws, and so on. Perhaps most important, however, there must be some means of protecting the individual against undue interference from other members of society and the state. The key is of course *undue*. Where the "rights" of society give way to those of the individual is a difficult line to draw, and one that will surely be drawn differently in China than in the United States. Indeed, reasonable people may differ as to the nature of rights. And they will surely differ as to how seriously rights are to be taken. But that they are to be taken considerably more seriously than they have been in China, few would deny.

Theories of natural law and natural rights, for all their philosophical warts, have served well in limiting the power of states to interfere in the lives of individual citizens. They may indeed be "nonsense on stilts," nothing more than philosophical myths. Yet, if nonsense, they are very valuable nonsense, if myths, life-saving myths. In the wake of the Tiananmen massacre, many Chinese might well wish they too had embraced such myths.[25]

Appendix: He Guan Zi and Huang-Lao Thought

I have argued that foundational naturalism and its corollary natural law constitute two of the defining characteristics of the *Boshu*, and by extension of Huang-Lao thought in general. Although I have discussed other texts that espouse one or more of the *Boshu*'s central tenets, none presents as complete a synthesis, particularly of foundational naturalism and natural law as does the *Boshu*. As a consequence, one might ask whether the synthesis of foundational naturalism and natural law is characteristic of the Huang-Lao school as a whole or simply of the *Boshu*. That no other Huang-Lao text maintains such a position might suggest that the *Boshu* constitutes an anomaly within the Huang-Lao tradition.[1] Fortunately, there exists another text that evinces a similar view—the *He Guan Zi*.

The Mawangdui discovery has rekindled interest in the *He Guan Zi*. The occurrence of numerous parallel passages between the *He Guan Zi* and the *Boshu* has forced sinologists to rethink the long-accepted view of the former as a post-Han apocryphal work. The emerging consensus is that, although the work may be a composite of the writings of multiple authors representing various schools of thought, much if not all of it belongs to the late Warring States to Han periods, though external evidence is only firm from about 500 A.D.[2]

The relation between Huang-Lao and *He Guan Zi* has long been suspected. Lu Dian of the northern Song (1042–1102) traced the text to Huang-Lao and the doctrine of *xing ming*.[3] A host of modern commentators, struck by the many parallel passages and the similarity of ideas found in the *He Guan Zi* and the *Boshu*, have followed Lu in characterizing the *He Guan Zi* as a Huang-Lao work.[4]

Yet despite the renewed interest, problems remain. Opinions differ as to what parts are authentic.[5] Authorship—both the immediate question of which chapters are written by whom and the ancillary issue of the relation of authorship to thought—remains problematic. Neugebauer divides the text into six sections, Ogata into at least eight. Graham thinks that, although all but two chapters are related, the text advances three different ideals of government: Legalist, Yin-Yang (Huang-Lao), and Daoist anarchist.[6]

There are methodological complications as well. In comparing the *He Guan Zi* to the *Boshu* and the Huang-Lao school, some authors have been content to simply select similar or contrasting ideas regardless of their location, taking them all as equally representative of He Guan Zi and ignoring the problem of authenticity and the possible presence of different strata or schools of thought within the text. Given the eclectic character of the text, if one is to analyze successfully its relation to Huang-Lao, one must first sort out, virtually on a chapter-by-chapter basis, the various schools or strata. To be sure this is no easy task. Indeed, the best efforts of several formidable sinologists to classify the various chapters has produced the decidedly mixed results noted previously.

In analyzing the text, scholars have employed various techniques. Some have turned to philological evidence, examining rhyme schemes, key terms associated with a certain geographical location, text or school of thought, parallel passages in the classical corpus, and so forth. Others have turned to historical and literary standards: the depiction of historical events or the championing of unorthodox quasi-historical exemplars—Cheng Jiu and Jiu Huang (the Nine Majesties)—as opposed to orthodox figures such as Yao and Shun. Many have taken similarity of thought as the standard for classification, with the *Boshu* serving as the primary source and standard of Huang-Lao thought.

Yet for this latter method to be effective, one must first state what constitutes the essence of Huang-Lao thought in general and the *Boshu* in particular. One needs, in short, to determine criteria for distinguishing Huang-Lao and the *Boshu* from other classical schools and philosophical works. Some—citing, for instance, the numerous parallel passages—have appealed to language and style to demonstrate that *He Guan Zi* is a Huang-Lao work, probably by Chu authors.[7] Yet this approach is open to the objection that late Warring States and early Han texts are often extremely eclectic, commonly borrowing ideas and passages from many texts and schools while turning them to their own ends. Indeed, one finds in the *He Guan Zi* passages from works of several schools (though the number of passages from the *Boshu* far exceeds that of any other text) as well as Confucian, Legalist, Mohist, Yin-Yang Five Phases, and School of Names ideas.

Given Sima Tan's description of Huang-Lao as the school that selects the best from the others, several commentators have made a virtue of necessity by taking *He Guan Zi*'s eclecticism as evidence of its Huang-Lao character.[8] Were eclecticism limited to Huang-Lao texts, this would be a more convincing argument.

Christopher Rand has focused on military theory, arguing that the *He Guan Zi* and the *Boshu* are examples of Huang-Lao or syncretic thought that calls for a complementary balance between the civil (*wen*) and martial (*wu*), and provides a metaphysical justification for warfare as part of the cosmic order.[9]

Others, most notably Wu Guang, have pointed to a similarity between the social and political philosophy of the *He Guan Zi* and the *Boshu*.[10] Based on analysis of the *Boshu*'s philosophy in Chapter III, one can identify the following salient similarities, not all of which are peculiar to Huang-Lao.

First, both the *Boshu* and *He Guan Zi* call for a centralized, unified state. Whereas the former turns to the Yellow Emperor as the legendary ruler who unified the empire, the latter turns to Cheng Jiu and the Jiu Huang (Nine Majesties). Nevertheless, the message is the same: by holding fast to the one and basing the political order on the natural order, one is able to rule over the four seas as one family without end.[11]

Although there is to be but one ruler,[12] he is to be a servant of the people: "the ruler of man treats his people as his children" (6/18b/3); "to act in accordance with the people is the essence of the way" (4/10a/4). The exemplary ruler is attributed virtues usually associated with Confucianism: benevolence (*ren*), moral judgment (*yi*), loyalty (*zhong* 忠), and trust-worthiness (*xin* 信) (6/16b/6). Further, he is required to balance martiality (*wu*) with civility (*wen*, 4/8a/8), punishments (*xing*) with rewards (*de*, 9/9a/6). As in the *Boshu*, punishments and rewards are to be coordinated with the natural order, with rewards dispensed in three seasons and punishments in one (10/16a/11). Finally, the ruler demonstrates his concern for the people by safeguarding their economic well-being, ensuring sufficient supplies and distributing the wealth of the state (6/16b/8).

Like the *Boshu*, the *He Guan Zi* attempts to justify a hierarchical society as natural (4/6a/7, 4/10a/10). At the same time, society is portrayed as meritocratic (4/6b/9, 4/10b/5, 6/15b/3). As for the relation between ruler and minister, each has his own role: "The way of the ruler is to know men; the way of the minister is to know daily affairs" (6/16b/8). With each performing his own duties, the ruler and ministers cooperate (6/18b/5). The animosity and mistrust that characterize the ruler-minister relation for Shang Yang and Han Fei are conspicuously absent.

All of the preceding approaches have their value, especially when taken together. By examining the collective results, a consensual portrait begins to emerge as to which chapters are indeed representative of Huang-Lao thought. For my purposes, however, it is not necessary to determine precisely each and every chapter properly classified as Huang-Lao. Even less is it my task to determine the proper school for those chapters that are not Huang-Lao. My more limited goal is to support the claim that foundational naturalism and natural law are characteristic of Huang-Lao thought and not simply idiosyncratic features of the *Boshu* by demonstrating that certain chapters of the *He Guan Zi* espouse these same ideas. Of course, to the extent that one accepts foundational naturalism and natural law as defining traits of Huang-Lao, one will in locating chapters that promote these views also be identifying the most likely Huang-Lao candidates.

Based primarily on these criteria, I have provisionally identified the chapters most likely to be Huang-Lao as 3, 4, 5, 6, 8, 9, 10, and 11.[13] Conversely, Chapters 1, 7, 13, 14, 16, and 19 are most likely not Huang-Lao.[14] Chapters 12, 17, and 18 share some characteristics of Huang-Lao thought, but because of differences in tone, style, emphasis or appeal to orthodox exemplary figures they appear to represent, if not a different school, at least a different sect than the core Huang-Lao chapters. Chapter 15 is eclectic, but other than that does not appear to be part of Huang-Lao. Chapter 2 simply does not provide enough information to locate it with any confidence.

It is worth mentioning that my assessments gain some support from a survey of the parallels between the *Boshu* and *He Guan Zi*.[15] There are parallels between the *Jing Fa* section of the *Boshu* and Chapters 4, 6, 8, 9, 10, and 14. All have been provisionally identified as core Huang-Lao chapters except 14. However, the parallel in 14 is questionable in that the phrase—*dao sheng fa* (道生法—the way gives rise to law)—is imbedded in a passage in the *He Guan Zi* whose meaning, as Tang Lan notes and I discuss later, runs counter to that of the *Boshu* passage.[16] Chapter 12, which Graham considers part of "Daoist anarchist" block, has two parallel passages with the *Shiliu Jing* section, not the *Jing Fa*. The *Shiliu Jing*, in addition to presenting several hagiographical anecdotes of the Yellow Emperor, places greater emphasis on military affairs than the predominantly political *Jing Fa*. Chapter 12, for its part, differs from the core Huang-Lao chapters of the *He Guan Zi* in its use of historical stories as a narrative device. Further, like the *Shiliu Jing*, it devotes considerable attention to military affairs.[17] Finally, Chapter 17 contains a parallel to the *Cheng* section. Although it evinces many Huang-Lao ideas, it appears to have been written by a different author than the core chapters and indeed has long been assumed to be a later addition.[18]

Foundational Naturalism in the *He Guan Zi*

In the *He Guan Zi*, *tian* and *di* refer to an impersonal natural order, not simply the firmament and earth: "What we call *tian* is not the azure *qi*; what we call *di* is not this conglomerated soil. When we say *tian* we mean that which lets things be so without suppression; when we say *di* we mean that which makes things even and cannot be disordered" (8/1b/5). The natural order is rule governed, constant, and regular: "What we call *tian* is the principled (*li*) actuality of things;[19] what we call *di* is that which being constant does not depart from it" (1/1a/10). One passage that also appears in the *Boshu* attests not only to the patterned regularity of the natural order but to the appropriateness of the natural order as a model for the human social order: "The sun reliably rises and sets, north and south have their extremities—these are the models for measurement. The moon reliably waxes and wanes, there is a constancy to advancement and withdrawal—these are the models for calculation. The stellar formations not deviating from their orderly progression, alternating without interference—these are the models for positions. Heaven illumines the three in order to fix the one" (10/16a/4).[20]

As in the *Boshu*, the natural order consists of the triad *tian-di-ren* (heaven-earth-humans): "The extreme of intuition and illumination (*shen ming*) is the affairs of heaven, earth and humans returning to the one" (10/15a/13). As such, it encompasses both the human order and that of nonhuman nature. Indeed, as part of the larger cosmic order, both the human order and that of nature are governed by the same rules (8/1a/12): "Heaven and humans share the same patternation (*wen* 文); earth and humans share the same principles (*li*)."

There are many general statements as to the need to predicate the human social order on the natural order (4/8b/6): "What lets things go and leaves all to positional advantage is *tian*. Let things go and leave all to positional advantage. Hence no one is capable of taking charge who does not *tian* (act in accordance with the natural order)." Similar sentiments are expressed in the *Boshu* (53:47b): "Where one treats heaven as heaven (*tian tian*), one attains intuition (*shen*)."

The sage is not to rely on his own judgment as to what is best in a given situation but to take as his model the natural order: "Heaven is that by which the myriad things get established. Earth is that by which the myriad things get stabilized. Thus heaven determines them. Earth places them. . . . The sage takes them (heaven and earth) as his model" (6/15a/6).[21]

As in the *Boshu*, there is a premium placed on timeliness. One must act in consort with the seasons and the rhythms of the natural order or else suffer the inevitable consequences: "There is a constancy to *qi*, it's principles determined by heaven and earth. Actions running contrary to natural timeliness (*tian shi*) are inauspicious and bring disaster" (6/15b/3).[22]

Specific social policies are determined by the natural order. As noted previously, rewards are to be disbursed in spring, summer, and autumn, punishments enforced and executions carried out in winter. Deployment of the military must likewise be coordinated with heaven and earth: "The method of using troops is to do so in accordance with heaven, earth and humans" (14/7a/12).[23] Perhaps most important, the laws adopted by the ruler and society are to be grounded in the natural order.

Natural Law in the *He Guan Zi*

Like the *Boshu*, the *He Guan Zi* promotes rule of law[24] as a primary means of effecting social order. "When an exemplary ruler adheres to established law, subsequent generations are long-enduring. When a negligent ruler does not comply, the present generation is destroyed" (6/18b/13).[25] Chapter 8 of the *He Guan Zi* presents a quasi-historical account of the descent from past utopias where law was unnecessary to contemporary realities where it is. Ideally, one is to govern through intuitive or spiritual transformation (*shen hua* 神化). Only as a last resort does one turn to rule of law. Unfortunately, the demands of the present age necessitate such harsh measures. Not only are rulers not always as wise as the legends of yesteryear, but people nowadays are not as cooperative and other regarding as they may have been in the past.[26]

Rule of law, although not ideal, has its merits, perhaps the greatest being impartiality: "Law causes the rejection of partiality (*si*) and the attainment of impartiality (*gong*)" (8/5b/9). When like cases are treated alike, fairness is enhanced.

As characteristic of natural law theories, that of the *He Guan Zi* posits an inseparable link between law and morality: "What is right is that to which the law is intimately related; what is wrong is that from which the law is distinct; what is right is intimately related to the law, and hence strong; what is wrong is distinct from law, and hence perishes" (5/12b/11). Law must uphold the way: "What protects the one way (*yi dao*) and regulates the myriad things is law. Law is what protects the inner [court]; ordinances are what outwardly regulate. Law does not defeat what is right (8/3a/6)."

Many commentators have pointed to another passage seemingly parallel to the *Boshu* that relates law to dao: "Worth generates sagehood,

sagehood the way, the way law (*dao sheng fa*), law intuition and intuition illumination/clarity" (14/8a/10). Although the phrase *dao sheng fa* does occur in the *Boshu*, it is part of a philosophy of law that is dramatically at odds with that expressed in this passage from the *He Guan Zi*. In the latter, the sage is arguably the ultimate source of the way, a notion best expressed in Confucius's dictum that "it is human beings who are capable of broadening the way, not the way that is capable of broadening human beings" 15:29). As discussed in Chapter IV, the sage-judge in the Confucian system relies on his own discretion and intuitive judgment as to what is best in a specific situation. In contrast, Huang-Lao law is a product of a discovered foundational way and grounded in a predetermined natural order. One does well to distinguish between (Confucian) coherence theories of law and (Huang-Lao) natural law in a strict foundational sense, both of which reject legal positivism and separability of law from morality. Both types of theory are present in the *He Guan Zi*.

The existence of a strict natural law theory of the type found in the *Boshu* is confirmed by the grounding of law in the discovered, normatively privileged, natural order: "Law is heaven and earth's instrument of proper order. When law is used incorrectly, original virtuous potency is not realized" (10/5b/2). The description of laws as the commands (*ming*) of the natural order attests to the predetermined character of *He Guan Zi*'s natural law: "What gives rise to law is command. What is given rise to by law is also command. Command is what is so of itself" (5/12b/12). Lest anyone mistake the predetermined commands of the natural order for positivist commands of the sovereign, the author adds, "Only the sage can thoroughly investigate the actualities of the Way. Only the law (*fa*) of the Way impartially governs and illumines. When the handle of the Dipper points East, South, West, North, it is spring, summer, fall, winter. With the handle of the Dipper circulating on high, affairs are established below. With it pointing in one direction, the four frontiers are completed. This is the employment of law by the Way" (5/12a/13).

In the epistemology of the *He Guan Zi*, the sage discovers the predetermined Way. He is not a creator of the way(s), but a mediator between the given natural order and the human social order; he is responsible for effecting through legislation a social order that reflects the natural order. He takes what he has discovered through intuitive reflection (*shen*) and translates it into enlightened social policies and laws that illumine or clarify (*ming*) the Way for others:

> As being here law is called near, as issuing forth to transform the other it is called far. From the near it arrives, so is called intuition (*shen*); from the far it

returns, so is called illumination (*ming*). The illumination is here, its radiance illumines the other. Its affairs are formed here, its achievements complete the other. What transforms the other from here is law. The generator of law is myself, the completer of law is the other. The generator of law is something which is present every day and never flags. One for whom the generating and completing are in himself is called the sage. (5/12a/4)

The price to pay for a wayward sage who generates or legislates law not in accordance with the Way cum natural order but in light of his own best judgment as to what is appropriate in the context is chaos, both social and cosmic: "When knowledge lacks the Way, the patternation of heaven is disordered above, the principles of earth obliterated below, harmony among humans cut off in the middle . . ." (8/2a/4). The final standard for proper order, the object of true knowledge, is heaven and earth, not man:

> The Supreme Majesty asked the Supreme One, "Of these three—heaven, earth, and man's work—which is most urgent?"
> Said the Supreme One, "Inward correction by care of the quintessence and nurturing of intuition are how one emulates heaven. 'Heaven' is that in which intuition and illumination is rooted." (10/15a/7)[27]

> Heaven and earth are the correct standards for forms and intuitive reflection (*shen*). (8/1b/2)

Significantly, Chapter 1, identified by Graham as Legalist, advances a contrary thesis. The ultimate authority is not heaven, the natural order, nor the Way, but the ruler: "The ruler is the one who constitutes the correct standard for intuition and clarity" (1/1b/2). As in the *Boshu*, the natural law philosophy of the *He Guan Zi* serves as a theoretical limit on the unbridled powers of the Legalist ruler.

Realism in the *He Guan Zi*

One offshoot of the *Boshu*'s foundational naturalism and epistemology of discovery is its realist philosophy of language. Rather than a matter of convention and pragmatic utility, names come preassigned, attached as it were to the determinate form of the real objects to which they refer: "When a thing is forthcoming, its form precedes it. Established in accordance with its form, it is named in accordance with its name" (81/142b). There is a passage in the *He Guan Zi* that suggests a similar realist view:

> There being the One there is *qi*, then the idea (*yi* 意), then the picture (*tu* 圖), then the name, then the form, then the affair, then the covenant. The

covenant being decided the time is born, the time being set the thing is born. Therefore superimpositions of *qi* make the time, of covenants the project, of projects the achievement, of achievements gain and loss, of gains and losses fortune and misfortune, and of the myriad things victory and defeat. All of them spring from the *qi*, interchange along the way, are covenanted for in affairs, are corrected by the time, are distinguished through names and completed by law. (5/11b/7, Graham [7], p. 514)

Graham, for one, toys with the idea that this passage presents "the rudiments of a 'Realist' theory of naming." He points out that "it would seem theoretically possible for ancient Chinese to conceive Heaven personified after the analogy of the human ruler as fixing the names of things by his decree before generating them." Yet in the end he dismisses the idea, claiming that "no school except the Mohists went as far as that in personifying Heaven, and it was in the Mohist school that the 'Nominalist' theory of naming developed."[28]

This difficult passage is surely open to a variety of interpretations. What exactly is one to make of *yi* (idea? intention? cognitive motive or plan?) or *tu* (picture? scheme? representation? plan?)? It is unlikely that *yi* means "idea" and *tu* "picture" in a Wittgensteinian sense. And what is the philosophical significance of the *He Guan Zi*'s inversion of names and forms? Perhaps it indicates a nominalist theory of naming after all: names are generated according to ideas-intentions and images-plans; how we name things determines how we cut up the world and hence generates forms that in turn shape our every day affairs.

On the other hand, the ultimate source of names and so forth is *qi*, the primal quasi-materialist energy that constitutes the stuff of reality. Further, one need not assume as Graham does that only a personified heaven can be a source of a realist theory of naming. As observed in the *Boshu*, names are grounded in an impersonal, rule-governed natural order. Indeed, the author states, "*tian* rectifies names and initiates them" (66:70a). Thus, in light of strong Huang-Lao character of the Chapter 5 of the *He Guan Zi*, it is possible that the author had in mind a realist theory of names similar to that of the *Boshu*. At the very least, such a position is consistent with his foundational epistemology and theory of a discovered natural law.

*

I have been concerned primarily to demonstrate that there is in the *He Guan Zi* a well-articulated foundational naturalism and natural law philosophy of the type presented in the *Boshu*. Yet the *He Guan Zi* is not the *Boshu*. There are differences, even between the core Huang-Lao chapters and the *Boshu*, and these differences deserve to be noted. Several have already been mentioned, such as the alternative line of mythic heroes. Others have been discussed elsewhere, notably the *He Guan Zi*'s introduction of the notion of *yuan qi* (元氣—primal or original *qi*), believed by some commentators to be a development of and advancement on the materialist ideas of the *Boshu*.[20] One difference that merits comment is the pervasive presence of an integrated yin-yang five phase theory in the *He Guan Zi*. As noted previously, there is little mention of the five phases in the *Boshu*, though much of yin-yang. The fully realized synthesis of yin-yang and the five phases in the *He Guan Zi* may indicate a later date of composition. Of course, this is highly speculative. The synthesis may have occurred before the writing of the *Boshu*, whose author may either simply not have known of it or deliberately decided not to make use of it.

Another difference is that, despite Lu Dian's comment, the doctrine of *xing ming* does not appear to be as developed or philosophically central in the *He Guan Zi* as in the *Boshu*. From an epistemological perspective, the *He Guan Zi* places less emphasis on the attainment of emptiness and tranquility (*xu jing*) as a means to eliminate biases and gain objectivity. Conversely, it pays closer attention to the role of the sage in the "discovery" of the way through intuition and illumination (*shen ming*), suggesting that the author(s) were less sanguine about the notion of objective and impartial discovery than the author of the *Boshu*.

Indeed, perhaps the biggest difference in the two texts concerns the role of the sage. In the *He Guan Zi*, the sage is able to subdivide as he pleases within the general framework given by nature:

> The lay-out of members and placing of joints, unchanging for a myriad ages, is from the positions of heaven and earth; the dividing of things and sequencing of names, so that patterns and principles are clear and distinct, is from the equalizing by intuitive sages. (11/21a/12)
>
> The multiple we ourselves make multiple. (10/19a/1)

The *He Guan Zi* seems to be grappling with a question raised earlier in conjunction with the *Boshu*: to what extent are the natural and human social orders given? In the *Boshu*, things come with forms and names preassigned, so there is little room for the creative input of humans. To be sure each thing may not have a unique form and name. Thus there might be some room to choose between several tokens of type *x*. And while the human social order must comply with the laws and principles set by the natural order, these laws may be underdetermining, thus allowing for more than one possible social order. Nevertheless, the choices appear to be more severely constrained for the *Boshu*'s sage than *He Guan Zi*'s in that the latter is responsible for sorting out the details of the human order within the overall guidelines set by the natural order.

The greater degree of input ceded the sage in the *He Guan Zi* is evidenced in the distinction between laws (*fa*) and ordinances (*ling* 令) encountered in a passage cited earlier: "What protects the one way and regulates the myriad things is law. Law is what protects the inner (court); ordinances are what outwardly regulate. Law does not defeat what is right" (8/3a/6). Whereas *fa* (laws) represent fundamental metaphysical cum moral principles, *ling* (ordinances) represent specific political decrees, policies, or orders based on the laws. Unlike laws, which are given in the natural law theory of the *He Guan Zi*, ordinances represent applications of the law as interpreted by the sage in the specific context.[30]

Whatever their differences, the *Boshu* and (parts of) the *He Guan Zi* share a common Huang-Lao heritage. No where is this more apparent than in their support of a philosophy of foundational naturalism and natural law.

Notes

*

I. Introduction

1. For an English introduction to the Mawangdui material, see Loewe, Jan Yun-hua (1), Tu Wei-ming (2), and Riegel. Riegel offers a partial bibliography of early works by Chinese scholars on the Mawangdui discoveries.
2. For references to Huang-Lao in the classical literature, see Zhang Weihua (1), Zhong Zhaopeng (2), Wu Guang (2), and Yu Mingguang (2).
3. Zhong Zhaopeng has scoured the historical records to compile an admirable summary in table form (name, nature of influence, and bibliographic citation) of Han political figures said to be influenced by Huang-Lao, see Zhong (2), pp. 94, 97.
4. *Shi Ji* 74.2347; 63.2146.
5. See VII.3.1.
6. See Tu Wei-ming (2); Riegel; Cheng Chung-ying; Schwartz, 237–254; and Jan Yun-hua (1–5). A recent article by Karen Turner advances a thesis similar to mine: namely, that Huang-Lao espouses natural law.
7. The first is a broad survey by Wu Guang; cf. Wu (2). The second is by Yu Mingguang who attempts to differentiate "*Lao xue*" (the classical Daoism of Lao Zi) from "*Huang xue*" (the doctrines of the Yellow Emperor, also referred to as "Huang-Lao"); cf. Yu (3).
8. Hu Xintian does offer a modern Chinese paraphrase of the text. (Hu died before completing his work. The task of editing and publishing fell to Li Zongtang.) Hu's version of the original text, however, often differs from the 1980 *Wen Wu* version. In addition, Hu frequently emends the text or supplies his own interpolation for missing characters without providing justification. The text is of little help to scholars seeking to understand the philosophy of Huang-Lao.

Jan Yun-hua (2) has translated into English the final short section labeled *Dao Yuan*. Takahashi has translated most of the first section, the *Jing Fa*, into Japanese and provided commentary and annotation. Guo Yuanxing has written an article explicating several difficult passages. Tang Lan provides a list of similar or identical passages to the silk manuscript in the classical literature. Yu Mingguang (3) provides extensive annotation and commentary to all four sections, but stops short of offering a modern Chinese translation. Random House will soon publish a translation by Robin Yates.

9. See Zhong Zhaopeng (2), p. 80; Yu Mingguang (3), pp. 9–12.

10. For more on the images of the Yellow Emperor, see Zhang Weihua (1), Wu Guang (2), LeBlanc (2), Jan Yun-hua (4), and III.2.1.

11. In tomb three a wooden writing slip was found that reads "in the twelfth year, second month, a month designated *yi si*, on the first day of the month, a day designated *mou zhen* . . . [all] has been presented to you, Lord, Master of the Grave." According to a recently discovered Han year chart based on the *zhuan xu* calendar used in Emperor Wu's time, the date of entombment is calculated to be April 4, 168 B.C. See Riegel, p. 11; Loewe, p. 100. I discuss further the title, authorship and dating of the text later.

12. See Wang Hsiao-po and Leo Chang.

13. See Kanaya, pp. 7–8; Schwartz, pp. 242–250; Jiang Ronghai; Gao Yinxiu and Zhang Zhihua; Yu Minguang (3).

14. See Saiki Tetsuro (1 and 2).

15. See Hu Jiacong (3, 4, and 6); also, Zhi Shui (2).

16. See Wu Guang (2), pp. 195–207.

17. Ibid., 166–191.

18. See Williams, pp. 115–126; Wu Guang (2), pp. 151–165; Graham (7), pp. 508–509; Tian Jiajian, pp. 58–60, Du Baoyuan, pp. 54–57; Li Xueqin, pp. 53–56; Tōru Ōgata (3), pp. 18–19; Chen Keming; and Hosokawa Kazutoshi.

19. See Hu Jiacong (2).

20. See Liu Xiaogan.

21. This term is defined and explained in detail in II.1.

22. Bodde and Morris, pp. 43–44.

23. See vol. 2, Needham, pp. 549, 560, and later, III.1.2.

24. See Hall and Ames, pp. 12–17; see also III.1.2 and IV.1.2.

25. See Hansen (3); also II.3.2.

26. Or, perhaps, "Standards of Regularity." The scope of *fa* is broad, ranging from method to standard to law. I opt for the more narrow rendering because of the importance of law in the text (see II.3.4, and III.1.1).

27. Yu Mingguang (3) notes that in 1976, Wen Wu Press published another version of the text with commentary.

28. See Tang Lan.

29. Tang Lan supplements his argument against the other possibilities based on the number of sections with the following reasons: "Since this text is not an engraved text, it obviously is not the *Yellow Emperor Engravings* (*Huang Di Ming*). Were one to say that it was the *Huang Di Jun Chen*, only the "Shi Da Jing" [now referred to as the *Shiliu Jing*] part would be similar. However, in

this part there are fifteen subsections of which only eight pertain to the ministers of the Yellow Emperor. In these eight chapters, there is a treatment of the mythologizing of the Yellow Emperor and a discussion of the story of the capture of Chi You. As for the names of the officials, there are Li He [that is, Li Mu], Tai Shan Zhi Ji, Guo Tong, Yan Ran and so on. There is also Gao Yang who according to tradition is the Emperor Gao Yang. Thus, this cannot be the text *Li Mu*. This leaves the *Miscellaneous Accounts of the Yellow Emperor (Za Huang Di)* whose fifty-eight parts cannot be accounted for. In addition, there are parts on the Yin Yang school, the novelist school, military, yin and yang, astronomy, calendars, five phases, various divination methods, a medical classic and so on. Of the fifty-eight parts, only twenty-eight are related to the Yellow Emperor. Hence the content does not coincide. Consequently, of these texts related to the Yellow Emperor, only the *Yellow Emperor's Four Classics* is in four parts. On the basis of the number of parts, therefore, this lost text in four parts coincides precisely with the *Yellow Emperor's Four Classics*" (Tang Lan, p. 9).

30. Tang Lan, pp. 9–10.
31. See Gao and Dong, p. 89.
32. See Wu Guang (2), Zhang Weihua (1), Tian Changwu, and Zhong Zhaopeng (2).
33. Tu Wei-ming (2), p. 103.
34. See Long Hui.
35. See Xigui, Qiu, p. 71; Uchiyama Toshihiko, p. 13.
36. See Wu Guang (2), p. 131; also Wei Qipang, p. 179.
37. In the egalitarian communal system of Shen Nung, all are to till the field without exception.
38. See III.2.2.
39. See also the "Ci Xiong Jie" section of the *Shiliu Jing*, where the author argues strongly in favor of feminine characteristics. In the "San Jin" section, he then argues that both masculine and feminine traits are needed: "As for whether the human way should be hard or soft, being hard is insufficient as a means while being soft is not enough to rely on either" (74:125b).
40. Similarly, the gender of the author is not known, but to avoid the stylistically awkward he/she, his/her, I will simply refer to the author as *he*.
41. See Long Hui.
42. Yu Mingguang devotes one chapter to the argument that Chu was the home not only of the author of the *Boshu* but also of Daoism, both that of Lao Zi and Huang-Lao. See Yu Mingguang (3), pp. 217–238. A. C. Graham has challenged the claim that Lao Zi and Daoism can be traced to Chu; see Graham (5), pp. 111–124.
43. Zhong Zhaopeng (2), p. 82. See also Wu Guang (1), pp. 19–20.

44. It may be that the author spent time at the academy. Alternatively, he may only have met people from the academy.

45. The Warring States period runs from 480 to 221 B.C., the Western Han period from 206 B.C. to 25 A.D. I follow Wu Guang in dividing the Warring States into early (480–395), mid (394–310), and late (309–221); see Wu Guang (2), p. 1. I give the end date for the composition of the *Boshu* in the Han as 135 B.C. because that is one year after the death of Empress Dowager Dou and about the time when Han Wu Di banned Huang-Lao thought from court. It is highly unlikely that the work would have been written after the banishment, and certainly none of the scholars who favor a early Han dating so contend.

46. See Tang Lan, Long Hui, Jan Yun-hua (2), Zhao Jihui, Liu Jingquan, Xu Kangsheng, and Yu Mingguang (3).

47. See Ge Ronjing, Zhong Zhaopeng (1 and 2), Gao Heng and Dong Zhian.

48. See Wu Guang (2), Uchiyama Toshihiko, Kanaya Osamu.

49. See Qiu Xigui, Nishikawa Yasuji, Jiang Guanghui, Saiki Tetsuru (2).

50. Tang Lan, p. 10, n. 1.

51. Creel, p. 1.

52. See Thompson (1 and 2); also VII.1.2.

53. See Kanaya Osamu, pp. 7–8; Schwartz, pp. 242–250; Jiang Ronghai; Gao Yinxiu and Zhang Zhihua.

54. Tang Lan, p. 11.

55. Ibid., p. 11.

56. See Long Hui, p. 30.

57. See Wu Guang (2); Yu Mingguang (2). Note also Sima Tan's statement, cited later, that Huang-Lao represents the best of all schools.

58. See Wu Guang (1), p. 19; Zhong Zhaopeng (2), p. 82.

59. See for instance, Graham (6), p. 217.

60. See Wu Guang (2), pp. 129–132.

61. Uchiyama Toshihiko, pp. 11–13.

62. Several have pointed out that Sima Tan does not distinguish between Daoism and Huang-Lao thought; for the most extensive and convincing argument, see Yu Mingguang (2) and particularly (3), pp. 205–216.

63. See Uchiyama Toshihiko, p. 11.

64. Namely, hot (yang) and cold (yin), wind and rain, dark and light; cf. Graham (6), p. 325.

65. See Graham (4), p. 91.

66. Graham contrasts causal and correlative thinking. Although the manner in which the *qi*-forces of yin and yang "cause" changes in the natural order for ancient Chinese may differ in significant ways from a modern Western scientific understanding of causation, the term *causal* is still useful to mark the shift

away from early classificatory correlative cosmologies to those of the late Warring States to early Han.

67. See VII.1.1 and 4.2. There is some debate among sinologists whether the ideas in the *Chun Qiu Fan Lu* attributed to Dong Zhongshu are in fact indicative of his thought. The *Shi Ji* presents an account of Dong's thought at variance with the mechanistic orientation of the *Chun Qiu Fan Lu*.

68. For more on yin and yang, see II.2.3 and VII; see also Graham (4), Peerenboom (1).

69. See IV.2.

70. See Wu Guang (1), pp. 14–15, and (2), pp. 9–15, 100–109; Zhong Zhaopeng (2); Gao and Dong, Tang Xin, Cheng Wu, and Yu Mingguang (3), p. 25.

71. *Li Ji* 1:35a.

72. This is, of course, the standard Marxist-Leninist view of law: cf. Lenin, "law is a political instrument. It is politics" (Hazard, p. 69); Marx states "society is not based upon law; that is a juridical fiction. Just the reverse is the truth. Law rests upon society, it must be the expression of the general interests that spring from the material production of a given society" (Stumpf, p. 52). Speaking to the bourgeosie, Marx asserts "your law is the will of your class given the authority of statute" (ibid., p. 53).

73. See Schwartz, pp. 238–239; Liu Yuhuang, pp. 7–8; Zhi Shui (1), pp. 82–84; Liu Weihua and Miao Runtian, pp. 26–27.

74. Schwartz, p. 238.

75. Cited by Guo Moruo (2), pp. 133–134. Guo was one of the first to argue for a historical connection between the Jixia Academy of Qi and Huang-Lao thought.

76. For more on the images of the Yellow Emperor, see Jan Yun-hua (4), LeBlanc (2), Zhang Weihua (1), Zhong Zhaopeng (2); and III.2.1.

77. See IV.2.3, V.1.2; see also Turner.

78. See Nishikawa Yasuji, pp. 31–37.

79. Jiang Guanghui, p. 138.

80. Needham and Bodde and Morris claim Confucian jurisprudence to be natural law; Wang and Chang claim Han Fei and Shang Yang to be natural law theorists. See IV.2.1, and V.1, respectively.

81. Moral validity, although a necessary condition for legal validity, is clearly not sufficient. Many acts that are moral, even morally obligatory, are not legally required. The necessary relation between morality and law simply entails that a rule be morally permissible if it is to be a law.

82. See John Austin's command theory put forth in *The Providence of Jurisprudence Determined*.

83. See Hart's theory of primary and secondary rules in *The Concept of Law*.

84. St. Augustine I, 5; Aquinas, Qu.xcv, Arts.2, 4. John Finnis, a modern natural law advocate and apologist, contends that no natural law theory need maintain that an unjust law is not a law, adding that this is but a subordinate theorem in every natural law theory he knows of; see Finnis, p. 351.

85. For Feinberg's articulation of the coherence methodology, see Feinberg, p. 18. The coherence component of Rawls, his notion of reflective equilibrium, is only one component of his methodology. Rawls's attempt to secure universality for his principles of justice through a thought experiment by "rational agents" who make life-plan choices from behind a "veil of ignorance" runs counter to the context-specific character of pragmatist ethics. See Rawls, particularly pp. 19–21.

86. Feinberg refers to them as *principles* rather than *judgments*, as does Rawls. Rawls, for his part, requires in addition that the justification or rationale for balancing one's judgments with one's moral beliefs and intuitions in a particular way be brought into equilibrium. That is, one seeks the most coherent set of intuitions, reflective judgments and rationales.

87. Feinberg, p. 18.

88. For a clarification of *transcendence*, see II.1.2.

89. This is Aristotle's distinction. Cf. *Nichomachean Ethics* V:7, 1134b18–20. Whether or not Aristotle is indeed a natural or proto-natural law theorist remains contested. For an argument that he is the former, see W. von Leyden; for an opposing view, see D. N. Schroeder, pp. 17–31.

90. I must caution that no single natural law thinker, much less everyone in that tradition, need subscribe to all of the points I have used to portray natural law theories. There will be paradigmatic cases that clearly fall within the tradition as described. But there will remain a penumbral area into which certain figures will fall who have one foot in the natural law tradition and one outside of it. This is to be expected when we examine thinkers in light of a hermeneutical framework that they not only did not have but could not have had in mind inasmuch as the framework had not yet been clearly elaborated. This does not nullify the usefulness of this distinction as a hermeneutical tool given our current perspective and purposes.

91. Needham, vol. 2, p. 582; see also Bodde and Morris, p. 10.

92. Murphy and Coleman (p. 17) offer two basic characteristics of natural law theories: (i) moral validity is a logically necessary condition for legal validity and (ii) the moral order is part of the natural order—moral duties being in some sense "read off" from essences or purposes fixed (perhaps by God) in nature. They further point out that many contemporary natural law theorists would accept the first clause while rejecting the second. Even though the author of the *Boshu* does accept the second clause in maintaining that the moral, sociopolitical, and legal orders are implicate in the natural order or dao, I

have not appealed to the second clause as a defining trait of natural law theories. More important, in my view, is the foundational nature of the justifications for the law.

93. See, for instance, Murphy and Coleman (p. 29), who state that positivist theories "insist on a sharp separation between law and morality." They add a further differentia, that positivist theories offer a pedigree test for legal validity—that is, a rule will count as law if, historically, it was generated in a certain way (passed by the legislature, commanded by the sovereign, and so forth). Others, as they point out, simply take the essence of positivism to be the existence of a test for law that is a conventional social rule, what Hart calls a *rule of recognition* (see Murpy and Coleman, pp. 62–63, n. 22; Hart, pp. 92–104).

94. Hart, p. 181. Hart points out that this simply means that there is no *logically necessary* relation between morals and the validity of the law, though of course the "ways in which law mirrors morality are myriad" (ibid., p. 199).

95. He himself sees it this way, see Dworkin (1), pp. 339–341. For an excellent review of the debate as to where Dworkin's theory falls on the positivist-natural law scale, see Ball.

96. I have argued elsewhere that in *Law's Empire* Dworkin advances two incompatible positions: a weak thesis, that law as integrity consists of a balance between justice, fairness, due process, and political integrity; and a strong thesis, that law as integrity requires justice, fairness, and due process be subject to the overriding constraint of political integrity understood as coherence in fundamental moral principles. In demanding that the law be made coherent in light of moral principles, the strong version prohibits pragmatic, utilitarian considerations of policy and social consequences. This considerably lessens the distance between Dworkin's coherence theory of the law as integrity and natural law theories, though in the final analysis it is still the judge who determines what moral principles are to be considered and what weight they are to be given. See Peerenboom (6).

Dworkin's claim that there is a single right answer in all legal cases also seems at first glance to push him in the direction of natural law. Over the years, he has been relentlessly attacked on this point. Many have pointed out that his problem is exacerbated in *Law's Empire* in that (i) law as an interpretive concept is inextricably tied up with larger issues of political morality (and even metaphysics), so that there must now be a right answer not only to legal problems but moral ones as well and (ii) one's conception of what the law is, and hence one's decision in hard cases, will depend on how one balances Dworkin's dual standards of fit and justifiability. These standards may, however, provide conflicting results: a conception that fits better may not score as high on justifiability. Dworkin does state that fit is merely a threshold test, but the degree of fit necessary to cross the threshold is itself a matter of interpretation. Furthermore, the right answer thesis requires not just that judges balance fit and justifiability, but that there is only one correct way to do so. This becomes a moot point, however, because Dworkin also contends that there is no available objective or conclusive test of correctness for a judge's decision. As Max Weaver has remarked, because a decision cannot be proved to be the right answer, the right answer thesis seems unnecessary and pointless. For our purposes, Dworkin's acknowledgment that there is no objective test ensures that his interpretive theory remains at heart a coherence and not a foundational theory.

97. Finnis, p. 25.
98. Ibid., pp. 23–24.
99. Ibid., p. 251.
100. Ibid., p. 23.
101. Ibid., p. 12.
102. Ibid., p. 127.
103. Legislators have indeed appealed to such natural principles to outlaw birth control devices. Cf. Houlgate (pp. 17–18), who points out that attempts to ground law in human teleological nature fail because people disagree over what are our ends as humans.
104. Aquinas, IaIIae, q.94, art.i; Ia, q.79, arts 12–13.
105. Donagan, p. 350.
106. Sellars, p. 169.
107. For a Confucian-like response to Dworkin, see Peerenboom (6).
108. This first stage builds on the groundwork of sinologists who perform the initial philological chores of transcribing the original manuscripts into modern characters and so forth.
109. These two stages can be combined in a single work, as they are to a certain extent in this one.

II. The Natural Way of Huang-Lao

1. Roger Ames has recently called into question the appropriateness of the organic or organismic metaphor as a characterization of Chinese philosophy on the grounds that it (i) entails a sense of wholeness typical of many Western cosmogonic traditions but absent in the self-generative cosmologies of pre-Qin China, (ii) imparts a potentiality-actuality distinction that obviates the sui generis character and unduly restricts the creativity of the particular, and most important, (iii) conjures up images of Aristotelian teleology and the notion of a progressive and steady advance toward a predetermined perfection; see Ames (7).

Although Ames's criticisms serve notice that one must take care in employing the organism metaphor—as one must with any metaphor, particularly one laden with philosophical associations from an alternative tradition—they do not require its abandonment. Its continued use may be justified in that it does bring out the contrast between the holistic world-view of much Chinese philosophy in which the cosmic natural order embraces both humans and nonhuman nature and a dualistic view in which humans are juxtaposed to nature. This also justifies, in my opinion, the use of the term *ecosystem* even though normative order does not emerge out of interaction among the members of the system but is conceptually predetermined. Dao as the de facto order is indeed the totality formed by the particulars that do exist in the given moment such that on a descriptive level dao is the result of an interaction of its constituents parts. Prescriptively, or normatively, however, dao cum the cosmic natural order is transcendent and predetermined; see II.1.2.

That an alternative tradition would have different conceptions of such concepts as ecosystem or organism is to be expected. If we are to translate the original terms into English so as to avoid burdening the reader with excessive transliterations, we must choose those terms that are most similar or appopriate and then state the relevant differences between the use in the Chinese text and a common use or uses of the term in English.

Further, Ames's criticisms are not all equally applicable to every school of Chinese thought. For instance, the creativity of the particular in the world of Huang-Lao, as we shall see, is considerably more restricted than it is for Confucius. Thus *organic* is more readily applicable to Huang-Lao than to Confucian thought.

2. *Boshu* 49:29a (two characters missing); see also 71:116b, 67:132a.

3. Some humanisms derive their ethical views from an account of human nature, thereby grounding morality and the social order in the natural order. Yet such humanisms need not evidence any concern for the nonhuman nature component of the natural order. The *Boshu*, in contrast, is less concerned about human nature than nonhuman nature.

4. There are many senses of *natural*: (i) that which conforms to the laws of nature, (ii) that which is in keeping with one's inner nature, (iii) that which is spontaneous, unforced, (iv) the opposite of artificial, (v) human behavior or social practices that imitate or are modeled on nonhuman nature, and (vi) human behavior or social practices that instantiate a predetermined role in the cosmic natural order. The last two are the primary senses of *natural* for Huang-Lao. That there are two reflects the conceptual equivocation of the author discussed earlier. The human order may be "natural" in the cosmic sense if humans realize their proper place in the cosmic structure. This need not entail imitating nature in that the human society may have its own way or

order within the cosmic structure and nature its own. See later, imitative versus nonimitative naturalism, II.1.1.

5. One is reminded of Aristotle's attempt to justify the social practice of slavery on the grounds that some people were born "natural" slaves.

6. It is, however, not clear that the natural-cosmic order itself could be destroyed in a descriptive sense. Even if humans destroyed all life—human and nonhuman—and radically altered the landscape and the makeup of the cosmos, there would still be a cosmos and ipso facto a cosmic natural order. In Daoist terms, there would be a dao, though the Huang-Lao prescriptive or normative dao that assigns a place to humans within the cosmic structure would not be instantiated. In short, even when the way is lost from a normative perspective, there remains a dao in a descriptive sense.

7. See *Boshu* 62:85b.

8. Adapted from Hall and Ames, p. 13.

9. The imitative-nonimitative distinction is not isomorphic with but rather cuts across the correspondence-interpretive distinction because it is possible for correspondence naturalists to contend that both the human and nonhuman nature components of the natural order are predetermined, and yet still argue that each has its own independent, nonimitative way. Similarly, it is possible for imitative naturalists to conceive of nature as evolving and emergent rather than predetermined and rule governed. In general, however, imitative naturalists tend to be correspondence naturalists because they usually consider nature—and ipso facto the imitative human social order—to be predetermined and rule governed.

10. Hansen (2).

11. One must, however, take care not to make Zhuang Zi out to be an anything-goes relativist. Whereas on a theoretical level no *shi* or *fei* can be proven to be absolutely and infallibly correct, from a practical or pragmatic standpoint, some ways work better than others. See IV.2.1.

12. See *Boshu* 58:74b: "There being a distinction between right and wrong, use the law to adjudicate between them."

13. "It is human beings who are capable of broadening the way. It is not the way that is capable of broadening human beings" (*Analects* 15:29).

14. Hall and Ames, pp. 16, 131–138.

15. For a further elaboration of the differences, see III.1.2.

16. Ames (5), pp. 116–117.

17. Ames (4), p. 70.

18. See 53:50b: "necessity characterizes the determinant conditions of nature."

19. See *Boshu* 87:168a–169b.

20. See Teng Fu (2).

21. One's lot may be that of a pawn in the political chess game such that one cannot assume the position of the king. On the other hand, whether one is the queen's pawn or the king's pawn may be left open. For a Huang-Lao theory that allows humans some discretionary latitude, see the discussion of *He Guan Zi*, Appendix.

    The bias toward *li* as particular in Teng's reading reflects his tendency to read Huang-Lao in terms of Han Fei for whom *li* does perform such an individuating function (as it does in Neo-Confucianism); see Han Fei's commentary on chapter 14 of the *Lao Zi* (Liao, 1:191–192). For a discussion of Huang-Lao and Han Fei, see Chapter V.

22. Some Platonists, Terry Penner among them, have questioned the soundness of this distinction. Penner argues that to talk of Aristotle's universals as immanent, as residing "in" things, whereas Plato's Forms exist "separately" somewhere "out there" in Platonic Heaven is to speak just as metaphorically in either case. He suggests that the notion of "transcendence" or "separateness" be taken in a nonspatial way and to indicate a logical or epistemological difference between particular things and universals: they are separate in thought. See Penner, pp. 97, 118–121. Similarly, I do not simply want to trade in the spatial metaphor for a temporal one. The notion of laws of nature being "prior," or "*pre*determining," is meant to indicate a logical or conceptual relationship, not a physically temporal one. That is, within the author's thought system, the natural order is conceived of as determining the social order; it has a normative priority as the foundation on which the social order is constructed.

23. One could, I suppose, refuse it the label *tian ren he yi* on the grounds that the essence of that conception is not simply organicism but nonfoundationalism; to count as *tian ren he yi*, it would have to be nonfoundationalist organicism in which the order is not predetermined in accordance with universal principles or laws of nature but emerges as an interaction between humans and their environment. Personally, I see no reason to limit the scope of the term in this fashion. As it stands, it is a perfectly useful concept for capturing an important insight into the general character of Chinese thought as opposed to certain dualistic cosmologies that draw a sharp distinction between humans and nonhuman nature. One can always further qualify the term, speaking, for example, of a Dong Zhongshu *tian ren gan ying* 天人感應 (mechaninstic interactive response of nature and humans) variety or Confucius's *yi*-based (義—aesthetic interpretation) type.

24. As pointed out, both interpretive and correspondence naturalisms—and all other naturalisms that fit my three criteria—are foundational in that they normatively privilege the natural order. However, Huang-Lao is foundational in

the more radical sense peculiar to correspondence naturalisms. When referring to Huang-Lao as a foundational naturalism, I intend the more radical sense of correspondence naturalism unless otherwise stated.

25. See Rorty (1), pp. 335–339.

26. One's conceptual framework need not be construed exclusively in individualistic terms. The standards a given person uses for evaluating epistemic claims are, except in those cases of geniuses, mad people, and some religious converts, social in character. One makes one's judgments as a member of a community, indeed, as a member of various communities, which are communities by virtue of the shared values, attitudes, and so forth of the members.

27. I use the term *epistemology* in a broad sense to refer to a subdiscipline in philosophy that focuses on knowledge, knowing, how we know, the criteria for knowing, and so on. Thus interpreted, epistemology embraces both the traditional search for foundational truth that has dominated Western philosophy from Plato through the Enlightenment thinkers of Kant and on to this day, and the postmodern, pragmatic, Confucian, and Daoist alternatives to foundationalism. Rorty draws a distinction between hermeneutics and foundational epistemology in the Enlightenment-Kantian sense; see III.1.1. I will not restrict the scope of the term in that fashion.

28. Although some have argued that Zhuang Zi's perspectivism commits him to anything-goes relativism, I do not agree. As an antifoundational fallibilist, Zhuang Zi rejects the notion of rational certainty and moral absolutes. Yet that there are no indubitable reasons for epistemic or moral claims does not entail that there are no reasons at all or that from a pragmatic perspective any reason is as good as any other. For a further discussion, see VI.2.1.

29. See 81:143a; also 66:97a, where *tian* is identified as the source.

30. Following Hansen (1), p. 62.

31. For Confucius' philosophy of language as a pragmatic, performative theory of attunement of names, see Hall and Ames, pp. 261–275.

32. For the anthropomorphic character of Confucius's *tian*, see *Analects* 3:13, 9:6, 9:12, 12:5, 14:35, 16:8.

33. See *Dao De Jing* 5.

34. See Asano Yuichi who argues that there are three sources for Huang-Lao natural law: the objective natural order, the dao of Lao Zi, and an anthropomorphic deity (*shang di* 上帝 or *tian*). See also Saiki Tetsuro (2) who takes the *Boshu tian* as similar to the anthropomorphic Confucian *tian*.

35. See II.4.1–2.

36. Bodde (1), p. 722; see also Bodde (2).

37. Needham, vol. 2, p. 562.

38. See III.1.2.

39. See Wei Qipeng.
40. See Hsu Fu-kuan, ch. 2. Graham has pointed out that since yin and yang are part of the six *qi* that include light and dark, their early meaning may have been warm and cold.
41. Two characters missing, for which I interpolate *gan* 幹—heaven's trunk—and *di*—earth's (norms).
42. One character missing, the meaning of which seems to be something like "pursue," "scrutinize," "investigate."
43. For further discussion of yin yang thinking in the *Boshu*, see VII.1.2.
44. Hall (2), p. 50.
45. See IV and VI for a discussion of Confucian and Daoist daos-orders as emergent rather than predetermined. For a discussion of Daoism as cosmic and social anarchism, see Hall (1 and 2). He notes that anarchy is to be understood in the etymologically primary sense of *an*: without + *arche*: ruler, rule, authority—that is, without a coercive source of order, be it determinant logical principles, dogmatic moral rules, or authoritarian political structures.
46. *Li* occurs in the *Han Fei Zi*, the eclectic "outer chapters" of the *Zhuang Zi* and in the *He Guan Zi*, a composite text with some Huang-Lao chapters (see Appendix).
47. Approximately nine characters missing.
48. See II.4.2.
49. Graham (1); Guan Feng, pp. 86–89.
50. For the Yellow Emperor as a symbol of centralized government and Shen Nung of communal anarchism, see Graham (5), pp. 94–100; and III.2.1.
51. See *Dao De Jing* chs. 39, 40, 42; see also VI.1.2.
52. Approximately ten characters missing.
53. Reading *kung* 空—empty—as *kung* 孔—opening, hole—in accordance with the *Huai Nan Zi* (Yuan Dao), which states: "The multitude of myriad things all pass through one opening (*kung*); the root of the many affairs all depart from the same door."
54. See Liu Xiaogan, pp. 61–63.
55. See Teng Fu (1).
56. Yu Mingguang (1), p. 71. Yu also disagrees with Teng's reading of Lao Zi's dao, contending that it is, *pace* Teng, materialistic.
57. Ge Ronjing, pp. 47–50.
58. Wu Guang (2), p. 137.
59. Jin Chunfeng, pp. 54–56.
60. For an explanation of the namelessness and unfathomability of dao, see VI.1.1.
61. Many mainland philosophers are aware of the limitations of the materialism-idealism dichotomy; cf. Mao Conghu and Gao Tingtai, p. 11.

62. One character missing.
63. One character missing, for which I supply *hao* 號—titles—based on a parallel passage in the *He Guan Zi* (2/2b/12).
64. Following the Mawangdui editorial group in taking *bu* 不—not—in the first clause as a copying error.
65. Hansen (3), p. 492.
66. Ibid., p. 516.
67. To be sure, in certain circumstances—introductory textbooks, speeches to an audience of nonspecialists, and so on—such characterizations may be not only appropriate but beneficial.
68. *Truth* is a concept. *Semantic truth* is a conception, one version, of the concept. *Warranted assertability* is another conception of truth. Given the strong tendency in our tradition to conceive of truth as semantic truth, one might well want to argue that it is more convenient and less confusing to reserve *truth* solely for semantic truth. But that is a pragmatic decision rather than a philosophical one. Those traditions or schools of thought that do not have the tendency to think of truth solely as semantic truth may use *truth* to mean warranted assertibility. Hansen himself admits as much elsewhere: "Thus, Chinese thinkers, relatively speaking, are concerned less about semantic truth and more about pragmatic acceptability. That is not to claim that their language is in some fundamental way different, such that the criteria of truth cannot be applied—it can" (Hansen [1], pp. 58–59).
69. Hansen (3), p. 496.
70. Ibid., p. 502, emphasis added.
71. Ibid., p. 516, emphasis added.
72. Ibid., p. 492.
73. Ibid., p. 500.
74. There are arguably other exceptions besides the Huang-Lao school, most notably the Later Mohists. See Graham (1).
75. Hansen (3), p. 516. He adds, however, that one may interpret *dang* as a pragmatic concept. This is to be accepted because one's philosophy of language is dependent not so much on the words one chooses as on one's epistemology for Hansen.
76. See 43:4b, 45:10a, 45:14b.
77. See 45:9b.
78. See 54:56b; see also 53:52a, 52:45b.
79. The nature of one's language may, of course, be an argument in favor of a certain interpretation of one's philosophy. But it is merely an argument, not a conclusive one unless one wishes to adopt some form of linguistic determinism.
80. Exceptions include four contested chapters of the *Han Fei Zi*, some of the

"outer chapters" of *Zhuang Zi*, and parts of the *Guan Zi* and *He Guan Zi*—all of which have been associated with Huang-Lao by modern scholars.

81. Four characters missing, though the phrase may be reconstructed on the basis of the subsequent contrary phrase.

82. Based on the subesequent contrary phrase, the missing character is most likely *shun* 順—compliance. A similar passage in the *Guan Zi* (Jun Chen shang) also suggests *shun*, as does the appearance of the damaged character (though based on appearance alone the character could also be dao).

83. For discussion of Huang-Lao military thought, see Lewis, particularly pp. 231–238; Rand, particularly pp. 211–218.

84. Nine characters missing.

85. Many scholars have commented on the importance of *yin*. Zhang Weihua, noting that Sima Tan and Qian took it as a defining characteristic of Huang-Lao thought, argues that it refers to following the objective laws of nature, which requires that the ruler be empty and vacant. Zhang adds that *yin* also entails going along with old customs and established laws (Zhang Weihua [2], pp. 204–206). Liu Weihua and Miao Runtian (pp. 28–29) demonstrate the importance of *yin* for Shen Dao, Shen Bu Hai, and the Guan Zi, all of whom they consider to be Huang-Lao thinkers.

86. See *Shi Ji* 130.3292.

87. Three characters missing. Emended according to the *Huai Nan Zi* (Zhu Shu), which states: "If one has a grand strategy, he cannot be burdened with quick craftiness. If one has little knowledge, he cannot be entrusted with large tasks. People have their respective abilities (*cai* 才); things have their respective forms. There is that which when entrusted to one is too heavy but when entrusted to one hundred is still light." This last phrase can be used to interpolate the missing three characters—*ren yi er* 任一而. The Mawangdui editorial group suggests that *zhong* 中—centrality—in the following *Boshu* phrase be emended to *cai*—abilities—on the basis of this passage as well.

88. Larre, p. 37.

89. For a more Confucian, coherence theory reading of *cheng*, see Tu Wei-ming (2), pp. 105–197.

90. See *Analects* 12:17; 13:13.

91. See Gao Heng and Dong Zhian; also Jin Chunfeng.

92. See Xu Kangsheng and Wu Guang (2) for a similar interpretation of Huang-Lao epistemology, Ge Rongjin for a more mystical one. Also, see Hu Jiacong (6) for a comparison of the epistemology of the *Boshu* to what Hu considers to be other Huang-Lao texts, particularly the *Guan Zi*.

93. Schwartz, p. 249.

94. *Ming*—names—followed by three missing characters.

95. One character missing.

96. *Shi*—also signifying "reality", or "substance" (as opposed to pretense).
97. Tu Wei-ming (2), p. 104.
98. *Dao De Jing* 47.
99. Jan Yun-hua (3), p. 214.
100. For a comparison of Huang-Lao epistemology to that of certain chapters of the *Guan Zi*, see VII.1.2; to that of Confucius, IV.1.2 and V.1; of Lao Zi and Zhuang Zi, VI.1.1 and 2.1, respectively.

III. The Social and Political Philosophy of Huang-Lao

1. See Needham, vol. 2, p. 562. Others have also argued that Huang-Lao espouses natural law, see in particular Turner.
2. See Needham, vol. 2, p. 544; Duyvendak (2), p. 81; Bodde (1), p. 709; Bodde and Morris, p. 20; Zhang Qiyun, p. 8.
3. Needham, vol. 2, p. 518.
4. For an explication of natural law theories in the strict sense, see I.2.1.
5. The term *fa* has a wide range of meanings in Chinese, from model to standard to law. One could make a case for all of these readings in the *Boshu*. One might contend, as James Sellmann has pointed out to me, that I have simply begged the hermeneutical question by translating *fa* as "law" in that in many, perhaps all, of the passages I cite, *fa* could arguably be rendered in a broader sense than *law*.

    To do so, however, would entail a radically different reading of the text than I offer. We can evaluate the relative merits of the various interpretations once they are produced. In the meantime, that there exists a continuum of possible meanings does not prevent one from opting for the more specific reading when it fits the context better in light of one's overall reading of the text while simultaneously according with the way we use *model, standard, law* in English. There is no reason to privilege a priori the broader meaning. Of course, one must remain sensitive to the connotations of the original Chinese word and not assume when reading "law" that it is isomorphic with *fa*. In any event, the distinction between law-standard-model tends to collapse on my reading because specific juristic laws are consistent with and an expression of the more general standards of the natural order. This may not be the case for the author of the *He Guan Zi*; see the Appendix.
6. See Tang Lan. The debate as to whether the text belongs to Legalism or Daoism was influenced, however, by the internal politics of the PRC during the "Cultural Revolution" as the various factions sought to use the Han court struggles between Confucianism and Legalism for their own ends; see,

for instance, Kang Li and Wei Jin. For relatively late accounts of the text as Legalism, see Cheng Wu, pp. 43–47; Tian Changwu, pp. 63–68; Wang and Chang, p. 90.

7. See Qiu Xiguin; also Saiki Tetsuro (2). Both Saiki and Qiu take the *Boshu* as part of "Dao-Fa Jia" and not Huang-Lao. Saiki, however, believes that the *Boshu* and Dao-Fa Jia represent mainstream Daoism of the Early Han whereas Qiu believes that that honor goes to Huang-Lao, which he takes to be a more politically passive philosophy.

8. One character missing.

9. Three characters missing.

10. One charactor missing, emended with *si* (私—partiality) accorting to *Guan Zi* (Jun Chen xia) and *Han Fei Zi* (Ren Zhu) passages cited by Mawangdui editorial group.

11. One character missing.

12. Hart, p. 181.

13. Augustine, 5; Aquinas, Qu.xcv, Arts.2, 4.

14. *De* has a wide range of meaning. Sometimes rendered as "potency," it is often translated as "virtue" in that the latter in its Latin root *virtus* connotes moral worth and excellence of character, as well as power, force, manliness. In this text, it is sometimes used in the more Confucian sense of moral worth, particularly when referring to the character of the sage-ruler. At other times it is used in the more Daoist sense of potency. And at still others it is contrasted with punishments to refer to rewards in the Legalistic sense.

   To further complicate the picture, John Major has noted that *xing* 刑 and *de*, although often appropriately translated as "rewards" and "punishments," are sometimes employed as cosmological terms best understood as universal principles rather than as acts of human government. He offers several instances where *xing de* if translated in terms of the human acts of reward-punishment render the passage unintelligible. He concludes that in such cases, one would be better served by the translation of "accretion" for *de* and "recision" for *xing*, though he allows that these terms do not sit well with his preference for plain English translations of classical Chinese. See Major (2), pp. 281–291.

15. Cf. Bodde and Morris (p. 497), who claim that "natural harmony was thought to flow from both the moral order and physical orderliness. Crimes produced discord; once a crime is committed, harmony is restored only by suitable punishment. An inept punishment is as bad as, or worse than, none; it will not restore natural harmony; on the contrary, it will disrupt order still further."

16. As noted in I.2.1, a second characteristic of classical natural law theories, and the reason for the adjective *natural*, is that the moral order is understood to be part of the natural order. The *Boshu* evidences this aspect as well. To allow for

greater refinement in contrasting the views of the *Boshu* and of Confucius, and to take advantage of advances in contemporary jurisprudence, I have stressed the foundational rather than the natural character of natural law.

17. "The way to respond to transformations is to leave off once the scales reach equilibrium. Where light and heavy are not weighed up, this is called losing the Way" (43:6a).

18. Needham, vol. 2, pp. 214–215.

19. Commenting on the reemergence of Confucianism in the Han, Needham states, "Law again became, as Duyvendak says, firmly embedded in ethics, and successive emperors . . . justified their mandates by invoking natural law, i.e. norms of behavior universally considered moral—in fact, *li*—and not positive law" (Needham, vol. 2, p. 214).

20. Bodde (1) and (2).

21. Needham, vol. 2, p. 549.

22. Ibid., vol. 2, p. 562.

23. See II.1.2.

24. For a discussion of correlative thinking in China and the shift around 300 B.C. to causal correlative cosmologies, see Graham (2), and VII.1.2.

25. The term first appears in the *Shi Ji*. For a discussion of its occurrences, see Zhang Weihua (1) and Liu Weihua and Miao Runtian.

26. See VI.1.2.

27. See VI.1.1.

28. See *Dao De Jing*, 5.

29. See VI.1.2.

30. See *Mo Zi*, ch. 35 (W118). The three tests have been much discussed. For a particularly interesting treatment, see Hansen (3), pp. 511–514.

31. Zhang Weihua (1), Zhong Zhaopeng (1), and Le Blanc (2) provide excellent tables in which they compile citations of the Yellow Emperor in the literature. See also Yu Mingguang (3), pp. 4–12.

32. Ding Yuanming (pp. 71–72) points out that the surprisingly many citations to the Yellow Emperor by such a wide variety of schools may very well be due to the policies of the infamous Qin Shi Huang Di. When Qin Shi Huang ordered the burning of the books, he exempted Legalist works along with those on prognostication, medicine, alchemy, and immortality. The Yellow Emperor, in the form of Huang-Lao thought, was associated with Legalism and Legalist thinkers favored by the Emperor, as evidenced by the *Shi Ji*, which links Han Fei, Shen Bu Hai, and Shen Dao among others to Huang-Lao. Further, Huang-Lao thought contains a yin-yang element and the naturalist cosmology that would later be developed into causal correlative cosmologies. Such cosmologies underlie many of the late Warring States–early Han immortality practices of the *fang shi* and other longevity seekers (see Peerenboom [2]). This

would also explain the popularity of the Yellow Emperor: it was politically safe to cite the Yellow Emperor because he was connected with both Legalist and immortality thought favored by Qin Shi Huang.

I would add to Ding's insightful comments that the Yellow Emperor was traditionally portrayed as a totalitarian ruler who unified the empire through military conquest (as discussed later). Such an image must surely have appealed to the Qin Shi Huang, who himself did precisely that, as it would to the rulers of Qi who usurped power. For the relation of Huang-Lao to the state of Qi and the Jixia Academy, see I.1.4, and VII.1.2.

33. See Zhang Weihua (1); Zhong Zhaopeng (1); Wu Guang (2), pp. 109–121; and Liu Weihua and Miao Runtian. In English, see Jan Yun-hua (4); Lewis pp. 137–148, 174–212; and Le Blanc (2). In addition to an extensive compilation of Yellow Emperor citations, Le Blanc provides a bibliography of earlier work of the Yellow Emperor.

34. Given the numerous citations to the Yellow Emperor by such a wide variety of schools, there is little point in attempting to reduce the symbolic value of the Yellow Emperor to a single image. His roles and functions are many, varying, as Jan Yun-hua (4) has demonstrated, across time and from school to school. Nevertheless, by examining certain recurrent themes, the use of the Yellow Emperor in philosophical texts of the certain genres (particularly Daoist and Legalist) and the images of the Yellow Emperor within the *Boshu* itself, one is able to appreciate why Huang-Lao is called *Huang-Lao*.

35. See also *Yi Jing* (Xi Ci, Wilhelm 331); *Shang Jun Shu* (Geng Fa, D172), *Zhuang Zi* (Shan Xing, W172).

36. *Shang Jun Shu*, ch. 18, (D284).

37. This is a common image of the Yellow Emperor: cf. *Shi Ji* ch. 5, p. 192; also Shen Buhai "Yi Wen Lei Ju" *juan* 54, *Tai Ping Yu Lan juan* 638 (Creel, p. 150).

38. Although Lao Zi is not the absolute pacifist that many make him out to be, he does not resign himself to the inevitability of war as readily as the author of the *Boshu*; cf. *Dao De Jing* 30, 31.

39. See both the *Shiliu Jing* "Wu Zheng" (65:94a) and "Zheng Luan" (67:104a) sections.

40. See Graham (4), pp. 67–110.

41. Lewis points out that Shen Nung, the Divine Husbandman, is the mythic creator of agriculture. The creation of agriculture freed ancient Chinese from the need to hunt, making possible a nonviolent life-style. The Yellow Emperor, as the mythic hero of Warring States rulers bent on unification of the empire through military conquest, reintroduced warfare as proper human behavior. As noted later, violence is sanctioned or justified on the grounds that it is natural: not only do animals battle, but so do humans. The Yellow Emperor

bought peace to the empire by subjugating rival clans. Warfare as proper social behavior was also naturalized by being grounded in the natural order, the cosmic cycles of yin and yang. See Lewis, pp. 137–241, especially 177–178.

42. The label *primitivist* is that of Graham, see Graham (1), pp. 200–223.

43. This is a standard reading of mainland scholars, see Wu Guang (2), pp. 67–78; Zhang Weihua (1), p. 13; Liu Yuhuang, p. 6. I do not hold this view. For my counterarguments, see VI.2.2.

44. The following story is from the "outer chapters" of the *Zhuang Zi*: "Zhuang Zi was fishing in the Pu River. The king of Chu sent, two grandees to approach him with the message: 'I have a gift to tie to you, my whole state.'"

"Zhuang Zi, intent on his fishing rod, did not turn his head. 'I hear,' he said, 'that in Chu there is a sacred tortoise that has been dead for 3000 years. His Majesty keeps it wrapped up in a box at the top of the hall in the shrine of his ancestors. Would this tortoise rather be dead, to be honored as preserved bone? Or would it rather be alive and dragging its tail in the mud?'"

"'It would rather be alive and dragging its tail in the mud.'"

"'Away with you! I shall drag my tail in the mud'" (45/17/81, G122).

45. See the *Sun Zi Bing Fa* (Huang Di Fa Chi Di) excavated in Shan Dong province and cited in Zhong Zhaopeng (1), p. 77. In that account the Yellow Emperor's military success is attributed to his attaining "the way of heaven, the appropriateness of earth and the affection of the people." Much the same idea is expressed in the "Bing Rong" (71:116b) section of the *Shiliu Jing*.

46. See also *Shu Jing* (Lu Xing); *Ji Zhong Zhou Shu*, 56, "Chang Mo Jie," *Sibu congku* ed., 12a; *Shan Hai Jing* 17/6b; *Guo Yu* 10/259; *Huai Nan Zi* 15/la. See also Lewis, pp. 183–195.

47. Interpolating *pi* (皮 —skin) for the missing character. *Gan hou*, according to the *Yi Li* (Da She), is the name of a kind of target.

48. Literally "meat sauce." Guo Yuanxing, finding it hard to accept that the Yellow Emperor could be so cruel as to make his people drink the bitter broth of Chi You, contends that he made a kind of alcohol that was used to prevent rotting. He then poured the alcohol over the bones and carcass of Chi You to preserve it as a reminder to the rest of the empire. See Guo Yuanxing, pp. 129–130.

49. Following the Mawangdui editorial group in emending *chen* 諶 to *kan* 戡.

50. For the role of the Yellow Emperor in sanctioning warfare and violence as proper human-social behavior, see Lewis, pp. 137–241. Lewis discusses at length the way in which warfare and violence are justified in the Warring States by being grounded in and predicated on the natural order. For the "metaphysical" underpinnings of warfare for Huang-Lao, see also Rand.

51. The portrait of the Yellow Emperor as the originator of the state, a warrior, and ruler is corroborated in a variety of texts from many different schools.

Although the various schools may give greater weight to one image as opposed to another, the biggest difference is in their assessments of shared images: what one takes to be laudable others find reprehensible.

52. For gardens, cf. *Zhuang Zi* (60/22/79, W246); for the *ming tang*, cf. *Guan Zi* 3:15.

53. For music, cf. *Zhuang Zi* (95/33/19, W365), *Guan Zi* 2:82. For rites, cf. *Shang Yang* (Hua, D285); for benevolence and righteousness, cf. *Shi Ji* (5.192), *Zhuang Zi* (26/11/19, W116).

54. Jan (4), p. 123. See also *Guan Zi* 41:14/242, 77:23/384; *Lu Shi Chun Qiu* 4/5a, 5/8b; *Shi Ji* 1.6.

55. *Zhuang Zi* (39/14/68, W164).

56. *Guan Zi* 2:89–90; the last sentence also occurs in a fragment attributed to Shen Buhai, "Yi Wen Lei Ju" *juan* 54, *Tai Ping Yu Lan juan* 638, (Creel, 150).

57. For the image of the Yellow Emperor as teacher of civilized institutions see *Guo Yu* 4/17; *Guan Zi* 41:14/242, 78:23/384; *Lu Shi Chun Qiu* 26/12b; *Shi Ji* 1.6, 5.192, 16.1256; *Han Shu* 21a/3b, 30/23b, 62/10b. I owe these references to Le Blanc (2), pp. 50–51.

58. See for instance the *Shan Hai Jing* 1:82. For a discussion of the divine images of the Yellow Emperor, see Jan Yun-hua (4), Le Blanc (2), and Zhong Zhaopeng (1).

59. See Le Blanc (2), p. 61.

60. Ibid., pp. 62–63.

61. For an explication of Daoist anarchism, see Hall (1 and 2).

62. For a similar point of view, see Jan Yun-hua (5), who focuses on the political philosophy of the *Shiliu Jing*; also Zhong Zhaopeng (1), Uchiyama Toshihiko, Tian Changwu.

63. It is interesting to note in this regard however that the *Guo Yu* (Lu Yu Shang) attributes the practice of naming to the Yellow Emperor, stating that he "was able to complete the process of giving names to the many things."

64. *Boshu* 51:35b.

65. See Yu Mingguang (3), pp. 44–46.

66. See also 83:164b–165b.

67. That each person comes into existence with a preassigned place in the normative hierarchy (which one may or may not live up to) argues against the blanket generality of Donald Munro's assertion that "any search for the concept of man in early China will lead at the same time to the idea of natural equality, which dominates that concept." Again, Huang-Lao serves as a challenge and corrective to universal statements about the nature of classical Chinese thought. Nevertheless, Munro may very well be correct that, by and large, the concept of natural equality in the sense he intends "is a central idea to any deep understanding of the Chinese world view" (p. 22).

68. See Saiki Tetsuro (1); Ōgata Tōru (3), p. 13.

69. *Xian guo* 县國 refers to the "prefectures" and "commanderies" in his empire. Hence he does not emphasize the number of prefectures in his empire; that is, the size of his empire.

70. The metaphor of the ruler as the hub controlling his ministers as the spokes is a common one. Cf. *Huai Nan Zi* (Zhu Shu); *Dao De Jing* (11); *Shen Buhai Zi* (CSCY 36/25b/5).

71. "I love the people and thus they do not perish" (61:79b).

72. *Boshu* 47:14b.

73. The most sophisticated treatment is by Wang and Chang, who base their comparison primarily on Han Fei. I agree with them that Han Fei's political philosophy in theory is designed to serve the interests of the people, as compared to that of Shang Yang, which is intended to serve the ruler. I also agree that Han Fei cannot be held entirely responsible for the practical abuses of his views by Qin Shi Huang Di. Therefore, to the extent that the comparison of Legalism and Huang-Lao thought is restricted to Han Fei and the author of the *Boshu* and the ends of government, the differences are perhaps less important than the similarities. However, there are other significant points of contention between Han Fei's views and those of the author; see Chapter V.

74. See *Shang Jun Shu* (Shuo Min, D211).

75. "Solemn and awful are mother nature's punishments. Yet without rewards one is sure to be toppled (69:109a). . . . Where magnanimity is absent, the meting out of punishments misses the mark" (69:111b).

76. Actually, the author sanctions both righteous (*yi* 義) wars—"assailing disorder and prohibiting cruelty, one promotes those of superior character and gets rid of those lacking in it" (75:128a)—and deployment of troops for beneficial (*li* 利) reasons–as when one attacks a mismanaged state where the people are starving and disorder abounds (75:127a).

77. Following the Mawangdui editorial group's suggestion that based on parallel phrasing one character has been omitted.

78. This point has been made by others. Ōgata Tōru (3), p. 12; Rao Xinxian, pp. 326–228; Shimamori Testsuo; and especially Turner.

79. Interpolating *li*—principle—for the missing character.

IV. The Anthropocentric Pragmatism of Confucius

1. *Shi Ji* 130.3289.

2. Hansen, defending the comprehensive coherence approach to interpretation, explains that "when we translate the language of Mencius in a particular way, we implicitly choose to attribute one set of beliefs to him rather than another. How can we prove which is the correct set of beliefs? We cannot simply say,

'This is what Mencius says in the text,' because if we had chosen one of the alternative interpretations, we would have had him saying quite different things" (Hansen, (4), p. 39). My only qualification would be to suggest that one abandon the notion of proving in a univocal, once and for all sense which theory is *the correct* one. Rather, we are better served by making fallible, comparative claims: on the evidence, this theory is better; given the data, this interpretation is the best of those on the table and so forth.

3. Although the development of pragmatism in terms of Rortean antifoundationalism is in effect a presentation of Confucius's epistemology, I do not explicitly take up his epistemology until Chapter VI, where I compare what it means to *zhi dao* (知道 -roughly, know the way) for Confucius, Huang-Lao, Lao Zi, and Zhuang Zi.

4. For a trenchant critique of convergent realism—roughly, the view that our scientific theories are increasingly close approximations of the truth-reality so that in the long run we will converge on the truth-reality—see Laudan (1).

5. One need not endorse all of Rorty's program, particularly his political agenda. For instance, his vociferous support of liberal democracy is at odds with the paternalism and deference to achieved excellence of Confucian society.

6. See Dewey (1) and (2).

7. See Mead.

8. See Rorty (l) and (2).

9. Rorty (2), p. xlii.

10. Rorty (1), p. 6.

11. Ibid., p. 159.

12. Rorty refers to them as, respectively, hermeneutics and epistemology (see later). Although foundational correspondence theories have dominated Western epistemology, I resist the temptation to conflate correspondence theories with epistemology, using the latter term to refer to the subdiscipline in philosophy concerned with the study of knowledge in a broad sense. This allows one to speak of pragmatist or Confucian epistemology even though they are not instances of foundational correspondence epistemologies.

13. Rorty (1), p. 159.

14. Ibid., p. 96.

15. Peirce, vol. 1, pp. 135–149. Rorty goes so far as to attack the incorrigibility of our own pain experiences. He argues that the criteria for evaluating claims of pain are or could be social. Imagine, he says, a machine that is able to measure back trouble. A controlled test of persons with and without back pain demonstrates that the machine is accurate: it indicates pain for all those who claim to have pain and no pain for those who do not over a period of years. Now somebody claiming to have back pains is hooked up to the machine and the machine indicates no pain. Whom would one believe? The machine? Or the person?

The point is that the criteria for assessing claims about personal experience ultimately social in nature, though at this point, in the absence of a pain-indicating machine, we have little basis for challenging the pain reports of others. See Rorty (1) pp. 114–127.

16. Conversely, of course, one cannot verify that one has *not* correctly apprehended reality either. As Robert Forman (p. 409) points out, whether or not a meditative technique can eliminate all subjective constructions is an empirical matter about which philosophers have no privileged information. Forman further notes that the view that all experience is inevitably con-structed—shaped and conditioned—by one's concepts, expectations, past experiences, and so forth is an assumption rather than a demonstrated conclu-sion of post-Wittgensteinian thought. One might wish to take issue with this latter claim, arguing inductively that one can demonstrate that many experi-ences do indeed reflect our concepts, previous experiences, and so forth and therefore one can conclude that all experiences are probably so constructed.

More important, however, philosophers do have a greater role than For-man would allow. Although they may not have any special access to all medita-tive experiences so that they can deny the unconstructed nature of the "pure consciousness event," they are in position to have access to, or at least to argue for or against, epistemic claims made on the basis of the experience. In the pragmatist view, epistemic claims are propositions that exist in a communal space and are judged by the criteria of a given community. Philosophers play an important, though not a legislative, role in criticizing and conditioning the epistemic standards of a community.

17. The Confucian program is internally regulating or "holistic" in the following sense intended by Rorty (1), p. 170: "[H]olism is a product of [the] commit-ment to the thesis that justification is not a matter of a special relation between ideas (or words) and objects, but of conversation, of social practice. Conversa-tional justification, so to speak, is naturally holistic, whereas the notion of jus-tification embedded in the [correspondence] epistemological tradition is reduc-tive and atomistic. . . . The crucial premise . . . is that we understand know-ledge when we understand the social justification of belief, and thus have no need to view it as accuracy of representation. Once conversation replaces con-frontation, the notion of the mind as the Mirror of Nature can be discarded."

Some have misconstrued Quine's remarks on holism and indeterminacy of translation to entail some sort of radical inability to communicate or under-stand the other's position, thereby making conversation, and choices based on mutual or shared standards, impossible. They claim, fallaciously in my reading of Quine, that he is committed to the position that comparative judgments are *never* possible because we never fully understand each other or share complete-ly the same standards and assumptions. But again, Quine's holism and indeterminacy of translation does not exclude *partial* understanding and communication. Nor does it deny that people of different persuasions often share common standards by virtue of which they can reach a consensus in theory choice.

Moreover, the real issue being addressed is not that of radical indeterminacy versus some degree of partial communication but of the nature of the justification one can claim for one's criteria or choices. In that we are inextricably bound up in a web of beliefs that precludes access to reality/nature/the other language, one's claims to have a determinate interpretation or reading must be justified conversationally, by appeal to our own theory-laden, conceptual scheme relative reasons, rather than foundationally, by appeal to correspondence.

18. William James was fond of pointing out that when new ideas threaten central tenets, the tendency is to cling to the endangered status quo equilibrium at all costs, resorting, if need be, to all manner of subterfuge, including sarcasm and ridicule. At some point, however, the sheer weight of counterevidence becomes so great that one is for all practical purposes compelled to realign one's system.

19. See Laudan (2), pp. 10–11. Laudan attributes this view to Rorty, Quine, Thomas Kuhn, Mary Hesse, and Paul Feyerabend among others.

20. Rorty (1), pp. 316–318.

21. See II.1.2.

22. Hall and Ames, p. 16.

23. Huang-Lao, though an instance of a logical order, shares with Confucianism the view of the cosmos as immanent. As we have seen, the cosmic natural order or dao embraces the way of both humans and nonhuman nature. The transcendence and hence "logical" character of the Huang-Lao system lies in the *normative* priority of the natural order. The way is conceptually prior and predetermined.

24. To be sure, contemporary neo-pragmatists such as Rorty have been criticized for ignoring the role of metaphysics in the philosophy of the classical pragmatists Peirce, James, and Dewey. I would argue, however, that it is not a question of ignoring but of deliberately downplaying that which is least tenable to accentuate the more defensible aspects of their thought.

25. Peirce, vol. 5, p. 398.

26. Ames has pointed out in personal communication that he and Hall reject predetermination "in an obligatory way." That is, they allow contingent determination, in the form of human-generated tradition, for example. Thus a person enters the world as part of a historical-cultural nexus defined in part by the traditions of his society. However, such conditions are not determinate in a strict sense in that they do not limit in an absolute fashion one's creative opportunities for self-disclosure: one can overcome the affects of nurture.

Even so amended, their position still discounts nature and genetics in favor of nurture and morphological factors. Further, allowing for the conditioning element of tradition neither speaks to nor renders more plausible their metaphysical assumption of a radically open multiverse.

27. See, for example, Hall (2), pp. 51–52, 57.

28. Rorty, for instance, states, "I think that [Nelson] Goodman's trope of 'many worlds' is misleading and that we need not go beyond the more straightforward 'many descriptions of the same world'" (Rorty [2], p. xlvii n. 47).

29. Joseph Margolis, following Peirce, refers to this as the persistence of reality. For more on the persistence of reality, see VI.1.2.

30. See III.1.

31. I have argued elsewhere that in demanding that the law be made coherent in light of moral principles, the strong version of law as integrity advanced by Dworkin in *Law's Empire* prohibits pragmatic, utilitarian considerations of policy and social consequences. This considerably lessens the distance between Dworkin's coherence theory and natural law theories, and increases the separation between him and Confucius. I contend that the weaker, more Confucian, position, allowing for consideration of social consequences, is superior—even by Dworkin's own criteria of fit and normative justifiability— and that Dworkin's dalliance with the weaker thesis suggests that he too is aware of the unpalatable implications of the strong thesis. See Peerenboom (6).

32. See Chan, pp. 3–8; also Mou Tsung-san (p. 20) who attributes transcendence to *tian ming*.

33. See Ames (1), pp. 15–16. He cites in support this *Zhong Yong* passage: "[Confucius] is comparable to the heavens in that there is nothing they do not overarch and over, and again the earth in that there is nothing that it does not support. He is comparable to the succession of the four seasons and the alternations of the moon. . . . Only the most sagacious in the world . . . are expansive like [*tian*] and are profoundly deep like an abyss. . . . Thus they are said to be the complement of [*tian*]."

34. The *Chun Qiu Fan Lu* articulates most clearly the notion of *tian ren gan ying* (mutual influence between humans and heaven-nature).

35. Tu Wei-ming, borrowing the term from Eliade, captures the interactive relation between humans and *tian* in his depiction of the Confucian world as an "anthropocosmic unity." See Tu (1), p. 8.

36. *Zhong Yong* 27.

37. To be sure, in the context of pre-Qin China the monetary value of a horse may have been greater than that of a peasant worker. Therefore in a way Confucius's not asking about the horses may be interpreted as indication of his concern for moral rather than monetary value. That said, it nevertheless

reflects a lack of moral concern for nonhumans that would not sit well with many animal rights advocates today.

38. Donald Munro (pp. 23–29, 32–48) interprets Confucian sociopolitical order as a rigid, rule governed hierarchy consisting of social institutions with predetermined roles and specified duties. Moreover, he argues (p. 84) that "*the* social hierarchy is natural" in that it is derived from the hierarchy present in nature, with heaven above, earth below, and so on. This view is problematic on two scores: first, that the natural order is hierarchical may contribute to the view that there is to be *a* hierarchical social order, but this in no way commits one to the view that the current or desired social hierarchy is a direct manifestation or reflection of *the* hierarchial natural order; and thus, second, Confucius need not be, and I will argue later is not, committed to a rigid, rule governed hierarchy with predetermined social roles. Rather, the best social order in the circumstances is the one that is able to most fully serve and reflect the needs, values, abilities, and so forth of the particular persons who form it. Thus one's social role will be a function of both one's own talents and unique traits and the relationship of that role to other roles (defined in part by the persons filling those roles) in the actual hierarchy.

39. Graham (1), pp. 32–33.

40. Hansen (2), p. 33.

41. For a more extended treatment of the pivotal role of Yang Zhu in the history of Chinese philosophy, see Graham (5), pp. 18–22; and (6), pp. 107–111.

42. Mencius also rejects Yang Zhu's basic assumption that it is human nature to seek self-preservation at all costs. See *Mencius* 6a10 where he argues that we do in fact rule out certain acts even if our life hangs in the balance: few would choose to subject one's parents, spouse, and children to death by torture even were it the only way to save one's own skin, for example.

43. Graham has pointed out that prior to Xun Zi, Confucians did not make the distinction between human nature as an abstract teleological tendency and as the concrete process of nurturing and developing one's character; see Graham (5), p. 15. Roger Ames, building on Graham's work, has argued at length that the conventional understanding of *xing*—"human nature"—as innate and determined blinds us to the dynamic, developmental side; see Ames (6).

44. Though Needham and Bodde speak of "Confucian" natural law, it is not clear to what extent their comments are meant to apply to Confucius's views rather than to later Confucians such as Mencius, Xun Zi, or even to Confucianism in post-Han China. Nevertheless, it remains illumining to examine Confucius in light of their arguments for ethics as a ground for "Confucian" natural law.

45. Needham, vol. 2, p. 214.

46. Bodde and Morris, p. 21.

47. As is often the case, there is an attempt to shore up the claim to universality by

arguing that the *li* are an outgrowth of human nature and the macrocosmic natural order. However, as we have seen, Confucius neither shows interest in nor holds the requisite view of nature—human or nonhuman—to justify an interpretation of the *li* as universal ethical principles.

Interestingly, Herbert Fingarette, in what at first blush seems to be an interpretation of Confucius that would militate against a foundationalist natural law view, belies this initial promise in claiming that the *li* originate from some "impersonal standard" in the tradition and that dao is a "Way without crossroads." See Fingarette (1), pp. 18–36, 62–63.

Munro (pp. 32–48) also takes the *li* as a cosmic principle that is universally valid and embodies an "antecedently determined [ethical] content to the evaluations made by the mind." Thus he argues, "Confucians were advocating adherence to a fixed, abstract standard" (p. 93).

48. This was Fingarette's initial assessment of Confucius, see Fingarette (1), p. vii.
49. Cf. *Analects* 4:10, 8:2, 13:5, 9:3, 17:11.
50. Fingarette (1), p. 63.
51. Needham (vol. 2, p. 544) sates, "Confucians adhered to the body of ancient custom, usage and ceremonial . . . this was the *li*" adding that "since correct behavior in accordance with the *li* always depended on the circumstances, such as the status of the acting parties in social relationships, to publish laws beforehand which could take insufficient account of the complexity of concrete circumstances, was an absurdity" (vol. 2, p. 545); see also pp. 214, 521, 544. The context-specificity of the *li* is brought out in Bodde and Morris's comment that "a government based on *li* functions harmoniously because the *li*, being unwritten, can be flexibly interpreted to meet the exigencies of any particular situation" (Bodde and Morris, p. 21).
52. Hall and Ames (pp. 87–89, 100), in arguing for the notion that an authoritative person is one who embodies the tradition, note, along with Peter Boodberg, the cognate relationship between the characters *li* and *ti* (body, to embody).
53. MacIntyre, p. 151.
54. Consider, for example, the maximin strategy of Rawls: "The maximin rule tells us to rank alternatives by their worst possible outcome: we are to adopt the alternative the worst outcome of which is superior to the worst outcome of the others. . . . The two principles of justice would be chosen if the parties were forced to protect themselves against [the] contingency . . . that their initial place in society [will be] decided by a malevolent person" (Rawls, p. 153).
55. "One feature of justice as fairness is to think of the parties in the initial situation as rational and mutually disinterested. . . . They are conceived as not taking an interest in one another's interests" (Rawls, p. 13). Rawls does so on the grounds that assuming people to be self-interested rather than altruistic is a more minimal condition, that it is "the simplest and most compelling way" to

put the original position. Yet is the claim that people are *not at all* altruistic any less objectionable than either the claim that they are completely altruistic or completely self-interested? Building in some level of altruism and concern for others could very well alter the results.

56. "Justice is the first virtue of social institutions" (Rawls, p. 3). It is on the basis of justice that an individual stakes a claim against the community, the state, or fellow beings: "Each person possesses and inviolability founded on justice that even the welfare of society as a whole cannot override" (ibid.).

57. Pincoffs, p. 15.

58. Fifth century B.C. Greece, for instance, witnessed the emergence of a secular legal system in response to the increasing complexity of society and the concomitant breakdown of the tribal mores and customs of the Ionians, Dorians, and other Hellenes. See Rosemont, (2), pp. 57–58. We have already seen that the response of Locke and Rousseau to the upheaval of the seventeenth and eighteenth century was to search for social contracts that defined justice in terms of legal entitlements. Similarly, the movement to the single, legalistic order that culminates politically in the unification of China by Emperor Qin—foreshadowed in the Xun Zi reinterpretation of Confucianism and in the Huang-Lao school that places increasingly greater emphasis on laws and objective order—is the result of the failure of the Confucian virtue-ethic to inspire a sense of common direction. As society became increasingly complex, the consensus broke down and laws became necessary.

59. These include appropriateness in interpersonal relations (*ren*), filial piety, parental commiseration, wisdom, courage, loyalty, earnestness, credibility, diligence, generosity, frugality, and propriety.

60. As Henry Rosemont, Jr., reminded me, this notion has come under attack in recent years by Peter Singer, Tom Regan, and many others.

61. Rawls, p. 3.

62. Mary Anne Warren was one the first in the contemporary literature to draw a similar distinction between "genetic humans" and "persons." She does not emphasize as clearly as does Confucius, however, that the achievement of personhood is a social one. Rather, her criteria such as consciousness, reasoning, and self-motivated activity are much more individualistic in nature. This is all the more peculiar in that she explicitly links personhood with the notion of "member of the moral community." See Warren, pp. 43–61.

63. Hall and Ames, p. 139.

64. See *Analects* 18:6, 10:17. Humans, of course, have the potential to differentiate themselves from animals.

65. Ames has suggested that the *xiao ren* or bestial person is particularly loathesome to Confucius—even more so than a member of the undifferentiated masses (*min*)—because he represents the failure to take advantage of opportuni-

ties presented to him. For one born into a relatively high socioeconomic class to descend to the level of a *xiao ren* is more reprehensible than the failure of those born into harsh conditions that limited their opportunities for achievement.

66. As MacIntyre (p. 169) observes, "the law is one and the same for all rational beings; it has nothing to do with particularity or circumstance."

67. That for Confucius the concept of *ren* plays a central role is evidenced by its occurrence more than a hundred times in the *Analects*. Though it has been translated in many ways, one can on the basis of its being cognate with *ren* (person), its graphic form (the character for "person" plus the character for "two") and its usage in the text, be assured that its core meaning centers around the notion of interpersonal relations. It refers to the kind of person you are, the quality of life you lead, as part of a community. That the small or bestial man (*xiao ren*) is not a person of *ren*—an authoritative person—indicates that, for Confucius, humanity entails the achievement of excellence. Thus I translate it as "excellence in interpersonal relations." Other translations include benevolence, love, agape, altruism, kindness, charity, compassion, magnanimity, perfect virtue, goodness, human heartedness, authoritative personhood, and humanity. All of these indicate a concern with one's relation to others.

68. Cua (2), p. 68.

69. See Ivanhoe, (pp. 26–29), who argues that *shu* (analogical projection) "is primarily concerned with mediating the application of rules. . . . It ensures that one will run the rules and not be run by the rules." In contrast, *zhong* (loyalty) "urges one to be a strict rule follower." In the end, *shu* must rein in *zhong*: one is context-specific discretion must check one's sense of universally binding duty.

70. For a discussion of shu, analogy and analogical projection in Confucianism see Cua (3); Hall and Ames, pp. 285–290; Fingarette (2), pp. 382–383; Ivanhoe. For the role of anology in the Chinese legal system of the Qing dynasty, see Bodde and Morris, pp. 32, 176–178, 517–538.

71. One cannot help but recall the famous words of William James: "A man's vision is the great fact about him."

72. See Xu Zhixiang, pp. 126–127; Wang Jie, p. 73. The latter argues that Xun Zi's legal philosophy is also best understood in term of rule of man, or, more specifically, rule of the sage.

73. *Yin Wen Zi*, p. 37. This passage is cited and partially translated by Duyvendak (2), pp. 109–110. For more on the *Yin Wen Zi* and its relation to Huang-Lao, see Hu Jiacong (2) and Chapter 7, section 1.2.

74. For an excellent analysis of Hobbesian theory in terms of contemporary game theory and a comparative study of the views of Hobbes and Rawls, see Kavka.

75. See II.2.2.
76. *Zuo Zhuan* (Chao, p. 29; Legge, p. 732).
77. *Zuo Zhuan* (Chao, p. 6; Legge, p. 609).
78. Even Xun Zi, the most legalist of all Confucians, places primary emphasis on the need for virtuous people who must interpret the law: "It is possible to have good laws and still have disorder in the state. But to have a gentleman acting as ruler and disorder in the state—from ancient times to the present I have never heard of such a thing" (26/9/14, W35). Moreover, he opposes the doctrine of the *Boshu* that juristic laws are grounded in the objective laws of nature, considering law instead to be a purely human product: "the law cannot exist by itself. . . . The superior person is the source of law" (44/12/2, D111).
79. The need for universal laws to be tempered by reason to fit the particular circumstance is a major point of Aristotle, see *Nichomachean Ethics* 5:10.

    Munro points out three additional reasons for Confucian insistence on *li* (rites) rather than *fa* (law) as primary means of social control. First, Confucians taught *li*: that was their job, and the source of their power and influence. Second, Confucians themselves belonged to the upper class, and hence naturally would have not wanted laws applicable to the lower class applied to them. Third, and more positively, they believed that whereas imposition of the law only altered outward behavior, study of the *li* changed character. Given the chance, people would try to circumvent the law and pursue self-interest unless inculcated with a sense of moral appropriateness embodied in the *li*, in which case they would be too ashamed to seek self-benefit alone. See Munro, pp. 110–111; also *Analects* 2:3.
80. Interestingly, the Confucian Xun Zi sides with the Legalists in this regard, favoring publicly promulgated and impartially applied laws.
81. *Li Ji* 1:35a. To be sure nobles were punished more severely than commoners for certain crimes that constituted violation of the moral order—frequenting prostitutes, violating the sumptuary regulations, and so forth. Cf. Bodde and Morris, p. 35.
82. This is of particular concern to many in the Critical Legal Studies movement. See, for instance, Balkin, pp. 431–432.
83. At least, it is so for Huang-Lao. As for the Qin Legalists, one could make a case that Han Fei Zi shares this concern for protecting the disadvantaged; see Chapter V. It would be difficult, if not impossible, however, to argue likewise for Shang Yang and Qin Shi Huang Di.
84. See III.2.3.
85. When all is said and done, of course, the nature of virtues for Huang-Lao is quite different than for Confucius. Take the example of *ren*—excellence in interpersonal relations. For Huang-Lao, *ren* entails instantiation of a predetermined order. It requires that each person treat the other as befitting his or her

place in the normative hierarchy. One's possibilities for expression of *ren* are closed; it is a matter of rightness, compliance with a given standard or norm. For Confucius, on the other hand, the manner in which one expresses interpersonal excellence is open. To borrow a distinction from Cua, *ren* constitutes an ideal *theme* rather than an ideal *norm*. An ideal norm is a particular standard of excellence: the Buddha did not drink wine nor eat meat so neither will I. One may want to adopt such traits "quite apart from the specific nature of one's life plan or policies of life" (Cua [2], p. 124). Whereas an ideal norm is a particular standard one aspires to, ideal themes inspire us in a broader sense. They are less determinate and restrictive. They refer to the quality of one's life, the style. They qualify the way one lives and color a wide range of one's actions. Consequently each person will give expression to an ideal theme in his or her unique way my acts of *ren* or compassion or nonviolence will not be the same as yours.

V. The Pragmatic Statesmanship of Han Fei

1. Wang and Chang, p. 92; for the claim that the thought of Han Fei is related to that of Huang-Lao, see Schwartz, pp. 343–345; Cheng Chung-ying.
2. Wang and Chang, p. 105.
3. Ibid., pp. 90–91.
4. See also Sun Shiming, pp. 42–47.
5. Of course, discretion can never be completely eliminated: sometimes, in the case of unforseen events, there will be no specific law; even when there is a law, laws need to be interpreted and applied to the specific case and so on.
6. See V.2.
7. *Li Ji* 1:35a.
8. The "sovereign" is the person or body that is habitually obeyed by others but is not in the habit of obeying others.
9. This is Hart's formulation of Austin's position (see Hart, p. 25); see also Austin.
10. See Hart, pp. 18–77, particularly p. 77 for a concise summary of his major objections.
11. See Hart, particularly p. 113; Hart's rule of recognition, a secondary rule, is especially important to the continuing appeal of legal positivism as a theory about what law is—as opposed to a theory about what *the* law of a particular society is, or to a theory of what the law *should* be.
12. Although much has been written on Mo Zi's alleged utilitarianism, little attention has been paid to Han Fei's utilitarian views.
13. One might be able to salvage Han Fei's theory by advancing a rule- rather than

an act-utilitarian defense. The merits and demerits of rule utilitarianism have been much debated in the literature; see, for instance, Bayles.

14. Of course, they might be wrong: others could argue that even on utilitarian grounds their system is immoral—as one would in the case of Han Fei's heavy punishments for supererogatory acts. But if Han Fei were to insist that over all greater benefit is gained, how could one disprove his claim? Such global claims are empirically unverifiable in practice. To allow global utilitarian claims to satisfy Hart's minimum separation thesis lends theoretical legitimacy to any legal system and undermines the thesis as an operable criterion of legal positivism.

15. Han Fei himself contrasts government by virtue (*de*) with government by an impartial ruler who relies on his position (*shi*) and laws rather than moral character or wisdom. And, as one would expect of a legal positivist, he sides with the latter, disparaging, as we have seen, those bound by conventional morality. On the other hand, he does add that in the end true benevolence requires a harsh and impartial rule by law so that the two extremes of moral government versus government by power of position are not incompatible. To pose them as either-or alternatives is a false dilemma (see 301:5, L2:206).

16. Wang and Chang, p. 81.

17. For a similar reading, see Cheng Chung-ying.

18. See Rong Zaozu, Kimura Eiichi, Hu Shi. Wang and Chang (pp. 87–109) discuss the authenticity issue in an appendix.

19. On the other hand, they may be nothing more than an attempt to gain a little respect for Legalist philosophy by riding piggy-back on the reputation of Daoism.

20. In Chapter IV, I noted that *pragmatism* has a broad range of meaning. Han Fei is a pragmatist primarily in the everyday sense of a practical person who assesses value by practical effects in light of one's chosen ends. Although Han Fei does not engage in extensive explicit discussion of epistemology, what he does say is sufficient to indicate that he is also a pragmatist in the sense that he rejects epistemological foundationalism. His social views, in particular his understanding of humans as self-interested individuals able to be manipulated in a mechanistic, behavioral fashion through punishments and rewards is at odds with the social views, particularly, the understanding of humans as irreducibly social beings, of Dewey and Mead.

21. See *Han Fei Zi* 326:6, L2:251.

22. For various senses of realism, see IV.2.3.

23. Ames (1), p. 51.

24. Wang and Chang, pp. 70–71.

25. Ibid., p. 77.

26. Han Fei may of course be referring not to Huang-Lao epistemology of emptiness but to that of Lao Zi or even Zhuang Zi. For a discussion of Lao Zi's
meditative epistemology in which one discovers the way to effect harmony
through the attainment of emptiness, see VI.1.1. For the importance of emptiness in Zhuang Zi's epistemology, see VI.2.1.
27. See II.1.2.
28. See *Han Fei Zi* 71:3, L1:122. For further discussion of Han Fei's technique of
wu wei, see V.2.1.
29. DeBary et al., p. 152.
30. According to Sima Qian (*Shi Ji* 63), the king of Qin was familiar with and
highly appreciative of the works of Han Fei. When Han Fei was sent by Han as
an envoy to Qin, the king took a liking to him. However, Han Fei met an
untimely death in Qin when his former fellow student Li Si turned the Qin ruler
against him.
31. Qian Mu, p. 63.
32. DeBary et al., p. 123; see also Chan: "The Legalists were primarily interested
in the accumulation of power, the subjugation of the individual to the state,
uniformity of thought, and the use of force. It is not surprising that they were
instrumental in setting up the dictatorship of Ch'in" (251); Graham, (6),
p. 290.
33. See, for instance, Peng Daxiong. Later I note in passing similarities between
Han Fei and Machiavelli. An immediate one is that Machiavelli, like Han Fei,
has not been treated kindly by history. And, as with Han Fei, one must take
care in assessing Machiavelli to distinguish between the received Machiavelli of
textbooks and the actual Machiavelli who wrote not just the infamous *Il Princi-
pi* but *Discorsi* as well.
34. Ames (1), p. 50.
35. Wang and Chang, p. 117.
36. Bodde and Morris, p. 18; see also Feng Yu-lan (1), vol. 1, p. 336.
37. Of course, to the extent that the historical failure of Qin can be attributed to
Han Fei's policies they form part of the "text" in the postmodern sense to be
considered in assessing Han Fei's Legalism. Even so, one cannot simply attribute, direct statements to the contrary, Qin's policies to Han Fei.
38. Machiavelli, pp. 44–45.
39. Machiavelli as well saw people as self-interested: "ungrateful, fickle, feigners
and dissemblers, avoiders of danger, eager for gain" (p. 59). To the suggestion
that there are two ways to govern—by argument or by force, with the former fit
for humans and the latter for beasts—Machiavelli replied that people are at
times like beasts so we must be prepared to be beasts in response. We should
be both fox (cunning and deceptive) and lion (strong and forceful).
40. See also 266:2, L2:144.

41. Ames (1), p. 72.
42. *Han Fei Zi* 210:9, L2:53.
43. Graham, (6), p. 290.
44. Hobbes himself was aware of this objection. His response was twofold. First, he argued that people are better off with a despotic tyrant than with civil war: "the state of Man can never be without some incommodity or other; and that the greatest, that in any forme of Government can possibly happen to the people in generall, is scarce sensible, in respect of the miseries, and horrible calamities, that accompany a Civil Warre" (*Leviathan* ch. 18, p. 94). Second, he argued, as did Han Fei, that the sovereign's job to is procure the "safety of the people," by which he means not just preservation of life but "all other Contentments of life, which every man by lawful Industry, without danger, or hurt to the Commonwealth, shall acquire to himselfe" (ibid., ch. 30, p. 175).
45. For an extensive compilation of quotes, see Wang and Chang, pp. 117–131.
46. See for instance, 84:10, L1:148.
47. *Shang Jun Shu* ch. 20.
48. For a similar line of criticism, see Young, pp. 91–92.

VI. *The Daoist Ways of Lao Zi and Zhuang Zi*

1. See Smith, pp. 121–123 (cited later in VI.2.2); and Needham, pp. 59–61. 94. For a counter view, see Ames (4) and Cua (1), both cited later in section 2.2.
2. For elaboration of these and other points, see Ames (8); also see IV.1.1, for an overview of the antifoundationalism epistemology of pragmatism.
3. Elsewhere Hall and Ames have developed this aspect of Confucius's philosophy in terms of the focus-field model. See Hall and Ames, pp. 237–244; and Ames (7).
4. Hall and Ames, in addition to explicating Confucian cosmology in terms of a focus-field model, attribute to Confucius a process ontology rather than a substance or essentialistic ontology. This militates against the view of objects as discrete ideas that could be copied by the mind. See Hall and Ames, pp. 237–239, 263–264. See also VI.1.2 for Peirce's doctrine of continuity.
5. See II.4.3.
6. Cf. Peirce's notion of abduction: pp. 71–74, vol. 5, p. 189, vol. 6, pp. 477, 522–528.
7. See II.1.2.
8. Shigenori Nagatomo's article is a welcome exception.
9. Most commentators—even those who read Daoism as a kind of nonduality and acknowledge the central role of meditation in many nonduality traditions—focus on postmeditative practice. See, for instance, David Loy's recent work, *Nonduality*.

10. More accurately, dao as the uncarved block, as the nameless, undifferentiated *wu* (無 —often translated "nothingness") is discovered, or uncovered, through apophatic meditation. Yet dao is not only undifferentiated *wu* but phenomenal *you* (有 —often translated as "being"). As I argue later, Lao Zi conflates the discovery of dao as *wu* with dao as *you* in that the sage, having attained *xu* (emptiness, or pure consciousness), is ipso facto able to enact harmony (*wu wei*) upon return to the phenomenal world.

   Examples of kataphatic meditation include Tantric mandala meditations, repetition of mantras, chanting, focusing on the breath, and visualization of colors.

   I am indebted to Michael Saso for suggesting and explaining the terminology apophatic-kataphatic. Although the term's primary associations with the Christian tradition are potentially misleading, I believe that, properly qualified, they can nevertheless be profitably employed for my purpose: to distinguish between two methods of meditation, one that empties the mind of all objects of consciousness and one that makes use of objects of consciousness.

11. See Forman, pp. 395–396, 403–405.

12. See also *Dao De Jing*, 10, 52.

13. Of course, the conscious intent of becoming empty must itself be abandoned along the way. Han Fei, as noted earlier (V.1.2), objects that to pursue emptiness as a goal is inconsistent and inherently self-defeating. Although that may be the case during the time and at the point that one is consciously doing so, the objection loses force once one empties oneself of any intention of becoming empty. Nevertheless, at the early stages, it may be useful as a didactic device. For the discussion of such instruction as deconstructive rather than constructive, see Forman, pp. 410–412.

14. Forman, p. 396.

15. Hall (2), p. 80.

16. "The way is constantly a nameless, uncarved block (32)."

17. See *Dao De Jing*, 10.

18. Hall (4), p. 108.

19. That is not to say that dao is not at all mysterious. Its role in the cosmogonic generation of life, in the generation of the phenomenal world of *you* from the undifferentiatedness of *wu*, remains a mystery. That the world should have evolved in the way it has is likewise a mystery.

20. See *Dao De Jing*, 1. That the way that can be named (or can be spoken of: *ke dao*) is not the constant dao does not mean that dao cannot be named or spoken of. On the contrary. It simply means that one cannot give a constant name to dao, a name that is always correct. This is to be expected of a dao that is emerging contextually rather than predetermined and absolute. Further, when one names, one does so from one's particular perspective. Thus there is

no privileged perspective of the emerging way: there are possibly as many appropriate "names" or images of the emerging way as there are namers and imagers.

21. Dao, of course, refers to both *wu* and *you*: the undifferentiated and the differentiated phenomenal world. Cf. *Dao De Jing*, 1, 40.
22. See *Dao De Jing*, 50, 52, 55.
23. *Dao De Jing*, 55.
24. For the differences in the relative weights of cognitive factors and reasoning as opposed to noncognitive factors in the epistemologies of Confucius and Zhuang Zi, see VI.2.2.
25. Graham, p. (6), 220; Graham, however, intends by *Daoism* both that of Lao Zi and Zhuang Zi.
26. There is one passage that is suggestive in this regard. In *Dao Yuan*, the section that most closely resembles the thought and style of the *Lao Zi*, the author states:

> Only the sage is able to investigate the formless and able to hear the soundless.
> Only once one has recognized the repleteness of emptiness will he be able to realize great emptiness.
> Thus, he will penetrate the essence of heaven and earth and thoroughly penetrate the seamless sameness . . . (87:171a).

27. To be sure there is also change in the world of Huang-Lao, and one does encounter new circumstances. However, there is also much more that is held constant and that need not be continually rediscovered. For instance, in the world of Huang-Lao, each person has a place in the natural order, but that place is assigned in the predetermined normative order. For Lao Zi, each person is a contributing factor to the way that emerges contextually. If that person were not present, or if that person were anything other than what he or she is, there would be a different moral order, a different harmony. At the same time one contributes to the moral order and serves as a conditioning factor for others, one is conditioned by the moral order and by others. One's attitudes, beliefs, and interests continually vary as one interacts with others, confronts new situations, encounters new ideas, and so forth. What constitutes harmony—and hence the moral order—changes accordingly.
28. This passage is, admittedly, cryptic, particularly in light of the author's claim that one of the six handles is "transformability" so that one who transforms is able to illumine *de* (virtuous potency, that which is beneficial) and eliminate harm (53:53b). Nevertheless, it would appear that the author is maintaining that although ever ready to transform in light of the changing circumstances of objective reality, once one has discovered the reality of the Way, one cannot be deterred from enacting it.

29. Illumination, although sudden, admits of degrees in that the scope of one's insight may be narrow or broad. One may have an insight that allows one to effect harmony in a narrow sphere or in a larger sphere, to answer a specific problem or a large one.

30. A second possible reason has already been noted: meditation may not be a necessary condition for the attainment of the proper attitude for effecting harmony. One may be able to adopt an attitude of nonegoic, objectless desire, unprincipled knowing, and so on without meditating; and this attitude may be sufficient to effect harmony. One would not then have the epistemological certainty, the personal feeling of conviction, that comes from discovery of dao in the meditative process. But the practical result of effecting harmony in praxis would be the same.

31. See also *Dao De Jing*, 50, 54.

32. See *Dao De Jing*, 10. Donald Munro (pp. 102–108) has challenged what he calls the "mana thesis," the reading of *de* as a magical force, potency, or charisma. He argues that it is virtue which attracts others, going so far as to claim that one assumption of pre-Qin thought is that humans have an innate attraction to virtue. For my part, it matters little whether humans are attracted to the *de* of a person or to the person of *de*. Nor is it particularly important that the ultimate source of the attraction of the person of *de* is virtue, broadly understood as the power or ability to effect social harmony in a way that benefits all, rather than a nonvirtue based magic power. Perhaps the best translation of *de* would be "virtuous potency."

33. See *Dao De Jing*, 2, 77, 81.

34. Some have suggested that the sage adopts a humble, seemingly selfless approach as a strategy to gain what he wanted all along. There is little reason, however, to foist such a cynical view on Lao Zi. This is, after all, a man who sings the praises of a simple life and who declares that one who understands that contentment is internal rather than external owns the greatest treasure. See *Dao De Jing*, 7, 9, 12, 33, 81.

35. As with *de*, there is a Daoist alternative to Confucian *ren*. See *Dae De Jing*, 8: "In interpersonal relations one is adept at *ren* (morally appropriate other-regarding behavior)."

36. See *Dao De Jing*, 38.

37. See also *Dao De Jing*, 62.

38. This contrasts with Confucius's politics of harmony that requires a minimum level of social and cultural achievement to gain the status of "human being" or political person.

39. This is not to make Confucius out to be a Kantian or a proponent of Enlightenment universal rationality. What counts as reasonable in Confucian discourse is a function of the traditions, beliefs, attitudes, and so forth of the particular

participants. Nor is it to claim that Confucius utilizes only reason, even reason broadly construed to embrace social historical, and affective considerations as discussed earlier. Character and charisma are, for instance, important factors in the Confucian as well as the Daoist sage's success.

40. This is, of course, not to say that Daoists do not speak, or do not engage in any verbal persuasion. They do. But when they do, their conversation reflects the characteristics of noncontention, open-mindedness, and the like.

41. Ge Ronjing, pp. 47–48.

42. Jan (3), p. 210; see also Jan (2).

43. See II.3.1.

44. Hansen (2), p. 36. However, one need not reduce Zhuang Zi's dao to a linguistic object to the extent that Hansen tends to do: "Chuang-tzu's dao is a linguistic rather than a metaphysical object" (ibid., p. 24). Although our linguistic practices affect the way in which we classify things and hence the way in which we act, so do many other factors—psychological, religious, cultural and so forth—that cannot be reduced to linguistic practice; that is, that may not be manifest in or through linguistic practices.

45. Chan (p. 152) renders it as "nature"; Lau ([1], p. 82) as "naturally so"; Graham as "so of itself," which he then explains as "pure spontaneity," see Graham (6), p. 226; Callahan (p. 172) as "action-discrimination from a particular perspective."

46. Although dao as the descriptive totality changes for Huang-Lao as well, as the normative way, it does not.

47. Of course, instantiation of a single order may itself be one kind of harmony, as it is for the author of the *Boshu*. Nevertheless, that does not undermine the claim that harmony entails many possible orders, one of which happens to be a Huang-Lao like order.

48. See *Dao De Jing*, 6, 7, 39, 40, 52.

49. For a reading of Daoist cosmology in terms of Whiteheadean process ontology, see Hall (1) and (3), pp. 212–223.

50. Peirce, vol. 1, p. 175.

51. In addition, the principle of continuity entails a dissolution of the mind-matter distinction such that matter "is not completely dead, but is merely hidebound with habits" (Peirce, vol. 6, p. 158). What Peirce means by this is the subject of some debate. As I read him, the defining characteristic of mind for Peirce is spontaneity. Whatever possesses spontaneity cannot be reduced to mechanistic laws. Such laws can account only for regularity, for habit-bound matter. As long as there is spontaneity in nature, in the universe, our scientific laws will be at best probabilistic. Thus Peirce states, "the principle of continuity is the idea of fallibilism objectified" (vol. 1, p. 171). Further, for Peirce the element of life or spontaneity in the cosmos accounts for the phenomena of change and diver-

sification. It is what makes the cosmos, if not open ended, at least evolutionary, emerging and contingent rather than predetermined and necessary. Because there is an element of contingency, of spontaneity, to everything, including nature, nature may be understood as mind. Of course, everything may be understood as mind. Within Peirce's monism, mind and matter are ends of a continuum, with mind being the most open and spontaneous, matter the most regular and habit bound. Thus, while a matter is mind, it is mind that has become "hidebound with habits."

I am indebted to Hank Skaja for pointing out the relevancy of Peirce's views for explicating Chinese cosmology and for his repeated attempts to help me understand what those views are.

52. Peirce, vol. 1, p. 175.
53. He also contends, however, that synechist philosophy is "forced to accept the doctrine of a personal God" (Peirce, vol. 6, p. 162).
54. Peirce, vol. 1, p. 409.
55. Ibid.
56. Ibid.
57. Peirce, vol. 6, p. 44.
58. See, for instance, Hall (1), p. 278.
59. See *Dao De Jing*, 5, 7, 76, 77.
60. Lao Zi's position is in this regard similar to not only that of Peirce but of Whitehead as well: "Since all laws of nature depend on the individual character of things constituting nature, as the things change, then correspondingly the laws will change. . . . Thus the conception of the universe as evolving subject to fixed eternal laws regulating all behavior should be abandoned" (Whitehead, p. 143).
61. Peirce, vol. 6, p. 55.
62. Bernstein, p. 10.
63. See for instance, Wu Guang (2), p. 78; Zhang Weihua (2), p. 199; Liu Xiaogan, p. 64, Gong Pixiang, p. 62.
64. Meditation in the *Zhuang Zi* is discussed only slightly more than in the *Lao Zi*; cf., for instance, Saso who offers an anthropological study of the use of the *Zhuang Zi* as a meditation manual by the Zhengyi Zitan Daoists of north Taiwan.
65. Both Lao Zi (ch. 10) and Zhuang Zi (15/6/7, G84) mention breathing exercises. Although concentration on one's breath and circulation of breath are themselves kataphatic meditation techniques, they may and often do serve a preparatory function in the apophatic process. Once the practitioner has relaxed and become tranquil, he or she need not continue to focus the mind on breathing
66. It is difficult if not impossible to imagine how one could survive permanently in this state. Zhuang Zi does relate stories of certain persons who appear to have

gone beyond the exemplary state of ecstatic roaming (*xiao yao you* 逍遙遊) in which one does not cling to fixed distinctions to a "final withdrawal into the impassivity beyond life and death"—to cite the apt description of Graham (1), p. 95. One such figure is Meng Sun who "took the step beyond knowledge." Another, a member of the Tai clan, "at one moment deems himself a 'horse,' the next an 'ox.'" But even these sages make *some* distinctions. Further, it would be a mistake to read the lyrical flights of a great writer such as Zhuang Zi as literally as one would an analytical philosopher. Although there is some value in the apophatic pure consciousness event—both as a way of clearing aside preconceptions and as a corrective to the notion that public debate and rational discourse are the means to solve all problems—Zhuang Zi does not advocate permanent residence in this state.

67. Hansen (2), p. 34.
68. This is not simply an empirical or psychological observation; namely, that certain people will stubbornly refuse to alter their views come what may. Rather, it is to claim that one could, at least in theory, stick to one's guns on legitimate epistemological grounds.
69. Or again, all sides might be wrong.
70. For Rorty's attack on incorrigibility of personal claims of pain, see Rorty (1), pp. 114–127. Zhuang Zi also challenges self-referential epistemic claims. "Last night Zhuang Zhou dreamt he was a butterfly, spirits soaring he was a butterfly, happy with himself and doing as he pleased. He did not know about Zhou. When all of a sudden he awoke, he was Zhou with all his wits about him. He does not know whether he is Zhou who dreams he is a butterfly or a butterfly who dreams he is Zhou. Between Zhou and a butterfly there is a necessary dividing; just this is what is meant by the transformation of things" (7/2/94, G61). Robert Allinson (pp. 78–110) has argued that there must be an awakening to a higher, privileged state, a state in which one can know with certitude whether one is dreaming or not. To make his case, Allinson is forced to emend the text. Yet there is a more straightforward, and consistent, reading. Zhuang Zi is not arguing that one can know absolutely reality from illusion. Quite the contrary. We will never know if our theories about reality, about nature, about our self, are dreams. The world we construct in and through our images and theories may be fiction not fact, dream, not reality. Because there is no way to escape one's perspective, one's human-constructed reality, there is no way to verify if the world is as we imagine it to be or not.

As for the so-called awakening passage, as Wu Kuang-ming points out, what one awakens to is not infallible knowledge of reality attained from a transcendent Archimedean point, but to the realization that all knowledge is knowledge from a particular perspective. "What Chuang Tzu attained by reflecting on his dream is the awakened knowledge that we cannot know our fixed identity. It is this knowledge that releases the dreamer (ourselves) from the tyranny of obsession with objective realism. This is a meta-knowledge, an awakening to ignorance" (Wu [2], p. 379; see also Wu [1], pp. 7, 20).

71. Hansen (1), p. 97.
72. Ibid., p. 92.
73. Graham (3), p. 6.
74. In fairness to Hansen, he does later add that "a *pien* [dispute] is not to be decided, but dissolved. This is accomplished by viewing it from other perspectives and perhaps from some all-encompassing perspective (the axis of *tao*s)" (Hansen, [1], p. 95). He never reconciles, however, his view of humans as incommensurable monads with the view of humans as social beings with shared lingistic practices and overlapping perspectives. It is only in light of the incommensurable view that one can make sense of his strong claim that "there is no sense in which we can hope to settle disputes that arise at any level because they rest on adopting arbitrary beginning points" (ibid., p. 97).
75. Smith, pp. 121–123. Cited in Ames (4), pp. 66–67. See also Needham (vol. 2, p. 59), who states "The Confucian and Legalist social-ethical thought-complex was masculine, managing, hard, dominating, aggressive, rational and donative—the Taoists broke with it radically and completely by emphasizing all that was feminine, tolerant, yielding, permissive, withdrawing, mystical and receptive."
76. Ames (4), pp. 67–68.
77. To be sure, some dynasties and rulers favored Daoism over Confucianism. But as a rule, the Confucian influence on Chinese political figures is predominant.
78. It also exaggerates the degree of similarity, if one is comparing rather than contrasting the two schools.
79. Of course, the label *Daoist* (*dao jia*) is a Han dynasty invention. There was never an actual school in which Lao Zi and Zhuang Zi instructed disciples and so forth.
80. See Ames (4), p. 69.
81. See Cua (1).
82. If it does result from the apophatic meditation process, emerging out of the pure consciousness event, it would appear to the practitioner to be from heaven—that is, from *tian*, that which is beyond human control—because the conscious ego-subject will have been eliminated. However, Zhuang Zi, as discussed previously, does not allow that the insight is completely independent of human construction and interpretation; it is one more *yin shi*. What the source of inspiration is for the constructed insight is another question. Zhuang Zi, it would appear, is willing to allow that the source is at least in part *tian*.
83. I am indebted to Bill Callahan for suggesting this reading of the axis of dao to me.

84. See Graham (6), pp. 109, 176.
85. Graham (3), p. 4.
86. Ibid., p. 11.
87. Graham (6), pp. 109–110.
88. Graham (3), p. 9.
89. Ibid., p. 10.
90. Ibid., pp. 9, 8.
91. Technically, Zhuang Zi denies that it is possible to know our minds mirror nature. One could argue, however, that although we cannot "know" in the sense of gaining independent access to reality by which to verify that our theories, decisions, actions, and so forth correspond to "the way of heaven," it is nevertheless possible that one does in fact mirror nature when one becomes empty. How would one "know" that one does not?

There are passages in the *Zhuang Zi* (and *Xun Zi*) that use the metaphor of the mirror (21/7/32, G98): "Become wholly identified with the limitless and roam where there is no foreboding of anything. Exhaust all that you draw from Heaven and never have gain in sight; simply keep yourself empty. The utmost man uses the heart-mind like a mirror: he does not escort things as they go or welcome them as they come, he responds and does not store." First, this passage may be interpreted as referring to the meditative process. One is exhorted to roam in the limitless and to keep empty. This might refer to the state of pure consciousness that on occasion gives rise to ideas, to insights—though when one becomes aware of such objects of consciousness one is no longer in the state of pure consciousness. As noted, these insights might appear to the practitioner to be "from heaven" in that they are not the product of his conscious mind or control. When such thoughts, ideas and so forth arise, the sage does not focus on or cling to them, but simply notes them.

Alternatively, with respect to postmeditative praxis, one can simply read the mirror metaphor in a nonfoundational fashion (as appropriate for Xun Zi). Just as one can interpret "objective" in a foundational and nonfoundational way (see II.1.2), so can one interpret the mirror metaphor. To "mirror" what one perceives, experiences, feels for Zhuang Zi is not to perceive, experience, feel in a completely unmediated, unconstructed fashion. That would be to have a *shi-fei* before it is formed in the heart-mind, something that Zhuang Zi declares to be as impossible as leaving for Yue today and arriving yesterday (4/2/22, G51). Rather, to mirror something is to be as unbiased and open minded as possible. The heart-mind that acts as a mirror does not impose dogmatic categories but remains ever ready to try out alternative approaches and points of view in hopes of finding a mutually acceptable way, one that lets both alternatives proceed.
92. If it did, it would be possible for even a beginner to attain the marvelous results

of a master such as Cook Ding, the famous butcher of the *Zhuang Zi* (see later). But in fact, even Cook Ding took several years before he was able to rely on his intuitive clarity to carve oxen.

93. Graham (3), pp. 7–8.
94. Graham (6), pp. 189–190.
95. See Graham (3), p. 21; (6), p. 193. The point for Graham, however, is somewhat different. It is not so much that all rationality is founded on intuition and unwarranted assumptions, and hence fallible rather than apodictic. Rather, in Graham's reading, rationality for Zhuang Zi, as for Hume, is itself inert. Reasoning cannot by itself stimulate one to act. There must be in addition an "impulse" that moves "one in directions which veer with changes in awareness" (Graham, personal communication).
96. Graham (3), p. 21.

VII.   The Evolution of Huang-Lao Thought

1. See Welch, particularly part three, pp. 88–163.
2. I limit my discussion of the relationship between Huang-Lao and religious Daoism to an examination of Han developments in naturalist cosmology and the emergence of immortality theories and practices that rely on these developments for their theoretical foundations. In this sense I will be treating merely the antecedents of religious Daoism in that a complete reconstruction of the bridge would require that I demonstrate in detail the specific influences of the immortality practices mentioned on particular sects of religious Daoism. The role of immortality within religious Daoism has, however, been dealt with at great length by many others. Shi Qin, for instance, takes up the discussion where I leave off, examining the influence of Han immortality practices on Zhang Daoling, one of the founders of religious Daoism. He argues that Zhang Daoling combines Han immortality practices with Huang-Lao thought to modify and transform the original shamanist belief structures into religious Daoism; see Shi. See also Zhao Zongcheng; Schipper (1); Maspero; Welch, pp. 88–123.
3. In keeping with the pragmatic character of the Confucian tradition, Xun Zi advises one to investigate nature only up to point where it is useful. He in no way denies the utility of having a sufficient understanding of the operations of nature to meet our practical needs. We need to know when to plant crops, beware of floods, and so forth. But this should be the extent of our study of nature: "When the wise man turns his thoughts to nature, he seeks to understand only those phenomena which can be regularly expected. When he turns his thoughts to earth, he seeks to understand only those aspects that can be taken advantage of. When he turns his thoughts to the four seasons, he seeks

to understand only the changes that will affect his undertakings" (63/17/16, W81).

4. According to the *Shi Ji* (74.2348), Xun Zi spent time at the Jixia Academy. If the Huang-Lao school did in fact emerge out of the Jixia Academy, as the evidence suggests, then Xun Zi would surely have encountered their ideas. In fact, some have suggested that Xun Zi's own beliefs reflect considerable influence from the Huang-Lao school; see, for instance, Hu Jiacong (4), p. 32.

5. Although there are passages in which Zhuang Zi draws a distinction between nonhuman nature and humans, seemingly privileging the former, his considered opinion is that one cannot privilege either. As we have seen, this is consistent with his antifoundational epistemology. See VI.2.1; *Zhuang Zi* 15/6/1, (G84).

6. Chen Guying, p. 34.

7. Duyvendak (1), p. 12.

8. Feng Yu-lan (2), pp. 100–101.

9. Watson (3), pp. 25 and 26.

10. See Peerenboom (5). The critique is set up in terms of the dichotomy of humans as part of nature or apart from nature. At the time, I had not yet thought out the ambiguity in nature-*tian*, *tian zhi dao*, where nature-*tian* may refer to either the cosmic natural order or to nonhuman nature only. This contributed in part to my failure to clearly distinguish between dao as the normative order and as the prescriptive order. Although many of the criticisms I make are still relevant, some would have to be modified if not abandoned.

11. That there are two senses of natural reflects the conceptual equivocation of the author discussed previously. The human order may be "natural" in the cosmic sense if humans realize their proper place in the cosmic structure. This need not entail imitating nature in that the human society may have its own way or order within the cosmic structure and nature its own. See imitative versus nonimitative naturalism, II.1.1.

12. Needham, vol. 2, pp. 36–37.

13. Feng Yu-lan (2), p. 177.

14. It is not clear that advocates of this position actually want to equate dao with the laws of nature in the natural science sense. As we have seen, Needham for one does not believe that early Chinese conceived of nature in such terms. Nevertheless, as the logos, the Order of Nature, the naturalness that controls the orderly process of change, dao does seem to be some kind of natural law. See II.2.3 and III.1.2.

15. Further, a corollary of this and indeed all naturalist interpretations is that humans realize the way-dao by being "natural." Expressed in Daoist terms, one is to *wu wei*. In that *wu wei* for the naturalist means to do what is natural,

which in turn means to comply with dao, one must inevitably *wu wei*. Since one cannot possibly *you wei* the term is meaningless: it has no possible referent. Because *you wei* is meaningless, the distinction between *you wei* and *wu wei* collapses. Yet this distinction is widely acknowledged to be a cornerstone of Lao Zi's philosophy. Indeed, Chen Guying (p. 23) declares, "the concept of complying with nature through non-action (*wu wei*)' must be taken as the very essence of the *Tao Te Ching*." That Needham's interpretation vitiates the crucial *wu wei–you wei* distinction casts doubt on its viability as a reading of Daoist philosophy. For the importance of *wu wei* as doing what is natural, see also Needham, vol. 2, pp. 68–69; Feng Yu-lan (2), pp. 100–101; Watson (3), p. 6.

16. The nonpurposive, nonartificial, and inherent nature interpretations are all attempts to redefine *wu wei* as compliance with the normatively privileged natural order—either an external nature-natural order as with the first two or an internal one as with the last; see Peerenboom (5).

17. Chan, p. 9.

18. Even Needham (vol. 2, p. 549) allows that, although "law cannot be said to be *in* non-human Nature . . . the laws of human society should be modelled *on* non-human nature." One would suspect given this view that Lao Zi would strongly favor investigation of nature. After all, if one is to model the human social order on the nonhuman order of nature, one must know what that order is. But Lao Zi evinces no interests in any such investigation. Indeed, his reluctance to embrace technology suggests just the opposite. Nevertheless, Huang-Lao may have developed Lao Zi's suggestion that human behavior or social practices imitate or model nonhuman nature in a broad sense into a full-blown imitative, correspondence naturalism in which human behavior or social practices instantiate a predetermined role in the cosmic natural order.

19. Chan, p. 153.

20. See *Dao De Jing*, 48.

21. Chen Guying, p. 122.

22. See Peerenboom (5).

23. See Chapter 1, section 1.4, also Guo Moruo (2), p. 152; Schwartz, pp. 238–240; Yu Mingguang (2); Liu Yuhuang; Zhi Shui (1).

24. See *Shi Ji* (79:2347): "Shen Dao came from Zhao; Tian Pian and Jie Zi were from Qi; Huan Yuan was from Chu. All studied the arts of Huang-Lao Daoism." For Zou Yan, see *Shi Ji* 79.2344.

25. See Rickett (1), pp. 12–13.

26. For dating and introduction to Zou Yan, see Chan, p. 244; Feng yu-lan (1), vol. 1, pp. 159, 283. Graham, however, following Qian Mu, dates Zou Yan much later (ca. 250 B.C.), contending that he was not a member of the Jixia Academy under King Xuan as claimed by Sima Qian; see Graham (4), pp.

11–13. Even assuming Graham's dating to be correct, Zou Yan could still have been a later member of the academy.

27. See *Shi Ji* 46.1895, which locates Zou at Jixia.

28. Needham, vol. 2, p. 273.

29. Graham (4), particularly pp. 70–91, 274.

30. Needham, vol. 2, p. 273; Graham (4), pp. 70–91.

31. Graham (4), p. 84.

32. Schwartz, p. 351.

33. See also *Boshu* 83:164b.

34. See Major ([1], p. 34), who argues that the doctrine, made popular by Dong Zhongshu, of mutual resonance (*gan ying* 感應, or *xiang ying* 相應) on the basis of like *qi* originates with the Zou Yan school. See also Le Blanc (1), p. 143. Graham ([4], p. 89) notes that "after 300 BC the philosophical schools came to accept the Yin and Yang as the *ch'i* which are the . . . influences behind chains of pairs," and that "the translation of *wu hsing* by "Five Phases" [cyclical cosmological forces] becomes appropriate with the full development of a cosmology in which they divide out of the universal *ch'i*, as in the *Ch'un-ch'iu fan-lu* ascribed to Tung Chung-Shu" (ibid., p. 89).

35. Graham (4), p. 70.

36. Ibid., p. 34.

37. Graham wanted to contrast causal and correlative thinking. Although acknowledging significant differences in the notion of causation between ancient Chinese causal correlative theories and, say, post-Galilean science, the term *causal* will nevertheless suffice as a means to mark the shift away from early classificatory correlative cosmologies to those of the late Warring States and early Han.

38. Following Huang in reading *you* 尤 as *qi* 氣. The *Huai Nan Zi* (Tian Wen) contains a similar passage using *di qi* rather than *di you*: "When the third month of fall arrives, if the earth's *qi* is not stored away then one will receive its killings (i.e. disaster) and the many insects and creatures will suffer. . . ." The *Guan Zi* (Qi Jun Qi Zhu) adds as well: "If in the winter governing is not restricted then the earth's *qi* will not be stored."

The *qi* of the earth is yin *qi*. Yin *qi* begins to build up in autumn and peaks in the winter. It is associated with death and decay and hence is responsible for the harvest that signals the end of the life cycle of the plant (as well as the end of the cycle of yang *qi* that is responsible for life).

39. There is, in addition to the passage cited earlier in which yin and yang constitute the forces structuring the natural order, one passage (62:81b) where yin and yang are incorporated into a cosmogonic scheme, though the text has suffered considerable damage at that point.

40. Cf. *Boshu* 53:48a; 62:81b; 66:96b; 69:109a.

41. Cf. 83:164b.
42. This is all the more to be expected in that in five phases theory, the Yellow Emperor assumes the pivotal central position. The author of a Huang-Lao text extolling the virtues of the Yellow Emperor would most likely make use of this notion.
43. For a Legalist reading, see Ban Gu in the *Han Shu* bibliography, "Yi Wen Zhi"; Xun Zi (15/6/8, W125); Guo Moruo, p. 164. For a Daoist reading, cf. *Zhuang Zi* (92/33/50, G280); Wu Guang (2), p. 84. The *Siku quanshu zongmu tiyao* classifies him as eclectic (*za jia*). For a Huang-Lao reading, see Sima Qian, *Shi Ji* 74.4b; Jiang Ronghai; Kanaya Osamu, pp. 7–8; Yu Mingguang (3), pp. 182–185.
44. See Jiang Ronghai pp. 111–112; Gao Yinxiu and Zhang Zhihua, pp. 87–88; Kanaya, Osamu, pp. 7–8. See also Schwartz who claims that "in Shen Dao . . . the 'constant war' and 'constant *fa*' are embedded in the very fabric of the sociopolitical order itself" (p. 245), and that "certain constancies of the human sociopolitical order . . . correspond to the constancies of the patterns of nature" (244). He concludes that with Shen Dao, "we find a vision which does seem to fuse Taoist and Legalist themes" (p. 247).
45. Thompson, *Shen Tzu Fragments*, pp. 1–3; *Boshu* 82:159b.
46. Jiang Ronghai, p. 111.
47. This is similar to Needham's reading of Lao Zi: if dao is the all-encompassing logos of nature that informs and controls the course of all things, then how can anything run counter to the way? It is worth noting that the *Zhuang Zi* criticizes this view ascribed to Shen Dao on grounds that Shen Dao's way "is not for live men to act on—he's attained the pattern which sets the course for dead men" (92/33/51, G280). That is, Shen Dao's way is not only too anti-rational to be practicable, but simply impossible. One cannot avoid making valuative distinctions in life. As argued in the last chapter, Zhuang Zi does not advocate permanent residence in a state of pure consciousness in which all distinctions are abandoned. But once one departs from that state, one has returned to the realm of perspectival discourse, of *yin shi*. In the everyday world of *yin shi*, there are some ways—for example, those that avoid conflict by letting both alternatives proceed—that are better, at least contingently, than others.
48. Gao Yinxiu and Zhang Zhihua, p. 87; see also Kanaya Osamu, pp. 7–8.
49. Jiang Ronghai, p. 112. Dao for Jiang refers to *tian dao*: the way of nature; cf. p. 111.
50. The *Zhuang Zi* (Tianxia) characterizations are problematic in general.
51. This is, of course, to greatly oversimplify. I am not so much interested, however, in the validity of Hobbes's argument as its general outline. For my purpose, it will suffice to establish the difference between the rational jus-

tifiability (reasonableness) of rule of law as a general social institution and that of particular laws.

52. For a discussion of the natural law side of Hobbes, see Benditt, p. 90, Stumpf, pp. 189–217; for the positivist side, Friedrich, pp. 84–91; both aspects of Hobbes's thought are developed by Cairns, pp. 250–267.

53. Like Han Fei, Shen Dao sees self-interest as the means by which one is able to establish an impersonal government of laws and mechanical rewards and punishments. It is the person who does not accept salary, that is not motivated by rewards and punishments, that is worrisome. See Thompson, *Fragments* 29, 30, 31, 32.

54. For the endorsement of these points by the author of the *Boshu*, see Chapters II and III.

55. This reminds one of Justice Brandeis's famous remark that "in most matters it is more important that the applicable rule of law be settled than that it be settled right" (dissenting opinion in Burnet v. Coronado Oil and Gas Co., 285 U.S. 393, 406).

56. *Shen Tzu Fragments*, cited by Asano, (p. 53, n. 5); also Jiang Ronghai, p. 112. See Thompson (1), pp. 206, 271.

57. See also the *Huai Nan Zi*: "Law has its origins in appropriateness (*yi*). . . . Law is not something sent down by heaven, nor is it engendered by earth. It springs from the midst of humans themselves" (Bodde and Morris, pp. 14–15). That both Shen Dao and the author of the *Huai Nan Zi* passage would feel compelled to deny that juristic laws are simply discovered in the natural order suggests that such a notion was influential in their times. Of the known schools of thought in ancient China, only Huang-Lao could possibly hold such a position.

58. As Gao Yinxiu and Zhang Zhihua point out, Shen Dao, like the author of the *Boshu* and Han Fei, favors a totalitarian ruler, albeit one who serves the interests of the people by using his position to appoint others to do what they are good at. In a passage that occurs in the *Boshu* as well, Shen Dao contends that the better the ruler is at taking advantage of people's skills, the more powerful he will be. See Thompson, *Fragments* 32; see also pp. 33–37, and *Boshu* 81:147a. The *Boshu* passage has suffered textual damage. Nevertheless, enough of the passage exists to verify the relation to *Shen Zi*. For the importance of *yin*—accommodation—see Chapter II.4.2.

One of the main reasons for sponsoring a rule of law for Shen Dao is to circumvent Confucius's rule of man where decisions are made according to the sage's discretion. Although Shen Dao favors a totalitarian ruler, he seeks to limit his power in the same way as Han Fei, by advising him to *wu wei* and let his ministers handle the actual affairs of daily government. Of utmost importance in this regard, the ruler is to steadfastly refrain from interjecting his personal considerations in the judicial process. He is to let his ministers impartially apply the publicly promulgated laws.

59. The popular notion that Shen Dao emphasized *shi* whereas Shen Buhai stressed *shu* (technique) and Shang Yang *fa* (law) originates with Han Fei, who claims *shi* is the main idea of Shen Dao. Actually, *shi* only occurs twice in the extant fragments (13 and 71), though there are other phrases and passages which suggest a similar idea: 11, 12, 14.

60. To be sure, he is warned that frequent changing of the laws will cause social disorder, endangering his reign. He is also advised to change laws in accordance with the way: but what constitutes the way is up to the ruler to determine.

61. *Xun Zi*, 15/6/8.

62. See Rickett ([1], pp. 1–36, particularly pp. 6–3, 33–35), who argues that the Jixia Academy is the likely place of origin of the *Guan Zi*.

63. Hu cites the "Xingshi" and "Banfa" chapter; see Hu Jiacong (6), p. 55.

64. Ibid.; for more on the epistemology of the *Guan Zi* and its relation to that of the *Boshu*, see Hu Jiacong (3), pp. 49–53.

65. Hu Jiacong (6), p. 56; see also Hu (4), pp. 46–53.

66. See Hu (6), pp. 56–57; see also Hu (2) where he discusses the ideas of another Jixia scholar, Yin Wen. Hu cites Yin Wen as instrumental in developing the theory of *xing ming* (forms and name) in its relation to dao and *fa* (law). However, the text ascribed to Yin Wen has long been considered an apocryphal work of the Wei-Jin. Although Hu contests this view, he does so primarily on the grounds that the text reflects Warring States ideas, concluding that it is most likely a compilation by Yin Wen's students.

Even were the *Yin Wen Zi* an authentic Warring States or early Han work, it would still represent a philosophy different in important respects from that of the *Boshu*. Whereas the *Yin Wen Zi* advocates a rule of law (see *Yin Wen Zi* pp. 33, 35, 37 and IV.2.2, where Yin Wen recounts favorably the discussion between Peng Meng and Song Zi in which Peng advocates rule of law over and against rule of man) and although it does base law on an theory of objective names (Wang, p. 24), arguably grounding both *fa* and *zing ming* in dao (ibid, p. 35), its dao is not a predetermined natural order. It espouses not natural law but a pragmatic legalism bolstered by Daoism: "Where the Way is not sufficient to effect proper sociopolitical order, use laws; where laws are not sufficient, use techniques; where techniques are not sufficient, use discretion (*quan*); where discretion is not sufficient, use power (*shi*)" (ibid., p. 22).

The difference between the *Yin Wen Zi*'s pragmatism and Huang-Lao's foundationalism is manifest in their views of warfare. For Huang-Lao, military and sociopolitical order are subject to the same normative standards. For the *Yin Wen Zi*, the two spheres are to be held separate: "Proper governing (*zheng*) refers to names and laws; use names and laws to rule the state and the myriad things cannot be disordered. Irregularity (*qi*) refers to expedients (*quan*) and techniques; using expedients and techniques to employ the military, the myriad things cannot be opposed. In general, where one is able to use stipulations, laws, expedients and techniques and thereby rectify the situation of cruelty and tyranny, there will be no affairs for one to look after. If one need not get involved with affairs, he will gain the empire" (ibid., p. 36). "Although what is right is always what is right, there are times when what is right is not to be used; although what is wrong is always what is wrong, there are times when what is wrong must be practiced" (ibid., p. 32).

Lewis (p. 232) argues that Huang-Lao also distinguishes between normative regularity in political affairs and the need for extraordinary measures (*qi*) in military action. However, as he himself points out, the *Boshu* attempts to bring warfare into accord with the normative natural order. Indeed, it is one of the best examples of the Warring States transition to justification of sanctioned violence on cosmic grounds: violence is intrinsic to the natural order; when it is time to make war, to refrain from doing so would be normatively unacceptable. Thus, the author of the *Boshu* does not permit irregularity (*qi*) in military affairs. On the contrary, those who violate the normative natural order, deploying the military at the wrong times or for the wrong ends, will have calamity redound on their own heads. See for instance, 45:9b; also 81:143b: "Irregularity follows from irregularity; regularity from regularity. Irregularity and regularity never share the same hall." Rand makes a similar point in claiming that Huang-Lao theory of warfare fuses ethical with metaphysical justifications. See Rand, pp. 216–217.

67. See Hu (6), pp. 57–58.

68. Creel (pp. 135–162) was one of the first to point out the need to differentiate these two basic types.

69. Kanaya Osamo argues that the law of Qin-San Jin is positive law whereas that of Qi is natural law. He suggests that Shen Dao was the initiator of Qi natural law, which grounds objective laws in a natural dao. Shen Dao then passed it on to other Jixia scholars. Further, Kanaya contends that Qin positive law, after a period of dominance under Qin Shihuang, gave way to the natural law of Qi that reemerged in the early Han as Huang-Lao thought. Qin law failed because it lacked a (moral) basis for law. As we have seen, Huang-Lao addressed this problem by grounding law in dao as the normative natural order. See Kanaya, pp. 7–10. The four contested chapters of the *Han Fei Zi* are "Zhu Dao," "Ti Quan," "Jie Lao," and "Yu Lao"; see V.1.2.

70. Hu Jiacong argues that Tian Qi or Jixia Legalism reflects greater influence by

Daoism and Confucianism than does Qin Legalism. In particular, laws are to be based on dao and the ruler is to love and serve the people. Hu points out that Han Fei studied both Qin and Qi Legalism, and that his philosophy is a synthesis of the two; see Hu (1) and (4), pp. 25–26, 32–33. This is consistent with my claim that Han Fei's Legalism is intended to serve the people and not the ruler, whereas the Qin Legalism of Shang Yang and Qin Shihuang Di is designed to further the interests of the ruler.

71. Jixia Daoists are distinguished from classical (early or "Lao-Zhuang") Daoists in that the former synthesize dao, *fa* (law), and *li yi* (rites and morality) whereas the latter reject both *fa* and *li yi*. Jixia Daoists also develop and clarify, Hu claims, the notion of materialistic *qi* present in the *Lao Zi*. Finally, Hu adds that Jixia Daoism serves the political interests of the rulers of Qi by providing an ideology supporting the newly arisen land-owning class and unification of the empire through military conquest. Lao Zi, on the other hand, is an apologist for the old order. See Hu (4), pp. 30–33.

72. Hu (4) includes in the category of Jixia Daoism the "Xinshu shang," "Xinshu xia," "Baixin," "Neiye," "Quanyan," "Yuhe," "Jiushou," and "Zheng" chapters of the *Guan Zi*. Jixia Legalism consists of the "Fafa," "Renfa," and "Junchen shang" chapters. At times he also speaks of Jixia Huang-Lao Daoism, though the distinction between Jixia Daoism, Jixia Legalism and Jixia Huang-Lao Daoism is not clear. It appears that both Jixia Legalism and Jixia Daoism are incorporated into Jixia Huang-Lao Daoism.

73. See Hu (4), pp. 25–26. Hu further suggests that Xun Zi synthesizes dao, *fa* and *li yi* but does so by grounding dao and *fa* in *li yi* rather than the other way around; see Hu (4), p. 32.

74. See Hu (4), pp. 27–29.

75. Hu (4), p. 26, and (6), p. 54.

76. Kanaya Osamu identifies four different schools or philosophies of law: (i) weak legalism heavily influenced by Confucianism (the "Mumin" chapter of *Guan Zi*), (ii) Daoist natural law ("Xinshu shang," "Shuyan," "Junchen shang," and "xia," "Banfa" chapters of *Guan Zi*; the four sections of *Han Fei Zi* mentioned previously and the *Huang-lao Boshu*), (iii) positive law of Han Fei Zi and parts of the *Guan Zi* ("Renfa," "Mingfa"), and (iv) the penal law of Li Kui and Shang Yang.

77. The clearest expression of dao as a predetermined natural order is in the "Xingshi" chapter, and even more explicit is the commentary appended to it: see *Guan Zi*, 2/4b2–3, 64/1b9–2b3, 64/8b6 (R122–123, 136). The author exhorts humans to comply with the way of heaven-nature (*tian dao*) in a general sense; see 64/11b3, 2/6b10, 2/7a10 (R142–143, 146). But he never depicts the laws or principles governing human society as grounded in the objective natural order.

78. See "Xinshu shang" chapter of *Guan Zi*, 4a6, 2a9, 5a9 (R175, 177, 179).
79. See Hu (3 and 4); Kanaya Osamu; Zhi Shui (2); Teng Fu (1); Wu Guang (2), pp. 93–99. Interestingly, Wu classifies the *Boshu* not as a Jixia Daoism or Qi Huang-Lao but as Chu Huang-Lao. His reasons for doing so are not clear, other than that the author seems on the basis of philological evidence to be if not from Chu at least familiar with Chu. From a philosophical perspective, such geographical classifications are not particularly important in and of themselves. The author may have developed his thought in Qi at the Jixia academy, regardless of his place of origin.

     The authorship and dating of these three chapters continues to be the subject of debate. Guo Moruo and Liu Jie argue that all three are the product of the Jixia philosopher Song Xing, a contemporary of Mencius (371–289 B.C.) See Guo (1), pp. 210–232; Liu Jie, pp. 238–258. Takeuchi Yoshio and Machida Saburo argue against this reading, the latter contending that all are Qin-Han works (see Rickett (1), p. 158). Rickett (pp. 156–157), although acknowledging the speculative nature of the claim, suggests a Qi official named Rao discovered "Neiye" and "Xinshu" and then wrote another version of the latter and a commentary. Hu, for his part, argues that there is little reason to expend great effort to figure out who wrote what; see Hu (3), p. 47.

     It bears mention that the *Guan Zi* chapter with the most linguistic parallels to the *Boshu* appears to be "Shi"—see Yu Mingguang (3), pp. 194–196. Despite this, it has received little attention by Huang-Lao commentators.
80. All citations of the "Neiye" are to ch. 49 of the *Sibu beiyao* version, of "Xinshu xia" to ch. 37, "Xinshu shang" to ch. 36.
81. The heart-mind is also described as *an ning* (serene and peaceful, 1b) and *zheng jing* (correct and tranquil, 4a).
82. Robinet has pointed out different senses of *shou yi* (hold fast to the one) in Daoist meditation practices. See Robinet (1), pp. 183–211. I have argued that with respect to the *Lao Zi* it may be taken to refer to the apophatic state of pure consciousness; Robinet points out how it may also be used as a kataphatic technique of focusing or concentration, as it seems to be in the "Neiye."
83. *Guan Zi* "Neiye," 2a, 1b, respectively.
84. One begins by controlling the breath (*qi*, 6a), expelling emotions (joy, anger, desire, self-interestedness, 8a), and eliminating thoughts (6a). This produces tranquility (*jing*, 7a) and leads to a refined state of breathing and concentration (*jing*, 6b), to potency (*de*, 5b9), to clarity (*shen*, 5b9), and to discovery of dao as oneness (*yi*, 6a). Significantly, no mention is made of dao as harmony. This is in keeping with the understanding in "Xinshu xia" of the epistemological process as one of discovery of an objective order. Less emphasis is given to the need to interpret the particular circumstances and to create a harmonious order in light of one's best judgment.

85. The emphasis in "Xinshu xia" again appears to be on the kataphatic meditative techniques of concentration on breath and focusing of the mind. As noted in regard to "Neiye," this is more in keeping with the *Boshu* than Lao Zi in that the former downplays the pure consciousness aspect of the meditation process in favor of the illuminative.

86. See Rickett (1), p. 156.

87. One is to empty oneself of desires (3a10), knowledge (3b2), preferences (4b4), sense perceptions (4b4). This leads to emptiness and tranquility (*xu jing*, 3a9), which in turn leads to impartiality (4a10), intuitive clarity (*shen*, 3a10, 4b4), and discovery of dao (3b7). As a result, one is able to *wu wei* (2b7, 3b7), respond to things in an *wu zhi* fashion (5a9), and match names to forms (4b9).

88. See for instance, Zhong Zhaopeng, (1), p. 66; and Asano, p. 43.

89. Other similarities include the belief that there is to be but one ruler; that one is to be appointed on the basis of merit, not family background or political connections; that laws are to be applied impartially, even to nobles; and that the ruler should listen to and get help from his ministers.

90. Although objective, dao is emergent in these texts.

91. Many have argued that Huang-Lao flourished in the early Han because its call for a strong, centralized government that serves the interest of the people fit the post-Qin conditions; see, for instance, Wu Guang (2); Zhong Zhaopeng (1); Jiang Guanghui; Zhang Weihua (2); Saiki Tetsuro (1), Ōgata Tōru; Hou Cunfu and Su Qin.

92. For the relation of these figures to Huang-Lao and the citation to the appropriate classical source, see the table compiled by Zhong Zhaopeng (2), p. 94. Yu Mingguang has pointed out that early bibliographers did not clearly distinguish between the Daoism of Lao Zi and that of Huang-Lao. Thus some of these figures may turn out on further analysis to be Lao Zi rather than Huang-Lao devotees. Yu makes an initial effort to sort out who belongs to which sect; see Yu (3), pp. 168–174.

93. See, for instance, *Shi Ji* "Biography of Zhang Shizhi" (102.2751–2756, W1:533–539). In his summary, Sima Qian states, "Zhang upheld the law without doing violence to larger principles." Indeed, Zhang is reported to have said to the emperor, "the law must be upheld by the Son of Heaven and by everyone alike. . . . I were to impose a heavier penalty in special cases, the people would cease to have any faith in the laws."

94. Dubs, vol. 1, p. 16.

95. Ibid., p. 19.

96. Several scholars have pointed out that Lu's thought reflects the influence of diverse schools, including Huang-Lao and Daoism. See Mei-kao Ku, pp. 2,

36–58; also Zhang Zhizhe and Luo Yijun. Like the author of the *Boshu*, Lu
Jia maintains that both laws and virtue are necessary for good government.
However, consistent with his predominantly Confucian orientation, he gives
pride of place to the latter.

97. Lu Jia, however, is reported to have had the last word, replying, "you got it
on horseback, but can you rule from horseback?" Lu then proceeded to cite
historical examples of rulers who lost their thrones through moral deficiencies. Liu, duly chastened, solicited from Lu a political treatise explaining such
matters. See Lu's biography in the *Shi Ji* 97.2699, W1:277; also Mei-kao Ku,
p. 2.

98. Most notable are Chen Ping and Cao Can. See their biographies in the *Shi Ji*
(56.2051–2064, W1: 152–156; 54.2021–2032, W1:421–426 respectively); also
Zhong Zhaopeng (2), p. 94; and later in this text.

99. Dubs attributes to Confucianism the willingness of Han rulers to serve the
interests of the people—to reduce taxes, lighten punishments, loosen the
laws, and so on. Yet these policies are consistent with Huang-Lao thought as
well. Given that Sima Qian reports the Emperors Wen and Jing and the
Empress Dowager Dou to have favored Huang-Lao, and that many of the
important officials are also said to have studied and practiced Huang-Lao
ideas and policies, it seems more likely that Huang-Lao is the dominant influence. Of course, Huang-Lao itself may very well have drawn on Confucianism for the notion of a virtuous government that serves the people.

100. Some scholars argue that Liu Bang was simply forced by circumstances to
adopt Huang-Lao-like policies. Saiki Tetsuro (1), for instance, contends that
with the toppling of Qin, the totalitarian political structure crumbled. In the
early years of the Han, Liu Bang was too weak to wield the power of Qin
rulers at their height. The economy was in shambles, the authority of the
government undermined. It would take time to rebuild. But local power
brokers and the military men who helped Liu defeat Qin did not want to wait,
demanding their share of the spoils. Liu, wishing to avoid the mistake of the
rulers of Qin and his rival Xiang Yu who tried to monopolize power, realized
that the best, perhaps the only, way to consolidate his own power was to share
it. Thus he divided up the territory among his supporters, enfeoffing those
who contributed to his victory.

There is some merit to this view. Initially, Liu Bang did not oppose the
feudal lords. However, over a period of time, he managed to replace local
potentates with his blood relatives and long-time followers from his home in
Pei, thus securing his rule. For my purposes, however, that Liu Bang may
have been forced by circumstance to adopt Huang-Lao-style rule is not as
important as the fact that he did.

101. As in the case of Liu Bang, one of Cao's first acts on becoming prime minister was to summon the local authorities to inquire how best to bring stability and peace to the people. See *Shi Ji* 54.2029, W1:422.

102. That Sima Qian explicitly discusses the legal policies and attitudes toward law of many of the Han political figures associated with Huang-Lao in the *Shi Ji* indicates not only the central role of law for Huang-Lao, but the extent to which Huang-Lao law differs from that of other schools, particularly that of Qin Legalism. Most Huang-Lao supporters are said to have practiced lenient law, like Cao Can. Ji An, for instance, is known to have emphasized *wu wei* hands-off management and to have enforced the spirit if not the letter of the law. He argued not only for lenient but constant laws. See *Shi Ji* 120.3105, W2:343. Zhang Shizhi insisted that the law be applied impartially and reliably according to the prescribed punishment. Sima Qian comments, "he upheld the law without doing violence to larger principles." See *Shi Ji* 102.2751, W1533.

  Strictly speaking, it is not Huang-Lao policy to modify punishments or to grant pardons. Rather, punishments are to be just, to match the crime. In contrast to the harsh laws of Qin, this meant that in practice Huang-Lao laws were less restrictive and its punishments lighter. But they were supposed to be executed strictly and reliably. Although Huang-Lao does incorporate Confucian benevolence, it does not, at least in theory, accept Confucianism's notion of amnesties and disregarding of minor offenses. See *Analects* 13:2; also McKnight, p. 5.

103. See *Han Shu* 39:11b, Ds1:186.

104. See for instance, Dubs, vol. 1, p. 186; Lewis, p. 70; Zhao Zongcheng, p. 44. For an excellent study of Han law, see Hulsewe (1).

105. Emperor Hui, concerned about Cao Can's allegedly lackadaisical attitude, sent Cao's son to protest. Cao became angry and beat his son. When the emperor summoned him to court, Cao poignantly queried, "how does your majesty compare to Gao Zu?" Emperor Hui of course responded that he was much the inferior. Cao then asked, "and how do I compare with Xiao He?" The emperor replied that Cao did not appear to be his match. Cao agreed, and then argued that since he was not the equal of Xiao He, the best that he could do was to follow the way of Xiao He without initiating change. See *HS* 39:11b, Ds1:186.

106. See Ōgata Tōru (1), p. 23. Much of this discussion of the relation between Cao Can and Xiao He follows Ōgata.

107. Emperor Wen is reported to have favored the doctrine of *xing ming*, which scholars previously took to mean Legalism. However, the discovery of the Boshu with its well-articulated doctrine of *xing ming* together with the nature of the Emperor Wen's policies and the fact that Huang-Lao was the dominant

ideology of the era suggests that Emperor Wen favored not Legalism but Huang-Lao. Further, the rule of both Emperors Wen and Jing was strongly influenced by Empress Dowager Dou, a confirmed Huang-Lao advocate. See *Shi Ji* 121.3117, W2:398. For the impact of Huang-Lao thought on the government of Wen and Jing, see Hou Cunfu and Su Qin.

108. At the same time, it was Emperor Wen who, acting on the advice of his only Confucian minister, Jia Yi, began to reclaim the power ceded local authorities by the first emperor, Liu Bang. He did so by dividing up the fiefs of potential rivals. This policy would eventually culminate in the highly centralized rule of Emperor Wu. Emperor Wen also showed interest in the supernatural and techniques for attaining long life that would so preoccupy Emperor Wu. See Dubs, vol. 1, pp. 217–218.

109. Ibid., p. 301.

110. See Dubs, vol. 2, pp. 341–353.

111. *Shi Ji* 121.3122, W2:403, Ds2:345.

112. See *Shi Ji* 121.2117, W2:398, Ds2:21.

113. Feng Yu-lan ([1], vol. 1, p. 16) claims the memorial was presented in 136 B.C., Zhong Zhaopeng ([2], p. 95) thinks 134. The latter would seem more reasonable in that Dong is unlikely to have risked the wrath of Empress Dowager Dou who died in 135. See also *Han Shu* 56:21a: "Dong Zhongshu wrote replies to the examination questions promoting and making glorious the teachings of Confucius and repressing and degrading advocates of the other hundred schools."

114. See *infra*.

115. Dubs (vol. 2, p. 9) argues that the curbing of potential abuses of power by the ruler through the policy of assigning day-to-day management to the ministers, although Legalist and Daoist in origin, "was furthermore not contradicted by Confucian teachings." However, he also points out that "at the same time it was possible for sincere Confucians to allege that this practise was one of the 'evils inherited' from the Ch'in dynasty (*HS* 6:39a) and to reinforce by this argument the Emperor's natural ambition to dominate the governmental mechanism of which he was the head, urging that only by such a change could this anti-Confucian practice be removed. Szu-ma T'an makes imperial initiative in government a Confucian teaching (*Shi Ji* 130.9)" (ibid.). This is consistent with my reading of Confucianism, which relies on the discretion of those in power, the ruler in particular, to determine what constitutes proper sociopolitical order.

116. *Han Shu* 4:22a, Ds2:12.

117. See Wu Guang (2), Jiang Guanghui, Saiki Tetsuro (1); Shimamori Testsuo.

118. Why did Huang-Lao use the doctrine of pure tranquility and nonaction to conceal their continued support for a rule of law, albeit one less severe than

that of Qin? Nishikawa suggests that it is because of their acceptance of the notion of "love the people" (*ai min* 愛民), that government is to serve the people, which he points out is a tenet of Daoism (as well as other schools, most notably Confucianism). I have argued, in addition, that by grounding law in the epistemology of an objectively discovered natural order, Huang-Lao attempts to legitimate its laws by providing ethical foundations and to bolster its claim to ultimate authority for adjudicating all conflicts that may arise in the unified empire.

119. The distinction between Huang-Lao as more active or positive (*ji ji* 積極) and classical Daoism as more passive or negative (*xiao ji* 消極) is not entirely felicitous. For instance, it is often suggested that Huang-Lao is more active because it permits deployment of the military for just causes. But Lao Zi as well allows for appropriate use of the military; cf. *Dao De Jing* 30, 31. Similarly, Lao Zi's *wu wei* does not mean literally no action in the realm of praxis, but rather action appropriate in the context and serving the end of harmony. In some circumstances, one will have to be more active, more aggressive, than in others. If anything, *wu wei* in the *Boshu* might be considered more "passive" on two accounts: first, the author adopts at times the Legalist reading of *wu wei* as a political technique whereby the ruler does not intervene in the day-to-day affairs of government but rather delegates responsibility to his ministers, thus making him a less "active" ruler; second, the standard for determining what constitutes *wu wei* behavior for Huang-Lao sage-ruler is the predetermined natural order, not personal discretion as to what constitutes an appropriate response conducive to the attainment of harmony. Therefore one might argue that the ruler "passively" instantiates a discovered predetermined order.

120. See Zhong Zhaopeng (2), p. 88; Cheng Wu, p. 46.

121. Karen Turner (p. 74), having argued at length that the natural law doctrine of Huang-Lao serves as a check (in theory) on the power of the ruler, cautions that "until a direct connection between principles and the creation of statutory law is found we cannot claim that ideals actually influenced legal practices." Even allowing that sufficient historical evidence has been amassed to conclude that Huang-Lao thought did effect early Han statutes, most notably under the supervision of Xiao He and Cao Can, one does well to bear in mind Turner's further observation that the Huang-Lao system did not provide legal sanctions, channels, or organized bodies to punish or overturn a ruler who behaved lawlessly.

122. Of course, he could claim that circumstances required changes in the law, but he could not do so simply on the grounds of political expediency. He would have to claim a change in the discovered natural order. But one of the features of the natural order, and of Huang-Lao law, is constancy; see III.1.2.

123. In any event, Emperor Wu circumvented this potential check on his power by continually dismissing his highest officials and replacing them with less formidable threats.

124. Dong Zhongshu himself does not seem to have shared Emperor Wu's preoccupation with immortality. Nevertheless, his theory of *tian ren gan ying*— mutual response between humans and the natural order—provides the theoretical foundation for Han immortality practices. See *infra*.

125. Dubs, vol. 2, p. 19.

126. Yu Yingshi (p. 97) points out that Wu sent expeditions not just to the East as others had before but to the West as well.

127. Wu's interest in alchemy grew out of a conversation with Li Shaojun, who convinced the emperor that he could become immortal by eating with utensils made of gold transformed out of cinnabar: "If you will make sacrifices to the furnace . . . you will be able to transmute cinnabar into gold. When the gold shall have been produced, you may make of it utensils for eating and drinking. Through using them your life will be prolonged, so that you may see the blessed immortals of the isle of Peng Lai. . . . When you have seen them, and have made proper sacrifice to high heaven and broad earth, you will never die. This is what the Yellow Emperor did." The *Shi Ji* adds that "it was after this discourse that the Son of Heaven for the first time performed in person the sacrifice of the furnace. . . . He occupied himself in experimenting with powdered cinnabar and all sorts of drugs in order to obtain gold" (28.1385, W2:39). For more on alchemy as means to immortality, see Davis; Sivin; Needham, vol. 5, p. 6.

128. See Yu Yingshi, pp. 97–98.

129. See Zhong Zhaopeng (2), p. 97. See also Hulsewe (2) for social welfare policies in the Han.

130. See Zhao Zongcheng, pp. 45–46; Peerenboom (2), pp. 38–46. Significantly, the "Yi Wen Zhi" mentions Lao Zi only in regards to Daoism. Not until later is he taken to be an immortal and deified within the circles of immortality seekers. See Zhao, pp. 45–48; Yu Yingshi, p. 104; Robinet (1), p. 20; Seidel. Zhong Zhaopeng notes that the *Lao Zi bianhua jing* discovered at Dunhuang sets an end date of 155 A.D. for the divinization of Lao Zi; see Zhong (2), p. 96, n. 3.

   The Yellow Emperor's association with calendars and astrology, and by extension divination based on study of natural phenomena such as earthquakes, comets, and so forth, can be traced back to his role as source or discoverer of a rule-governed natural order that contains within it the proper social order. See III.2.1.

131. See *Zhuang Zi* 29/12/18 (W129); 46/18/20 (W192); see also *Lie Zi* (Zhou Mu Wang).

132. *Zhuang Zi* 16/6/33.
133. See *Shi Ji* 28.1385, W2:39.
134. There is some debate as to whether or not Huang-Lao Jun originally referred to the Yellow Emperor and Lao Zi as one deity or as separate deities. Akizuki Kanei argues that the term refers to both the Yellow Emperor and Lao Zi combined into a single deity. At any rate, that "Huang-Lao" came to be associated with immortality and Daoist religion is clear. See Akizuki Kanei, p. 77; also Yu Yingshi, p. 116; Zhao Zongcheng, p. 48.
135. See Zhang Weihua (1), p. 23.
136. See Yu Yingshi, p. 104, *Shi Ji* 28.1393; see also 80.2436, which gives the lineage of Huang-Lao masters from He Shang Zhang Ren to An Qisheng and on down to Gai Gong and Cao Can.
137. See Wen Yiduo, pp. 170–172, n. 12; also Yu Yingshi, p. 104.
138. *Hou Han Shu* (Fangshu zhuan); see DeWoskin, p. 62; cf. Yu Mingguang (3), p. 170, for another account of a *fang shi* versed in Huang-Lao.
139. See *Shi Ji* 28.1385, W2:39; 28.1293–1297, W2:49–52; 28.1403, W67; *Han Shu* 25a.12b.
140. See *Shi Ji* 28.1368, W2:25–26, where Sima Qian associates the *fang shi* of Yan and Qi with Zou Yan. DeWoskin points out that Zou's influence does not extend to all varieties of *fang shi*, and that only a minority of the *fang shi* documented in the historical records are from Yan and Qi, see DeWoskin, p. 6. However, as he himself notes, the historical records are far from complete. Further, it matters little for my argument whether most or only a few *fang shi* would have spent time at Jixia.
141. See Graham (6), p. 171; Zhang Weihua (1), pp. 20–24; Zhong Zhaopeng (2), pp. 97–98; Zhao Zongcheng, pp. 45–48; DeWoskin, p. 176, n. 79. For the most extensive treatment of the *fang shi* in English, see DeWoskin, who points out the role of Dong Zhongshu's New Text Confucianism in the development of *fang shi* practices. He also notes that the *fang shi* were adept at a wide range of practices, and that pursuit of immortality was not an interest of all *fang shi*.
142. See Chen Guying, p. 27; Welch, p. 76; Chan, p. 291; Feng (1), vol. 1, p. 425.
143. Zou Yan is linked to the *fang shi* by Sima Qian: "Song Wuji, Zhengbo Qiao, Zhong Shang, Xianmen Kao and Zui Hou were all men of Yan who practiced magic and followed the way of immortals, discarding their mortal forms and changing into spiritual beings by means of supernatural aid. Zou Yan won fame among the feudal lords for his theories of yin and yang and the succession of the five phases, but the *fang shi* who lived along the seacoast of Qi and Yan, though they claimed to transmit his teacings, were unable to understand them" (*SJ* 28.1368, W2:25–26). Some scholars, Hsu Fu-kuan among them,

have questioned Sima Qian's account of Zou Yan, arguing that Zou did not play as significant a role in the development of ying-yang five phases theory as Sima would have one believe. Nevertheless, the *fang shi*'s use of yin-yang five phases theory in their divinatory, medical, and immortality practices remains unchallenged. See DeWoskin, pp. 11–13, who also notes the importance of Dong Zhongshu's *Chun Qiu Fan Lu* and New Text Confucianism among the *fang shi.*

144. Strictly speaking, his theory expressed in its most general form entails "mutual response between like things," with nature and humans being one instance of like things. For a study of the notion of mutual response, especially in relation to the Han Daoist text, the *Huai Nan Zi*, see Le Blanc (1), particulary pp. 191–197. Le Blanc contends that the "*Huai-nan tzu* was a major expression of the new [Huang-Lao] Taoism' of Former Han" (ibid., p. 7). He argues that the main theme of Chapter 6, "Peering into the Obscure," is the application of the Zou Yan-naturalist school's doctrine of resonance or mutual response to the Daoist political theory of government by nonaction: "the idea of resonance is shown to derive from *Tao* and to be of universal extension. The universal character of resonance imposes itself as normative and binding in the particular field of government, where it appears as non-action" (ibid., p. 193).

145. The extent to which humans could control the natural processes in this theory, and the extent to which Dong Zhongshu and others actually believed in the notion of mutual response as a practical theory, is difficult to gauge. It is virtually impossible to accept nowadays that anyone would really believe the actions of one person could upset the order of the seasons, making it snow in summer and so on. On the other hand, many immortality seekers went to great lengths to practice techniques based on this theory. And much of the behavior as well as many of the policies of Han rulers such as Emperor Wu were calculated to accord with yin-yang five phases theory: amnesties tended to correspond to yang periods with more executions occurring during the fall and winter yin seasons, the emperor wore certain colors and performed certain sacrifices in keeping with five phase theory, and so on. Cf. McKnight, pp. 19–24, 40, 119. McKnight points out that of Han rulers, Emperor Wu adhered most strictly to the yin yang five phase pattern of behavior, indicating the depth of his commitment to naturalist theory and the powerful influence of New Text Confucianism.

It is worth noting that yin-yang five phases theory did not go unchallenged. Skeptics from the Old Text school such as Wang Chong and Wang Fu pointed out the many errors, discrepencies, and failures of the New Text school's predictions. Yet the Old Text school, although it shunned metaphysical speculation, did not attack the central tenet of the New Text school: that the natural order was rule governed and could be known by humans. This assumption was called into question by the *xuan xue* (玄學—mysterious learning) philosophers of the Six Dynasties who maintained that the mysteries of the universe would never be fully comprehended. Thus Wang Bi, known for his mystical reading of the *Lao Zi* emphasing the notion of *wu* (nothingness, undifferentiatedness), also wrote a commentary on the *I Jing* in which he argues against the correlative cosmology reading of Jing Fang. Cf. DeWoskin, p. 13.

Even though the Huang-Lao reading of the *Lao Zi* as a rule governed naturalism discoverable by humans and Wang Bi's mystical reading are in their understanding of the nature of order and their view of the possibility of knowledge of the world perhaps at opposite ends of the hermeneutic continuum, they represent the two dominant interpretive strains of the *Lao Zi*: Lao Zi as naturalist and Lao Zi as mystic.

146. Veith, p. 97.

147. See *Guan Zi* 64/3b10, Rickett (1), p. 126; *Huai Nan Zi* 2/31/6; Morgan, p. 52.

148. This method occurs in the *Taiping jing*; cf. Needham, vol. 5, p. 31.

149. See *Yu Fang bijue* 1a; Needham, vol. 5, p. 194; also Schipper (1), p. 24; Harper, pp. 549, 576. The Yellow Emperor is a common figure in sexual yoga lore. See Seidel, pp. 50–51; Harper, pp. 546–547.

150. *Su Nu Jing* 1a; Needham, vol. 5, p. 193.

151. For more on the use of sex for health and immortality, see Needham, vol. 2, pp. 146–152, vol. 5, p. 5; van Gulik, pp. 35–47; and Harper (particularly pp. 546–549) who, in discussing the sexual techniques described in the medical treatises discovered along with the *Huang-Lao Boshu* at Mawangdui, treats the relation of the Yellow Emperor to sexual yoga and immortality.

152. Veith, pp. 138–139.

153. An excellent example of this merger of naturalism, immortality theory and Daoism during the Han is the He Shang Gong commentary on the *Dao De Jing*, one of the earliest and most important of the commentaries on Lao Zi and perhaps the most influential of all commentaries for religious Taoism. See Zhao Zongcheng, pp. 48–53; Needham, vol. 5, pp. 5, 130–135; Peerenboom (2), pp. 43–46.

The identification of He Shang Gong with He Shang Zhang Ren, the alleged founder of Huang-Lao, has long been asserted by many scholars, including Wang Yinglin in the Song, and is now, according to Erkes, generally accepted; see Erkes, p. 124, n. 2. Yu Mingguang, however, denies the identity, though he does so largely on the basis of highly dubious datings. See Yu (3), p. 151.

154. See note 2.

VIII. *Epilogue*

1. See, for instance, Watson (2), vol. 1, pp. 311–314.
2. See Yu Mingguang (3), pp. 168–174. Yu both calls attention to and begins this necessary task. See also Hou Cunfu and Su Qin who examine the impact of Huang-Lao thought on the rulership of Han Emperors Wen and Jing. Zhang Zhizhe and Luo Yijun discuss Huang-Lao elements in the *Xin Yu* of Jia Yi, one of Liu Bang's foremost advisers.
3. That is Confucianism, Daoism, and Legalism.
4. See Cua (2), who attributes to Xun Zi an ethical reasoning process very similar to that I have attributed to Confucius; see also Wang Jie, who argues that despite greater reliance of impartial law, Xun Zi's legal philosophy remains rule of man or, rather, rule by sages.
5. See Bentham, vol. 2, p. 501.
6. Murphy and Coleman, p. 13.
7. See Li Maoguan. That the *Beijing Review* is an official organ of the state needs to be underscored. R. Randle Edwards has noted the special role of the government sponsored press in the legal process: "The official Party press . . . in effect performs a wide variety of legal functions: it acts as a finder of fact; judges the validity of claims; and acts in a quasi-legislative fashion by widely publicizing negative and positive, model cases, illustrating how or how not to construe new Party directives" (Edwards [1], p. 60).
8. An in-depth study of the influence of classical legal philosophies on contemporary jurisprudence must await another forum; (cf. Nathan [2]). In this section, I will be able to adumbrate only a few salient points that shed light on the historical and philosophical value of Huang-Lao jurisprudence.
9. See Li Maoguan, pp. 17, 19; see also Leng and Chiu, pp. 34–84.
10. Li Maoguan, p. 18.
11. See Nathan (1), pp. 101–102, 108–112; also Nathan (2), pp. 132–137; Leng and Chiu, pp. 98–104. Although in theory the 1982 constitution limits party authority, the ultimate authority of the party is explicit in the 1975 and 1978 constitutions. Further, during all periods since 1949, the party has in practice dominated the people's congresses, courts, and other organs of state.
12. Li Maoguan, p. 18.
13. The ancient practice of executing not only one found guilty of serious offenses but also the offender's immediate family, grandparents, aunts, uncles, and so on would surely have made the thought of prosecution intimidating.

    For an excellent "insider's view" of the Chinese legal system of the Qing, see Hang Liuhong's *Fuhui quanshu* (translated by Djang Chu). Liu describes frankly the corruption plaguing every level of the judicial system.
14. For "extralegal" methods of conflict resolution in contemporary China, see

Victor Li's *Law Without Lawyers*, pp. 14–16, 44–65; Edwards (2), pp. 45–46; for such methods in the Qing dynasty, see Bodde and Morris, pp. 5–6; Cohen; Hsiao Kung-chuan.

15. The doctrine of equality before the law has had a troubled history in China, particularly since 1949. Some constitutions have explicitly denied equality to all groups, specifically those constituting the enemies of socialism. As a consequence, because of their class background, members of some groups (landlords, rich peasants, counterrevolutionaries, rightists, and other "bad elements") have been punished more harshly than others for similar crimes. On the other end of the spectrum, high-level cadres and their families have received special treatment. See Leng and Chiu, pp. 20–21, 104–111; Edwards (1), p. 62.

16. Nathan attributes this in part to the traditional ethical belief, also propagated as a primary socialist value, that people are to willingly and selflessly restrict their legal rights in deference to the normatively superior interests of the community or state. See Nathan (2), p. 144.

17. See Henkin, pp. 25–26; see also Nathan (1), pp. 79–80. One right notably absent in Chinese communist constitutions is freedom of thought; see Edwards (2), p. 59.

18. Li Maoguan, p. 19.

19. Article 51 states that individuals must not "infringe upon the interests of the state, of society, and of the collective, or upon the lawful freedoms and rights of other citizens." Cf. Edwards (2), p. 55.

20. See Nathan (1), p. 82. For a table of the constitutions and the rights they provide, see Nathan (1), pp. 79–80. Nathan (ibid., p. 99), Edwards ([2], p. 52), and Henkin (pp. 26–27) all note that Chinese constitutions are political manifestos, charters that promise future rights as benefits the state hopes to deliver once certain material or sociopolitical conditions have been attained. Thus rights are considered "programmatic" rather than present checks on legitimate state interference with individuals. They also note that all constitutions attach some proviso by which the interests of the state can override the rights provided. As Edwards ([2], pp. 44–45) explains, "China's leaders today, like the imperial and bureaucratic rulers of the past, hold that rights flow from the state in the form of a gratuitous grant that can be subjected to conditions or abrogation by the unilateral decision of the state." In contrast, in many Western theories, rights are derived from one's status as a human being and not a grant from the state. The state is designed to protect the rights attached to its members as human beings and hence cannot override these rights without meeting stringent political and legal standards and demonstrating clear and compelling state interests; cf. Nathan (1), pp. 122–123.

21. Victor Li points out an additional advantage: it allows for earlier intervention

in deviant social behavior. One need not wait for the individual to overstep his area of constitutionally protected autonomy—his sphere of privacy and individual rights that act as trumps, in the memborable phrase of Dworkin, against the interests of the state. At the first sign of inappropriate behavior, community elders and watchdogs can begin to educate and persuade. Greater pressures can be brought to bear should one, resisting the early gentle urgings, behave in an increasingly unacceptable fashion. Cf. Li, pp. 38–65. For more on the "mass line" method, see Leng and Chiu, pp. 24–25.

22. Indeed, "overcome official profiteering" (*da dao guan dao* 打倒官倒) was one of the leading rallying cries of the 1989 populist uprising. After crushing the fledgling democracy movement, Beijing sought to appease the masses by implementing a much publicized anticorruption campaign in which several prominent officials were arrested, tried, and sentenced. Li Maoguan (p. 18) also discusses this "tilting of interests" by officials toward self-enrichment at the expense of the masses. See also Leng and Chiu, pp. 104–111.

23. Victor Li (pp. 20–31) discusses the political background of the twentieth century debate over rule of man versus rule of law. With modernization as their slogan, early reformers such as Liang Qichao declared ideological war on Confucianism, arguing for *fa zhi* (rule of law) over and against *li zhi* (rule by rites) and *ren zhi* (rule by man). As Li points out, in the early years after the Communist victory, the new regime was forced to turn to legal specialists, most of whom were Nationalist supporters, to design and implement a legal system. At the same time, however, many important positions within the legal system were filled by "new cadres" appointed not for their legal skills but for ideological dependability. The specialists favored a rule of law; the new cadres, supported by the central authorities, a rule of man.

Ironically, the politics of the Cultural Revolution provided an interesting twist to the debate, with the post-Mao government siding with "revolutionary" Legalism and rule of law and opposing "revisionist" Confucianism and rule of man. These terms continue to dominate the discussion, as evidenced by the 1980 volume *Fazhi yu renzhi wenti taolunji* (Collected Papers on the Question of Government by Law versus Government by Persons), which followed a major conference on the same theme. See Leng and Chiu, pp. 18–19, 49.

24. The 1982 constitution gives the power to interpret and enforce the constitution not to the judiciary but to the supreme legislature and its standing committee. Because the National People's Congress drafts and adopts laws in the first place, it is unlikely that that body would interpret any statute or amendment as inconsistent with the constitution or the basic principles of the statutes. At any rate, the party remains the de facto authority. See Leng and Chiu, p. 43, also Nathan (1), p. 120.

25. Of course, not all rights theories are theories of natural rights. That one take

rights seriously does not entail that rights be considered absolute, inalienable, a trump against any and all interests of the state, or as invariably of greater moral weight than matters of policies or social consequences. In short, one need not agree with Rawls (p. 3) that "each person possesses an inviolability founded on justice that even the welfare of society as a whole cannot override," or with Nozick (p. ix) that "individuals have rights, and there are things no person or group may do to them (without violating their rights)." To be sure, once one allows rights to be compromised or traded off to secure other normative considerations, one has cracked the lid on Pandora's box. There may be no way to guarantee that powerful political parties will not abuse this window of discretionary opportunity to inappropriately override legitimate individual rights. No system is foolproof. And as absolute power in the hands of fools is a real and ominous possibility, there should be many and stringent institutional safeguards. Decisions as to when state interests are sufficiently compelling to override rights granted to individuals by the constitution should not be in the hands of a single branch of government, much less a single person. One could also require majority or perhaps even quorum vote by the appropriate legislative bodies and implement a system of judicial review, for example. Although more complex than traditional natural rights theories, a contingent rights doctrine would have the advantage of philosophical viability.

Appendix: He Guan Zi and Huang-Lao Thought

1. Of course, the loss of most Huang-Lao texts makes it difficult to verify one way or the other the central tenets of Huang-Lao thought.
2. See Williams, pp. 1–69; Graham (7), pp. 497–509; Ōgata Tōru (3), Wu Guang (2), pp. 151–158. Of course, given the imprecise dating of both the *Boshu* and the *He Guan Zi*, it is difficult to determine who was citing whom.
3. See his "Preface to the *He Guan Zi*" (*He Guan Zi* xu), included in *He Guan Zi* (Zhonghua Press).
4. See Williams pp. 115–126; Wu Guang (2), pp. 151–165; Graham (7), pp. 508–509; Tian Jiajian, pp. 58–60, Du Baoyuan, pp. 54–57; Li Xueqin, pp. 53–56; Ōgata (2), pp. 18–19; Chen Keming; and Hosokawa Kazutoshi.
5. Neugebauer rejects as additions sections 14–19; Ōgata Tōru 12, 13, 16, 17, 18, 19; Wu Guang 12, 16, 19; Graham only 16 and 19.
6. He is, however, only able to locate ten of the ninteeth chapters within these three schools. Excluding 16 and 19, which he believes are not original, that leaves seven chapters unclassified.
7. This method is nearly universal among commentators, see Graham (7), p. 508; Williams, p. 116; Li Xueqin, p. 57; Ōgata (3), pp. 18–19.
8. Williams, p. 115; Du Baoyuan, pp. 53–57; Li Xueqin, pp. 54–56; Tan Jiajian, pp. 58–60.

9. In Rand's terms, both *He Guan Zi* and the Boshu represent syncretic-rationalist-metaphysical-ethical-pragmatic military philosophies; see Rand, pp. 206–218. *He Guan Zi* is categorized as a military text in the *Han Shu*, though later deleted as a repetition of a text listed under Daoism. He Guan Zi the person is often thought to have been a military man, in part because his pseudonym refers to a pheasant cap which "had a definite military significance" (Williams, p. 4).

10. Wu Guang (2), pp. 162–166; see also Tan Jiajian, p. 59.

11. See Chapter 9, 10, 11 and 4/16b/2.

12. See 4/11b/2; 6/16a/12.

13. This of course does not mean that all are the product of a single hand or authentic Warring States to Han works.

14. Although I am primarily interested in the *He Guan Zi* as an example of a Huang-Lao text that evidences and hence lends credibility to my reading of Huang-Lao, I owe perhaps at least a brief statement as to my reasons for excluding these chapters from the Huang-Lao camp. A. C. Graham has identified Chapter 1 as Legalist. That the ruler is the standard for the primary epistemological notions of *shen ming*—intuition and illumination (or clarity)—puts it at odds with the core Huang-Lao passages in which *shen ming* refer to discovery by the sage of the way cum natural order. That the way-natural order is the standard for political order and the ground for laws differentiates the foundational naturalism and natural law theory of Huang-Lao from the pragmatic legal positivism of the Legalists. Chapter 7 rejects the notion that humans are to follow nature. And although acknowledging that laws may be necessary to ensure proper order, the author denies that they are sufficient. In the end, proper order is dependent on the judgment of a sage. Similarly, Chapter 14 advances a rule of man rather than a rule of law, as discussed more fully later. Chapter 13, identified by Graham as "Daoist anarchist," is similar to the "primitivist" chapters of the *Lao Zi* and *Zhuang Zi*, which is inconsistent with the centralizing and unifying direction of Huang-Lao political theory. In addition, the author denies that there is one right way to govern. Rather, the right way to govern depends on the particular circumstances and the characteristics of those in power. This is more in keeping with the position of Confucianism and classical Daoism than the foundationalism of Huang-Lao. Chapter 16, long suspected to be a military text of Pang Huan, repeats the passage of 13 denying the existence of one right way to govern. Chapter 19 is also believed to be part of the military text of Pang Huan. It advocates military conquest without fighting. However, Huang-Lao insists that conflict is inevitable, part of the cosmic order, and hence one must wage war when the time is right or perish.

15. This line of argument is obviously limited. In some cases, the parallel passages contain ideas that are also the basis for claiming a similarity in content, and hence for identifying the chapters as Huang-Lao.

16. The thrust of the *He Guan Zi* passage is that the sage is the source of the way and in turn of law. Therefore this passage advocates a rule of man rather than a rule of natural law, and hence is closer to the position advanced in the "Xinshu shang" chapter of the *Guan Zi*: "laws are derived from authoritative discretion (*quan*) and authoritative discretion is derived from the way" (1b11, R175). See Tang Lan, p. 17.

17. It also contains a parallel passage to Chapters 13 and 16. Chapter 13 is not consistent with the Huang-Lao chapters, as Graham has observed. Perhaps 13 was included on the basis of the parallel to 12, which, given its Huang-Lao characteristics, served as a bridge to the core Huang-Lao chapters. Similarly, 16 is a military discussion that many believe to be part of the military text of Pang Huan mentioned in the "Yi Wen Zhi." Given the military focus along with the mention of Pang Huan in Chapter 19, there is reason to believe that it too originally belonged to the Pang Huan text. It may have been inserted along with 16—which in turn may have been inserted because of its parallel to Chapter 12, which, despite its Huang-Lao characteristics and parallels to the *Shiliu Jing*, appears to be somewhat out of step with the core Huang-Lao chapters of the *He Guan Zi*.

18. See Ōgata Tōru (3), p. 22.

19. Graham translates "the pattern in things as it essentially is."

20. The *Boshu* reads, "the stellar formation have their quantifiable relations, and do not deviate from their paths—these are the models for reliability (*xin*). Heaven illumines the three in order to fix the one." For the rule governed natural order in *He Guan Zi*, see also 11/21b/12.

21. Only when heaven and earth (i.e., nature) move and act within his breast is the work accomplished outside. Only after the myriad things come in and out of him is the generation of things unharmed. He opens and shuts the four seasons, pulls on and shifts the yin and yang. . . . And the world supposes them so of themselves" (11/22b/7).

22. See also 2/3a/4: "The exemplary ruler . . . moves at the right time and does not act carelessly."

23. More literally, to "heaven it, earth it, and human it." See also 17/16a/8: "In regards to warfare, there is heaven, earth and man." For a discussion of the "metaphysical" or natural-cosmic justification for war in the *He Guan Zi*, see Rand, pp. 206–211; for the Huang-Lao school in general, Lewis, pp. 213–241.

24. That law in the *He Guan Zi* is natural law is suggested by Tan Jiajian, p. 59; Hosokawa Kazutoshi, p. 12; Rand, p. 208; Ōgata Tōru (2), pp. 50–51; Williams, p. 122.

25. See also 7/21a/9: "If the ruler's understanding is not clear he takes the nobles as the way, his own intentions as the law. . . . What calamity exceeds this? One such as this, on the day of retreat, subsequently understands his command is

lost." However, Chapter 7 advances not rule of foundational natural law but a rule of law that depends in the final analysis on the judgment of sages.

26. For *He Guan Zi*'s concern with the limitations of average ruler, see Ōgata Tōru (2). For discussion of the five forms of government as a quasi-historical descent from past utopia to present realities, see Graham (7), p. 523.

27. See also 10/14a/4: "The Supreme One is that which maintains the organization of the same-on-the-widest-scale, tunes the *qi* of the Supreme Immensity, and corrects the positions of the intuitive and illumined."

28. Graham (7), p. 514.

29. See Guang Wu (2), pp. 158–161; see also Tan Jiajian, p. 59.

30. For a similar view, see Tan Jiajian, pp. 59–60.

Bibliography

※

Akizuki Kanei (秋月觀暎). 黄老觀念の系譜 "Kōrō kannen no keifu" (On the Geneology of Huang-Lao Ideology). *Tōhōgaku* (1954): 69–81.

Allinson, Robert E. *Chuang-Tzu for Spiritual Transformation*. Albany: SUNY Press, 1989.

Ames, Roger T. (1). *The Art of Rulership*. Honolulu: University of Hawaii Press, 1983.

———. (2). "Is Political Taoism Anarchism?" *Journal of Chinese Philosophy* 10, no. 1 (1983): 27–48.

———. (3). "Religiousness in Classical Confucianism: A Comparative Analysis." *Asia Culture Quarterly* 12 (1984): 7–22.

———. (4). "The Common Ground of Self-Cultivation in Classical Taoism and Confucianism." *Qing Hua Journal of Chinese Studies* 17, nos. 1 and 2 (1985): 65–97.

———. (5). "Getting the *te* Back into Taoism." In *Nature in Asian Traditions*, ed. J. Baird Callicott and Roger T. Ames, pp. 113–144. Albany: SUNY Press, 1989.

———. (6). "The Mencian Conception of *renxing*: Does It Mean 'Human Nature'?" In *Chinese Texts and Philosophical Contexts*, ed. Henry Rosemont, Jr. La Salle, Ill.: Open Court, 1990.

———. (7). "The Confucian Focus Field Conception of Self." In *Self and Person in Asian Theory Practice. Perspectives*, ed. Roger Ames, Wimal Dissanayake, T. P. Kasulis. Albany: SUNY Press, 1993.

———. (8). "Meaning as Imaging: Prologomena to a Confucian Epistemology." In *Culture and Modernity: East-West Philosophically Perspective*. Ed. Elliot Deutsch pp. 227–274. Honolulu: University of Hawaii Press, 1991.

Aquinas, Saint Thomas. *Summa Theologica*, trans. A. S. Benjamin and L. H. Hasckstaff. New York: Macmillan, 1964.

Aristotle. *The Complete Works of Aristotle*, trans. Jonathan Barnes, 2 vols. Princeton, N.J.: Princeton University Press, 1984.

Arima Takuya (有馬卓也). 《淮南子》原道の位置 "Enanji gendōken no ichi" (The Status of the *Huai Nan Zi* 'Dao Yuan Xun'). *Nihon Chūgoku Gakkaiho* 39 (1987): 41–55.

Asano Yuichi (浅野裕一). 黄老道の政治思想—法術思想との對比 "Kōrō-do no seiji shisō—hōjutsu shisō no taihi" (The Political Thought of Huang-Lao Daoism: A Comparison to the Art of Law Thought). *Nippon Chugoku Gakkaiho* 36 (1984): 40–54.

Augustine, Aurelius, Saint. *De Libero Arbitrio*. N.P. Christian Classics, 1981.

Austin, John. *Providence of Jurisprudence Determined*. London: J. Murray, 1932.

Balkin, J. M. "Taking Ideology Seriously: Ronald Dworkin and the CLS Critique." *UMKC Law Review* 55 (1987): 392–433.

Ball, Stephen W. "Bibliographical Essay/Legal Positivism, Natural Law and the Hart/Dworkin Debate." *Criminal Justice Ethics* 3 (1964): 68–89.

Bayles, Michael, ed. *Contemporary Utilitarianism*. Garden City. Anchor Book, 1968.

Benditt, Theodore. *Law as Rule and Principle*. Stanford, Calif.: Stanford University Press, 1978.

Bentham, Jeremy. *The Complete Works of Jeremy Bentham*, ed. John Bowring. New York: Russell and Russell, 1962.

Bernstein, Richard. "Pragmatism, Pluralism and the Healing of Wounds." *Proceedings and Addresses of the American Philosophical Association* 63:3 (1989): 5–18.

Bodde, Derk. (1) "Evidence for the 'Laws of Nature' in Chinese Thought." *Harvard Journal of Asiatic Studies* 20 (1957): 709–727.

———. (2). "Chinese 'Laws of Nature,' a Reconsideration." *Harvard Journal of Asiatic Studies* 39 (1979): 139–156.

Bodde, Derk, and Morris, Clarence. *Law in Imperial China*. Cambridge, Mass.: Harvard University Press, 1967.

Cairns, Huntington. *Legal Philosophy from Plato to Hegel*. Baltimore: John Hopkins University Press, 1949.

Callahan, W. A. "Discourse and Perspective in Daoism: A Linguistic Interpretation of *ziran*." *Philosophy East and West* 39, no. 2 (1989): 171–189.

Chan, Wing-tsit. *A Source Book in Chinese Philosophy*. Princeton, N.J.: Princeton University Press, 1963.

Chen Guying. *Lao Tzu: Text Notes and Commentaries*, trans. Rhett Young and Roger T. Ames. Taibei: Chinese Materials Center, 1981.

Chen Keming (陈克明). 试论《鹖冠子》与黄老思想的关系 "Shilun *He Guan Zi* yu Huang-Lao sixiang de guanxi" (Examination of the Relation of the *He Guan Zi* and Huang-Lao Thought). *Zhexueshi luncong* (1981): 224–244.

Cheng Chung-ying. "Metaphysics of *Tao* and Dialectics of *Fa*." *Journal of Chinese Philosophy* 10 (1983): 251–284.

Cheng Wu (程武). 汉初黄老思想和法家路线 "Hanchu Huang-Lao sixiang he fajia luxian" (On the Early Han Huang-Lao, Legalist Line). *Wen Wu* 10 (1974): 43–47.

Ch'u T'ung-tsu. *Law and Society in Traditional China*. Paris: Mouton and Co., 1961.

Chun Qiu Fan Lu (春秋繁露). Sibu beiyao edition. Taibei: Zhonghua shu-ju, 1982.

Cohen, Jerome Alan. "Chinese Mediation on the Eve of Modernization." *California Law Review* 54 (1966): 1201–1226.

Creel, Herlee. *Shen Pu-hai*. Chicago: University of Chicago Press, 1974.

Cua, A. S. (1). "Forgetting Morality: Reflections on a Theme in *Chuang Tzu*." *Journal of Chinese Philosophy* 4, no. 4 (1977): 305–328.

———. (2) *Dimensions in Moral Creativity*. University Park: Pennsylvania State University Press, 1978.

———. (3) *Ethical Argumentation: A Study in Hsun Tzu's Moral Epistemology*. Honolulu: University of Hawaii Press, 1985.

Dao De Jing. Zhu zi yinde. Taibei: Nanyu Press, n.d.

Davis, Tenney L. "The Chinese Beginnings of Alchemy." *Endeavour* 2 (1943): 154–160.

Davis, Tenney L., and Wu Luqiang. "Chinese Alchemy." *Scientific Monthly* 31 (1936): 225–235.

deBary, William, et al. *Sources of Chinese Tradition*. New York: Columbia University Press, 1960.

Dewey, John. (1). *Reconstruction in Philosophy*. Boston: Beacon Press, 1920; reprint, New York: Mentor Books, 1954.

———. (2). *Experience and Nature*, 7th ed. La Salle, Ill.: Open Court, 1925.

DeWoskin, Kenneth. *Doctors, Diviners and Magicians of Ancient China*. New York: Columbia University Press, 1983.

Ding Yuanming (丁原明). 齐学与汉初黄老之学 "Qixue yu Hanchu Huang-Lao zhi xue" (State of Qi Thought and Huang-Lao Thought). *Guan Zi xuekan* 4 (1988): 70–76, 64.

Donogan, Alan. "Wittgenstein on Sensation." In *Wittgenstein: The Philosophical Investigations*, ed. George Pitcher. New York: Anchor Books, 1966.

Du Baoyuan (杜宝元).《鹖冠子》研究 "He Guan Zi yanjiu" (*He Guan Zi* Studies). *Zhongguo lishi wenxian yanjiu jikan* 5 (1984): 51–60.

Dubs, Homer H. *The History of the Former Han Dynasty*, vols. 1 and 2. Baltimore: Waverly Press, 1938.

Duyvendak, J. J. L. (1). *Tao Te Ching*. London, n.p., 1954.

———. (2) *The Book of Lord Shang*. San Francisco: Chinese Materials Centers, 1974.

Dworkin, Ronald. (1). *Taking Rights Seriously*. Cambridge, Mass.: Harvard University Press, 1977.

———. (2) *Law's Empire*. Cambridge, Mass.: Harvard University Press, 1986.

Edwards, R. Randle. (1). "Reflections on Crime and Punishment in China, with Appended Sentencing Documents." *Columbia Journal of Transnational Law* 18 (1977): 45–103.

———. (2). "Civil and Social Rights: Theory and Practice in Chinese Law Today." In *Human Rights in Contemporary China*, ed. R. Randle Edwards, Louis Henkin, and Andrew J. Nathan, pp. 41–76. New York: Columbia University Press, 1986.

Erkes, Eduord. *Ho Shang-kung's Commentary on Lao-tse*. Ascona: Artibus Asiae, 1950.

Fang Ke (方克). 《经法》等篇中的朴素辩证法思想 "'Jing Fa' deng pian-zhong de pusu bianzhengfa sixiang" (The simplistic dialectics of the 'Jing Fa'). *Xueshu luntan* 4 (1982): 20–23, 30.

Feinberg, Joel. *Harm to Others*. New York: Oxford University Press, 1984.

Feng Qi (冯契). 《管子》和黄老之学 "*Guan Zi* he Huang-Lao zhi xue" (*Guan Zi* and the Huang-Lao School). *Zhonggua zhexue* 11 (1984): 1–10.

Feng Yu-lan (馮友蘭). (1). *A History of Chinese Philosophy*, trans. Derk Bodde, 2 vols. Princeton; N.S.: Princeton University Press, 1952.

———. (2). *A Short History of Chinese Philosophy*. New York: Macmillan, 1984.

Fingarette, Herbert. (1). *Confucius—The Secular as Sacred*. New York: Harper and Row, 1972.

———. (2). "Following the 'One Thread' of the *Analects*." *Journal of the American Academy of Religion* 47, no. 3 (1979): 373–406.

Finnis, John. *Natural Law and Natural Rights*. Oxford: Clarendon University Press, 1980.

Forman, Robert K. C. "Paramārtha and Modern Constructivists on Mysticism: Epistemological Monomorphism Versus Duomorphism." *Philosophy East and West* 39, no. 4 (1989): 393–418.

Friedrich, Carl J. *The Philosophy of Law in Historical Perspective*. Chicago: University of Chicago Press, 1958.

Gao Heng and Dong Zhian (高亨, 董治安). 《十大经法》初论 "'Shi Da Jing' chulun" (Preliminary Discussion of the "Shi Da Jing"). *Lishi Yanjiu* 1 (1975): 89–97.

Gao Yinxiu and Zhang Zhihua (高银秀, 张志华). 慎到法治思想简论 "Shen Dao Fazhi sixiang jianlun" (A Brief Discussion of the Rule of Law Thought of Shen Dao). *Jinyang xuekan* 6 (1988): 87–93.

Ge Ronjing (葛荣晋). 试论《黄老帛书》的"道"和"无为"思想 "Shilun *Huang-Lao Boshu* de *dao* he *wu wei* sixiang" (On *Huang-Lao Boshu*'s Thought of *dao* and *wu wei*). *Zhongguo zhexueshi yenjiu* (1981): 47–50, 53.

Gong Pixiang (公丕祥). 《庄子》法哲学思想概括 "*Zhuang Zi* fazhexue

sixiang gaiguan" (An Overview of the Legal Thought of *Zhuang Zi*). *Zhexue tansuo* 1 (1989): 62–65, 55.

Graham, A. C. (1). *Later Mohist Logic, Ethics and Science*. Hong Kong: Chinese University Press, 1978.

———.(2). *Chuang-tzu: The Inner Chapters*. London: George Allen and Unwin, 1981.

———. (3). "Taoist Spontaneity and the Dichtomy of 'Is' and 'Ought.'" In *Experimental Essays on Chuang-tzu*, ed. Victor H. Mair, pp. 3–23. Honolulu: University of Hawaii Press, 1983.

———. (4). *Yin-Yang and the Nature of Correlative Thinking*. Singapore: Institute of East Asian Philosophies, 1986.

———. (5). *Studies in Chinese Philosophy and Philosophical Literature*. Singapore: Institute of East Asian Philosophies, 1986.

———. (6). *Disputers of the Tao*. La Salle, Ill.: Open Court, 1989.

———. (7). "A Neglected Pre-Han Philosophical Text: *Ho-kuan-tzu*." *Bulletin of the School of Oriental and African Studies* 52, no. 3 (1989): 497–532.

Guan Feng (关锋). 庄子哲学讨论集 *Zhuang Zi zhexue taolunji* (Discussion of Zhuang Zi's Philosophy). Peking: Zhonghua Books, 1962.

Guan Zi (管子). *Zhu Zi yinde*. Taibei: Nanyu Press, n.d.

Guo Moruo (郭沫若). (1). 宋钘尹文侠初考 "Song Xing Yin Wen yi chu-kao" (On the Remnants of the Writings of Song Xing and Yin Wen). In *Qing Tong Shi Dai* (The Bronze Age), pp. 210–232. Chungking: Wenzhi chubanshe, 1945.

———. (2). 十批判书 *Shi pipan shu* (Ten Critiques). Beijing: Kexue chu-banshe, 1962.

Guo Yuanxing (郭元兴). 读《经法》 "Du 'Jing Fa'" (On Reading the *Jing Fa*). *Zhonghua Wenshi lun zong* 2 (1979): 125–136.

Hall, David. (1). "Process and anarchy: A Taoist vision of creativity." *Philosophy East and West* 28, no. 3 (1978): 271–286.

———. (2). "The Metaphysics of Anarchism." *Journal of Chinese Philosophy* 10, no. 1 (1983): 49–63.

———. (3). *The Uncertain Phoenix*. New York: Fordham University Press, 1982.

————. (4). "On Seeking a Change of Environment." In *Nature in Asian Traditions*, ed. J. Baird Callicott and Roger T. Ames, pp. 99–112. Albany: SUNY Press, 1989.

Hall, David, and Ames, Roger T. *Thinking Through Confucius*. Albany: SUNY Press, 1987.

Han Fei Zi (韓非子). *Zhu zi yinde*. Taibei: Nanyu Press, n.d.

Hansen, Chad. (1). *Language and Logic in Ancient China*. Ann Arbor: University of Michigan Press, 1983.

————. (2). "A *Tao* of *Tao* in Chuang-tzu." In *Experimental Essays on Chuang-tzu*, ed. Victor H. Mair, pp. 24–55. Honolulu: University of Hawaii Press, 1983.

————. (3). "Chinese Language, Chinese Philosophy, and 'Truth.'" *The Journal of Asian Studies* 44, no. 3 (1985): 491–519.

————. (4). "Individualism in Chinese Thought." In *Individualism and Holism: Studies in Confucian and Taoist Values*, ed. Donald Munro, pp. 36–55. Ann Arbor: University of Michigan, 1985.

Harper, Donald. "The Sexual Arts of Ancient China as Described in a Manuscript of the Second Century B.C." *Harvard Journal of Asiatic Studies* 47, no. 2 (1987): 539–593.

Hart, H. L. A. *The Concept of Law*. Oxford: Clarendon University Press, 1961.

Hazard, John N. *Communists and Their Law*. Chicago: University of Chicago Press, 1969.

He Guan Zi (鶡冠子). Sibu beiyao edition. Taibei: Zhonghua Press, 1970.

Henkin, Louis. "The Human Rights Idea in Contemporary China: A Comparative Perspective." In *Human Rights in Contemporary China*, ed. R. Randle Edwards, Louis Henkin, and Andrew J. Nathan, pp. 7–40. New York: Columbia University Press, 1986.

Hosokawa Kazutoshi (系田川一敏). 《鶡冠子》と漢初黄老思想との関係との意義 "*Kakkanshi* to Hansho Kōrō shisō to no kankei to sono igi" (The Relation of *He Guan Zi* to Early Han Huang-Lao Thought and Its Significance). *Bungei ronsō* 14, no. 2 (1979): 1–14.

Hou Cunfu and Su Qin (霍存福, 粟勁). 黄老的法律思想與文景之治 "Huang-Lao de falu sixiang yu Wen Jing zhi zhi" (Huang-Lao Legal

Thought and the Rule of Emperors Wen and Jing). *Jilin daxue shehuike-xue xuebao* 4 (1985): 15–21.

Houlgate, Lawrence. *Family and State*. Totowa, N.J.: Rowan and Little-field, 1988.

Hsiao Kung-chuan (蕭公權). *Rural China, Imperial Control in the Nineteenth Century*. Seattle: University of Washington Press, 1967.

Hsu Fu-kuan (徐復觀). 陰陽五行觀念之演變及若干有關文獻的成立時代與解釋的問題 *Yin yang wuxing guannian zhi yanbian ji ruogan youguan wenxian de chengli shidai yu jieshi de wenti* (The Evolution of the Concepts Yin Yang Five Phases and Several Problems Relating to the Dating and Explanation of Relevant Texts). Taibei: Minzhu Pinglu Press, 1961.

Hu Jiacong (胡家聪). (1). 田齐法家法治理论的主要特点 "Tianqi fajia fazhi lilun de zhuyao tedian" (The Important Features of the Theory of Legal Control of the Legalist School of Tian in Qi). *Qilu xuekan* 2 (1984): 36–40.

———. (2). 《尹文子》与稷下黄老学说 "*Yin Wen Zi* yu Jixia Huang-Lao xueshuo" (*Yin Wen Zi* and the Jixia Huang-Lao School). *Wen Shi Zhe* 2 (1984): 21–28.

———. (3). 从《心术上》看早期的黄老学说 "Cong 'Xinshu shang' kan zaoqi de Huang-Lao xueshuo" (Early Period Huang-Lao Doctrine from the Perspective of the 'Xinshu shang' Chapter of *Guan Zi*). *Zhongguo zhexueshi lunzong* (1984): 47–57.

———. (4). 《管子》中道家黄老之作新探 "*Guan Zi* zhong daojia Huang-Lao zhi zuo xintan" (An Explanation of the Works of Daoist and Yellow Emperor Daoism in the *Guan Zi*). *Zhongguo zhexueshi yanjiu* 4 (1987): 24–32.

———. (5). 《管子》中以法治国的法理之学 "*Guan Zi* zhong 'yi fa zhi guo' de fali zhi xue" (The Legal Philosophy of 'Using Law to Order the State' in the *Guan Zi*). *Guan Zi xuekan* 3 (1988): 20–26.

———. (6). 黄老帛书《经法》的政治哲学 "*Huang-Lao Boshu* 'Jing Fa' de zhengzhi zhexue" (The Political Philosophy of the *Huang-Lao Boshu* "Jing Fa"). *Zhongguo zhexueshi yanjiu* 4 (1988): 54–60.

Hu Shi (胡適). *Zhongguo gudai zhexueshi* (Ancient Chinese Philosophy). Taibei: Shang Wu, 1961.

Hu Xintian (胡信田). 黄帝經通釋 *Huang Di Jing tongshi* (Commentary of the *Yellow Emperor Classic*). Taibei: Tian Gong Shu Ju, 1984.

Huai Nan Zi (淮南子). Yang Jiage edition. Taibei: Shijie Press, 1985.

Huang Liuhong (黃六鴻). 福惠全書 *Fuhui quanshu* (A Complete Book Concerning Happiness and Benevolence), trans. Djang Chu. Tucson: University of Arizona Press, 1984.

Hulsewe, A. F. P. (1). *Remnants of Han Law*. Leiden: E. J. Brill, 1955.

———. (2). "Han China—A Proto 'Welfare State'?" *T'oung Pao* 73 (1987): 265–285.

Ivanhoe, Philip. "Reweaving the 'One Thread' of the *Analects*." *Philosophy East and West* 40, no. 1 (1990): 17–34.

Jan Yun-hua. (1). "The Silk Manuscripts on Taoism." *T'oung Pao* 63, no. 1 (1977): 65–84.

———. (2). "*Tao Yuan* or *Tao: The Origin*." *Journal of Chinese Philosophy* 7 (1980): 195–204.

———. (3). "Tao, Principle, and Law: The Three Key Concepts in the Yellow Emperor Taoism." *Journal of Chinese Philosophy* 7 (1980): 205–228.

———. (4). "The Change of Images: The Yellow Emperor in Ancient Chinese Literature." *Journal of Oriental Studies* 19, no. 2 (1981): 117–137.

———. (5). "Political Philosophy of the *Shih Liu Ching* Attributed to the Yellow Emperor Daoism." *Journal of Chinese Philosophy* 10 (1983): 205–228.

Jiang Guanghui (姜广辉). 试论汉初黄老思想 "Shilun Hanchu Huang-Lao sixiang" (Examination of Early Han Huang-Lao thought). In *Zhongguo zhexueshi yanjiu jikan* 2, ed. Editorial Department of *Zhexue yanjiu*, pp. 136–155. Shanghai: Shanghai People's Press, 1982.

Jiang Ronghai (江荣海). 慎到应是黄老思想家 "Shen Dao ying shi Huang-Lao sixiangjia" (Shen Dao Must Be a Huang-Lao Thinker). *Beijing-daxue xuebao* 1 (1989): 110–116.

Jin Chunfeng (金春峰). 论《黄老帛书》的主要思想 "Lun 'Huang-Lao Boshu' de zhuyao sixiang" (A Discussion of the Important Ideas of the *Huang-Lao Boshu*). *Qiusuo* 2 (1986): 54–60.

Jing Fa (经法). Peking: Wenwu Press, 1976.

Kanaya Osamu (金谷治). 先秦における法思想の展開 "Senshin ni okeru

hōshisō no hatten" (On the Development of Legal Thought in the Pre-Qin Era). *Shūkan Tōyōgaku* 47 (1982): 1–10.

Kang Li and Wei Jin (康立, 工今). 法家路綫和黄老思想 "Fajia luxian he Huang-Lao sixiang" (The Legalist Line and Huang-Lao Thought). *Wen Wu* 7 (1975): 1–7.

Kavka, Gregory. *Hobbesian Moral and Political Theory*. Princeton, N.J.: Princeton University Press, 1986.

Kimura Eiichi (木村一). 法家思想の研究 *Hōka shisō no kenkyū* (Study of Legalist Thought). Tokyo: Kobundo, 1944.

Ku Mei-Kao, *A Chinese Mirror for Magistrates: the Hsin-yu of Lu Chia*. Canberra: Australian National University, 1988.

Larre, Claude. "The Empirical Apperception of Time and Conception of History in Chinese Thought." In *Cultures and Time*, ed. L. Gardet et al. Paris: UNESCO Press, 1976.

Lau, D. C., trans. (1). *Lao Tzu: Tao Te Ching*. Hammondsworth, England: Penguin Books, 1963.

———. (2). *Confucius: The Analects*, 5th. ed. Suffolk, England: Penguin Books, 1979.

Laudan, Larry. (1). "A Confutation of Convergent Realism." In *Scientific Realism*, ed. Jarret Leplin, pp. 218–249. Berkeley: University of California Press, 1984.

———. (2). "Demystifying Underdetermination." In *Scientific Theories*, ed. Wade Savage, pp. 267–297. Minneapolis: Univ. of Minnesota Press, 1990.

Le Blanc, Charles. (1). *Huai Nan Tzu*. Hong Kong: Hong Kong University Press, 1985.

———. (2). "A Re-Examination of the Myth of Huang-ti." *Journal of Chinese Religions* 13 and 14 (1985 and 1986): 45–63.

Legge, James. *The Chinese Classics*, 5 vols. Taibei: Southern Materials Center, 1985.

Leng, Shao-chuan, and Chiu, Hungdah. *Criminal Justice in Post-Mao China*. Albany: SUNY Press, 1985.

Lewis, Mark Edward. *Sanctioned Violence in Early China*. Albany: SUNY Press, 1990.

Li Ji (禮記). Taibei: Chinese Materials and Research Aids Service Center, 1966.

Li Maoguan. "Why 'Laws Go Unenforced.'" *Beijing Review* 32, no. 37 (1989): 17–19, 26.

Li, Victor H. *Law Without Lawyers*. Boulder, Colo.: Westview Press, 1978.

Li Xueqin (李学勤). 马王堆帛书与《鹖冠子》"Mawangdui boshu yu *He Guang Zi* (Silk Manuscripts of Huang-Lao and the *He Guang Zi*). *Jianghan kaogu* 2 (1983): 51–56.

Liang Qichao (梁啟超). 先秦政治思想史 *Xianqin zhengzhi sixiangshi* (A History of Pre-Qin Political Thought). N.p.: 1922.

Liao, W. K. *The Complete Works of Han Fei Tzu*, 2 vols. London: Arthur Probsthain, 1959.

Liu Jie (劉節).《管子》中所見之宋鈃一派学说 "Guan Zi zhong suo jian zhi Song Xing yi pai xue shuo" (Theories of the Song Xing Group Seen in the *Guan Zi*). In *Gushi kaocun*, pp. 238–258. Beijing: Renmin chubanshe, 1958.

Liu Jingquan (刘景泉). 黄老之学述考 "Huang-Lao zhi xue shukao" (Study of the School of Huang-Lao). *Nankai shixue* 1 (1988): 122–137.

Liu Weihua and Miao Runtian (刘蔚华, 苗润田). 黄老思想源流 "Huang-Lao sixiang yuanliu" (Origins of Huang-Lao Thought). *Wen Shi Zhe* 1 (1986): 24–33.

Liu Xiaogan (刘笑敢). 庄子后学中的黄老派 "Zhuang Zi houxue zhong de Huang-Lao pai" (The Huang-Lao Sect Within the neo-Zhuang Zi School). *Zhexue yanjiu* 6 (1985): 59–63, 77.

Liu Yuhuang (刘毓璜). 试论"黄老之学"的起源 "Shilun 'Huang-Lao zhixue' de qiyuan" (On the Origins of the Huang-Lao School). *Lishi jiaoxue wenti* 5 (1982): 6–9.

Loewe, Michael. "Manuscripts Found Recently in China." *T'oung Pao* 63, no. 2 (1978): 99–136.

Long Hui (龙晦). 马王堆出土"老子"乙本前古佚书探原 "Mawangdui chutu 'Lao Zi' yibenqian guyishu tanyuan" (A Philological Study of the Lost Ancient Treatise Before the *Lao Zi* 'A' Manuscript Unearthed at Mawangdui). *Kaogu xuebao* (1975): 23–32.

Loy, David. *Nonduality*. New Haven, Conn.: Yale University Press, 1988.

Lun Yu (论语). In *The Chinese Classics*, 5 vols., ed. James Legge. Taibei: Southern Materials Center, 1985.

Machiavelli. *The Prince*, ed. Quentin Skinner and Russel Price. Cambridge: Cambridge University Press, 1988.

MacIntyre, Alasdair. *After Virtue*. Notre Dame, Ind.: University of Notre Dame Press, 1981.

Major, John. (1). "Topography and Cosmology in Early Han Thought: Chapter Four of the Huai-nan-tzu." Ph.D. diss., Harvard University, 1973.

———. (2). "The Meaning of Xing-te." In *Chinese Ideas about Nature and Society*, ed. Charles Le Blanc and Susan Blader, pp. 281–291. Hong Kong: Hong Kong University Press, 1987.

Mao Conghu and Gao Tingtai (冒从虎, 高庭台). 十年来西方哲学史研究的新进展 "Shinian lai xifang zhexueshi yanjiu de xinjinzhan" (New Advancements from Ten Years Study of the History of Western Philosophy). *Lilun yu xiandaihua* 5 (1989): 11–13.

Margolis, Joseph. *Pragmatism Without Foundations*. New York: Basil Blackwell, 1986.

Maspero, Henri. *Taoism and Chinese Religion*, trans. Frank Kierman. Amherst: University of Massachusetts Press, 1981.

Mawangdui Editor's Group, ed. 長沙馬王堆漢墓出土《老子》乙本前佚書釋文 "Changsha Mawangdui Hanmu chutu *Lao Zi* yi ben qian yishu shiwen" (Transcription of the Lost Text Before the *Lao Zi* B Excavated from the Han Tomb at Mawangdui). *Wen Wu* 10 (1974): 30–42.

Mawandui Hanmu Boshu vol. 1 (馬王堆漢墓帛書). Beijing: Wen Wu Press, 1980.

McKnight, Brian E. *The Quality of Mercy*. Honolulu: University of Hawaii Press, 1981.

Mead, George Herbert. *Mind, Self and Society*, ed. Charles Morris. Chicago: Chicago University Press, 1934.

Mencius. Zhu zi yinde. Taibei: Nanyu Press, n.d.

Mo Zi (墨子). *Zhu zi yinde*. Taibei: Nanyu Press, n.d.

Morgan, Evan. *Tao: The Great Illuminant*. Taibei: Chengwen Publishing Co., 1966.

Mou Tsung-san (牟宗三). 中国哲学原论, 原道第一 *Zhongguo zhexue yuan lun, yuandao di yi* (On Chinese Philosophy: Yuan Dao Number One). Taibei: Student Book Store, 1963.

Munro, Donald. *The Concept of Man in Early China*. Stanford, Calif.: Stanford University Press, 1969.

Murphy, Jeffrie, and Coleman, Jules. *The Philosophy of Law*. Totowa, N.J.: Rowman and Allenheld, 1984.

Nagatomo, Shigenori. "An Epistemic Turn in the *Tao Te Ching*: A Phenomenological Reflection." *International Philosophical Quarterly* 23, no. 2 (1983): 173–189.

Nathan, Andrew J. (1). "Political Rights in the Chinese Constitutions." In *Human Rights in Contemporary China*, ed. R. Randle Edwards, Louis Henkin, and Andrew J. Nathan, pp. 77–124. New York: Columbia University Press, 1986.

―――. (2). "Sources of Chinese Rights Thinking." In *Human Rights in Contemporary China*, ed. R. Randle Edwards, Louis Henkin, and Andrew J. Nathan, pp. 125–164. New York: Columbia University Press, 1986.

Needham, Joseph. *Science and Civilization in China*, vols. 2 and 5. Cambridge: Cambridge University Press, 1956.

Neugebauer, Klaus Karl. *Hoh-kuan tsi: Eine Undtersuchung der dialogischen Kapitel*. Frankfurt am Main: Peter Lang, 1986.

Nishikawa Yasuji (西川靖二). 漢初における黄老思想の一側面 "Hansho ni okeru Kōrō shisō no issokumen" (One facet of Huang-Lao thought in the early Han). *Tōhōgaku* 62: 26–39.

Nozick, Robert. *Anarchy, State, and Utopia*. New York: Basic Books, 1974.

Ōgata Tōru (大形徹). (1). 漢初の黄老思想 "Hansho no kōrō shisō" (Early Han Huang-Lao Thought). *Taikenzan ronsō* 13 (1979): 19–36.

―――. (2). 鶡冠子―不朽の國家を幻想した隠者の書 "*Kakkanshi*―fukyū no kokka o gensō shita inja no hon" (*He Guan Zi*―the Book of a Hermit who Fantasized an Imperishable State). *Tōhōshūkyō* 59 (1982): 43–65.

————. (3). 鶡冠子の成立 *Kakkanshi* no seiritsu" (The Formation of the *He Guan Zi*). *Ōsaka furitsu daigaku kiyō, Jimbun shakai kagaku* 31 (1983): 11–23.

Peerenboom, R. P. (1). "Han Dynasty Cosmology: The Emergence of Naturalism." *Asian Culture Quarterly* 16 (1988): 13–40.

————. (2). "Naturalism and Immortality in the Han: The Antecedents of Religious Daoism." *Chinese Culture* 29, no. 3 (1988).

————. (3). "Confucian Justice: Achieving a Humane Society." *International Philosophical Quarterly* 30, no. 1 (1990): 17–32.

————. (4). "Beyond Naturalism: A Reconstruction of Daoist Environmental Ethics." *Environmental Ethics* 13, no. 1 (1991): 3–22.

————. (5). "Natural Law in the *Huang-Lao Boshu*." *Philosophy East and West* 40, no. 3 (1990): 309–330.

————. (6). "A Coup d'État in Law's Empire: Dworkin's Hercules Meets Atlas." *Law and Philosophy* 9 (1990).

Peirce, Charles Sanders. *Collected Papers of Charles Sanders Peirce*, 6 vols., ed. Charles Hartshorne and Paul Weiss. Cambridge, Mass.: Harvard University Press, 1931–1935.

Peng Daxiong (彭達雄). 韓非和馬凱維里 *Han Fei he Makaiweili* (Han Fei and Machiavelli). Gaoxiong: Da Zhong Publishers, 1973.

Penner, Terry. *Ascent From Nominalism*. Boston: D. Reidel, 1987.

Pincoffs, Edmund. *Quandaries and Virtues*. Lawrence: University of Kansas, 1986.

Qian Mu (錢穆). 中國思想史 *Zhongguo sixiangshi* (History of Chinese Thought). Taibei: Zhonghua Wenhua Publishing, 1952).

Qiu Xigui (裘錫圭). 馬王堆《老子》甲、乙本卷前后佚书与"道法家" "Mawangdui *Lao Zi* jiayiben juanqianhou yishu yu 'Dao fa jia' (The Lost Texts Before and After Mawangdui Lao Zi A and B and the 'Daoist-Legalist' School). *Zhongguo zhexueshi yanjiu* 2 (1980): 68–84.

Rand, Christopher C. "Chinese Military Thought and Philosophical Taoism." *Monumenta Serica* 34 (1979–1980): 171–218.

Rao Xinxian (饒鑫賢). 漢初黃老学派法律思想略說 "Hanchu Huang-Lao xuepai falu sixiang lueshuo" (On the Legal Thought of the Early Han Huang-Lao School). *Faluxhi luncong* 3 (1983): 326–338.

Rawls, John. *A Theory of Justice*. Cambridge, Mass.: Harvard University Press, 1971.

Rickett, W. Allyn. (1). *Kuan-tzu*. Hong Kong: Hong Kong University Press, 1965.

———. (2). "*Kuan-tzu* and the Newly Discovered Texts on Bamboo and Silk." In *Chinese Ideas About Nature and Society*, ed. Charles Le Blanc and Susan Blader, pp. 237–248. Hong Kong: Hong Kong University Press, 1987.

Riegel, Jeffrey. "A Summary of Some Recent *Wenwu* and *Kaogu* Articles." *Early China* (1975): 10–15.

Robinet, Isabelle. (1). *Meditation Taoiste*. Paris: Dervy-Livres, 1979.

———. (2). "Metamorphosis and Deliverance from the Corpse in Taoism." *History of Religions* 17, no. 1 (1979): 37–70.

Rong Zaozu (容肇祖). 韓非子考證 *Han Fei Zi kaozheng* (Textual Criticism of the *Han Fei Zi*). Taibei: Tailian Guofeng Publishing, 1972.

Rorty, Richard. (1). *Philosophy and the Mirror of Nature*. Princeton, N.J.: Princeton University Press, 1979.

———. (2). *Consequences of Pragmatism*. Minneapolis: University of Minnesota Press, 1982.

Rosemont, Henry, Jr. (1). "On Representing Abstractions in Archaic Chinese." *Philosophy East and West* 24, no. 1 (1974): 71–88.

———. (2). "Notes for a Confucian Perspective: Which Human Acts Are Moral Acts?" *International Philosophical Quarterly* 16, no. 1 (1976): 49–62.

Saiki Tetsuro (斎木哲郎). (1). 黄老思想の再檢討 "Kōrō shisō no saikentō" (A Reexamination of Huang-Lao Thought). *Tōhō Shūkyō* 62 (1983): 19–36.

———. (2). 馬王堆帛書より見た道家思想の一側面 "Maotai hakusho yori mita dōka shisō no issokumen" (One Aspect of Taoist Thought as Seen in the Mawangdui Silk Manuscripts). *Tōhōgaku* 69 (1985): 44–58.

Saso, Michael. "The *Chuang-tzu nei-p'ien*: A Taoist Meditation." In *Experimental Essays on Chuang-tzu*, ed. Victor H. Mair, pp. 140–157. Honolulu: University of Hawaii Press, 1983.

Schipper, Kristofer. (1). "Science, Magic and the Mystique of the Body."

In *The Clouds and the Rain: the Art of Love in China*, ed. M. Beurdeley, pp. 10–24. London: Hammond and Hammond, 1969.

———. (2). "The Taoist Body." *History of Religions* 3, no. 14 (1978): 355–386.

Schroeder, D. N. "Aristotle on Law." *Polis* 4 (1981): 17–31.

Schwartz, Benjamin. *The World of Thought in Ancient China*. Cambridge, Mass.: Belknap Press, 1985.

Seidel, Anna. *La Divinisation de Lao Tseu dans le Taoisme des Han*. Paris: Ecole Francaise d'Extreme Orient, 1969.

Sellars, Wilfrid. *Science, Perception and Reality*. London: Humanities Press, 1963.

Shi Ji (史記—Historical Records), 4 vols. Taibei: Dingwen Press, 1989.

Shi Qin (郝勤). 张陵与养生 "Zhang Ling yu yangsheng" (Zhang Daoling and the Cultivation of Longevity). *Zongjiaoxue yanjiu* 2 (1986): 58–67.

Shimamori Testsuo (島森哲男). 黄老思想の構造と位置:經法等四篇ち讀てぐ考える "Kōrō shisō no kōzō to ichi: *Keihō* nado shihen o yonde kangaeru" (The Structure and Position of Huang-Lao Thought: On Reading the Four *Jing Fa* Chapters). *Shūkan tōyōgaku* 45 (1981): 1–16.

Sivin, Nathan. *Chinese Alchemy*. Cambridge, Mass.: Harvard University Press, 1968.

Smith, Richard J. *China's Cultural Heritage*. Boulder, Colo.: Westview Press, 1982.

Stumpf, Samuel Enoch. *Morality and the Law*. Nashville: Vanderbilt University Press, 1966.

Sun Shiming (孙实明). 韓非自然观浅探 "Han Fei ziranguan qiantan" (A Brief Examination of Han Fei's Naturalism). *Zhongguo zhexueshi yanjiu* 2 (1985): 42–47.

Takahashi Yoichiro (高橋庸郎). 馬王堆帛書《老子》乙本卷古佚書《經法》釈文解法 "Maotai bosho 'Rōshi' otsobun kenzen koissho 'Keihō' shakubun chūkai" (An Annotated Translation of the *Jing Fa*, the Ancient Lost Text Before the Mawangdui Silk Manuscript *Lao Zi* B). *Shōnan Kokuban* 30 (1980): 101–199.

Tan Jiajian (潭家健).《鶡冠子》试论 "*He Guan Zi* shilun" (Examination of the *He Guan Zi*). *Jianghan luntan* 2 (1986): 57–62.

Tang Lan (唐兰). 马王堆出土《老子》乙本卷前古佚书的研究 "Mawangdui chutu Lao Zi yiben juanqian guyishu de yanjiu" (Research on the Lost Ancient Text Preceding the *Lao Zi* B Discovered at Mawangdui). *Kaogu xuebao* 1 (1975): 7–38.

Tang Xin (汤新). 法家对黄老之学的吸收与改造 "Fajia dui Huang-Lao zhi xue de xishou he gaizao" (The Legalist's Adoption and Reformation of the Huang Lao School). *Wen Wu* 8 (1975): 18–22.

Teng Fu (滕复). (1). 黄老哲学对老子"道"的改造与发展 "Huang-Lao zhexue dui Lao Zi 'dao' de gaizao he fazhan" (The Improvement and Development of Lao Zi's 'dao' in Huang-Lao Philosophy). *Zhexue yanjiu* 9 (1986): 64–69.

———. (2). 黄老之学的方法论与政治思想 "Huang-Lao zhi xue de fangfalun yu zhengzhi sixiang" (The Methodology and Political Thought of the Huang-Lao School). *Zhejiang xuekan* 1 (1986): 182–188, 82.

Thompson, Paul. (1). *The Shen Tzu Fragments*. Oxford: Oxford University Press, 1979.

———. (2). *The Shen Tzu Fragments*. Photocopy.

Tian Changwu (田昌五). 再谈黄老思想与法家路线 "Zaitan Huang-lao sixiang he fajia luxian" (Reexamination of the Huang-Lao-Legalist Line). *Wen Wu* 4 (1976): 63–68.

Tian Jiajian (谭家健). 《鹖冠子》试论 "'He Guan Zi' shilun" (Preliminary discussion of *He Guan Zi*). *Jianghan luntan* 2 (1986): 57–62.

Tu Wei-ming. (1). *Centrality and Commonality: An Essay on Chung-Yung*. Honolulu: University of Hawaii Press, 1976.

———. (2). "The 'Thought of Huang-Lao': A Reflection of the Lao Tzu and Huang Ti Texts in the Silk Manuscript of Ma-wang-tui." *Journal of Asian Studies* 39, no. 1 (1979): 95–110.

Turner, Karen. "The Theory of Law in the *Ching-fa*." *Early China* 14 (1989): 55–76.

Uchiyama Toshihiko (內山俊彥). 馬王堆帛書《經法》《十大經》《稱》《道原》小考 "Maotai bosho *keihō*, *jūdaikyō*, *sho*, *dōgen* shōkō" (A Brief Study of the silk Manuscripts Unearthed at Mawangdui—*Jing Fa*, *Shida Jing*, *Cheng* and *Dao Yuan*). *Tōhōgaku* 56 (1978): 1–16.

van Gulik, R. H. *Sexual Life in Ancient China*. Leiden: E. J. Brill, 1961.

Veith, Ilza. *The Yellow Emperor's Classic of Internal Medicine*. Taibei: Southern Materials Center, 1982.

von Leyden, W. *Aristotle on Equality and Justice*. London: Macmillan, 1985.

Wang, Hsiao-po, and Chang, Leo. *Philosophical Foundations of Han Fei's Political Theory*. Honolulu: University of Hawaii Press, 1986.

Wang Jie (王杰). 礼治、法治抑或人治 "Lizhi, fazhi ihuo renzhi" (Rule of Rites, Rule of Law or Rule of Man). *Lilun tansuo* 6 (1988): 70–73.

Warren, Mary Anne. "On the Moral and Legal Status of Abortion." *Monist* 57 (1973): 43–62.

Watson, Burton. (1). *Hsun Tzu*. New York: Columbia University Press, 1963.

———. (2). *Records of the Grand Historian of China*, 2 vols. New York: Columbia University Press, 1961.

———. (3). *The Complete Works of Chuang Tzu*. New York: Columbia University Press, 1968.

Weaver, Max. Review of *Law's Empire*, by Ronald Dworkin. *Journal of Law and Society* 14 (1987): 266–271.

Wei Qipeng (魏启鹏). 《黄帝四经》思想探原 "*Huang Di sijing* sixiang tanyuan" (Examination of the Origin of the Thought System of the *Yellow Emperor's Four Classics*). *Zhongguo zhexue* 4 (1980): 179–190.

Welch, Holmes. *Taoism: The Parting of the Way*. Boston: Beacon Press, 1957.

Wen Yiduo (聞一多). 神话与诗 *Shenhua yu shi* (Myths and poems). Beijing: Zhonghua shuju, 1959.

Whitehead, Alfred North. *Adventures of Ideas*. New York: Macmillan, 1933.

Williams, Bruce C. "*Ho-kuan tzu*: Authenticity, Textual History and Analysis Together with an Annotated Translation of Chapters 1 Through 4." Master's thesis, University of California, Berkeley, 1987.

Wu Guang (吴光). (1). 论黄老学派的形成与发展 "Lun Huang-Lao xuepai de xingcheng yu fazhan" (On the Formation and Development of the Huang-Lao School). *Hangzhoudaxue xuekan* 14, no. 4 (1984): 14–20, 59.

————. (2). 黄老之学通论 *Huang-Lao zhixue tonglun* (General Survey of the Huang-Lao School). Hangzhou: Zhejiang People's Press, 1985.

Wu Kuang-ming. (1). *Chuang Tzu: World Philosopher at Play.* New York: Scholar's Press, 1982.

————. (2). "Dream in Nietzsche and Chuang Tzu." *Journal of Chinese Philosophy* 13, no. 4 (1986): 371–382.

Xu Kangsheng (许抗生). 略说黄老学派的产生和演变 "Lueshuo Huang-Lao xuepai de chansheng he yanbian" (A Brief Comment on the Origin and Evolution of the School of Thought of Huang Di and Lao Zi). *Wen Shi Zhe* 3 (1979): 71–76.

Xu Zhixiang (徐志祥). 孔子法律学说述评 "Kong Zi falu xueshuo shuping" (Discussion of Confucius's Philosophy of Law). *Jilu xuekan* 6 (1985): 124–128.

Xun Zi (荀子). *Zhu Zi yinde.* Taibei: Nanyu Press, n.d.

Yin Wen Zi (尹文子). Siku quanshu edition. In *Zhou Qin Mingjia sanzi jiaoquan* (Collation of Three School of Names Philosophers of the Zhou Dynasty State of Qin), ed. Wang Qixiang. Shanghai: Zhonghua Shuju, 1975.

Young, Stephen. Review of *The Philosophical Foundations of Han Fei's Political Theory*, by Hsiao-po Wang and Leo S. Chang. *Philosophy East and West* 39, no. 1 (1989): 83–93.

Yu Mingguang (余明光). (1). 黄老思想初探 "Huang-Lao sixiang chutan" (Preliminary Exploration of the Thought of Huang-Lao). *Xiangtandaxue xuekan* 1 (1985): 71–75.

————. (2). 《论六家要旨》所述"道论"源于"黄学" "'Lun Liujia yaozhi' suoshu 'daolun' yuan yu 'huangxue'" (The "Daoist Theory" of the *Liu jia zhiyao* Originated in "Yellow Emperor Studies"). *Xiangtan daxue xuebao* 1 (1987): 34–38.

————. (3).《黄帝四经》与黄老思想 *Huangdi sijing yu Huang-Lao sixiang* (*Yellow Emperor's Four Classics* and Huang-Lao Thought). Heilong-jiang People's Press, 1989.

Yu Yingshi. "Life and Immortality in the Mind of Han China." *Harvard Journal of Asiatic Studies* 25 (1964–1965): 80–122.

Zhang Qiyun (张其昀). 孔子的法律哲学 "Kong Zi de falu zhexue" (Confucius's Philosophy of Law). *Huaxue yukan* 17 (1977): 1–20.

Zhang Weihua (张维华). (1). 释"黄老"之称 "Shi 'Huang-Lao' zhi cheng" (Explication of the Appellation 'Huang-Lao'). *Wen Shi Zhe* 4 (1981): 13–24, 38.

———. (2). 西汉初年黄老政治思想 "Xihan chunian Huang-Lao zhengzhi sixiang" (The Political Philosophy of the Early Western Han Huang-Lao School). *Zhongguo shehui kexue* 5 (1981): 199–208.

Zhang Zhizhe and Luo Yijun (张志哲, 罗义俊). 论《新语》的黄老思想 "Lun Xin Yu de Huang-Lao sixiang" (On the Huang-Lao Thought of the *Xin Yu*). *Jianghan luntan* 6 (1981): 110–114.

Zhao Jihui (赵吉惠). 关于《黄老之学》《黄帝四经》产生时代考证 "Guan yu 'Huang-Lao zhi xue' *Huangdi sijing* chansheng shidai kaozheng" (Concerning the Era of Origin of the "Huang-Lao School" *Huangdi si jing*). *Dongbei shidaxuebao* 3 (1987): 25–29.

Zhao Zongcheng (赵宗诚). 道教尚黄老探源 "Daojiao shang Huang-Lao tanyuan" (Investigation of Religious Daoism's Veneration of Huang-Lao). *Zongjiaoxue yanjiu* 1 (1985): 43–54.

Zhi Shui (知水). (1). 论稷下黄老之学产生的历史条件 "Lun Huang-Lao zhi xue chansheng de lishi tiaojian" (On the Historical Conditions of the Origins of the Jixia Huang-Lao School). *Nanjingdaxue xuebao* 2 (1988): 81–87.

———. (2). 稷下黄老玄学体系新探 "Jixia Huang-Lao xuanxue tixi xintan" (A New Look at the xuanxue system of Jixia Huang-Lao Thought). *Guan Zi xuekan* 2 (1988): 52–56.

Zhong Zhaopeng (钟肇鹏). (1). 黄老帛书的哲学思想 "Huang-Lao boshu de zhexue sixiang (The Philosophical Thought of the *Huang-Lao Boshu*). *Wen Wu* 2 (1978): 63–68.

———. (2). 论黄老之学 "Lun Huang-Lao zhi xue" (An Examination of the Huang-Lao School). *Shijie zongjiao yanjiu* 2 (1981): 75–98.

Zhuang Zi (莊子). *Zhu zi yinde*. Taibei: Nanyu Press, n.d.

Index